For Ruth —
with warm personal
regards,
Suzanne Massie

ALSO BY SUZANNE MASSIE

The Living Mirror: Five Young Poets from Leningrad

Journey (co-author with Robert Massie)

Land of the Firebird: The Beauty of Old Russia

Pavlovsk: The Life of a Russian Palace

Trust but Verify

Reagan, Russia and me

A personal memoir

Suzanne Massie

MAINE AUTHORS PUBLISHING

ROCKLAND, MAINE

Copyright ©2013 by Suzanne Massie

All rights reserved. No part of this book may be reproduced in any form or by any electronic or mechanical means, including information storage and retrieval systems, without permission in writing from the author, except by a reviewer, who may quote brief passages in review.

Book and cover design by Phil Schirmer

Produced by Maine Authors Publishing
558 Main Street, Rockland, Maine 04841
www.maineauthorspublishing.com

Manufactured in the United States of America

ISBN 978-1-938883-68-2

Cover photograph: Courtesy Reagan Presidential Library

www.trustbutverifybook.com

To Vicki and Mikk
whose devotion and loyalty beyond the call of duty
made possible the writing of this book

and to Mary and Phil
whose faith, support and sustaining friendship gave me
the courage to finish it

ACKNOWLEDGEMENTS

Nine years ago, shortly after the death of President Reagan, I began work on this book, interrupted in December, 2006, when my husband, Seymour Papert, MIT professor, mathematician, visionary and pioneer in his field of technology and education, suffered a catastrophic accident in Hanoi, Vietnam after delivering the keynote address at the International Mathematics Education Conference. He was hit by a speeding motorcycle while attempting to cross a street in the mortally dangerous and unregulated traffic of Hanoi. Barely escaping death, he suffered severe brain injuries that cut short his brilliant career and left him, a recognized genius and educationist, unable to continue his lifelong work. Flown home in a coma, he survived, but remained a near invalid requiring constant care. I spent the next three years in hospitals and when he was finally able to return home, was left to face financial ruin in our society which offers little support for those who need constant care at home. My deep gratitude goes to those who have generously contributed to the Seymour Papert Recovery Fund that has helped to provide him with the essential care he has needed and continues to need. Without this help and that of priceless friends, this book could never have been written.

Any words of thanks for the support they brought us is inadequate, for it is due to them that we both have been able to survive and I, finally able to write again.

My gratitude goes to my husband's caregivers Vicki Dulong and her multi-talented son Mikk Wardwell who, by their quick action, not only saved his life three times, but without missing a single day of work have cared for him for the past six years. Thanks to them, during my long days of writing, I always have had the precious certainty of knowing that my beloved husband was safe. Also my thanks to Dan Hays who cared for him on weekends and was always ready to step in day or night when he was needed to help in many ways. My thanks go also to George Markowsky, professor and Chair of Computer Sciences at the University of Maine who has remained an ever-loyal friend to my husband, never failing during seven years to visit him regularly, bringing him appreciation for his unique leadership and life, and giving contact with the world of his work. And to Rick Greenblatt, Seymour's former colleague at the MIT Artificial Intelligence Laboratory (which Seymour founded), who has worked with him twice a week via Skype for close to four years. Also thanks to David Cavallo and Chris Myers.

My fulsome thanks go to the Reagan Presidential Library and the benefit of their comprehensive museum exhibits and extensive research library where I spent many hours in the preparation of this book, and particularly for the help of library archivists, Sherrie Fletcher, Cate Sewell, Ray Wilson and Steve Branch, audiovisual archivist.

My grateful thanks go to my Blue Hill office team headed by my long-time assistant Carolyn Waite who, during these many years has brought her talent for organization, attention to detail, creativity, patience with the ups and downs of my complicated existence and precious help for many details of my work. Gayle Cambridge, our bookkeeper, organizer and locomotive of Heart Tree Press and much else, whose cheerfulness, humor and colorful sweaters brought sunshine whenever she walked in the door, and to Nichole Hammet whose extraordinary energy and wealth of practical suggestions kept our house clean and our garden blooming.

In Washington, to Marilyn Swezey, my friend of thirty-five years, my thanks for the inspiration of her religious faith, kindness and generous hospitality and her reading of my chapter "The Achilles Heel" and for providing important details about the church. Wren Wirth, who, while traveling the world, never forgot me with her cards and phone calls. John Evans, former U.S. Ambassador to Armenia and one of our most talented diplomats who read my manuscript with his experienced eye, and our former Ambassador to Moscow, John Beyrle who took time to read and check up on my Russian transliteration. Any faults or errors are due only to me.

In Maine, I thank Dr. John Bradford and his wife Margie who offered me the warmth of their home in Bangor when I was kept late at night at the hospital, to my neighbors Darrell and Jeannette Gray in Blue Hill who drove me to the hospital in the middle of the night and Butch and Patty in Deer Isle who dug me out of the snow and changed my flat tires, also for the generous help of Roger and Marissa Olsen. Sergei Breus and his family kept me close to Russia with encouragement from Dr. Vodka, salted cucumbers and mushrooms from the woods. A special thanks for the support of my priest Father John Pawelchak whose prayers and concern for my welfare provided me with a constant example of Christian compassion and faith. Grateful thanks to Tom Tootill and Bill and Lee Tootill for their careful reading of my manuscript and helpful suggestions. Maine Authors Publishing has been a pleasure to work with—Jane Karker, Genie Dailey, and Cheryl McKeary. Thanks also, for the assistance of Joe Gardner, Northeast Historic Films and Jenny Smick, who typed my final manuscript.

From Russia, encouragement came from Rostislav Ordovsky-Tanayaevsky, Tatiana Stukalova, Leonid and Olga Garber.

I owe a very special debt of gratitude to two gifted artists who define the term "best friends"—who shared their meals, their sense of beauty and their lives with me: Mary Schirmer who, during the past four years, pulled me through the darkest moments of my soul, always giving me love, comfort and hope, and her husband, Phil Schirmer, a master of tempera painting, who generously found time in his busy career to give his abundant talents to the design of this book and its cover.

My beloved husband, Seymour, always comforted and encouraged me in his inimitable way. Overflowing thanks to my children—all three talented writers. Although far away in London and New York and burdened with an enormous load of work and responsibilities, my daughter Elizabeth read several versions of my manuscript, offering her precious professional suggestions and ideas; my daughter Susanna in Kentucky gave me steady encouragement and constant faith. My son Bob in Boston always provided me with the example of his courage, and his keen intelligence and suggestions sharpened my wits. My grandchildren always filled me with a sense of pride in their accomplishments and the hopeful joy of youth.

Now that it is finished at last, I owe this book to all of you.

CONTENTS

Acknowledgments
Prologue 13
1 The Long Road 21
2 The Worm Turns 38
3 Back in the USSR 55
4 Back in the USA—A Step Closer 77
5 First Meeting with the President 90
6 Mission to Moscow 103
7 Lunch in The Oval Office 115
8 The Achilles' Heel 134
9 Moscow Invites and Washington Calls 157
10 Geneva: Reagan and Gorbachev Meet 174
11 Lunch on the Patio 207
12 Long Lunch with the President 218
13 Trust But Verify—Reykjavik 232
14 Nancy 243
15 Gorbachev Comes to Washington 258
16 KGB "Princes" 270
17 The Ambassador Flap 287
18 Crocodiles in Washington 295
19 Secretary Shultz 304
20 Reagan Wows Moscow 329
21 Millennium of Russian Christianity 349
22 A Few Last Words 361
23 The President Leaves 370
Epilogue 378
Bibliography 381
Footnotes 384

PROLOGUE

Life is what happens when you've made other plans

Today there are two questions that I am asked everywhere by just about anyone I meet. The first is: Why did I become interested in Russia?, quickly followed by the second: How did I meet President Reagan?

Both are strange and improbable stories.

There was nothing in my background that would have indicated my future interest and intense connection with Russia. Although people I meet keep insisting that *surely* there must have been someone Russian in my family back ground, that is not the case. I was born in New York City. That makes me American, but my late father and mother were both Swiss citizens, and all my relatives are Swiss. When I was born, my father was working in the Swiss foreign service at the New York consulate, and in later years became Swiss consul general and dean of the Consular Corps in Philadelphia. So although I have a dual nationality, by blood I am Swiss, one hundred percent. My maiden name is Rohrbach, my paternal origin the little mountain town of Guggisberg in the canton of Bern, and, since the 13th century, I am descended from a long line of alpine folk once known to be among the best soldiers in Europe. The Bernese are renowned for their long memories, stubbornness, courage, and, above all, perseverance, all needed for scaling the snow-covered peaks that stand as inspiration and goal before them.

I always had a vivid imagination. As a child, I wrote fairy tales in which the tears of the princess turned to diamonds, and I dreamed of an adventurous life. But nothing prepared me for the way it was to happen. And yet…there was something that happened before my birth that held the seeds of the future.

When my mother was a teenage girl from the watchmaking town of La Chaux de Fonds in Switzerland, she merrily went to Russia to spend the summer in Moscow with a family who were friends of my grandfather. It was 1914, not a propitious summer as on August 3, Germany declared war and World War I began, preventing her from returning home. She ended up staying not for three months, but for five years, finally escaping from the Russian Revolution in 1919 along with the family who had invited her. Despite this harrowing experience, mother always kept fond memories of her days in that great and mysterious land she called "the country of the heart." As a result, my first fairy tale books were Russian, and she passed on to me her stories and a passion for ballet and dancers that has remained one of the great joys of my life.

Yet, apart from this unusual event, there was nothing else that would indicate the course of what was to be my future career. I grew up bilingual, speaking French at home and accustomed to visitors from many lands. On my father's home leaves, I traveled with my family to Switzerland, where I happily hiked in the mountains and bicycled with my many cousins. I went to school at Germantown Friends School in Philadelphia, to college at Vassar, where I studied English history, French and English literature, and spent my junior year in Paris at the Sorbonne and the École des Sciences Politiques. After college I went to work for *TIME Inc.* in New York, and in 1954 married Robert Massie, whom I had met in Paris when he was a Rhodes Scholar at Oxford. I settled down to a life as a housewife in the suburbs of New York. My idée fixe was to return to Paris.

Then came a decisive blow. In 1956, our first child, a boy—like Alexis, heir to the throne and only son of the last tsar of Russia Nicholas II—was unexpectedly born with hemophilia.[1] This, despite the fact that there had never been a single case of hemophilia in our large extended family. When this catastrophe happened, I was in despair, certain that my life and youthful hopes were over forever. How wrong I was! Fate had forged a critical link with the history of Russia that was to alter the course of my life.

Because of the unceasing demands of my son's condition, I had to reinvent myself. My life, like the lives of so many women, was completely dominated by the demands of my family. I had to give up all ideas of a career.

Instead, I spent many years coping with hospitals, crises, transfusions, and pain. Due to my circumstances, I was never able to pursue a normal path of study about the country that was one day to become as familiar to me as my own. It was to be a crooked road with many detours that eventually led to my path of learning. Yet, following an unconventional and winding path, I was to end up with a personal knowledge of Russia and an understanding of the Russian people that was given to few in the tense years of the Cold War.

The first step came in 1958 when Bobby was two years old. After he suffered a particularly severe medical crisis, to save my sanity I enrolled in an adult education course in Russian language at the local high school. Why Russian? I don't know. Maybe just because it was available and cheap, only $8.00 a semester, which even in our miserable financial state we were able to afford. The teacher looked at me and declared, "Suzanne, you have a Russian soul." Through her I met her family and a whole village of Russian émigrés in the town of Nyack, across the Hudson River from Irvington, where we lived. During those acutely painful years and critical times, they were to help me, support me, pray for us, and inspire in me a gratitude which I never forgot.

Everyone we met in those days was curious about hemophilia, so one day in 1964 when my husband was discouraged about the direction of his magazine writing career, I suggested that he write a book about the experience of the last tsar and his wife, and how their hopeless fight against the condition of their son had been a factor leading to the Russian Revolution. After a while he exclaimed, "Put it on paper!" I did. In those days there was little knowledge and virtually no interest in a Russia that no longer existed. There was only the Soviet Union. The Enemy. Only one publisher reluctantly agreed to our idea and offered my husband a minuscule $2,500 advance.

To support us, I had to give up the idea of my own writing, and I landed a job as a researcher at *Time/Life* Books (in those days, only men were writers; women were always researchers) for a book in the series called

The Rise of Russia, and was lucky enough to be assigned for almost a year to work with the academic advisor for the book—a top professor of Russian history at Columbia University. Thus began the four years of my husband's and my total concentration and work on the book that became *Nicholas and Alexandra* and led to our first trip to Russia. Every day I commuted to New York and every night I read and edited my husband's pages after the children went to sleep.

So how did I come to meet Ronald Reagan? Although it remains a persistent American myth that in our democratic society an ordinary citizen can talk to the most powerful man in the land and he will listen, ordinary citizens don't usually come in off the streets to be brought into the center to interact with presidents on matters of national security. Improbably, this happened to me and might have come from one of Frank Capra's films. Some accounts of my encounters with President Reagan have been written in books and the press, most piecemeal and sometimes downright wrong, so I finally decided to set it down as it happened.

My story is a personal one, and not in any way an evaluation of the entire Reagan administration. I was and am today a private citizen, a writer. Politically, I consider myself an independent, leaning toward conservative Democrat, and never then or now have I shared the extreme opinions of the right or the left about President Reagan—neither those of my liberal friends who rant about what they consider his negative domestic legacy, nor the current Reagan adulation of the conservatives. The only Reagan I am qualified to talk about at all is the one I came to know: the peacemaker.

When I first met President Reagan in early January 1984, I did not know that it was a critical time, one that historians now consider the most dangerous time in U.S.–Soviet relations and the Cold War. During the last years of President Carter's term, tensions between the United States and the Soviet Union had escalated sharply. The Soviet Union had invaded Afghanistan in 1979, resulting in the end of all U.S.–Soviet cultural exchanges and an American boycott of the 1980 Olympic games in Moscow. By 1982, after President Reagan—a fervent anticommunist surrounded by hard-liners—took office, relations had reached an unprecedented level of hostility. There had been a massive American military buildup, and after the Soviets shot down a Korean airliner with Americans aboard in September 1983, angry rhetoric from both sides went into high gear. Reagan called the Soviet Union an "evil empire," proposed a controversial initiative called "Star Wars," and the United States began installing Pershing missiles in Europe, steps that the Soviet Union took as an ultimate threat. As a result, in December 1983, for the first time in fourteen years, the Soviets broke off all arms negotiations.

By the time I met President Reagan, I was an author who had written books on Russian history, and was a Fellow at the Harvard Russian Research Center. But my life and approach were highly unconventional. I was not a traditional Ph.D.-carrying academic, and my views were far from the establishment view of the time. This was the result of what had happened to me over several years in the frigid Cold War period of little or no close contact between Americans and ordinary Russians. I had traveled often to the Soviet Union and had been lucky enough to get to know a wide variety of Russian people in their own environment, to share their conditions of life, learn about their problems. I was deeply touched by them and what I had experienced. I learned firsthand how Soviet propaganda and our isolation from their long-suffering people had blinded us to the harsh reality of their lives. In fact, it is not too much to say that we in the United States had swallowed Soviet propaganda more completely than the Russians themselves.

What spurred me to try to reach President Reagan was an accidental and dramatic meeting in Moscow with a high Soviet official in the fall of 1983. After this, I became increasingly worried—indeed fearful—about the toxic state of relations between the United States and the Soviet Union. Something had to be done about it, and I believed that I had something to contribute. My motive was simple: I did not want us to bomb each other to smithereens as the result of basic misunderstandings between our two countries. I went to Washington on my own initiative and my own nickel, solely as a private citizen, and during the entire four years was never paid by anyone. It didn't enter my mind to ask for anything—not even my shuttle fare. I thought I was doing a small part to serve my country. My father had taught me to believe that every citizen has a responsibility to act. So on my own, I acted.

This book is not only about my meetings with the President and the events that followed, but a personal adventure story about those extraordinary years in my life, about those people, both American and Russian, who helped me, and the series of seemingly unrelated events that were to eventually lead me, a nonpolitical woman, to the White House and the most powerful man in the free world.

In Washington I was to confront a foreign policy establishment dominated by hardliners and Kremlinologists who had viewed the Soviet Union as an implacable foe for decades, as well as some who saw a political upside in heightened tensions. My interest in and study of Russian culture, art, and the religion of the Russian people made me not only an unusual voice, but, indeed a unique one in the foreign policy establishment. Their opinions often contrasted diametrically with mine. I found the accepted orthodoxy about the Soviet Union/Russia limiting and in many instances just plain wrong. My position was always clearly very different and not popular in the official circles of both nations: I was *anti* Soviet regime but *pro* Russian people.

From personal experience, I had learned how much Russians hated being referred to as a synonym for a regime that most felt had been imposed on them by force. Russian citizens regularly referred to their government as *them* and themselves as *we*. They suffered from having their ancient culture vulgarized, their history falsified, their religion destroyed, and their language cheapened by communist doublespeak. The common Western use of *Soviet* and *Russian* interchangeably was not unlike lumping all Germans together as Nazis. Indeed, it was striking that in their own schools Russian teachers were careful to differentiate between "German people" and "Fascists."

During the four years (1984–88) that I was to serve President Reagan, I made several trips to the Soviet Union carrying secret diplomatic messages and working to convince top officials there that our government wanted peace and not war. In the United States, I spent many hours with the president sharing my insights about the Russian people, including the role of religion in their lives—a fact that was entirely unrecognized in the U.S. government and our media and that helped the president, a man of deep faith, connect with the millions of citizens behind their intractable communist leadership. I gave him suggestions to help prepare him for his world-changing meetings with general secretary Mikhail Gorbachev, and provided my perspective on the meaning and impact of *glasnost*[2] for ordinary Russian people. I taught him the Russian proverb "Trust but Verify," which he adopted and famously used to great effect in many of his meetings with Gorbachev. But I believe that my most significant contribution was offering him a deeper understanding of the Russian people, humanizing them so that he no longer viewed them as faceless communists. It was this extraordinary opportunity to share my love for both America and Russia and the effort to bring them to a better relationship with each other as fellow human beings that I am most proud of and grateful for.

The United States is a country of upstarts and rebels, famous for being a place where unconventional ways of learning are recognized and celebrated. Our great President Lincoln and many of our finest presidents were known for their gumption and the courage of an independent approach that often went against the conventional thinking of their time. Alas, over the years, our government has swollen with excessive admiration for bureaucratic titles and academic think tanks. That President Reagan was unconventional enough to be open to the ideas of an unconventional woman and to enlist me, a virtually unknown person who had never served in government, as an unofficial advisor was in the best tradition of traditional American independent thinking. In those four years of his second term, there was to be a dramatic change in Ronald Reagan's approach to a country that he had once called an evil empire, and when he left office in 1988, relations between the Soviet Union/Russia and the United States were better than they had been since the beginning of the Cold War—or, for that matter, have been since.

CHAPTER 1

THE LONG ROAD

"God writes straight on crooked lines."
—Portuguese proverb

On a cold January day in 1984 in Washington, Bud McFarlane, President Reagan's National Security Advisor, led me up the stairs from his basement West Wing office to the first-floor Oval Office. Everyone we met along our way greeted him with a cheery hello. For them it was routine; for me, cataclysmic. It was a short walk through the narrow corridor that led to the Oval Office, but even in my paralyzed state I managed to notice the fine George Catlin watercolors that lined the walls. A reverent hush falls upon everything that surrounds a president: a palpable atmosphere of power like entering the anteroom of an emperor. Before the tightly closed, tall white doors that led to the inner sanctum, Secret Service men with their ever-present earphones whispered into their mouthpieces. A photographer stood at the ready. Then the impressive white doors slowly opened. I was to meet the most powerful man in the world, a famous hawk, to talk to him about a country I had come to know intimately and love. Could I say it right? My tongue felt frozen. Silently, efficiently, the photographer's light bulb flashed.

That first meeting with Ronald Reagan had taken a very long time to come about. It was the result of a completely unplanned road along with a series of events that gave no inkling that they would eventually lead me to the Oval Office—the culmination of a journey that had begun seventeen years before, in March, 1967, when I first went to Russia.

So let me set the stage in the next few chapters by telling you why Russia and how this improbable meeting ever happened at all.

In the spring, the ice of the Neva River in St. Petersburg cracks with the sound of a cannon shot that reverberates through the city, and the river begins to live again. Huge floes of gray-blue ice, pushed by the swift currents of the newly liberated river, rush toward the Baltic Sea. In the life of every human being there is a moment when everything that has gone before seems to have been leading to a single awakening. In the spring of 1967, this happened to me during my first trip to Leningrad and was the beginning of a voyage of personal discovery that changed my life. That first encounter with the country that was to become the passionate dedication of my life remains burned in my memory, as if it had happened yesterday.

My husband and I had decided that since what we simply called "the book" (*Nicholas and Alexandra*) was nearly finished, we needed to see for ourselves the city that had been the setting for the events that had lived vividly in our minds during four years of work. To pay for the trip, we borrowed on our life insurance. We flew to Helsinki, there to change planes to go on to Leningrad. Helsinki airport was modest and small in those days: no chrome halls or fancy shops. Dusk was falling. Far across the airfield, a solitary plane with the ominous blood-red letters CCCP stood waiting. It seemed a very long walk. At the top of the small ladder stood a sloppily dressed stewardess who, with a baleful glance, ushered us into the old plane. The seats were worn and dirty. There was a strange smell: a mixture of disinfectant and some kind of sweet orange candy, a pervasive odor that I would inhale over and over again in hotels and restaurants in the Soviet Union. We were the only passengers except for a lone British salesman on his way to try to sell shoes.

I was filled with apprehension about going to the Soviet Union. I remembered Stalin and the bloodbaths and horrors I had read about, the stories my mother had told of what Russia had been before the Revolution. Would any of that Russia still exist? What would I find there now? Yet, as we flew and I looked down on the vast dark forests below, I felt a strange stirring of recognition. When the plane landed and I stepped out and sniffed the air that smelled of fresh snow, I had a powerful sense that I had been traveling toward this land for a very long time. When I confronted the customs inspector with his fur hat and gold teeth and the old porter in his worn boots it seemed that I had seen them all before.

The Leningrad airport was shabby, little better than a shack. "Have you pornography or the Bible?" the lone inspector asked gruffly.

Waiting for us was a young man from Intourist. We didn't have a clue what to expect. It was, after all, the Cold War. But as soon as we were safely in the car with him and a driver who couldn't understand English, our guide eagerly asked, "Do you know Salinger?"

Not exactly the first question I would have expected. I thought for a moment he meant the well-known journalist Pierre Salinger, but no, it was J.D. Salinger, the author. We weren't much help. He knew a lot more about Salinger and his work than we did, and told us proudly that he was doing his dissertation on the famous author. It was not what we had been taught at home to expect about the Soviet Union.

In the dark streets we drove through there were almost no streetlights, but I could sometimes make out people muffled in heavy coats standing in long lines. We were deposited at the Hotel Astoria.

Built in 1911 when St. Petersburg was the proud cosmopolitan capital of imperial Russia, the Astoria had once been the most modern and elegant hotel in the city, with a large English library and a map of the London tube system on the wall of its grand lobby. Emperor Nicholas II and his beloved wife, the Empress Alexandra, their four daughters and young son Alexis were at the height of their popularity and the nation was preparing to celebrate 300 years of the Romanov dynasty in 1913. Russia was prosperous and industrializing rapidly. *National Geographic* that year devoted an entire issue to "Russia: Land of Unlimited Promise."

Then in 1914 came World War I, followed in Russia by revolution, chaos and a savage civil war. The tsar and his entire family were brutally assassinated in a distant Siberian town on the night of July 16/17, 1917—a bloody stain that was to spread all over the land. St. Petersburg was reduced to a provincial city, and, in 1924, its name was changed to Leningrad. Stalin, who always viewed the city as a potential threat, began his first murderous purges in the 1930s "time of terror" there. In 1941 came World War II and the invasion of the Nazi armies. Leningrad was subjected to a relentless 900-day siege—the longest and greatest siege in world history—that annihilated ten times more people than perished in Hiroshima and Nagasaki. Mercilessly bombed daily by the invading armies, at its height more than 3,000 people perished every day from cold and starvation, their frozen bodies pulled in sleds during the bitter winters to be buried in mass graves.[1] The Astoria served as a hospital for the wounded and dying. So certain were the Nazis of their victory, they had already printed invitations to the victory celebration that was to be held in that hotel. Yet because of the extraordinary heroism of the city and its inhabitants, they were never able to take the city, and in 1944 finally had to retreat, relentlessly pursued by partisans and the Red Army.

When we arrived at the Astoria that night in 1968, it was a far cry from the glory days of its past. Leonid Brezhnev ruled the Soviet Union from 1964 until 1982, a time known today as the "period of stagnation." It was a time of increasing pressure and repression of dissidents and a sharp economic decline in the nation. Leningrad was a dark and gloomy place, almost a ghost city. The great wartime siege still dominated the minds of its citizens, most of whom had lost many members of their families. There were shortages of everything; stores were empty. Foreigners were a rarity; there were few foreign consuls, no journalists. The few remaining hotels in the city were segregated, and the dilapidated Astoria limited to English-speaking foreign visitors only.

A soldier met us at the door. Where today there is an elegant lobby and a fancy antiques store, then there was only a cloakroom with an elderly man taking coats, and most of the remainder of the space was occupied by Intourist desks. After a monosyllabic checking of our papers by the clerk at the reception desk, we were handed a relic of the old days: a heavy key five inches long crowned with a large inscribed head. There was one other leftover of the hotel's glamorous past: an old but still elegant elevator, big as a room, with comfortable upholstered banquettes lining three of its gilded walls. An elevator lady with frizzy hair dyed a startling red had it set up as if it were her home, with newspapers and her knitting strewn about. She flashed a welcoming smile at us and ushered us into her golden cage. In our room we found a lumpy bed in a curtained alcove, a none-too-clean bathroom with leaky faucets, and the same smell as on the plane. But the room had a breathtaking view. Silhouetted against the evening sky was St. Isaac's Cathedral with its massive dome and huge granite columns. Throwing open the window, I inhaled a deep breath of that strangely familiar air and said, "I like it." We knew no one and yet I had a sure sense that I was waiting and that someone would find me.

It happened in a palace.

Shortly before our trip, I had been looking for photographs for our book at Hillwood Museum in Washington. The courtly chief curator, Marvin Ross, one of the few people in those days who knew any Russian museum curators, advised me. "You must go to Pavlovsk Palace," said he. "It is one of the finest restorations of the world. Take these names." The chief curator was Anatoly Kuchumov, who, said Ross, had saved the uniforms of Nicholas II.

So the next day, I went to the main Intourist representative sitting at her desk downstairs and said we wanted a car to go to Pavlovsk. "*Nyet*," said she firmly, "Pushkin[2] first and then Pavlovsk."

I kept repeating, "No. Pavlovsk first, then Pushkin," and added, "No guide, we can't afford one."

I finally wore her down and we left with a driver who spoke only Russian. When we got to Pavlovsk Palace, we found that no one there spoke English either. We were met by a gracious lady who greeted us repeating, "*Gostya, gostya*," meaning, I gathered, "Be our guests." At that early juncture, my Russian was limited to the alphabet and a few memorized poems, so I could only repeat, "Kuchumov, Kuchumov."

What to do? We waited. Then, a little distance away, I saw her go up to talk to a tall, bearded young man in shabby clothes. He approached us and in strongly accented English said the welcome words, "Can I help you? I am a poet of *Saint Petersburkh*.[3] They are looking for Kuchumov. He is in Pushkin now. In the meantime, be our guests. Look at the palace."

It did not occur to me then to wonder what a poet was doing as a tour guide in a palace. I learned later that, in those bleak days, a severe "parasite law" existed that decreed: "He who does not work does not eat," meaning that those with no regular employment risked being sent to a labor camp. To avoid this fate, unofficial poets and artists, excluded from the approved official unions of the Party and hard-pressed to be able to do their creative work, took on all manner of lowly jobs. Sympathetic museum curators like Kuchumov tried to help by managing to provide them with minimal employment. The result was that the museums of the city numbered among their janitors, sidewalk-snow cleaners, and occasionally guides (for Soviet citizens only, never for foreigners) some of the finest artists and poets of the city.

As I walked through Pavlovsk's magnificent rooms for the first time, how could I have imagined that in the future every painting, every piece of furniture, would one day become as familiar to me as my own home? My husband, Bob Massie, was impatient. From his point of view it was the wrong palace. He wanted to go to Pushkin, only a few miles away, where Nicholas II and his family had lived in the Alexander Palace. After all, we had borrowed on our life insurance to get there. Insisting it was time to go, he rushed me through and whisked me out of the palace, not giving me time to thank the gracious lady or the poet. But just as we were about to reach our waiting car and our dour driver, I heard someone running behind me. It was the poet, who asked, "Will you come back?"

I tried to explain that my husband was more interested in the palaces of Nicholas II, but not giving me time to finish, he continued, "But you must come back soon because tonight I am reading my poems."

I did not hesitate. "Can I come?" I asked.

"Yes," he said, pulling out of his pocket a small printed program in Russian and handing it to me while the driver looked on suspiciously.

In the car, my husband, irritated, grumbled, "I didn't come here to meet the population."

"Well I did."

Many years later, when I asked Constantine why he had decided to come after me that day, he answered cryptically, "Because you wore no bracelets. Western women wear many gold chains." This chance encounter and observation were to be the keys that would open the door to the people of the Soviet Union.

I was determined to go that evening, and although we did not know how to use public transportation, we knew the city's layout well from having studied it for so many years, and so we set out walking. The distance from the Astoria to the *Dom Kino* (House of Film) where the reading was to take place was some two miles. As we walked, Bob kept saying pessimistically, "They won't come."

I insisting, "They will!"

When we got to the small square opposite the building, there was no one in sight. We sat on a bench to wait with Bob continuing his litany: "They won't come," and I, "They will!"

And sure enough, at the last minute a taxi drove up, tires screeching, and an improbable number of people spilled out, among them the bearded poet.

That night I would go through the looking glass that separated foreigners from Russians. We all hurried up the stairs to a large hall where a few hundred people were waiting. For him. His name was Constantine Kuzminsky, and he read his translations of Byron to a rapt crowd. After he was through, he said, "And for you, Suzanne, my poems in English," which he proceeded to declaim in front of the bewildered audience. At the end, we sat with his friends in the *Bufett*[4] (Russian for French *buffet)* drinking bad coffee. Since we could not talk to them, they drew their professions on paper (a painter drew a paint brush, a musician, a guitar). Then Constantine dramatically announced, "And now we will see the courtyards where Dostoevsky wrote!" and we soon found ourselves on the dark streets, wandering into smelly courtyards heaped with garbage while Constantine, waving his arms, exclaimed grandly, "These are the courtyards where Dostoevsky wrote!"

Without any idea where they were taking us, we who had been working on a book about Nicholas II ended up almost next door to the gigantic Winter Palace on the Neva River Embankment. We entered a dark hallway and into the ground-floor room of a communal apartment. Shabby coats and hats smelling of sweat and dust were piled high on the floor by the door. Sitting around a table by candlelight were ten or twelve Russians waiting to meet us. That moment reminded me of the scene in *Snow White and the Seven Dwarfs* when she finds herself in a dark wood confronting the curious eyes of a host of friendly woods creatures. With his little daughter Julia asleep on a couch behind a makeshift screen, Constantine introduced us and explained proudly that we were in the basement of the "palace of Great Prince Vladimir."[5]

That was the first night. In those days, foreigners traveling on individual visas were not permitted to spend more than four days in any city—to ensure that meeting Russian citizens was virtually impossible. "They love tourists," commented Constantine dryly, "as long as they come in groups, speak no Russian, and spend a lot of money." During those few permitted days, we snuck out every night to the communal apartment on the Neva and met a whole group of interesting people, among them a doctor, a young man working in the port, a restoration specialist, young scientists, and several artists. A few spoke some English, but we were the first foreigners they had ever met. They produced a guitar player, and I sang "On Top of Old Smoky." Something happened to me then. The French call it "*un coup de foudre*" (a lightning stroke). I suddenly felt I had found a family that I had never known existed, and my eyes filled with tears.

Just after Labor Day in 1967, *Nicholas and Alexandra* was published and swiftly became a best seller, at last giving us some cash. So in early 1968, my husband and I, along with our three children, decided to move to Paris. Being bilingual myself, I wanted them to learn to speak French. We were to stay four years. But something had happened to me in Leningrad. In the West we were always supposed to be "cool." I was not. I had been profoundly touched by Russia. Tumultuous and intense feelings I had never experienced before had been awakened in me there, leaving me upset and bewildered, so contrary were they to everything in my earlier existence. One day, a mysterious Turkish woman I met by chance in Paris said calmly, "What you have, my dear, is a passion—and a passion takes a whole lifetime to live out." She was right. It has.

During our Paris years, I continued to study Russian. My Russian teacher drilled me over and over saying, "Russians talk very fast." (They do.) "They have a lot to tell you. Even if you cannot answer right away, you must understand." Twice a year for those four years, I traveled to the Soviet Union. It was a little schizophrenic. In Paris, the success of *Nicholas and Alexandra* had resulted in our being lionized by admiring Russian émigré nobility, French aristocrats, the Duke and Duchess of Windsor, and Prince Paul of Yugoslavia and his wife, Princess Olga. So startling was the contrast between Russia and the luxurious social life and lavish dinner tables of Paris, it was like navigating between two totally different planets.

Always calling it my "worm's eye view," in Leningrad I eagerly soaked up every experience. I learned about my new friends. I saw the miserable conditions in which they lived. Communist law decreed that each citizen was entitled to only nine square meters (eight and a half by ten feet) of living space. Whole families often lived in one room and used a communal kitchen. Stairwells were filthy and smelled of urine. A forest of doorbells greeted you at the door, each connected to an individual room inside. Once, when I was visiting friends in their communal apartment, one of them asked, "What is a 'slum'?" Thinking of the leaky toilet and the garbage-filled stairwell, I didn't know what to say. Noticing my hesitation, one said sadly, "We know. It is this."

I learned, too, about their moral sufferings. People were routinely called in for interrogations. One young man I met lost his job after receiving a single postcard from a Western foreigner. Some were thrown into psychiatric hospitals for a harrowing weekend or longer. But I also discovered their humor, generosity, ingenuity, and courage. Although anyone found with prohibited works by authors like Solzhenitsyn could be sentenced to three years in prison, I once witnessed a man carrying an innocent-looking shopping bag come silently into a room where people were gathered, read a few chapters of one of Solzhenitsyn's books, and then leave, on to read somewhere else. The test of a radio was whether it could be listened to through the jamming. People would go far into the countryside for a chance to hear the Voice of America, and once, in a distant park, we danced to Duke Ellington's music.

I shared the lives and hospitality of unofficial poets, artists, and just plain ordinary folks and their families. I was touched by their overwhelming generosity, how despite their meager rations they immediately put on the table whatever they had. I soon stopped even casually expressing interest in an object I saw in their homes because if I did, it was instantly given to me. It seemed as if Russians had developed a sixth sense. They were able to trust their instincts and perceive people instantly, to sense unspoken desires and fulfill them before they were even expressed. Considering the fact that they lived with the constant knowledge that an informer was always somewhere in their midst, perhaps they had to sharpen senses that in the West had long been dulled.

Strangely, I had recognized them and felt at home immediately—and they with me, accepting me as *nash* (ours). I was told, "Every foreigner comes to us with his own aura and we can sense his attitude toward us." There is no rational explanation for this mysterious attachment I felt, or why it seemed I had found a family that I had never known existed. Perhaps my years of living with the pain of my son's hemophilia had helped. It had taught me about suffering, about helplessness before an arbitrary force one could not change. I had learned about despair and insecurity and what it was to live in an uncertain world of permanent fear and anxiety. I had learned how to fight and how to appreciate the precious beauty of a good hour. It was perhaps the best preparation I could have had in the West for the state of mind of the Russians. I recognized them and they me. They comforted me and gave me courage.

A quote I read struck me deeply: "The place to which you feel the strongest attachment may not be the country you're tied to by blood or birth; it's the place that allows you to become yourself." Despite barriers of language and geography, I who had always felt like a mid-Atlantic orphan shuttling between Europe and America never quite fitting in anywhere, found that place in Russia. And from the first, lasting through all these forty-six years, that feeling has never left me. Ironically, I found myself, the best and most authentic self I had always wanted to be, and my personal freedom in that totalitarian country. They said of me that I had a Swiss head and a Russian heart. They loved me and I loved them back. In the years that followed in St. Petersburg and elsewhere in Russia, adventures, flowers, magnificent experiences were showered on me along with a beauty and poetry of life in an intensity that I had never known existed. In short, I was transformed.

At first I was led by Constantine. Then, as I became more independent, I walked through every door that was opened to me. Often I was frightened as I rode out on a bus to some obscure suburb, never quite knowing what I might find behind the door I was going to enter. I was to discover another world, a city of poets—unseen heroes of the people— and meet the finest poets and artists of the city: poets Victor Sosnora, Alexander Kushner, Gleb Gorbovsky, and Joseph Brodsky, and painters Mikhail Chemiakin, Anatoly Belkin, and many others, all of them struggling then, many world-famous today. I think I was helped by an unusual fact I never understood: for some reason, from the beginning of my travels to the Soviet Union, I was not seen as a foreigner or even taken for one on the street. Later, when I became fluent in Russian, I was told over and over by Russians that I spoke with no accent. I think they exaggerated, but if so, I attribute it to having listened to underground poets read for hours. Nothing melts the ice more with Russians than being able to speak their language. Unlike the French, who wince if one uses *le* instead of *la*, Russians are overflowingly generous toward even the most awkward attempts of foreigners to speak their difficult tongue.

I could never have imagined that one city could contain so many poets and artists. In those days, they were idolized like underground rock stars among the city's population. In packed, smoke-filled rooms of communal apartments, they were begged, "Recite your poems." That they did, often for two or three hours at a time. Whatever drink was available was drunk. Packs of Byelomorkanal cigarettes were consumed, and their words were absorbed thirstily as if they were the stuff of life itself. Young scientists, then the privileged members of Soviet society, kept them alive by giving them money, buying their paintings, listening to their verses. The only names then known at all in the West were Evgeny Evtushenko and Andrei Voznesensky of Moscow, who were permitted to go to the West to the Pen Club and other New York literary organizations to demonstrate that there was no "repression" of creative artists in the Soviet Union. There, they were plied with champagne and the adulation of admiring women.

I decided that somehow these Leningrad poets I was meeting should be known in the West. Even though I was a weak reed, I was the only one they had, so I decided to go to England and seek out the great Russian scholar and linguist Max Hayward at St. Anthony's College in Oxford and suggest to him that a book with the poems and biographies of the young poets of Leningrad, all of them unknown in the West, should be done.

He asked, "Of course you know the language?"

I had only an elementary knowledge of Russian at the time, but, gulping hard, I answered, "Yes."

"You know the structure of the language?"

Again I answered as bravely as I could, "Yes."

He fell silent. I thought he was going to turn me down, but after scrutinizing me for what seemed a very long time he said, "It is a good idea. I will help you all I can."

We worked together for four years. While I assisted and learned, Max translated seventy-five poems, some of them several pages long. I wrote a foreword about the Leningrad scene and a short biography of each poet. Max became my mentor and close friend, and thanks to his invaluable help and guidance, *The Living Mirror: Five Young Poets from Leningrad* was published in 1972. It was then, and remains today, the only book about the poets of Leningrad at that time.

And then there was the ballet! All my life I have loved ballet. Even during the most painful days of Bobby's illness, if I could see a ballet, I was restored. Through the years, ballet has never failed to nourish and inspire me. The combination of iron discipline and daily work that transcends the limitation of space and body to create ephemeral beauty touches the soul in its deepest, wordless recesses. Gesture is, after all, what we first know long before we can speak. In Russia I, who had loved ballet all my life and had studied it for ten years, suddenly was able to spend as many enchanted evenings as I wished in the exquisite silver and blue Mariinsky Theater,[6] that unique theater that my idol, George Balanchine, whom I knew in New York, always called "the most beautiful theater in the world." There, often sitting in what had once been the tsar's box, I was transported into another world by the most sublime ballets the world has known.

Thanks to a Swiss dancer I knew who was training there, I was introduced into the former Imperial Ballet School (today called the Academy of Russian Ballet) and granted the rare privilege of spending hours watching classes and rehearsals. I met all the greatest dancers of the city, among them Natalia Makarova, Valery Panov, and Alexander Mintz. One day, the great ballerina Natalia Dudinskaya, who was then, along with her husband and partner the great dancer Konstantin Sergeeyev, the co-director of the school, took me to the large old rehearsal room so I could see what she said was "a good young lad...the best we have now." I watched spellbound as the then nineteen year old Mikhail Baryshnikov whirled around the hall doing his manège.[7] At the Bolshoi in Moscow, I was taken on a tour by the head of the theater's ballet museum, and there found what had been my mother's box. He showed me old photos of the great ballerina Balashova, whom she had idolized. In Moscow I also met the incomparable Maya Plisetskaya. And once, Maris Liepa, the greatest male star of the Bolshoi, brought me roses and I was able to see his immortal performance as the Roman commander Crassus in *Spartacus*. Those were magical days.

How lucky I was! But none of it was easy. In Leningrad, every effort was made by the Soviet government to ensure that Russians and foreigners did not meet. Restrictions abounded. No ordinary Russian citizen was permitted to enter a hotel where foreigners stayed, and all phone calls from the hotel were monitored. Hotel clerks at the obligatory official currency exchange offices even went so far as to try to make sure one did not get any two-*kopeck* pieces that were necessary to dial a number from a booth on the street. When I would ask for one, the usual answer was, "We have none." (My friends collected them for me and gave me a little bag entirely filled with those precious two-*kopeck* coins so I could use street telephones to contact them.)

Only rudimentary maps were available for tourists. Phone books did not exist. Yet despite all this, I had wandered the streets and gotten to know Leningrad in the finest way anyone can come to know and love a city—through the eyes and words of its poets. I fell in love with that unique capital, birthed from the dreams of Peter the Great, that had inspired so many and had once been called the "Northern Palmyra" and the "Babylon of the Snows." Despite its battering by revolution and war, its beauty and magic had endured. That city, always called by its inhabitants simply "Peter," became my own and there I made friendships that have now lasted forty-six years.

In those years, the city was dark at night, its huge empty buildings standing like specters. Late at night, I had to make my way back alone across the deserted square in front of the looming St. Isaac's Cathedral to the door of my hotel while my friends, hidden in the shadows behind trees, watched to see that I made it safely. It was a scary business. I would confront a tightly locked door. I would ring and ring, terrified that no one would let me in. When it finally opened, I faced a glowering doorman and behind him an armed soldier who looked me over suspiciously. Making an effort to look unconcerned and slip by him as quickly as I could, I would flee upstairs to my room only to confront the watchdog floor lady, usually an elderly woman with sharp and unfriendly eyes, who begrudgingly handed me my heavy key and, as I started down the hall, carefully noted my room number and the time in her ledger.

Leaving Leningrad was a terrible wrench. No ordinary citizen was permitted to accompany a foreign tourist to the train or plane, only Intourist—usually in the person of a dour, dark-suited man. As the train pulled out I would look at the disappearing city, knowing that my friends were there somewhere, but now invisible. After I was gone, there was no communication. Only silence, as if they had disappeared, left behind on an alien planet.

All I wanted was to be able to continue to see them. Then, in June of 1972, with no warning and just before I was to leave for another trip, my visa was abruptly refused. Why? Who knows? As a Russian friend had once warned me, "There are no whys. Only Westerners ask for reasons." Perhaps it was reason enough that I had managed to slip through the net and meet too many Russians.

I should have known it would end. On my winter trip in 1971, I had noticed the famous "black raven" car following me wherever I went, so obvious that one friend told me philosophically, "When we didn't see the car in front of our house, we thought you had left." On one of my last evenings, at a party with a group of poets and their friends, I saw mysterious figures nonchalantly "reading" on every landing of the building where the party took place. A shiny black car stood outside in the street, motor running. When I left that night accompanied by a friend, a soft snow was falling, and the contrast between the beauty of the city and the sinister presence, the constant humiliation of Russian citizens, seemed unbearably obscene, filling my independent Swiss soul with such a torrent of anger that I impetuously slammed my umbrella as hard as I could on the trunk of the shiny car. Terrified as a rabbit, the man in the car roared off.

Another night, when I was visiting a poet and his sister in a distant working-class part of the city where foreigners never set foot, we saw the sinister black car waiting under the window with its motor idling. Silent and apprehensive, we watched from behind the curtains of the darkened room as a lone man got out and circled the building as if to take its number. Frozen in fear, I was sure that this would be followed by the dreaded knock on the door. Instead, we saw him return to his waiting car and watched as he reentered the car, placed a call from his car phone, and then, after a short time, roared off. I was terrified of what the consequences might be. But the poet remained calm and quietly said, "Do not be afraid. These men know nothing of good and nothing of God. If it is really your destiny to help Russia, they will never be able to touch you."

And somehow, who knows, under the protection of what benign star, he turned out to be right.

And yet, not quite. At the airport in Moscow that spring of 1972, which was to be my last trip for many long years, all seemed normal until suddenly several men in uniform appeared and confronted me. I was thoroughly searched and forced to miss my plane. I had nothing to hide, but even so they confiscated two or three books on ballet that friends had given me. "Too old," they said also confiscating a copy of *Leningradskaya Pravda*, the city newspaper I had bought in the street. When I asked why, the curt answer was, "Because it is not sold in the West." After I was finally released I was left sitting on the floor of the airport, helpless and penniless. (No one was allowed to take so much as a *kopeck* out of the country. Money was carefully counted at the border and notebooks and address books minutely scrutinized.) I managed to convince a sympathetic airport desk clerk to let me make a phone call and then found my way to a friendly European embassy. A few days later, accompanied by the American consul who escorted me to the airport I was permitted to leave. The next time I applied for a visa, it was refused.

I knew that I had done nothing wrong—unless making friends with Russians was wrong. The Soviet authorities could not conceive of the idea that anyone, an American in particular, would simply like their country and their people. Thanks to their constant level of paranoia, they assumed I had to be up to something dangerously suspicious. So I learned in a minor way what so many Russians experienced in far more tragic and deadly ways: in the Soviet Union it didn't matter what you did; innocence was no defense. The blow could land in any way at any time, unexpected, treacherous.

After my visa was revoked, I cried for three days. I wept because I knew in my heart that I would go back someday but that it would be a very long time. I wept because I knew that when I did go back, it would be different—those five bohemian years with the poets of Leningrad were gone forever. I knew that the lowliest employee in the mysterious "organs" could put an X on your name—and that no one higher up the ladder would take the chance of removing it. Why should they risk it? Only the man at the very top could do it—but how in the world to get to the top? Nevertheless, I was totally determined to somehow find a way to go back.

The plain fact is that if the Soviet government had not refused me that visa, none of the rest of this story would have happened, and I certainly would never have met President Reagan. Yet perhaps, as Mikhail Bulgakov wrote in his book *The Master and Margarita*, "It was the work of they who always try to do evil but always end up doing good."

CHAPTER 2

THE WORM TURNS

I was not the only one having trouble getting a visa. In the Soviet Union, for those trying to obtain an exit visa, the situation was far worse. Shortly before I lost my visa in the spring of 1972, the Brezhnev government arbitrarily imposed what was called the "diploma tax" on would-be emigrants who had received a higher education in the Soviet Union. At the time, the only possibility for emigration for any Russian was for Jews requesting permission to emigrate to Israel. This required an invitation from a close relative living there. These were passed through the Dutch Embassy, as Israel had no embassy in Moscow. The lucky ones (Jewish or not) who were able to somehow obtain the precious invitation from a "relative" (dead or alive), having sold their worldly goods and preparing to leave the country, were suddenly asked to pay the entire cost of their state-financed "free education." I began getting anguished pleas for help from Russian friends, some of whom I had not even known were Jewish, and realized that a lot more than my little visa problem was happening. Yet when our family returned to the United States in the fall of 1972, I had only one wish: to get back to Leningrad, to my friends, to that beautiful city and broad sky. Selfishly, for me, U.S.–Soviet relations boiled down to that single goal. But how was I to do it?

The Soviet government very effectively used the visa as a weapon to ensure that the West would be prevented from knowing the true nature of things. Beginning with the advent of the Cold War in 1945, travel to the Soviet Union had become ever more restricted and its people more isolated. The result was that by 1972, with the Cold War intensifying, fewer and fewer people were allowed to travel to the Soviet Union: diplomats, rare business people, tourist groups (as Constantine had said, "as long as they come in groups, speak no Russian, and spend a lot of money"), and a few hardy and courageous language and history scholars, mainly in Moscow, rarely in Leningrad. But by 1967–68, individual travelers were almost never allowed, and then only to a few carefully selected cities. Seventy-five percent of the country was closed. As for Soviet citizens wishing to travel outside the Soviet bloc: that was well nigh impossible except for a strictly limited number of officials or approved scientists. The result was that the Russian people virtually disappeared from sight in the Western world. Our journalists could walk the streets in Moscow, but were systematically prevented from seeing anything that the authorities could not control, and were forbidden to travel more than 25 miles out of the city without permission. There were no American journalists in Leningrad. When I was in Moscow in those early years of 1968–72 and visited journalists I knew, I observed the convoluted way they often were forced to try to cover the news. Each journalist had his informer, and they would call each other to check on the information given to them.

The Soviets' restricted visa policy had its intended effect on the formation of American impressions and lack of knowledge about the life and the people of the Soviet Union. Insidiously, it caused a self-censorship in academia and the media. Professors in our universities whose careers depended on "publish or perish" and who needed to do research in the Soviet Union were obliged to adjust their studies to what was possible and permitted to them there. The result was a narrowing of information. It became virtually impossible to get a master's or a doctorate in any subject dealing with pre-Revolution Russia, as there were virtually no professors left whose field it was.[1] Thus gradually the subject of "Kremlinology" came to dominate the field, along with an ignorance about a pre-revolutionary Russia that became a stock in trade and the Soviet Union's best weapon against those who would change the calcified status quo. Kremlinology professors and students hired into the bureaucracy brought their models with them. The result was that Washington was dominated by think tanks and Kremlinology "experts"—all, it seemed of the opinion that "Russia" (not the Soviet regime) was by its very nature threatening and expansive. The few scholars at the Hoover Institute, such as Robert Conquest, who thought and wrote differently were regarded as "retrograde." The testimony of Russian émigrés, even such notable figures as George Balanchine, Igor Stravinsky, and Igor Sikorsky, were dismissed as being from another era, glamorous but passé.

The cornerstone of President Richard Nixon's foreign policy with the Soviet Union was called "détente" (relaxing of tensions), formulated in 1971 by Henry Kissinger, his national security advisor. It was founded on the German principle of *realpolitik* (often referred to in the U.S. as "power politics"), and was a policy based on practical and material factors rather than ideological, moralistic, or ethical premises. As it applied to the Soviet Union, it coupled expanded East–West trade with other enticements (most significantly, the vast shipments of grain sent from the West to the Soviet Union each year to help make up for the failure of Soviet collectivized agriculture.) Some arms treaties were concluded, but with no challenges whatsoever to the Soviet system and human rights policies. After our return to the United States from Paris, and as I became better informed based on my own experiences in the Soviet Union one question nagged at me: At what point does a country's internal treatment of its own citizens spill over and become a concern to the wider world? I thought the Soviet Union's actions qualified for that concern, and that this "détente" policy was the wrong approach. To me it seemed only common sense that the test of how well a government would keep its international agreements depended a lot on how they treated their own people. If they lied and betrayed them, it followed that they would find it easy to lie and betray others, and a policy that ignored that basic fact and called itself "realistic" was not.

My view was that it was important for our government to champion the rights of individual Americans and ordinary Russians to know each other in order for the United States to more clearly see and experience the truth of life as it was really lived in the Soviet Union. Although I knew nothing about the Washington scene and its power players, one evening in 1974 I happened to go to a cocktail party in New York where I met a woman who was then president of the Democratic Women's Club, along with her companion, a friend of Senator Henry (Scoop) Jackson. She asked me if I would be willing to give a talk at the club about my experiences in the Soviet Union, and he suggested I get in touch with Senator Jackson, who had just introduced the Jackson-Vanik amendment under the Federal Trade Act as a response to the Soviet "diploma tax." (The amendment did not specifically mention Jews, as the tax applied to all Soviet citizens, not only Jews.) This amendment contained a provision aimed at communist countries, including the Soviet Union, that denied them "most favored nation" trade status with the U.S. until they changed their emigration policy. It has the distinction of being the first and only gesture of the United States at that time toward human rights in the Soviet Union. The amendment was a direct challenge to the détente policy and anathema to Kissinger[2] (then Secretary of State) and the conservatives. I agreed to give a speech about my view at the Democratic Women's Club and to get in touch with Scoop Jackson, which I did. He invited me to his office, and in the course of our conversation asked me whether I thought he had gone too far with the amendment. I said no. This first meeting began a friendship with him that was to continue until his death in 1983.

Introduced by Senator Jackson and House Majority Whip John Brademas, in 1974 I gave my first political speech at the Democratic Women's Club. Titled "No Détente Without a Human Face," I argued against the policy of détente with the Soviet Union unless also pressing for human rights. In the audience was Helmut Sonnenfeldt,[3] then known as "Kissinger's Kissinger" and adamantly opposed to Jackson's amendment. To press my argument, I determined to get an interview with him, and finally made it to his vast office in the Old Executive Office Building, where he proceeded to outline the benefits of their détente policy. One phrase he used has stayed glued in my memory: "We are building webs of trade that will keep them from tilting to the right or the left, and while we are building these webs of trade, your friends and all others in the Soviet Union will have to take the hardest *knout*[4] (a lethal whip used in old Russia) that system can administer."

I was shocked to hear that word in the Old Executive Office Building. When he was through, I answered icily, "Mr. Sonnenfeldt, your policy may be brilliant, but there is an old Russian proverb that says, 'The well-fed wolf does not become a lamb.'"

To which he growled, "Nonsense!"

So went my first days in Washington.

The struggle to regain my visa lasted eleven years. During that time, my friends and I could not communicate with each other. Censors opened all letters or confiscated them. Phone calls were impossible. And yet, being totally cut off as if we were on another planet perhaps only deepened the friendships and made them more precious. During those long years, I always called myself a *refusenik* in reverse, and tried in every way to find some help in getting back my visa. I was certain that if I could make my case to higher-up Soviet officials, I could succeed. But how to get to them? I tried the State Department. That I was received at all had taken strong letters requesting assistance on my behalf from Dorothy (Dickie) Fosdick, Jackson's chief foreign policy advisor, as well as from three powerful senators—Henry Jackson (D), Hubert Humphrey (D), and Hugh Scott (R).

It wasn't easy to find one's way in those long corridors of the State Department, all hospital-blue like the inside of an asylum, so monotonously identical that a long horizontal stripe is painted on the walls to keep hapless souls, hopelessly lost, from starving to death in that maze of anonymous halls. Every office identical, impersonally marked with numbers and incomprehensible initials, impressed me as being more Soviet than the Soviets. The State Department officials I met were no help at all. In fact, they seemed as suspicious of me as the KGB. I was looked at incredulously and told disapprovingly by a stone-faced bureaucrat, "You are the single American citizen who knows the most Soviet citizens *personally*"—as if this were some kind of crime. (I remember thinking then that we were really in trouble if that were true.)

They were definitely not interested in my argument about the importance of Americans getting to know Russian people, certainly not by helping an American who was crazy (or, it was implied, disloyal) enough to associate with (gasp) Soviet citizens personally and struggling to get back to see them again (potentially troublesome, obviously… or who knows what?). The head of the Soviet Desk, rubbing his hands together nervously, said, "It would be inappropriate for us at the present time to do anything," the clear implication being the fact that my visa had been taken away meant I must have done *something*, and I was a nobody anyway. It all added up to the fact that they wouldn't—or couldn't—get the Soviets to pick up the phone.

To be fair, this was indeed a general problem. In those days, the Soviet Embassy phones were always busy or rang incessantly with no answer, and if one happened by remote chance to get a gruff, unpleasant voice, it was sure to say that the person you were calling was not there. With that, the Iron Curtain would slam shut. The Soviet Embassy was then on 16th Street, housed in what had once been the elegant mansion of the tsar's ambassador to the United States,[5] but it was now a gloomy fortress. Heavy curtains always drawn, gate locked, security cameras staring down, and the occasional stern face peeping suspiciously from behind the draperies.

Desperate to get back in somehow, I went to Finland and, using my Swiss passport, applied for a visa and waited in Helsinki the ten days necessary to process one. I received the visa only to face the chilling experience of being stopped and held at the frontier by the Soviet authorities for many tense hours. They finally refused me and sent me back to Helsinki. I did manage to sneak in visa-less three times for a couple of days while lecturing on cruise ships by slipping away from the excursion bus for ship passengers. Always expecting a heavy hand to land on my shoulder, I managed to meet a few of my friends and timed my return to the ship precisely so as to slip back unnoticed into the line of passengers returning from their excursions.

It is a shameful indication of the prevailing atmosphere of the time that in the mid-'70s when Alexander Solzhenitsyn came to the United States, he was officially viewed as a potential troublemaker in the brave new world of détente. Winner of the Nobel Prize in 1970 for his searing book, *The Gulag Archipelago*, which definitively exposed the truth of the horrors of the Soviet system and shattered forever the apologist argument that "you had to break a few eggs to make an omelet," he had been brutally expelled from the Soviet Union in 1974. When he first came to the United States, no organization invited him to speak publicly except for the AFL-CIO in San Francisco. *The New York Times* refused to cover the speech except for a small mention on a back page. *Times* columnist Hilton Kramer objected strenuously, and insisted that when Solzhenitsyn spoke again before the AFL-CIO in Washington in 1975 he would personally cover it. I attended that speech sitting at a table with a group of tough labor leaders who seemed a bit bemused by the Nobel laureate's words.

So deluded were we by our wishful détente policy that, backed by Henry Kissinger, President Gerald Ford refused to receive the great writer and Nobel Prize winner in the White House because it "might anger the Soviets" and jeopardize "progress" and the "continuation of détente." Privately, Ford called him "a horse's ass," "only out for publicity."[6]

Our policy makers had their minds made up and did not want to be confused by facts that did not support their convictions. The prevailing doctrine was that the Soviet Union could be "contained" but never challenged, and the conviction was that the regime was there to stay. This at a time when anyone who traveled there could see that it was already crumbling and that there was widespread dissatisfaction among the Russian people. Solzhenitsyn was attacked in our media, implying that he was a retrograde nationalist and anti-Semite (which he was not), and for having the nerve to criticize some aspects of America in a speech at Harvard graduation in 1978, until he was gradually almost as isolated and discredited in the United States as he had been in the Soviet Union.

Our relations with the Soviet Union were bleak. Leonid Brezhnev was securely in power, outlasting five U.S. presidents, and the Brezhnev years saw a sharp turn toward a forceful repression of Soviet citizens: dissidents (I have always preferred the Russian term "those who thought differently"), unofficial poets thrown into insane asylums, writers prohibited from any publication, the work of painters bulldozed in Moscow. By 1980 it was rumored that the ailing Soviet leader was undergoing treatments administered by an exotic female Georgian faith healer.[7] In the U.S., the détente policy postulating that webs of trade would soften up the regime was getting nowhere. The emigration issue that had exploded in 1972 was now at a stalemate. Soviet recalcitrance was blamed on the Jackson-Vanik amendment, which had, according to our Kremlinology specialists, had 'hardened the Soviet position."[8]

Then, in 1976, I got an unexpected phone call from Jacqueline Kennedy Onassis, who had been a couple of years ahead of me at Vassar and had sat next to me in the advanced French literature class we both attended. She was going to the Soviet Union—could I tell her anything about what to see? Thanks to my advice, she visited Pavlovsk Palace, where her visit is remembered fondly to this day. After her return, she called again to ask if I would give a lecture at the Metropolitan Museum of Art. Too ashamed to say that I had never actually been to a lecture at the Met, I agreed.

My work at *Life* magazine had taught me how to tell a story in pictures, so I decided to tell the story of the development of Russian culture through the eyes and work of Russian artists. I went to start my work at the photo library of the Met only to find that not a single slide of a Russian painting was catalogued there, a measure of the isolation of the Cold War. Luckily, I had precious albums and books that my friends in Russia had given me, and I was able choose among them to make several hundred slides. (I left a set for the museum library.)

This lecture was a public success and the nucleus from which grew what would become *Land of the Firebird*. In the four years it took me to write that book, so buried and forgotten was the history of an earlier Russia, it was a bit like doing an archaeological dig. I searched for the testimony of travelers, scoured hundreds of books on art, textiles, customs, music, ballet, crafts, photographs, paintings, even pre-Revolution Baedeker guides to check on train schedules, store addresses, and names of restaurants, as well as pre-Revolution phone books when those in Russia were considered among the best in Europe. (Those I found in the rare books department of Columbia University Library.)

As 1980 began, my hope of ever going back to the Soviet Union had never looked bleaker. Doggedly, I kept sending in visa applications only to have them denied or get no answer whatsoever. Despite all my efforts and repeated requests, I was getting no help. The few rare communications I received from acquaintances returning from the Soviet Union gloomily reported that they had been told by my friends that I was *zapresheno na vsegda* (forbidden forever). With my publisher, things looked no better. I had turned in my manuscript in the early fall of 1979 and had been promised that my book would be published early in 1980, but then my editor put my book aside to work on her husband's forthcoming book and *Firebird* was put off. I agonized. To no avail.

Land of the Firebird: The Beauty of Old Russia finally appeared in September 1980. Its reception provided chilling evidence of how out of step I was in the prevailing atmosphere of the time. The reviewer of *The New York Times* daily wrote a savage review that went for the jugular. I was ridiculed on every count—content, writing style—with remarks that today would be considered outrageously sexist: The book was a "lollipop" by "a woman who understood nothing about Russia... a romantic woman who loved only Russian men." It was so violent I felt as though I had been raped.

The book party held for me that evening at the elegant apartment of Pat Patterson, a leading New York society hostess, was more like a wake. Humiliated, trying hard to pretend I was okay and handling it well, I stood in a corner steeling myself for condolences when a man I did not know came up to me and introduced himself, "My name is Hilton Kramer and I think that the use of literary pages for political attacks is outrageous. I will do what I can." He was then the influential cultural critic for *The New York Times* with a regular column, and he wrote a strong criticism of the review. *The New York Times Book Review* came out later with a measured review by an English historian that brought me a glimmer of hope. Still, I was so wounded that I didn't dare show my face and thought I would never be able to write anything again. *Land of the Firebird* seemed totally annihilated and buried.[9]

But the Russian community felt differently. With the battle cry, "This book has been attacked!" Russians in the United States, even priests in the Orthodox Church, took up my defense and I received grateful letters from Russians all over the world. I had sent my manuscript to Alexander Solzhenitsyn, living in seclusion in Vermont, and received a touching letter from him that brought me to tears.[10] A few days after the review, Alexander Ginzburg, a leading heroic Soviet dissident and a darling of *The New York Times*, called me saying encouragingly, "Good that it is so harsh. Everything that Alexander Isayevich [Solzhenitsyn] has always said." Then he added, "I could write a letter to the *Times*—but I don't think they would print it. We will fight. But we will use different weapons." In his lectures all over America, Ginzburg held up my book in colleges and universities as recommended reading.

And thank goodness most of America doesn't read *The New York Times*! *Firebird* became a public success and has remained in print for thirty-three years, used in colleges and universities and carried by tourists. The book even made it to the farthest reaches of the Soviet Union, where English-speaking guides used it to inform both their countrymen and foreigners, and continue do so today.[11] I began to be asked to lecture, although in 1980 the lecture agent told me that "men do not like to hear about politics from women" and booked me only in women's clubs or art museums.

With all the problems in my life, I hardly noticed when, in November 1980, Ronald Reagan was elected to his first term. I didn't vote for him and echoed the views of my liberal journalist friends who considered him a Hollywood lightweight. I had campaigned for the nomination of Senator Henry Jackson. When Reagan took office in January, he was surrounded by a phalanx of hardliners: Secretary of State Alexander Haig, National

Security Advisor Richard Allen, and Richard Pipes, head of Soviet–East Europe at the National Security Council. The few cultural contacts who fitfully brought ballet dancers along with their KGB spear-carriers to the U.S. to exhibit "Soviet culture" and make money for the state were all that remained.

The United States continued its policy of treating the communist regime as if it legitimately represented the Russian people, refusing to even consider the possibility of change. *Russian* and *Soviet* were merged in an all-purpose synonym, when in reality the two were very different. How the Russian people thought, the importance of culture and religion—all were ignored or dismissed as non-relevant. "Why is it always Soviet sputniks and Russian tanks?" one of my Leningrad friends had once sadly asked me, a remark that neatly sums up the situation. Stereotypical thinking dominated our pronouncements and our media. To cite a few random examples: "tsars and commissars" are the same; Russian people are "apathetic" and have a "slave mentality"; everything was "sunk in the mud before the Revolution"; Russians have "always lived under despotic rulers"; the Orthodox Church is "corrupt"; "communism, while brutal, brought social advances where none existed before." (After all, one must break a few eggs to make an omelet. How many eggs? What kind of an omelet?) I had seen that this was quite contrary to the thinking of the majority of Russians in the Soviet Union, who felt that they had been victimized by the Soviet regime more cruelly than the other republics: they were the majority, and, in order to create a new Soviet man, they had to be crushed, their culture vulgarized, their religion exterminated.

This is a taste of the atmosphere at the time of Ronald Reagan's election to office. Not in my wildest imagination could I have conceived that this event would not only lead me back to the Soviet Union, but also to the Oval Office, that my life would be changed dramatically by a set of adventures for which the previous years had been only prologue. My efforts to return to Russia seemed utterly hopeless. But just as I was about to give up, I was rescued by the United States Army.

THE MILITARY DENTS THE WALL

Ever since my days at Vassar, I have felt comfortable with military men. I like their courtesy, discipline, and crisp no-nonsense approach. With their shiny polished shoes, squeaky-clean knife-creased trousers, and erect posture, they reminded me of boy scouts and the best of our firefighters and policemen. Most of them join not for the money, but because they want to serve. Their motto, "Duty, Honor, Country," states concepts that have a noble 19th century ring in the babble of our shallow tele-speak society.

West Point was a short hour's bus ride away from Vassar, and my first contact with military men was with the cadets I dated there. I also got to know midshipmen at the Naval Academy at Annapolis, and was elected the editor of their once-a-year issue called *The Femmes Log*. I remember the Ring Dance at Annapolis as one of the crowning social occasions of my college years. In fact, I have nothing but happy memories of those days at both academies, and have always regretted that my two daughters did not have the chance that I had to attend those dances (called "Hops" at West Point). Wearing a ball gown and long gloves, with a dance card around my wrist, I would be danced off my feet by eager white-gloved cadets in their dress-gray uniforms with a double row of gold buttons, followed by a stroll out to the wide veranda to admire the majestic Hudson River by moonlight.

It was our military who were to give me my first serious toehold in my early days as a Russia hand. By chance, I met Colonel William Odom and his wife at journalist Hedrick Smith's house in 1976. Rick had just published his best-selling book, *The Russians*, in 1975, and had met Odom when he served as assistant Army military attaché (1972–74) in Moscow. At that time, Bill was assistant professor of government at West Point and from our first meeting I began a lasting friendship with him and his wife Anne. Bill was an outstanding military intellectual with a razor-sharp mind, an expert on Russian and Soviet affairs, and from late 1977 to 1981 served at the White House as military assistant to Zbigniew Brzezinski, NSC advisor to President Carter and in 1981 was promoted to major general. Bill was outspoken and could be acerbic in his opinions and criticism. There were those who feared his sharp and searching arguments, but I always enjoyed parrying with him, saying that I needed him to "get the fuzz out of my thinking." Among his many crisp and succinct statements I have never forgotten this one: "The job of the military is to stay out of war—but if we are in one, to win it."[12]

It was Bill who first invited me to come and address the political science classes of West Point about the dissident movement in the Soviet Union, and I was later instrumental in bringing to lecture at West Point two of the leading figures of that movement, Pavel Litvinov and Major General Petro Grigorenko.[13] Both were extremely impressed by the Academy. Surrounding Bill were an outstanding group of instructors, all then majors, among them Tyrus Cobb and John Concannon, an outstanding linguist who used some of the poems in my book, *The Living Mirror: Five Young Poets from Leningrad*, to teach the cadets Russian. Some years later, as army military attaché in Moscow, John would be a great support. Another was Robert Ivany, the son of Hungarian immigrants and former star of the Army football team, who went on to be the carrier of the atomic suitcase at the White House and was later promoted to major general. In 1976 he came with a group of officers to hear my initial lecture on Russian art and culture at the Metropolitan Museum, where his good looks and impressive military bearing caused frissons of admiration among the ladies of the program department, one of whom trilled, "Oh, Hungarians! They make the most wonderful military men!"

In 1977 Bill Odom invited me to participate in the West Point SCUSA Conference,[14] where, in my baptism of fire, I took part for the first time in a seminar where I was the only woman among thirty men—military, State Department officials, and civilians. At this conference, I had as my escort Major Tyrus Cobb. We got to know each other well, and he and his wife, Suellen, also became good friends of mine. Ty was promoted to lieutenant colonel in 1983, and he was appointed to the staff of the National Security Council.[15]

The military consistently supported me, and if it had not been for them, I might not have gotten any further. I learned a great deal from the military officers I met. I admired and tried to emulate the direct way in which they could discuss difficult questions and opposing views without getting hot under the collar, and those encounters taught me a lot about how to voice my opinions in a calmer but more forceful way.

In June 1981 Bill invited me to come to West Point to meet Ursula and Edwin Meese,[16] there for the graduation of their son. It was on that occasion that I first glimpsed President Reagan, who gave the address. I was seated directly behind Nancy Reagan, who, even in the broiling sun, remained immaculate and bandbox fresh in her pink jacket and knife-pleated pastel-plaid skirt. Never could I have imagined that just a few years later I would meet and get to know them both.

In subsequent years, I was invited to lecture at three War Colleges, and these remain fond career memories.[17] At the Army War College in Carlyle, Pennsylvania, I participated in a seminar where I was the only woman among twenty-one U.S. colonels—plus a Saudi general who was understandably surprised to see a woman present. Of all the senior officers I was privileged to meet, the one who impressed me most was General Andrew Goodpaster. In his brilliant speech at Carlyle, he quoted Churchill, Plato, Roosevelt, and Shakespeare, and never once used *Soviet* and *Russian* incorrectly. An imposing and elegant man, Goodpaster was a great soldier statesman in the tradition of George Marshall. A decorated hero of World War II, during his brilliant career he had served as adjutant to George Marshall and close advisor to General and then President Dwight Eisenhower, and was the first Supreme Commander of NATO. When I met him, he had just taken over as Commandant of West Point.[18] With the wise words, "In order to know what people will fight for, you have to know what they love," he invited me to give a lecture on Russian art and culture to the assembled cadets at the Academy.

The military officers I came to know were more open, less doctrinaire, and, paradoxically, more anti-war than the civilian bureaucrats that they (and I) often had to deal with. If I had to use two words to describe my impression of the top military cadres I had the good fortune to meet, they would be *responsibility* and *restraint*. Unlike civilian officials, they know directly what it means to send men into battle to be injured or killed. For them, it is never abstract. And unlike many other nations, our country has never had to worry that the military would challenge or overthrow our government. We are lucky to have them.

The military always treated me respectfully, in contrast to many bureaucrats who, jealous and often insecure, devoted to their own advancement and position, and always needing to be one up, tried to denigrate me and sweep me out of the way. The military were different, often seeking differing information because, as they told me, "it helped them to do their jobs better." One colonel at the Army War College said, "Our computers give us a lot of information, but they don't tell us how to put it together."

I once asked a psychiatrist why it was that the military seem to have less trouble than bureaucrats accepting a woman with strong differing views. "My dear," he said jovially, "it's because they wear their testicular credentials on their chests." Ever since, I have felt that I should modestly cover my eyes when I see a high-ranking officer's beribboned jacket. But there is truth in his facetious remark: the military had no fear that somehow I might take their jobs.

I was to find that our military were consistently better informed and more abreast of developments in the Soviet Union, often light-years ahead of the bureaucrats who remained narrowly locked in their one-dimensional political science models, their devotion to the status quo, and their conviction that nothing could ever change.[19]

Very early, members of our military perceived the trend of Russian (vs. Soviet) feelings that I had also seen, the first to sense the growing interest in nation and identity that was beginning to preoccupy the Russian people. All who were sent to the Soviet Union spoke and read Russian well, whereas many of our diplomatic officials, even some of our ambassadors, could barely speak a word. For the State Department, the Soviet Union was classified as a "hardship post" that brought the incentive of higher compensation. Not so for our military. None were sent who were not qualified, and only those who really wanted to be there went.

President Jimmy Carter's forgiving Christian stance, his public kissing of Brezhnev, confused the Soviets, convincing them that we were ineffectual. Once again, a Russian proverb sums it up: "No matter how often you feed the wolf, it always keeps looking at the woods." The Soviets intensified their steady push into various borders (Angola, Afghanistan), which resulted in growing tensions and the U.S. withdrawal from the Moscow Olympic Games in 1980.

When Reagan took office in January 1981, his reputation was well known in the Soviet Union. Although it would be two years before he was to call them the "evil empire," his strong, uncompromising anti-communist position, along with his conviction that America was the example that would bring peace and prosperity to all, made the Soviets very uncomfortable. The men in the Kremlin were curious about this new leader and anxious to take his measure. In that time of deteriorating relations, they began to rethink their position and extend some feelers through our military. In 1980 Ty Cobb was the first military officer to be awarded an IREX[20]-sponsored research grant to the Soviet Union. He had wanted to conduct dissertation research on the Soviet general staff, but was denied access to the Ministry of Defense archives. Reformulating his project to focus on the Soviet energy sector, he was accepted. When he got to Moscow he found opportunities to talk to Soviet analysts at IMEMO[21] and the Defense Institute during the final phase of the Brezhnev period, just as the first rumblings of change were being felt beneath the surface of the moribund Soviet system. He remembers that "Russian policy analysts began preparing analyses that were fairly stark and frightening about their country's future." He had the feeling that many of the Russians he met "were searching for ways out of their country's dilemma even before the leadership was prepared to recognize the need for change."

Ty Cobb had been the only person who had taken a real interest in my efforts to get back my visa, and it was he who, with a stroke of informed imagination, was to make a dent in the stone wall of silence and refusal I had encountered during nine long years.

When *Land of the Firebird* came out in the fall of 1980, I had been attacked, vilified, and ridiculed by *The New York Times*, but not by my friends in the military, who bought a great many copies. Nevertheless, I was surprised when, just before he left for Moscow, Ty called and asked noncommittally, "Could you give me seven copies of your book?" (I thought his request rather a heroic act as the hardbound books were quite heavy.) "And could you sign them?"

"Of course," said I, and he gave me a list of names that startled me even more: Georgy Arbatov, General Nathan Milstein, and other luminaries of the USA Institute.[22] I didn't ask him why.

When he returned from Moscow some months later, he called to report that he had scattered the books on the desks of the various gentlemen to whom I had signed them. At first, he said, they made no comment. But later he was asked, "Do you know this woman?" Indeed he did, he answered. "Interesting woman," they continued, "we would like to talk to her."

"Well," said Ty, "as a matter of fact, she would like to talk to you, too, but unfortunately she can't get a visa."

Then he went on to suggest to me cryptically, "Go see…," and named someone connected with the Soviet Embassy in Washington.

I asked only, "Is he high enough?"

"I think so," answered Ty.

Knowing that Ty was connected with military intelligence, I figured he knew what he was talking about. So I took down the name of the man in question and once again set out for the capital, ready to try anything.

CHAPTER 3

BACK IN THE USSR

"Relations between the Super Powers were not simply bad, they were nonexistent."
—Secretary of State George Shultz, 1982[1]

After my experiences of harassment in the Soviet Union and all my fruitless visa efforts over the years, I had to screw up my courage to pick up the phone. Amazingly, the Soviet Embassy phone that was ordinarily kept on busy was actually answered. I introduced myself, and, after a short interval, was connected with a suave man who spoke fluent English only slightly tinged with a Russian accent. Yes, he would meet me, he said pleasantly, and suggested the Soviet Embassy. After my tangles with the mysterious "customs officials" in the airport in the Soviet Union, I wasn't anxious to go there, so I demurred and said I would rather it be elsewhere. He suggested the lobby of the Jefferson Hotel across the street.

"How will I know you?" I asked.

"Well," he said, "I have white hair. I will be wearing a blue suit and will have my raincoat over my right arm."

It sounded so much like a caricature of the spy movies I had seen that I answered facetiously, "I am short, blonde, round, and will be carrying my raincoat over my *left* arm."

So I met Valentin Mikhailovich Berezhkov, who would play a key role in getting me back to the Soviet Union. He did indeed, as he had said, have a fine shock of white hair, very bright, searching blue eyes, a soft voice, and a silky manner, very different from the gruff Soviet officials whose sartorial style ran to baggy (and often sweaty) suits and scuffed shoes that I had met before in the years when my former husband Bob Massie had been *Newsweek's* UN correspondent, Berezhkov was dressed nattily in a well-tailored navy-blue suit, white shirt, and silk tie. He suggested a Spanish restaurant and drove me there in his powder-blue Cadillac. I didn't know what his position was, nor why Ty had seemed so sure he was the right one, but it was clear that he was secure in his authority. Indeed, I was later to learn that he was the only man associated with the Soviet Embassy who had permission to live outside the wire-fenced compound that members of the Soviet delegation in Washington called home. I don't remember the details of our conversation that day, but I do remember that, unlike the narrowly ideological Soviet bureaucrats I had collided with before, he knew the United States well, and despite the fact that he sometimes mouthed the obligatory Soviet propaganda criticism, he admired and liked America and Americans.

Things always moved slowly at first with the Soviets. There had to be a lot of schmoozing and jockeying for position before one got to the point. I told him something of my experiences in the Soviet Union, but we did not talk about my visa problems that day; in fact, it was a long time before we ever did. Still, I had made a direct contact and I trusted Ty.

We did not get down to the essentials for over a year after that first meeting—until Leonid Brezhnev's death on November 10, 1982. The television cameras caught his wife making the sign of the cross over his body. How odd, was the comment of our newsmen, who then promptly dismissed it as irrelevant.

Yuri Vladimirovich Andropov, then head of the KGB and known in the U.S. as the "butcher of Budapest" because of his brutal role in suppressing the Hungarian revolution of 1956, became the General Secretary of the Communist Party and leader of the Soviet Union on November 12, 1982. In hindsight, looking back on this still mysterious leader who lasted only fifteen months in power before his death, it can be seen that he marked the beginning of the end of communism in the USSR. Reliable facts about him remain scarce. Still today, almost nothing is known of this enigmatic man, his education or war service, his preferences in music and literature, his ideas or his linguistic abilities—not even agreement on how tall he was. So little was known about his family that he was assumed to be a widower until his wife, Tatiana, appeared at his funeral. A loner, as head of the KGB he was an oddity to the top party leaders. But as time has passed his reputation in Russia has grown. He brought many of the younger generation into the higher reaches of government, among them was Mikhail Gorbachev. Today, a list of his protégés reads like a who's-who in the list of those who became the forefront of change in the Soviet Union.[2] In my lectures during those days, I used to say that every Soviet citizen wore a mask, and the higher the official, the tighter the mask, adding, "If there is anyone there now who may make a change, we will not know it." Although the Western establishment, preoccupied as usual with the status quo and the old Kremlin dinosaurs, did not pay much attention to this tip of the iceberg, Gorbachev was that man, the first of the young "Khrushchev spring" generation to gain the higher echelons of power.

With the coming to power of Andropov the former chief of the KGB, I reasoned that perhaps my man might be in a more powerful position than before. So although I had not seen or spoken to him for several months, I took a chance and called Valentin.

He greeted me warmly. "Ah, Suzanne, I have been thinking of you!"

I replied sweetly, "And I of you." Although I had no plans to go to Washington, I decided to try my luck so I lied. "I will be in Washington next week and wondered if I could see you."

To my surprise he invited me enthusiastically. "Oh, yes, you will come to us at home and Lera will cook you a good Russian meal!" In those Cold War days, this was an extraordinary invitation, so of course I flew to Washington.

As soon as I entered his comfortable apartment, I saw a group of photographs on the wall that made clear his exceptional position. One showed the familiar image of the triumvirate at the Yalta Conference of 1945, but this photo was a little different from the usual ones. Official shots show only Stalin, Churchill, and Roosevelt sitting on chairs on the veranda of Livadia, the former vacation home of Nicholas II, but this shot was a little wider. Leaning on a pillar near Stalin stood a dapper, elegant young man in a dark suit, Stalin's translator—whom I immediately recognized as Valentin Mikhailovich Berezhkov. There was another photograph, this one of Ribbentrop and Molotov preparing to sign the 1939 Nazi–Soviet Non-Aggression Pact. There, at Molotov's elbow, was an even younger version of Valentin, who, fluent in both English and German, had been Molotov's translator, too.

Lera had indeed prepared a fine Russian meal, well lubricated with vodka. Thus fortified, at the end of the meal I decided to screw up my courage again and at long last bring up the subject of my visa. "Valentin," said I boldly, "any other country would have given me a medal for the books I have written about you."

"Ah, yes," he replied smoothly, "but would you have accepted it if we were to give you one? Would you like to be a hero of the Soviet Union?"

From somewhere I found words to answer. "No. I would so much rather be a hero of the *Russkaya Zemlya*. It is so much more poetic, don't you think?" (Here I must explain that the words *Russkaya Zemlya*—the Russian Land—is the expression used in the great medieval epic poems of Russian heroes battling the nomads of the Asiatic steppe and evoke the early days of Rus[3] and what is sometimes called the "Golden Dream of the Slavs"—the antithesis of Soviet communism.)

So it was after this dinner table exchange, when Lera had discreetly vanished into the kitchen that at last I asked, "All right, Valentin, what is this about my visa? I am perfectly aware of what Americans sometimes do in the Soviet Union and I have done none of this." This time, he pulled out a notebook and scribbled busily as I told my story with all its convolutions.

When we were through, to my astonishment he pulled out a copy of *Land of the Firebird* and asked me if I would sign it for Andropov himself. I hesitated. I had no inclination to sign, "To Yuri Vladimirovich with best wishes." So, after some thought, I signed, "To Yuri Vladimirovich, with hope for the future of the great Russian land." No Soviet Union. And I left.

That was December 1982. Ty had accomplished what the senators and the State Department could not. He had connected me with the right man. Why did he do it? I have always wondered. Could it be that he was following Odom's maxim about the job of the military to stay out of war? Whatever the reason, this time there would finally be results.

As 1983 began, I was spending my writing days in a friend's apartment at the Hotel des Artistes on 67th Street in New York, working on a novel that wasn't going well. I was still fixated on one thing: I wanted to get back to Leningrad and do a book on the history of the palace of Pavlovsk, to write something honest about the Soviet Union that the West could understand and share: the remarkable story of the work and dedicated devotion of the Russians in restoring the treasures of their past destroyed in World War II, a story that the West ignored entirely. It was a subject light-years away from the preoccupations of Washington, the Cold War, and the deteriorating U.S.–USSR relations. No publisher wanted it. How the Russian people thought, the potential importance for them of their pre-communist history and culture were dismissed as "not relevant." My book was a direct challenge to these assumptions. Dissidents were the cry of the day. Who cared about the painstaking restoration of a Russian tsarist palace? I kept trying to get my visa, but that looked more hopeless than ever. Because of the collapse of the cultural exchange agreement, there were no academic routes left. That was where things stood when out of the blue, I got some news that was to set in motion a series of events that would ultimately propel me into the middle of superpower relations.

At home in Irvington on a cold winter night in early February, I got a phone call. I heard the suave accented voice of Valentin Mikhailovich Berezhkov on the end of the line. I had not spoken to him since our dinner the previous December in Washington. With no preamble, he simply said, "I have heard from Moscow. Everything is all right. You may go whenever you like. You may make concrete plans." Just like that, after eleven years of exile and all my frustrated efforts with bureaucrats on both sides.

My years of disappointment and wariness with all Soviet officials was so deeply ingrained that, overcoming my astonishment and surging elation in a masterpiece of understatement I answered coolly, "Thank you. I'll think it over."

After I hung up, I sat on the floor stunned. Could it really be true? Was it really possible that I could go back once more? I have jokingly said since that only the Soviet Union could do a retrospective Suzanne Massie photographic exhibit by lining up my passport pictures Andy Warhol–style from all those abortive visa attempts over the years. Three passport pictures were obligatorily required, but as two were placed on the visa, which was taken away upon leaving, I have always wondered what they did with the third. Was it thrown away or perhaps filed in some dim basement of KGB archives? What for? Despite having heard from the poet Victor Sosnora through a friend returning from the Soviet Union that the KGB had told him that I was prohibited "forever," I had somehow succeeded. But how? Years would pass before I would learn the answer.

Anyway, hope springing eternal, I followed his instructions and applied again. I wanted to go for Orthodox Easter, which was on April 25.[4] But once again I was rejected, this time turned down by Intourist. Their excuse: no hotel room. I called Berezhkov and said, "Valentin, it seems there is not a room for me in all the Soviet Union."

This time his voice turned angry and impatient. "They [Intourist] have nothing to do with these things!" he growled.

"Seems they do," I said. "Over to you, Valentin Mikhailovich."

A few weeks later, he called to tell me that Georgy Arbatov, the powerful director of the USA Institute, the highly regarded think tank in Moscow, was to be in New York. Arbatov, a frequent visitor to the United States, was considered to be the horse's mouth on matters of Soviet–American relations. A fixture on American television panels and a favorite of interviewers and conferences, he was said to have been Brezhnev's closest advisor on all matters of American policy, and although I was dubious, Valentin strongly urged that I should see him. There was to be a reception at the Soviet Mission to the UN in New York and he invited me to come.

Dressed in power black, I approached the building on 67th Street with its tightly locked, menacing doors with apprehension. I had often demonstrated in front of that forbidding building with Carole Channing, Joel Grey, and other show-business personalities, carrying placards of support for dissidents in the Soviet Union, including the great ballet dancer, my friend Valery Panov, who was languishing under house arrest in Leningrad. Multiple all-seeing cameras were mounted outside, and masked men in white coveralls, looking like sinister snowmen, stood on the roof photographing all of us below, but I had never actually been inside the place. Nervously summoning my courage that cold winter night, I knocked hesitantly. The door was unlocked and opened by a surly security guard. The entry was bare except for a coat rack. Another dour man looked me over suspiciously, checked my name, and took my coat without a word. Feeling as if I had somehow landed back in Moscow, I walked down the long official halls with their dark-red leather Soviet-style armchairs, passing under looming portraits of Lenin and Andropov, and entered a large reception hall where a crowd was assembled. On a long table were spread a variety of hors d'oeuvres and a small forest of bottles of vodka, wine, and soda. Valentin was there, thank goodness, and he swiftly brought me over to meet Georgy Arkadyevich Arbatov.

Arbatov was a tall man in his late fifties whose long nose and even longer jowly face gave him the look of an aging bloodhound. With the smooth manner of Soviet officials accustomed to dealing with foreigners, he did not mention the question of my visa directly, greeting me with a slight smile and saying, "I understand you have had some trouble with our bureaucrats." (*You bet*, I thought.) Affably, he continued, "I have, too. Apply again." I told him that I could not go until September. He only repeated, "Apply again," and moved on. The whole exchange took less than two minutes. I stayed a short while longer, exchanged a few words with other Soviet officials, shook the hand of Oleg Troyanovsky, Soviet Ambassador to the UN, and beat a quick retreat, relieved to be out of the oppressively

Soviet atmosphere and again on the bustling streets of New York.

Following Arbatov's advice, I applied again a few months later, expecting to once again be turned down. This time there were no glitches, and I got the long-awaited visa. As it turned out, the forced delay proved to be providential, although at the last minute a tragic international catastrophe almost prevented my trip.

On September 1, 1983, a Soviet fighter pilot shot down a civilian Korean airliner that had mysteriously wandered into Soviet airspace, killing 269 passengers, including 61 Americans. The world community was outraged. A firestorm of international protests and bitter denunciations exploded. In the United States, a demonization of the Soviet government and Russians in general escalated. In Long Beach, California, longshoremen prepared to attack any Soviet seamen whose ships docked in the port. The governors of New York and New Jersey refused to allow the plane carrying Soviet Foreign Minister Andrei Gromyko to the UN to land. In Texas, Americans took to shooting at Russians on their television sets. In Vermont, a hapless young woman who happened to be of Russian descent was shot dead.

A few months earlier, the Reagan administration had made overtures to the Soviet government about opening a consulate in Kiev and resuming the Cultural Exchange Agreement that had lapsed under President Carter after the Soviet invasion of Afghanistan, but after the KAL catastrophe, all negotiations collapsed. Newspapers and politicians denounced the Soviets as barbarians with no respect for human life. Over strong Soviet protest, the U.S. redoubled its plans to install Pershing missiles in Europe. All diplomatic contacts between the U.S. and USSR came to an abrupt halt. The temperature of the Cold War plunged to a deep and ominous freeze.

The Soviets emphatically insisted that the airliner was a spy plane that had ignored all warnings. Seymour Hersh in his book, *The Target is Destroyed* chronicles in meticulous detail that it was due to tragic miscalculations by both the pilots of Flight 007 and the suspicions and fears of the panicked Soviet military. He also tells that a small group of U.S.

Air Force analysts prepared a secret presentation using slides showing that air force intelligence realized within hours that the Soviets did not deliberately shoot down the plane, but due to the heat of the moment their presentation got little attention and Hersh ends with "The sad fact is those in Washington who chose to increase international tension and their counterparts in Moscow who responded in kind were acting in ignorance of the facts. Flight 007 was a crisis made far more dangerous by the extent of misunderstanding and anti-Soviet feeling it engendered." So was it a tragic mistake inflamed by Cold War paranoia, or could it perhaps have been something more sinister? Knowing from experience that happenings were rarely what they seemed on the surface in the Soviet Union, I have continued to wonder. The incident occurred at the end of the summer, a critical time in the USSR when leaders were generally away on vacation. Andropov himself was gravely ill and absent from Moscow. Could it have possibly have been an attempt at a coup from hard line elements in the Kremlin? In subsequent years, I was given hints in Moscow that this might have been the case. In any event, after the first flurry of Soviet assurances that the catastrophe would be thoroughly investigated and those responsible for ordering the strike found and punished, and in spite of the hordes of investigative international journalists who attempted to get additional details, in the end, little were to be had. If any other shadowy figures might have been involved in the tragedy, they remain unknown to this day.

Michael Deaver who was with the President in California at his beloved Rancho del Cielo when the incident occurred told me this interesting story of Reagan's reaction: "It was always hard to get Reagan away from his ranch, but I insisted that the American people expected him to be in Washington and so reluctantly, with Reagan still in his jeans, boots, and Stetson we flew to Washington and went directly to the White House Situation Room where everyone was anxiously waiting to see what he would do. What would he order? Call out the Sixth Fleet? What? He could have done anything! Instead, he stretched way back in his chair and said "We will do nothing. The world will do it for us. We need to think of our long term interests." So, although publicly Reagan harshly condemned the Soviet action, he took no direct retaliation against the Soviets.

As for me, even the highly contentious and volatile atmosphere sparked by the KAL disaster was not going to deter me from returning to the USSR after eleven long years of absence. Friends exclaimed incredulously, "You aren't planning to go to that country *now*, are you?" I answered that I would walk if I had to.

On my way to Moscow I first stopped briefly in Paris, where there was to be a gathering of the Friends of the New York City Ballet, a group of super-rich American socialite donors who traveled about the world following the ballet. Members in various cities of the world outdid each other to provide lavish cocktails, dinners, and divertissements before and after the ballet performances to which these stylishly attired birds of paradise in their velvets, sequins, and furs would alight in a perfumed flock, chirping and kissing. Because of my books, I was included as a kind of mascot, since I obviously didn't have the deep pockets it took to become a member.

The evening before I was to leave for Moscow after a ballet performance, Pierre Cardin, the famous Parisian designer, hosted a gala champagne dinner at Maxim's restaurant that went on until the wee hours. Furious talk about KAL and the barbaric Russians swirled. The defense minister of France angrily declared that the Soviets had called it an "unknown plane" and that civilized nations did not shoot down "unknown planes," exclaiming heatedly, "There can be no dealing with them!" At about 2 AM, I slipped out to pack and try to catch a couple of hours of tense sleep in order to get up at 5 AM to go to the airport. Officially, there were to be no planes as there was a two week international moratorium on all air traffic to the Soviet Union, and French pilots had joined the protest. But having lived in France long enough, I knew that, with the French, there might always be an exception, so I went out to try anyway and groggily sat in the airport for several hours until, sure enough, a single Air France plane to Moscow was announced and I got on it. Aside from one member of an African embassy, I was the only passenger.

I was full of turbulent emotions and yes, fear. Eleven years had gone by, but that was not enough to erase the memories of the harrowing treatment I had received at the hands of Soviet customs officials who had once searched me at the airport, as well as the faceless men who lurked in the shadows whenever I went to see Russian friends in Leningrad. But despite all that, I was moved to tears when, after so many years, I looked out and saw once again the dark forests dotted with ramshackle villages that announced the approach to Moscow's Sheremetyevo Airport.

On September 23, after my long years of exile, I was back in the USSR. An eerie sight greeted me, so unreal that the memory has never left me. The enormous mausoleum-style airport with its long dark halls, sky-high ceilings, huge maroon marble columns, and dark-gray marble floors was cavernously empty. Not a soul was to be seen except a couple of lonely soldiers forlornly standing guard. My footsteps echoing in the vast halls, I anxiously made my way to the passport control. The drill hadn't changed there. Just as I remembered from before, a stone-faced soldier wearing the green epaulets of the KGB frontier guards sat in a closed booth. Silently, suspiciously, he peered up at me, his face half-illuminated by the light of his small desk lamp. For what seemed an eternity, I shifted my weight and tried to look unconcerned as he scrutinized my documents and filled in forms with slow deliberation, looking first at the papers, then up at my face, up and down, up and down, over and over as I tried to quell my growing conviction that something was seriously wrong. Then he picked up a phone to call some mysterious higher authority. After a muffled conversation, it was once again up, down, up. Finally, when I was sure all hope was lost and I was about to be arrested, there was the welcome metallic clunk of a mechanical stamp. My passport was handed back to me, and with a wave of dismissal and a click, the barrier opened.

In those days, an official Intourist representative still met all foreigners, but since no planes were supposed to arrive, no one was there. With rising panic, I wondered how I would negotiate the hour-long ride into the city. All change booths were locked. With no money (bringing in rubles was prohibited even if one could have gotten hold of any, since they did not exist in the outside world, I looked around at the empty airport and made my way to a shabby kiosk marked INTOURIST. Waving my transfer vouchers, I came face to face with a harpy with a garishly made-up face, intently buffing her scarlet nails.

Time has obliterated how I managed to make my way to the Intourist Hotel on what was called Gorky Street at the time (today back to its original name, Tverskaya), a stone's throw from Red Square and the Kremlin walls, where I had been assigned a room. The hotel was even more run-down and shabby than when I had last seen it eleven years before. It was 4 p.m. on a hot and sticky Friday afternoon, and I was drained from emotion and lack of sleep. After a long discussion at the desk with an unpleasant clerk ("You should have been met. Where is your Intourist guide?"), I finally convinced her that I actually existed, and, after a lot of shuffling of papers, she grumpily assigned me a room. With much clanking, the huge old hotel elevator lurched its way up, finally coming to rest with a heart-stopping jolt. I was ushered into the typical Soviet-style cubicle: narrow hard bed hidden in an alcove behind a slightly soiled, badly hung curtain, a bathroom with leaky faucets, and the odd cockroach for company. None of it mattered. Smelling that familiar scent of orange disinfectant, hearing the sounds of traffic on Gorky Street, I was overcome with emotion. I had made it back to the USSR.

Politely brought-up Swiss girl that I was, I thought that I should call the USA Institute to thank them for helping me with my visa. I didn't really think I would get anyone, as Muscovites usually head out to the country on Friday afternoons and it was well after 5 p.m. by the time I was settled. But I took a chance and called. Not only was I immediately put through to Berezhkov, but even more startling, he said urgently, "Can you come right over? We'll send a car." Such a thing had certainly never happened to me before. No official in the Soviet Union had ever paid me such attention, and considering I had been barred from the country for more than a decade, it was an astonishingly warm welcome.

Grimy and sweaty, exhausted from the trip, operating on no sleep, and awash with turbulent emotions, I gulped and asked meekly, "Can I take time to wash my hands?"

"Yes," was the answer, but in less than twenty minutes, a shiny black Volga and its driver were waiting for me downstairs. I was whisked off to the mighty USA Institute, which I had never seen. Considering its august reputation in the United States, I was surprised to find it housed in a run down yellow and white 19th century Russian building with an old fashioned porte cochère, tucked away on a narrow back street that ran parallel to the bustling skyscraper-lined Kalininsky Prospect (now called Novy Arbat). In the small dark entry, I was politely greeted by a grizzled wardrobe attendant who led me up a wooden staircase to a room where I found Berezhkov waiting along with Vitaly Zhurkin, one of the deputy directors of the Institute whom I had met long ago in New York. I had no idea what to expect.

To my surprise, they greeted me warmly and asked solicitously, "What can we do for you?" Bubbling over with the euphoria of being back, I said cheerfully that I would like to go to churches and markets. This request seemed to stump them. Neither of them knew of any nearby. Zhurkin got on the phone to inquire, and finally Berezhkov was dispatched to a nearby bookstore to buy a guidebook. It was obviously not what they'd had in mind. I asked to see Arbatov. They said he had already left. "Perhaps next time," they said, and suggested we meet again "so we could talk," on Monday.

After the meeting, in the gathering dusk as the lights twinkled on Kalininsky Prospect and I was bidding farewell to Berezhkov on a street corner, I exclaimed, "I can't believe that I am standing on a corner in Moscow—with you!" He looked at me quizzically. "It took some doing," he said wryly.

I thought at first that I had been received so swiftly because they were desperate to talk to someone, anyone, from the U.S., and I was the only one at hand. Thinking it over later, it couldn't have been that simple. There had to have been other reasons: perhaps Berezhkov had reported that I knew a lot of people in Washington, senators and such, that my book, *Land of the Firebird*, had been a success with the American public. Even the fact that I had gotten there at all, suddenly appearing during an official moratorium on all flights, on the only plane that flew in, was in itself significant. Or perhaps it was because of something I learned three years later when I was told by a high KGB official that the copy of *Firebird* I had inscribed to Andropov had reached him, and that it was Andropov himself who had made the decision to give me back my visa. Maybe that was reason enough for them to send a car.

On Monday the mood was very different. Forget markets and churches. They wanted to talk politics—especially about the horrendous state of Soviet–American relations. I was dismayed by the distortions of their perceptions and the degree of suspicion and hostility toward the United States. When they brought up the subject of the downing of the Korean airliner, Zhurkin was bitter and angry, obsessively trying to blame it on the United States. "We consider that President Reagan is at war with us! A state of war mentality brought this on! We believe that he wishes to destroy us!" Hissing like a cornered cat, he continued defensively, "We have lived with isolation before. We are accustomed to it. We don't need anybody!"

Yet under the bombast, I discerned extreme anxiety and desperation, along with a desire to find some way out, to reconnect without loss of face. Reagan's reference six months before calling the Soviet Union an evil empire had stung deeply. Over and over again, they came back to it, seeming to take every word our president uttered as gospel, and although I tried to remind them often to look at his deeds, not his words, I was brushed aside. I urged them to think about resuming the lapsed cultural exchange. "Never!" I was told adamantly, "Not until the missiles are out!"

Russians, especially Soviets, are by nature conspiratorial, quick to look for complicated and sinister explanations for everything. Yet later that week I found that not only bureaucrats but ordinary people were apprehensive about Reagan's motives. Although all the Russians I saw were shocked and horrified by the plane incident, they nevertheless kept asking me, "But why fly two hours over our territory?" There were ominous rumblings of a gathering storm. An experienced member of the French diplomatic corps in Moscow told me worriedly that he had never seen such a "psychosis of war" as was then being stirred up in the Soviet media.

That day at the USA Institute, I was told that there was no hope of my seeing Arbatov. "Very busy." Read: he didn't think I was worth seeing, so I tried another tack. The name of Rodomir Bogdanov, First Deputy of Georgy Arbatov at the USA Institute, had been mentioned to me in the respectfully muted tones reserved for a man of great power, both at the Institute and beyond. In the Soviet Union of those days it was well known that the *Zam* (short for *zamestitel*) First Deputy Director was usually the person to know, the one who could get things done, most often the KGB representative. At that time, the KGB was a gargantuan organization numbering some 750,000 people. It was essentially a shadow government, with its own statesmen and diplomats, journalists, soldiers, actors, priests, janitors, cleaning women, and assassins. No organization in the Soviet Union was free of its watchful presence. Ty Cobb had told me that Bogdanov was indeed powerful. Rumor had it that he was a KGB general who had been in charge of all KGB operations in India. Some in our embassy believed him to be a high officer of the GRU (military intelligence). Whichever it was, it equaled power and connections all the way to the very top. My friend, the eminent Harvard professor Adam Ulam, later told me that he had met him at international conferences in Europe and had great respect for his intelligence. Bogdanov, I was told, had never been given permission to come to the United States, a fact that seemed to confirm the rumors. Ty had told me to try and see him if I could.

So, at my second meeting with Berezhkov and Zhurkin, I asked to see Bogdanov, but was told this was impossible. He was "too busy." Suddenly a light bulb went off in my head. I took a chance and insisted, "But I have a message for him from Colonel Cobb." That seemed to do the trick, because a short time later I was told that Bogdanov was not too busy after all, and I was ushered into an anteroom and then into his office.

He was in his fifties, a stocky, black-haired balding man built like a tank. Unlike most Soviet bureaucrats, who always received foreign visitors with solemn ritual formality, facing their visitors across a table separated by an Iron Curtain of bottles of mineral water, Bogdanov was sitting at his desk tie-less and in his shirtsleeves, surrounded by a snow flurry of papers.

His searching dark eyes fixed on me fiercely and impatiently. He was obviously a man of authority accustomed to being obeyed. With what I hoped was a beguiling smile, I said, "Colonel Cobb sends his best regards and hopes to see you at the conference in Vienna."

"Is that all?" said he, incredulous that anyone had dared to take his time for such trivia.

"Yes," I answered, "that's all he said."

I thought he was about to throw me out when he paused and once again assessed me intently with his sharp eyes. I seized the moment and jumped in. "The relationship between our two countries is very bad and getting worse. Some kind of dialogue needs to be initiated. We are ready. What about the cultural exchange?"

"This is out of the question," he retorted. "Not until all the missiles are out" (referring to the Pershing missiles that the United States was about to install in Europe in November).

He brought up the question of Reagan's forthcoming run for reelection. Would he be reelected? I told him firmly, "He will be. He is popular. You know he will win."

I went on to the problem of conjecture surrounding the KAL tragedy. Who was responsible? He assured me that everything was being done to ascertain this. I said, "You did a terrible thing, but such is the cynicism of the world that you could have gotten away with it, but you handled it badly."

"I agree," he said. Then suddenly, his eyes flashing, and punctuating his remarks by shaking his fist, he exploded, "You! You don't know how close war is!"

Startled by his vehemence, I initially rejected his words, thinking, *He lies. They always lie. Take his words with twelve poods of salt.*[5] Yet the intensity and sincerity of his unexpected outburst chilled me. So shocked was I by those warning words that I cannot remember much of what we talked about after that.

That was my first encounter with this enigmatic man. I certainly could not have suspected that there would be many more, nor that without him I might never have been able to write *Pavlovsk*. I cannot say that we became friends. Rather, despite the fact that we stood on very different sides, I think we had mutual respect for each other. That day we parted as adversaries, but not enemies. I noticed that when he got up to escort me out, he had a pronounced limp. I asked him what was wrong and he told me he suffered from severe arthritis. I mentioned my son Bobby and his hemophilia-related joint pains, for which he was taking a new medicine, Motrin. He expressed great interest and wrote it down. I promised to bring him some the next time I came. Yet afterwards, his vehement words kept playing over and over in my mind and I couldn't rid myself of the thought: *What if he is who everyone says he is? What if he actually knows something!*

The rest of that week in Moscow I did my best to break through the adamant Soviet refusal to allow me to do research in Leningrad for the book that I was so anxious to write about the history and miraculous restoration of Pavlovsk Palace from the ashes of war. I tried every avenue I knew, laboriously working my way up the bureaucratic ladder, only to meet everywhere those all-purpose negative expressions in Russian: "He just stepped out." "He is in a meeting." "He is a little ill." "He has been called away on business, military duty, rest, sanatorium." "Perhaps tomorrow…tomorrow…tomorrow…next week." Even when I did finally make it to the head of the Writer's Union, I had no luck. The answer was, as always, *nyet*.

I called on our ambassador Arthur Hartman and his willowy wife,

Donna, at Spaso House, the official American ambassador's residence, a cavernous place almost as large as Grand Central Station, built by a rich Moscow merchant of the 19th century. The ambassador was tall, distant and haughty, dressed in a crisply tailored suit, his gray hair immaculately coiffed, the epitome of a State Department career officer. He spoke little Russian. He received me courteously, but was no help in solving my problem.

Blocked in my efforts, I left Moscow for Leningrad, wondering if, after eleven years, I would find any of my friends. In those earlier years, I had often been in that train station, looking up at the huge red neon sign high above the building that read LENINGRAD, feeling that my life took place between those two stations. I was of course accompanied by a monosyllabic Intourist representative. Tourists were only allowed to travel in "Soft" (1st) class—and even in 1983, were forced to occupy a compartment alone. No Russians. The Intourist watchdog (always male) waited until I was on the train, and then, to make absolutely sure, did not leave until the train pulled out.

Covering the nearly 400 miles between Moscow and Leningrad were several trains called the Red Arrow, leaving at intervals between the hours of 11 p.m. and 12 a.m. The train for the elite that I was on glided smoothly out of the station exactly as the large clock hanging on the track bonged midnight and the strains of the Soviet national anthem played over the loudspeaker. In that vast nation, the network of railroads built in the mid to late 19th century crisscrossing the country was central to Russian life. In Moscow alone, there are nine large train stations. Russians could hardly believe it when I told them that a great city like New York had only two.

There still were marvelous pre-revolutionary trains with wide cars. My compartment was spacious, with a bunk almost as wide as a double bed, neatly made up with sheets and pillows. By the windows hung with lace curtains, were comfortable red-velvet seats facing a cozy table over which hung a lamp with a red-fringed lampshade. An attendant brought me a glass of tea from the end of the car where a samovar bubbled. Looking out over the snowy countryside, I could easily imagine Anna Karenina casting her eyes over the same scenery as she returned to Petersburg after her fateful meeting with Count Vronsky. Alas, those comfortable old trains have disappeared forever (although rumor had it that they kept some of the cars for top communist officials), replaced by Soviet "modern," narrower cars with stuffy, overheated compartments for four with only a smelly toilet at the end of the car that held a tiny sink into which trickled a thin stream of water from the faucet.

Mine was one of two adjoining compartments that were connected to the once elegant large bathroom with a wide old-fashioned metal sink that had seen better days. I had noticed when I boarded that the adjoining compartment was occupied by two generals. (Before retiring for the night, I accidentally surprised one in his underwear in our shared bathroom. He gasped and fled like a startled maiden.)

I lay wide awake for a long time, listening to the rhythmic sound of the train wheels that seemed to repeat *"eleven years, eleven years."* Would I, could I, find my friends again? In Moscow I had risked making a clipped phone call to an artist friend to let him know I was in the country and, as casually as I could, that I would be coming to Leningrad. Finally, as the train rumbled along, lulled by the muffled sounds of the generals next door talking about their grandchildren, I fell into a fitful sleep.

It was a cold misty morning, still dark, when we arrived in Leningrad at 7 a.m. As we filed out of the train, I found that I had been traveling in one of several cars full of high-ranking military men, and that I was trudging alone among a mass of army officers in their long gray coats and high astrakhan hats and naval officers in their dark-blue uniforms with gold buttons and caps covered with gold braid, all silently trooping out in the early morning fog. Never in all the years that I had traveled on that train had I seen anything like it. The ominous words of Bogdanov echoed in my head. Apprehensively I wondered what this meant. Why had all these officers been called to Moscow? Was there to be a war?

I was lodged at the Astoria Hotel once again. Nothing had changed there. I stood in the lobby wondering what to do next.

Against all reason, I was certain that my friends were waiting, but how to connect? Despite the early hour, something made me decide that I would go outside and walk. A soft fog enveloped the silent, sleeping city. Not a soul was in the streets. Crossing the square I remembered so well in front of St. Isaac's Cathedral, I made my way toward the river and the park where the famous statue of Peter the Great, "The Bronze Horseman," stands. As if I were in a dream, surrounded by mist and silence, I began walking along a path that was shielded on both sides by tall bushes. Then, just before I reached the statue, like a ghost the poet who had been my closest friend noiselessly appeared from behind the tall bushes where he had been waiting for me. Time had stood still. Nothing had been forgotten.

In the same communal apartments, I was reunited with my friends. Their children were growing up but their lives and struggles were unchanged—or, if anything, worse. Yet despite my happiness at finding them again after so many long years of separation, I could not banish the warning words of Bogdanov, forget the sight of those massed officers at the station, or chase away the persistent feeling that there were far more serious things at stake than whether one American citizen was able to see her friends.

It was only several years later, after I had learned that a series of fateful events were occurring during those autumn months, and it was a time when the United States and the Soviet Union were blindly sliding to the brink of war, that I fully appreciated that my own sense of foreboding and Bogdanov's warning had been dead on. In that critical period of rising tensions between the U.S. and USSR, the tragedy of KAL on the first of the month had been one warning of the mounting danger, but there was another incident, even more perilous, that occurred three weeks later on September 26, 1983—the day I first met Bogdanov who, I later surmised had been in a position to know, but was kept secret in the Soviet Union and unknown in the West until the 1990s.

It happened in a secret bunker at the closed military facility south of Moscow: Serpukhnov-15, the Ballistic Missile Early Warning System command and control post (BMEWS), the Soviet forward defense line set up to detect U.S. Minuteman missiles at launch as they emerged from their silos. A forty-four year old Soviet lieutenant colonel, Stanislav Petrov, operations duty officer, sat in the commander's chair. It was he who had written the instructions prescribing the particular course of action to be taken in case of a U.S. launch, but that night he was there by accident, just to keep his hand in and keep in practice. Suddenly one of the Soviet satellites sent a signal to the bunker that a nuclear missile had been launched from the United States. The responsibility to evaluate whether it was real or not fell to Petrov, who was situated at a critical point in the chain of command. At first he dismissed it as a mistake, but then it quickly got worse. The satellite reported not just one missile but another and another. The system, Petrov said, was "roaring," indicating that five intercontinental missiles had been launched from the United States. It was his duty to push the fateful red button labeled START to begin the process of sending Soviet missiles in retaliation. Yet within five minutes, under enormous pressure with electronic maps flashing, phones and intercoms ringing Petrov decided that the launch reports must be false and later explained his rationale saying" You can't possibly analyze things properly within a couple of minutes. All you can rely on is your intuition. I had two arguments to fall back on. First, missile attacks do not start from just one base. When people start a war, they don't start with only five missiles. Computers are brainless, after all." There are lots of things it can mistake for a missile launch."

He knew that the satellite system had flaws, that it had been rushed into service and was, as he said, "raw." So entirely on his own, he decided that it was a computer error and not a missile attack, and chose not to follow the rules that dictated he should take the action that could have led to obliterating us all. Petrov underwent intense questioning by his superiors about his judgment. The false alarm was eventually tracked to a complicated computer error traced to the satellite, which had picked up the sun's reflection off the tops of the clouds and mistook these for a missile launch. Initially, he was praised for his decision by General Yury Votintsev, then commander of the Soviet Air Defense's Missile Defense Units, who was the first to hear Petrov's report of the incident (and the first to reveal it to the public in the 1990s). He stated that Petrov's "correct actions" were "duly noted and initially promised him a reward for his courageous action which he never received. Instead, he was reprimanded for improper filing of paperwork because he had not described the incident in the military diary. Reassigned to a less sensitive post, he took early retirement and suffered a nervous breakdown. He lives as pensioner in Russia in the town of Fryzino today.

In 2004, twenty-one years after the incident, the San Francisco Association of World Citizens awarded him their World Citizen Award and in New York in 2006 at a special meeting at the United Nations the same association gave him a special second World Citizen citation. He was interviewed by Walter Cronkite and many other journalists. In 2013 the Germans awarded him the Dresden Prize. In an interview, the modest Petrov explained, "I had obviously never dreamt that I would ever face that situation. It was the first and, as far as I know, also the last time that such a thing had happened. In a general way I had wondered if the Americans would actually attack us. We were trained by the military system to believe that the Americans easily might decide to do that. We had no way of judging by ourselves. We learned written English, but not the spoken language, because we were not supposed to be able to speak to anyone from the West. As a military man I never traveled outside the country; I did not even have a passport. The Cold War was ice cold.... I wish I could say that there is no chance of an accidental launch today. But when we deal with space—when we play God—who knows what will be the next surprise?[9]

CHAPTER 4

BACK IN THE USA— A STEP CLOSER

Leaving Moscow on October 7, it seemed as if an iron door clanged shut. So tense and unpleasant were the exit formalities in those days, and so relieved were the departing passengers in a Western plane, that they broke into applause as the plane left the ground. I flew to Geneva where my relatives were preparing to celebrate the sixtieth birthday of my cousin, Pierre Lalive, Swiss jurist and noted professor of law. As I was driven through the familiar peaceful streets of the city of the land of my ancestors by my good friend Johanna Hoerler, it was such a contrast to the intense emotions of my weeks in the Soviet Union, I once again had the sensation that I had landed on a different planet. As we drove, she chatted cheerfully, catching me up on the news of the family and plans for the forthcoming birthday festivities, the biggest problem being what restaurant would be selected. Her words seemed to come from a great distance. Instead, ringing in my head was the stern warning of Bogdanov: "You don't know how close war is!" Despite the fact that I had dismissed his warning as an exaggeration, a disturbing thought kept intruding: *What if it were true? What if he knew something?*

Johanna deposited me at Pierre's spacious house surrounded by its large garden. I was greeted with that particularly Swiss quality of joyful and contented certainty that nothing could ever go wrong. The house was overflowing with children and their friends, and I was ushered up onto the top floor into the little sewing room where there was an extra bed. That night, trying to calm my overwrought nerves, I looked out over the peaceful environs. Finally, exhausted, I fell asleep, only to awaken suddenly with perfect clarity in the middle of the night. I sat bolt upright in the dark room, my faculties as sharp as midday, and heard what seemed to be a stern command: "Go home!" And then, almost as abruptly as I had awakened, I fell asleep again.

The next morning the impulse of the strange night command remained just as strong. Of course it was out of the question to try to explain to my Geneva relatives that I heard voices at night. But I did tell Johanna that because of pressing obligations in the U.S., I would stay for the birthday lunch but needed to leave right after. I didn't want to make a fuss, but could she help me find out about trains to Paris? I had a place on a charter flight and knew my chances of changing it were slight, but when I got to Paris, miraculously, I was told that yes, there was one place on Pakistan Airlines going to New York that day and I could have it.

As I flew home over the dark Atlantic thinking over all the strange events and talks in Moscow, my father's words about the responsibility of every citizen to act came back to me. As the miles flew by, my deep conviction grew that it was a dangerous time—indeed, a critical time—and that I must somehow speak out about what I had seen and experienced in the Soviet Union—the mounting demonization between the two sides, the intense hostility that had been expressed—and voice my belief that we had to begin some kind of discourse with the Soviets again as soon as possible. An idea that seemed to come unbidden straight out of the air began to grow stronger and stronger in my mind. Bureaucrats wouldn't do: I had to go to the top, to President Reagan himself. I have no idea where this incongruous thought came from. Yet there it was, asserting itself. But how to do this?

I had always encouraged my children to be confident about their path in life and told them that they could get to anyone, that any person in the world no matter how mighty was only two introductions away. Why did I pick the number two? I don't know, but clearly it was time to put my words into practice. So shortly after I got back to the States, I went to Washington and stayed with my close friend Marilyn Swezey, a warm and generous woman whom I had first met after the publication of *Nicholas and Alexandra*. A Russophile, specialist in the art of Fabergé, Marilyn had converted to the Orthodox faith and as few other Americans, possessed a deep understanding of the mystical and often mysterious emotions that Russia could evoke. But when I, perched on a stool in a corner of her pristinely white kitchen sipping a small glass of ice-cold vodka, announced, "I have to see Reagan," even Marilyn said indulgently, "Yes, dear," clearly thinking I was a little mad.

"No," I continued, "I'm serious." Whom did we know who could help? We thought of Mstislav Rostropovich, the famous cellist, whom I had met several times and who had expressed admiration for *Land of the Firebird*. He lived in Washington at that time and was reputed, said Marilyn, to be a friend of Judge William Clark, then Reagan's National Security Advisor. She called Rostropovich's number only to learn disappointingly that Slava was away on an extensive overseas tour. We could think of no one else who could help. I went home. For the moment, I was stymied but determined. There had to be another way.

I had received an invitation to attend the christening of the new Trident submarine in New London from Helen Jackson, widow of my old friend, Senator Henry Jackson, who had died on September 1. All of the previous Tridents had been named for states, but in a break with tradition this latest one was to be named for Senator Jackson as a tribute to his firm support of the creation of these mighty weapons of war. I saw on the invitation that Judge Clark was to be present, and with a surge of hope, I went to New London, convinced that I would find a way to buttonhole Clark at the reception following the christening.

At the entrance to the naval base in New London, I made my way through an eerie assembly of demonstrators protesting atomic weapons, dressed as skeletons and wearing ghostly skull masks, then through multiple security points, and finally saw the fearsome and enormous submarine: 560 feet long, 18,750 tons, larger than many a cruise ship and able to cruise deep under the ocean for two years if necessary, carrying atomic missiles that could, I was told, annihilate 10 million people. It was an invulnerable weapon, and the United States at that time had more than a dozen[1] of these behemoths. Officers and sailors, smartly dressed in their best blues, were lined up on the top deck of the great submarine that lay like a gigantic gray crocodile, awaiting only the smash of the champagne bottle before sliding into the water.

Whenever I have traveled between two continents, I feel for several days afterwards as if I have left half of me behind, and the physical sensations of the other world stay with me. It had only been a few short days since I had been in Leningrad, packed into a city bus so crowded that my feet were lifted off the floor. Desperately trying to keep my footing, I had reached out for the belt of the nearest person who was crushed against me, a Soviet Army major. Swaying precariously for several stops, he held me firm, and when we both got off, he courteously helped me from the bus. When I thanked him, he gave me a jaunty salute. I remembered the young recruits in their heavy coats who sat tired and lonely in the back of the bus. Listening to the martial music, the ceremonial speeches, looking at our spic-and-span officers and men standing so straight and tall, the two scenes seemed to merge into one.

I was jolted from my reverie by an announcement on the loudspeaker. "Judge Clark will not be with us today. He has just resigned as National Security Advisor and has been replaced by Colonel Robert McFarlane." So much for that introduction. Discouraged, I went to the reception that followed, greeted Helen and her daughter, Anna Marie Jackson, and watched our blue-uniformed officers sipping drinks, laughing, and joking with friends while Glenn Miller music of the forties serenaded us. Again the dark words of Bogdanov echoed in my head. I had to keep trying.

I decided that if I could not get to the president, I did know quite a few senators. Scoop had introduced me to many of his senate colleagues, and several had invited me to come and talk to them, among these Senators Sam Nunn of Georgia, John Warner of Virginia, Ted Stevens of Alaska, Bob Dole of Kansas, and young Al Gore of Tennessee, along with a number of congressmen. But the one I knew best, dating from the time he had been a newly minted congressman in 1973, and having seen him after he became senator in 1978, was Bill Cohen from my beloved state of Maine, where I had summered since early childhood. So I went to Washington again, and on October 20 went to see Bill, who was at that time a senior member of the Armed Services Committee with long experience in questions of arms control. I was buoyed by the beautiful photographs of Maine on the walls of his office and by the warm reception of his top administrative assistant.

Providence was with me. For some reason, Bill was in a mood to talk that day, and we chatted over a period of several hours, interrupted occasionally by his rushing off for a vote and then returning. In his spacious office in the Russell Building, we talked about many things—the novel he was working on, his visit to the Soviet Union, his poetry and meeting with the Soviet poet Evgeny Evtushenko. I told him about my encounters in Moscow and my conviction that we were seeing not just the usual Soviet truculence but something more serious. My message was *Fire! Fire!*

"Stop thinking about the budget," said I. "We have to find a way to resume some kind of talking with the Soviets about *something.*" I went on to say that after my recent visit, despite all their hostility and belligerence, I thought they just might be ready to find a way out—the cultural exchange, for instance.

Suddenly he stood up and said, "You know, you've got to talk to Bud McFarlane," and went straight to the phone. "Hello, Bud," said he. "I have a woman here who knows a lot about Russia. You ought to see her."

The voice on the other end agreed, and Bill gave me the number and told me to call for an appointment. Thanks to Bill, I was one introduction closer.

When I look at my agenda for that week, I see how many things were set in motion and am amazed how many people I managed to see: Jack Matlock and Ty Cobb in the National Security Office; Madeleine Albright, then a professor at Georgetown, who invited me to come and address her class; Bill Odom, who was then assistant chief of staff of Army

Intelligence; Bishop Basil Rodzianko of the Orthodox Church of America; and Father Victor Potapov at the Voice of America. But the most unexpected of these meetings was one that came about thanks to Helen Jackson.

The question of Jewish emigration from the Soviet Union had been a crusade of her late husband, and there existed an active women's organization called Congressional Wives for Soviet Jewry, who were meeting at the Dutch Embassy in Washington that week to report on their recent trips to the Soviet Union. Only congressional wives were invited, but Helen made an exception for me. Of all the reports I heard that day, the eloquent and passionate remarks of two of the women present were outstanding. One was by Wren Wirth, wife of Democratic Congressman Timothy Wirth of Colorado,[2] and the other by Teresa Heinz, wife of Republican Senator John Heinz[3] of Pennsylvania. I was enormously impressed, and went up to compliment them both on their spirited words and knowledgeable speeches.

Starting from that day, we began a friendship that has lasted these many years. I admire both of them and their many achievements extravagantly. Powerhouses of organization, wives of powerful men as well as leaders in their own fields, they managed to do all this while remaining beautiful, elegant, and charming. Around them, I often feel like the dwarf to a pair of *infantas*.[4] During the Reagan years when I was so regularly in Washington, I often stayed with either the Wirths or the Heinzes, who were extraordinarily hospitable, supportive, and generous to me. Their wide and informed knowledge of Washington helped immeasurably to guide me through the perilous shoals of the capital.

I had accomplished a lot more than I had dared to hope for, but my ultimate goal was still distant. I have always loved Churchill's gritty phrase, "Success is going from failure to failure without loss of enthusiasm." I had to keep trying. Thanks to Bill Cohen, at least now I had a White House number to call, so even though I didn't expect much, try it I did.

A STEP CLOSER

When I called the number at the White House, a friendly no-nonsense voice informed me that I would be granted twenty minutes with Colonel McFarlane. Not long, but a precious toe in the door. I went back to New York and worked to hone my remarks to exactly the time allotted. I am not a very good typist. Alas, in a burst of youthful feminist bravado, when my father insisted I must learn shorthand and typing in order to qualify as an office secretary, I had rebelled and exclaimed, "Never!" Stupid. I have regretted it ever since. Laboriously (pre-computer age), I typed out my memo for the colonel. As he was known to everyone as "Bud," I found I couldn't remember what his real first name was, so I called my friend Hedrick Smith, who was then chief of the Washington bureau of the *New York Times*. Without hesitation, he confidently answered, "William." (If *The New York Times* didn't know, who would?)[5]

Rick then proceeded to give me a quick newsman's analysis. "Bud is matter-of-fact, straightforward. Likely to listen but not give much of an indication of what he is thinking. He is the opposite of you. You are emotional, intuitive. He is reserved, rational."

Rick didn't know me as well as he thought he did—or for that matter, Bud. So without checking further, I dutifully typed out: "To: Colonel William McFarlane."

How often fate turns on a detail. I had learned as a reporter that people simply freeze when they see their names spelled wrong. I know now that when someone tells me, "I loved your book," and proceeds to spell my name incorrectly, I don't believe a word they say afterwards. On November 2, flying down on the shuttle the day of my meeting, by chance I looked over at *The New York Times* article my neighbor was reading titled "Military Men in the White House." To my horror, one name leapt out of the page: Colonel *Robert* McFarlane! Not William. And I was on my way to his office! My heart sank. I felt sure that when he saw that I could not be trusted to even know his correct first name, all my carefully worked-out remarks would be discounted. What to do?

Going to the White House, no matter how many times, let alone the first, is an awesome business. First there is the close scrutiny of security guards at the gate, their searching questions, followed by phone calls to recheck the information, then the official-looking ID hung around your neck, and finally entering under the awning to the basement office into the hushed, cool atmosphere redolent with unseen power, the halls lined with large photos of the president waving, greeting crowds, smiling. Worried about my faux pas, trying desperately to look at ease, I walked into the basement office of the National Security Advisor (later to be moved into fancier quarters upstairs in the West Wing). There I was greeted courteously by a friendly woman who introduced herself as Wilma Hall, secretary to Colonel McFarlane. (Wilma has always used the word *secretary* with pride, rather than the more fashionably feminist *assistant*.) Thinking fast, marveling at how baldly I could lie, I took a deep breath and said, I hoped smoothly, "Mrs. Hall, I noticed on my way down that my secretary (of course I had none) typed Colonel McFarlane's first name incorrectly."

Quietly she said, "I'll take care of it."

Amazingly, in the few minutes it took for me to walk from her desk to the door of the inner sanctum office, she returned the memo to me with the name invisibly corrected. Had it not been for Wilma, who knows? The rest of this story might never have happened.

I will always be grateful to Wilma for saving me that first day. With her brown hair, soft brown eyes, and modest, ladylike demeanor, she could easily be taken for a well-bred suburban matron, a pillar of the Junior League, and not the most senior member of an unknown, unsung, unseen sisterhood of formidably efficient career civil-servant executive secretaries that make the Big Wheels of Washington run smoothly. During those Reagan years, I was to get to know her well, to admire and respect her tact and diplomacy. Over twenty-seven years, she served as executive assistant to some of the most powerful men in government, among them Henry Kissinger, Alexander Haig, Bud McFarlane, and Colin Powell. She knew everyone by their first names and could find anyone in the government in minutes. Patiently, cheerfully, she answered hundreds of phone calls every day and somehow managed to make every caller, no matter how lowly, feel that there was no one the great man would rather speak to, but unfortunately he was "tied up in a meeting just then," always making certain the caller went away feeling great, self-respect intact.

Wilma had started in 1960 at the Pentagon, worked for the Secretary of the Air Force for ten years, and then was asked to come over to the White House to work "temporarily" for the Henry Kissinger night shift from 7 p.m. to 2:30 a.m. while Ron, her husband, chief photographer of the Air Force records and history, stayed home with their children. She was asked to stay on, and over the ensuing years worked for twelve National Security Advisors, both Democrat and Republican, from Kissinger to Berger, becoming in 2003 the most senior member of that exclusive sisterhood. Modestly, she once explained her role: "Political people come and go, but they need people with administrative continuity. It takes a long time for them to get up and going, so they need people to function as facilitators, to start and make things go." Now retired, always totally discreet, she knows a thousand secrets. What stories she could tell—but never will.

Thus saved by Wilma, I walked in and found McFarlane sitting at his desk, a low light half-illuminating his face. On the shelves behind him were lined up books on international affairs. Courteously, he got up to greet me in his quiet, slow voice. He was a man of medium height with close-cropped sandy hair and blue eyes that held an expression of pained intensity. Marine-neat in his blue blazer, precisely creased gray trousers, and mirror-shined shoes, he had the squeaky-clean-just-out-of-the-shower look that always seems to distinguish military men. Rick had been right, up to a point. Clearly, he was a well-trained Marine officer who kept his emotions under tight control, but I felt his integrity and underlying sensitivity and liked him immediately. Mindful of the ticking clock, I went through my well-rehearsed twenty minutes.

I explained that I was just back from the Soviet Union and, as a result of the discussions I had had at the USA Institute, I felt it extremely important to find some means of defusing the tense situation as soon as possible. My talks had led me to cautiously hope that there might be an opening to resume discussions on the lapsed cultural agreement. Watching the clock, I delivered my remarks in exactly the allotted minutes, but to my astonishment, when I was through he didn't get up. Instead he said, "What you have to say is so interesting. Would you be willing to come back and talk longer? Would you come back and talk for two hours?" I should call Wilma to schedule the date. And so, two weeks later, I walked into that same office again, this time more confidently, and we did talk for two hours. After that meeting, Bud asked, "Could you put it on paper?" I could and did.

Struggling with the unfamiliar form of communication that is governmentese, and not trusting myself, I called my son Bob to ask for his help. He was adept at that form of expression, having spent a year as an intern in Senator Jackson's office working with the young Elliot Abrams and Richard Perle, both to become future luminaries. All of them were under the expert tutelage of Dorothy (Dickie) Fosdick, the feisty and famous woman who was the senator's chief advisor on foreign policy. Bob, who was then an Episcopal priest at Grace Church in New York, met me in a modest pizza parlor in Grand Central Station and helped me polish and edit my memo. I sent it to Bud, and shortly afterwards Wilma called and I was asked to come again to Washington.

This time I found Bud sitting with my memo in his hand. "I have talked to the president about this and he was very interested."

As we went over the various points in my paper, I found myself suddenly saying, "Send me. I can talk to them." I don't know how I found the nerve to suggest this, but after my recent experience in the Soviet Union and my many years of contact with a wide variety of Russians, I was certain that I could.

Bud grew thoughtful and answered, "If we can engender a kind of dialogue with the Soviets to make it clear that this renewed sense of purpose, strength, and resolve is not oriented against their system and that we are not seeking to alter it, then dialogue can lead to a modus vivendi."

After the meeting, as we were saying goodbye Bud said, "I want so much for them to know we are not hostile."

He uttered this so intensely and with such evident anguish that I, trying to lighten up his dark mood, said jokingly, "Well, if you send me, they'll know you're not hostile."

I was to see Bud frequently and grew to admire him greatly. Privately I always called him "the White Knight." A religious man, he was active in his Presbyterian church, devoted to his wife and family. Someone once remarked to me that he thought that Bud had the romantic soul of his Scottish countryman, Robert Burns. This seemed true when I remember one evening as dusk fell and we were finishing a meeting. He stopped abruptly, looked at his watch, and said, "Twenty-six years ago I proposed to my wife."

An internationalist, a seeker of peace and reconciliation, he was a model military man, disciplined, honorable, devoted to serving his country and his president. While he was National Security Advisor, he was often attacked by more hawkish White House types who went so far as to spread scurrilous rumors about him. When he resigned his post in 1985 as a result of the Iran-Gate scandal President Reagan lost a great and unselfish advisor, and I, a rare supporter in the White House.

When I first met McFarlane in those declining Indian summer days of 1983, American families were preoccupied with the World Series and getting their children back to school. The hit movie was *The Big Chill*, about the angst of Baby Boomers. Between them, the United States and the

Soviet Union had more than 20,000 warheads, and in hindsight a number of historians of the Cold War now believe that it was a time when the superpowers were imperceptibly edging to the brink of nuclear war.

How little I knew when I boldly suggested, "Send me"! There had been the tragic downing of Korean Air Liner 007 on September 1, and it is now known that Andropov, terminally ill and growing increasingly paranoid, had been urged on by the hardliners in his government and become acutely aware that his country was losing the technological race. He was obsessed with the idea that the U.S. was planning a first strike. Reagan's "evil empire" speech in March 1983 plus his announcement of SDI, a plan thought by American scientists to be implausible, were taken seriously in the Soviet Union. My experience had been that the Soviets firmly believed that Americans could accomplish anything if we put our minds to it. This, along with U.S. plans to deploy Pershing II missiles in West Germany, was seen by the Soviets as shortening warning of a strike to six minutes, poured fuel on their suspicions.

A Soviet KGB informer, Oleg Kalugin, reported that Andropov's distrust of American leaders was profound. Among the elderly and ailing leadership of the Soviet Union, paranoid fears of a surprise attack took hold. Oleg Gordievsky, a KGB colonel who was working as a double agent in London, wrote that extensive secret orders were issued to the KGB to try to detect and report on signs of such an attack, some of these completely far-fetched and outlandish. The top KGB agent in London received instructions from Moscow that an "important sign of British preparations for war would probably be increased purchases of blood...," and was also ordered to watch for signs that "church and bankers" had been given advance warning of a nuclear attack. Gordievsky warned the British that Soviet paranoia was rising to a dangerous point, but his warnings were discounted.

That November, a ten-day NATO military exercise known as AbleArcher 83 (November 2–11) further excited Soviet fears. These exercises were an annual event that involved NATO allies and NATO's command control procedures during a nuclear war, simulating a period of conflict orientation and culminating in coordinated nuclear release. In that period of deteriorating relations, the Soviets increasingly believed that this exercise might be a disguise for an actual first strike. This fear was exacerbated because, for the first time, there were to be several important changes, a unique new form of coded communication, and, most importantly, actual heads of state, including President Reagan, were to participate. Soviet protests grew increasingly shrill.

There was a great reluctance on the part of Reagan advisors to believe the Soviet fears were genuine, and many dismissed them as empty propaganda. Who could imagine that we would launch a first strike? Shultz thought it "incredible, at least to us." England's Prime Minister Margaret Thatcher and German Chancellor Helmut Kohl had agreed to participate, and Reagan, Bush, and Weinberger were also to do so. In an interview with me, McFarlane spoke of his apprehension at that time. When Secretary of Defense Cap Weinberger commented to him, "They would never think we would do that," he had answered, "But what if they do?" McFarlane, National Security Advisor, realizing the dangerous implications of such participation, prudently rejected the idea of Reagan's involvement in the military exercise. This relatively obscure incident is now considered by many historians to be the closest the world has come to nuclear war since the Cuban Missile Crisis of 1962.

I, of course, was oblivious to all this when I walked into McFarlane's office, boldly suggested I could talk to the Soviets, and urged that something had to be done quickly. I don't know why I felt this so strongly, but since that early morning in October when I was suddenly awakened in Switzerland, I felt impelled by a profound sense of urgency, and events were to follow in quick succession.

CHAPTER 5

FIRST MEETING WITH THE PRESIDENT, JANUARY 17, 1984

My last meeting with McFarlane took place on November 23. A few weeks later, one evening shortly before Christmas, Jack Matlock[1] called. Sounding nervous and somewhat reluctant, he told me that "it had been decided" that I was to go to Moscow to talk to the Soviets along the lines I had suggested in my meetings with Bud. I was to leave in three weeks and was to come to Washington in early January to prepare for my trip. Right away I said that because the Soviets were extremely rank-conscious, in order to be taken seriously I would have to have some designation—special envoy from the President or some such. (After our meeting, I had written to Bud about this.) Perhaps I was mistaken, but I had the feeling that my getting "rank" did not suit Jack. He demurred and told me that this would need congressional approval and would take a long time. I knew he was right about that, and in all my talks with Bud, I had insisted that time was important and that there was a need to move quickly. So I agreed that I would go as a private citizen.

There is no doubt in my mind that it was because Bud McFarlane was a military man, a Marine colonel, that he recognized the possibility that I might make a contribution and was singly responsible for my initial meeting with President Reagan and that first back channel[2] trip to Moscow. No bureaucrat would have done it. (Quite the contrary. I was told by executive secretaries in the White House that a certain high-level foreign policy official, hostile and jealous, used to storm in and ask, "WHO authorized this meeting?" "Bud used to ignore him," I was told by a witness to this outburst.)

FIRST MEETING WITH THE PRESIDENT 91

When I had so boldly said, "Send me. I can talk to them," I am very glad I didn't know how bad the situation was or I would never have had the courage. In the final months of 1983, relations between the U.S. and the USSR had reached an impasse. In September there had been KAL, and in November, U.S. Pershing Missiles aimed at the Soviet Union had been installed in Europe. In mid-December 1983 in Geneva, the Soviet negotiator Yuli Kvitsinsky stomped out of negotiations with the angry words, "Everything is finished." Nuclear arms control negotiations were suspended indefinitely, leaving the U.S. and the USSR with no arms control negotiations of any kind for the first time in fourteen years.

Even regular diplomatic relations were in a deep freeze. "Both sides settled in," wrote *TIME* magazine, "for a long period of immobility in superpower relations and an escalating arms race." Hurling verbal missiles at each other, Reagan had called the Soviet Union an evil empire that had "committed a crime against humanity," and Andropov declared that the Reagan administration had "finally dispelled illusions that it could be dealt with." American caricatures depicted Andropov as a mutant from outer space, and in the Soviet Union, swastikas and ghostly faces of Hitler were added to their drawings of Reagan as a gun-slinging cowboy. As 1984 opened, the deterioration of relations was virtually complete.

On January 2, 1984, *TIME* magazine's "Man of the Year" issue showed a frowning Reagan and Andropov back to back. James Cracraft wrote in an issue of *The Bulletin of Atomic Scientists* that "1983 was a bad year for U.S.–Soviet relations, and 1984, by most current indications, promises to be even worse." William Kincaide, Executive Director of the Arms Control Association in Washington added, "Soviet–American relations are in a more poisonous state that at any time since the 1962 Cuban missile crisis and perhaps since the 1946 war scare in Europe." Bernard Field, Editor in Chief of *The Bulletin of Atomic Scientists* agreed: "Not since the frightening days of the Cuban missile crisis has the world been so perilously close to WW III." In January 1984, declaring that humanity stood "at a fateful juncture in nuclear history," the editors of the *Bulletin* moved the hands of the Doomsday Clock forward by one minute, to three minutes before midnight.[3] It was an ominous measure of the situation that only once in their thirty-nine-year history, in response to the advent of the hydrogen bomb in 1953, had the warning hand been any closer to midnight than at that point. The mid-1980s in the United States was a time of apocalyptic fear and anxiety over nuclear weapons. People built bomb shelters and school children were taught to hide under their desks in case of an attack.

The first week in January I went to Washington to prepare for my trip with Bud and Jack. I was told that these meetings were to be absolutely confidential, and that only Bud, Jack, and Tom Simons, head of the Soviet Desk at the State Department, were informed. I was sure of my knowledge of Russia and my ability to talk to Russians, with whom I had always found a way to connect, even with the most doctrinaire communist ideologues. And yet I, who had consulted with powerful senators and military officers in the U.S. and tangled with tough bureaucrats and thinly veiled KGB officers in the Soviet Union, wasn't so confident about how to behave with State Department officials. Perhaps it was because my style was so different from their professional opaqueness. In polite but unmistakable terms, it was made clear to me that they didn't trust out-of-the-network unknown quantities and potential "loose cannons" like me. I didn't fit into the mold and might rock the boat. For these champions of the status quo, familiarity was of key importance, as were stability and predictability; the greatest fear was uncontrolled, unexpected change. (Thus their fondness for policy White Papers.)

More concerned with the known quantity of the sitting leadership of a given nation, they discounted the importance of the aspirations of the population with whom, certainly in the case of the Soviet Union, they had virtually no direct contact. There was a tendency to interpret national strength only in terms of military might, dismissing all other forms of strength as "unrealistic." Above all, in a system geared first to allegiance to department methods, nothing was to be colored with emotions or feelings. Developing close ties with the nations in which they served ("clientitis" in

State Department parlance) was discouraged by brief stays and incongruous postings (Burundi to Leningrad, for instance). This was the very antithesis of the Russians, who valued long association and close ties with the country in which they were placed. (A prime example was Anatoly Dobrynin, who served as Soviet Ambassador to the U.S. for twenty-four years, from 1962 to 1986.)

I represented the direct opposite of this way of thinking, concerned with the feelings, culture, and ways of thinking of people—"soft" as opposed to the "hard" subjects of arms control. I had seen many signs that communism was weakening, that Russians were increasingly seeking their lost roots, and was convinced that, with a growing younger generation change was coming sooner rather than later. With every trip, I had seen a larger gap between American perceptions and reality. I had stepped through the looking glass and observed a world that was out of sync with the prevailing image in the U.S., an image fostered and nurtured by men with a certain mindset and style, whose careers depended on the continuation of the status quo. I was to learn that Reagan also was not comfortable with this approach and had a different style based less on policy papers and more on human instincts and emotions.

I was acutely aware that I was not privy to their confidential information, nor did I know anything about how such back-channel messages were conducted. As a member of a generation in which women were encouraged to defer to men, it was very difficult for me at first to have confidence about how much I could or even should insist on my own sense of how such a mission should be accomplished. (In 1984, there were no women directly involved in Soviet Union policy planning.)[4] So I decided that since everyone else had advisors, I needed my own. I carefully chose two on whose confidentiality and superior intellect I could rely completely.

For an insight into the American position, I called Admiral Bobby Ray Inman, a man I admired greatly and had known in Washington. He was then in Texas, having resigned from his post as Deputy Director of the CIA. When I told him that I had some very definite feelings about how this mission was to be handled and I was getting some flak, he chuckled, "A lot of crocodiles down there." I explained to him that when I was told I would have only three days for the mission, I had objected strenuously saying that one couldn't get the Russians to pick up the phone in three days, and that I had to have time to walk away. In his quiet Texas-accented voice, Inman counseled that when they started pushing, "that is your cue to lean back, smile and say, 'This is not to criticize anything that has gone before, but I did think that when you asked me, you wanted to do things a little bit differently.'" Then he added that if they pressed on "a little steel is never amiss." I followed his advice. It worked, and it was finally agreed that I was to have two weeks, ten working days. Considering that none of our establishment had had much luck in penetrating the iron curtain of Soviet recalcitrance, it was not a whole lot of time—but better than three days.

The other was my friend Bishop Vasily Rodzianko of the Orthodox Church of America. A member of a great Russian family that had numbered among them a distinguished general and the head of the pre-revolution Duma,[5] his stalwart defense of believers and regular broadcasts and sermons to the Soviet Union on the Voice of America had won him a devoted following there. His perceptive knowledge of human nature and his vast experience with Soviet officials and diplomats at the UN had given him a unique perspective. He gave me invaluable advice about different categories of Soviet officials and how best to talk to each category, as well as suggesting an argument that turned out to very important. "President Reagan considers himself a Christian. He is a genuinely religious man. He considers that he is the defender of Christian beliefs—principles of equality and human rights. As you know, Christians can be very peaceful, but if their beliefs are challenged, they can take up the sword. He is influenced by his religious feelings sometimes toward peace. Sometimes, to move to the defense of Christian beliefs, he would use a sword. Do not be deceived. Do not disregard this factor or your own Christians. Better for you to bring out the pacifier than the crusader." And, he counseled, "Remember, a hundred pairs of eyes will be watching you. You will be like

Daniel in the lion's den. Reach for the particle of humanity in each person. Appeal to this particle, but remember that the demons are at work side by side in the same person."

Strengthened by the astute advice of my two expert advisors, I steadily gained confidence, and at the end of these preliminary meetings, I took a bold step and insisted that I had to see the President himself before I left. "The Russians are very personal people. I do not mean to diminish anyone, but all the president's men don't add up to the president. Not for my credibility but for his, I have to be able to say truthfully to anyone whom I am to see in the Soviet Union that this comes from him. I don't need to take much of his time; five minutes will do. I only need to ask him one question, but I must be able to say I looked him in the eye and that the answer came from him."

"Put it on paper," said Bud—which I did.

In my letter, I wrote, "... for Russians, personal contact is far more important than it is for us, a psychology that we do not completely understand or share. For them, everything is decided at the top.... They simply do not understand our president and do not trust him. Because of this, they are deeply suspicious of his motives and all of his initiatives, however reasonable. Given the state of communications between our countries at this time, this will not be an easy perception to dispel. My task of persuasion will be much more difficult if I have to say that I have never actually met him. Their reaction may well be, 'We trust you but you have never met him. Why do you trust him? How do you know this is a genuine gesture?' It will make it much easier for them to dismiss this initiative as 'just another American ploy.'"

A week later I was called and told to report to the White House for a meeting with President Reagan at 9:30 a.m. on January 17, 1984.

I had learned that on January 16, the President was to deliver a major address to the nation on Soviet policy. I wanted to be prepared, so I called former colleagues at *TIME* magazine to get an advance copy of the speech, which I read carefully. I liked it, especially his strong emphasis on peace, its warmer and more personal tone. The press was unimpressed and even derisive of its folksy, pure-Reagan story of Ivan and Tanya and Sally and Jim meeting in a waiting room and comparing notes about children and jobs, and dismissively called it his "peace speech." Conventional wisdom declared that "he didn't mean it."

With hindsight, it is apparent that he meant every word. It was, in fact, a key speech that laid the foundation of his policy toward the Soviet Union a full year before Gorbachev appeared on the scene. I was later told by Jack Matlock, who had seen the original speech, that it was "not staff written," and that the President had gone over the speech three times at great length and crossed out and rewritten entire sections himself.

As any woman would, I wondered what to wear to meet the President. In my diminished financial situation, I didn't have a lot of power clothes and couldn't afford to go buy any, so I went through my skimpy wardrobe. The only even vaguely suitable thing I could find was a simple black dress with a schoolgirl white collar and plaid bow, which I hoped would be okay. I was terribly nervous, and, remembering that day, I still find it surreal. I know I spent the night with Marilyn, who, faithful friend as always, drove me to the White House the next morning, dropping me off at the back security entrance. Then I was back in the basement office with Bud McFarlane, by now at least a familiar face and presence.

When I walked into the Oval Office that memorable day, I knew only that I had an overwhelming feeling that it was vital to end the icy relations with the Soviet Union, and to act quickly. I had no other agenda than my own conviction that the situation called for some gesture and a resumption of some kind of talk and, improbably perhaps, that I could do something about it. Now I was to meet the most powerful man in the world to talk to him about a country that I had come to know intimately and to love.

As I walked in, numb with nervousness, I was at first dazzled by the strong light coming in the tall windows of the Oval Office and the startling sight of the famous face of the President in his blue glen-plaid suit. I was too struck by how tall he was, how bigger than life he seemed, to notice anything else. I blessed the strong supportive presence of Bud, who introduced me. The President greeted me courteously in his warm, familiar voice and shook my hand, and only then did I become fully aware that he was surrounded by a whole gaggle of well-known faces: Vice President Bush, White House Chief of Staff James Baker, Deputy Chief of Staff Michael Deaver, Counselor to the President on Policy Edwin Meese, and, from the NSC, Bud, Jack, and Ty Cobb.

I was petrified. No one had prepared me for such a crowd, and I had no idea why they would be there. In my state of shock, they all seemed unnaturally tall, oozing with masculine power and importance. I wondered whether they had just come out of a meeting and had decided not to leave, or whether they had been convoked. Either way it was bad for me, and it got worse. I didn't know what to expect, but somehow I had imagined that it would all pass very swiftly: I would go in, the camera would go click-click, and the President would shake my hand and say, "Hello, Mrs. Massie." I would ask my question and then he would pat me on the shoulder: "Good luck, Mrs. Massie. Goodbye, Mrs. Massie," and that would be that. A question of a few minutes.

But, to my growing apprehension, it didn't happen like that at all. Instead the President said, "Sit down, Mrs. Massie," and escorted me to those famous white presidential armchairs in front of the fireplace that I had seen in countless news photographs and television programs, always occupied by some world leader. Now, incredibly, it was to be me. He escorted me to the chair on his left and sat down. Those chairs are big, and that day they seemed so big that I thought my feet wouldn't touch the ground. All the assembled president's men proceeded to sit down, too, in pecking order on those famous facing white couches. Bush, Baker, Meese (known as the "Troika"), with Deaver[6] on a chair alone at the end. On the side, Bud, Jack, and Ty. All expectantly waiting. For me.

I had a moment of pure panic. *I am not prepared*, I thought. I had only planned and prepared for five minutes—one question—and now? *I am nervous*, I thought. *I burble when I'm nervous. All those guys are going* to think, "Look at that dumb broad burbling." In a panic-filled instant, I sized up the situation. If I tried to address both the President and the assembled group and turn back to talk to the President, I would be forced to wag my head from left to right and it would be like a ping-pong game. In that moment I made up my mind. I was not giving a lecture. I had come to ask the President a question, so I decided to forget the others, look into his eyes, and pretend we were alone. Mentally holding my nose, I jumped into the unknown waters that confronted me.

When a person is as terrified as I was at that moment, pure animal instinct takes over and one can feel the atmosphere, the aura of the other. The President had his head slightly lowered and was looking at me sideways a little uncertainly. To my astonishment, I felt for some unbelievable reason that he was somewhat nervous about meeting *me*! Somewhere in the back of my mind, I remembered that I had read that the President was ill at ease when meeting "experts." Could it be that someone had told him I was one of those "experts"? I wanted to reach out, to put my arm around him and say, "Mr. President, I'm not an expert. I just know a little about this one thing. There are so many things you know about that I don't know—like being president, for one thing." Of course I said nothing, but hoped I was sending comforting vibrations.

He opened the conversation with a totally unexpected question: "How much do they [the leaders] believe in communism?"

It was a very good question, in fact, a key question, one that no one had ever asked me before. I thought for a moment about how to answer, and then I said, "Mr. President, of course I can't tell you how all Russians think, but I can tell you what many of them say. They call them [the communist leaders] 'the big bottoms' and say, 'they love only their chairs.'" Instinctively, I was stating the difference between the Russians and their communist bosses that was natural to me but an essential difference between my outlook and the Kremlinologists—that ideology was gone, only the form remained, and Russians and their Soviet leaders were not the same.

In retrospect, I imagine now that it might have been a new idea for the

President then. It turned out that, as usual the Russians knew more than we did, as we were to discover only a very few years later when the regime collapsed like a decayed tree.

After that, the conversation flowed easily. President Reagan was able to put people at ease—so much so that I could almost forget the intimidating masculine phalanx on the couches. I began to find myself as comfortable with him as if we had met before. I told him I thought his speech had been very good. I told him about the lack of direct knowledge of the United States among the top leadership in the Soviet Union, how they remained locked in their own nightmares, many having attended only technical universities (if any), knowing little but their own propaganda, and never having learned any foreign languages or left their own country except to visit their satellite communist nations.

"When I am in the helicopter," the President said, "I often think, as I look down on the houses, the people, our country, that if I could be with Soviet leaders and they could see how our people live, I would say, 'Look, why would we want to destroy this?' People forget that in 1946 the United States offered to turn the atomic bomb over to an international authority. When we had it exclusively we did not use it to conquer the world."

He went on to talk about his experience with communists in Hollywood when he was president of the Screen Actor's Guild, about their terror tactics and how poisonous and dangerous he had found these to be. He remembered a high school textbook he saw then in which there was a chapter telling young people that they should give up God, family, and country to join the Communist Party.

I spoke about the deep religious feeling that existed among many Russians in the Soviet Union, the importance of spirituality, despite all the restrictions and persecutions of the government, and that religion was still the strongest ideology, what men would fight for, die for. Mike Deaver, who was listening intently, spoke up and asked, "Do you mean the Pentecostalists?" (A group of them had managed to penetrate the U.S. Embassy in Moscow and were living in the embassy basement at the time.)

I replied a little sharply, "No, Mr. Deaver, I am speaking of the Orthodox Church."

"I never thought about this," said the President. "It's interesting if they should be hoisted on their own petard."

I emphasized my own belief in the importance of having an American presence in the Soviet Union and how enthusiastically young people still remembered our American exhibitions. Our contacts had been too elitist, too narrow, preventing us from seeing life as it really was lived there. We needed to push for far broader contacts between ordinary people on both sides—square dancers, cops, high school students, housewives, small business owners. The Soviet Union, I said, would no doubt fight against this, but we should fight for it because it was important for our nation and future. (When occasionally I stole a look at the couch sitters, at Vice President Bush, he did not look very enthusiastic.)

The President asked me about my visa, adding, "Did you know that only Russia required passports in the past? The passport is actually a new idea." I told him about Will Rogers and his both characteristically comical but penetrating observations in his book, *There's Not a Bathing Suit in Russia*, written in 1927 after his visit to the new Soviet Union, that I thought he might enjoy.

The President stayed not for five minutes but for twenty-five minutes, and had to be reminded twice that he was late for his schedule. As he stood up to leave, I looked him straight in the eye and asked my question: "When I go to the Soviet Union, I want to be able to say that I asked you this question and to give them your answer. If you are elected to another term, will the policy you spoke of, small steps to improve relations, be a continuing policy of your administration?"

Without a moment's hesitation, he gave a strong definitive reply. "Yes. If they want peace, they can have it."

I told him I would be in touch as soon as I returned.

As we parted, I couldn't resist joking, "And Mr. President, don't forget, they have their experts about the United States as we have our experts on the Soviet Union, and they don't necessarily know anything more about us than we know about them!" He laughed. We shook hands and he, followed by his men, swept out of the room leaving me standing there shell-shocked with Bud.

I had been awed and intimidated by the President, surrounded by all his advisors and worried that I might not have said the right things. As Bud escorted me down the narrow stairs again I asked him anxiously, "Did I do all right?"

"You did just fine," said Bud. "I know him well, and you lit a spark in him."

"I don't have a lot of experience in the Oval Office," said I, stating the obvious.

Again Bud laughed and said, "We'll have to see if we can't get you some more."

And soon I found myself on the street, blinking in the sunshine, stunned by the experience.

Five days later, I left for the Soviet Union.

I had asked Bud whether it would be all right for me to say I had met the President, and he assured me that I could. But apart from my family and closest friends, I told no one then about our meeting or why I was going to Moscow. To anyone else, I said that it was for research on my proposed new book. Later, when I was asked how I met the President, I always answered, "He read my book" (*Land of the Firebird*). He hadn't on that first day but did later.

As the superpowers began warily inching toward each other, there was one last bureaucratic impediment, which brought to mind the Russian proverb, "It would be funny if it weren't so sad." Before my departure, Bud had called Ambassador Dobrynin and advised him that I was going to the Soviet Union and that "they" (the White House) would be interested in what I had to say when I got back. As it turned out, because of the problems of Intourist bureaucracy, Dobrynin couldn't personally get me a room and Bud could not sign a check for my travel expenses because this had to go through and be signed by the Secretary of the Treasury. So I ended up putting the whole trip on my credit card to be reimbursed by the government later.

CHAPTER 6

MISSION TO MOSCOW, 1984

"The superpowers often behave like two heavily armed blind men feeling their way around a room, each believing himself in mortal peril from the other, whom he assumes to have perfect vision."
Henry Kissinger

On the long flight to Moscow, I had time to think over carefully the extraordinary events of the preceding few days: the meeting with the president, my last conversations with Jack Matlock and Bud McFarlane. Eleven weeks after I had first walked into Bud's office, the impossible had happened. I was on my way to Moscow to try to elicit a positive reaction from unknown figures in the Soviet Union. Who would they be? I had no idea what I would confront when I arrived, or even if there would be any response at all. I had confidence in my ability to talk to them. But would I get that chance? Before I left I had asked, "What am I supposed to do? Sit in my hotel room and wait for the phone to ring?" The answer was yes.

Despite my feeling that I needed to have some kind of "rank" to strengthen my position, Matlock's argument that this would take a long time, as well as my own urgent sense that time was essential, made this impossible. So I agreed to go, whatever the personal consequences might be, as a private citizen ostensibly to discuss the necessary permissions to do research for my new book, *Pavlovsk*. But I worried. For me, accepting such a back-channel mission was a personal risk and sacrifice, as I felt certain that, from then on in the Soviet Union, my status as a private citizen would be officially ended. I would be a marked woman, watched constantly. My friends might be questioned or harassed because the tough Communist Party boss of Leningrad from 1964 to 1970, Vasily Tolstikov, had declared,

"Leningrad is the cradle of the Revolution and no one will be allowed to rock the cradle." The Leningrad KGB was well known for being especially suspicious and brutish. I was just plain scared—and yet, there was that certainty in my mind that something had to be done.

Exhausted, I arrived in Moscow's lugubrious Sheremetevo airport and went through the usual lengthy gauntlet of Soviet immigration procedures. As always, I was first left to anxiously shift my weight from one foot to another, trying hard to look relaxed while the passport control guard, wearing the KGB green epaulets of border guards, looked skeptically from my face to my passport over and over. The wait—for him to lift his hand, for the staccato sound of his stamping machine, for the return of my passport—seemed interminable. Never a word of welcome, no "have a nice day."

Another long wait around the groaning and lethargic baggage belt was followed by the intense scrutiny of the baggage control inspector. In those days, all travelers were required to fill out a lengthy customs declaration on which one had to meticulously list every piece of jewelry and an exact accounting of every nickel and dime in all currencies one might be carrying. (Woe to anyone who made a mistake!) Finally I was spewed out into the cavernous hall. There was, of course, no one there to meet me, so I made my way over to the Intourist desk, where I handed my vouchers to the usual bored and surly woman. (Nothing in the Soviet Union was permitted without the proper tourist voucher.) After yet another long wait, a driver appeared and I was driven on the long dark road into Moscow, once again to the Intourist Hotel[1] on what was then still called Gorky Street.

There, after another tedious examination and exchange of vouchers, I was at last ushered into the usual room with its narrow hard bed tucked in an alcove and prudishly separated from the rest of the small room by a not-very-clean curtain.

The next morning, I called Warren Zimmerman, the deputy chief of mission in the absence of Ambassador Hartman.[2] He put me in touch with Ray Benson, U.S. cultural attaché, who invited me to lunch. In Washington, I had been told that only three people besides the president knew the real reason for my trip; our Embassy was not to be informed in advance. I don't know if this was true or if Ambassador Hartman *had* been informed. In any case, when I arrived, he was away on a skiing trip. When I asked Ray Benson whom I interviewed for this book, he told me that the Embassy did know the purpose of my trip: "We have our ways," and that "you were coming in an informal way to judge how things were going generally and the background against which we could negotiate a new cultural agreement."

Ray would become a great support and friend. In later trips, I stayed with him and his wife, Shirley, in their comfortable Embassy apartment, which became my oasis. In a period of little Embassy contact with Russian citizens, he and his wife were rare exceptions, both interested and knowledgeable about Russia and Russians. This was in marked contrast with many other Embassy personnel I had met through the years who tried to have as little interaction with the population as possible.[3] As I was officially there only as a private citizen, I was to receive no help from our embassy and had to get around as I could on public transportation—no easy matter in that gargantuan capital when one had a lot to accomplish in a short time.

To add to that complication, I had gotten my period on the plane on the way over and suddenly began to hemorrhage, something that had never happened to me before. With my condition not improving, I finally told the Bensons, who promptly sent me to the Embassy doctor. He checked my fingernails and advised, "Keep your feet up, and if your nails get white and it gets worse we'll send you to Finland." I had definitely not come all the way to Moscow to put my feet up, let alone get packed off to Finland, and I was not about to let this annoying health issue get in the way of my mission.

The Bensons invited me to accompany them to a milestone event at the Bolshoi Theater. It was the first performance since the Revolution of Nikolai Rimsky-Korsakov's 1904 opera, *The Invisible City of Kitezh*, with sets designed by the controversial nationalist painter Ilya Glazunov, whom

I had met on several occasions on my previous trips. He was a strange man who enjoyed mysterious support from high-level personalities, and whose openly nationalistic themes in his paintings were wildly appreciated by the Russian public.[4] His wife, Nina, whom I also knew happened to sit in front of us that night.[5] The opera caused a sensation. Glazunov had designed sets with traditionally Russian motifs. Religious banners and icons were paraded on the stage, the first such dramatic demonstration of the burgeoning nationalist Russian (as opposed to Soviet) feelings that I had observed. The next day, the Soviet newspapers were full of virulent criticism, but it was one more sign of the growing cultural cracks in the monolith of socialist realism.

On my own, I had sent a cable to Rodomir Bogdanov announcing my arrival and had received a cordial reply. So I called the USA Institute and was told to come over to meet with Valentin Berezhkov and Vitaly Zhurkin again. I had no idea whether they had been advised of my purpose in advance. I told them that after my last trip, I was so concerned about the atmosphere and the great misperceptions I saw on both sides, I had gone to Washington on my own as a private citizen to talk with several senators and congressmen. I also had met several times with Robert McFarlane, who asked me to come back and to carry a message to my friends here. I told them that funds for my trip were provided through the government agency overseeing cultural affairs. I explained that I had come to listen to their thoughts and suggestions as to how we might resume our talks on the lapsed cultural exchange programs between our countries, and to explore any suggestions they might have as to how such a new dialogue might proceed. Were they interested? Whom should I talk to—someone at the Central Committee secretariat perhaps, or the Minister of Culture? Was there anyone in authority who might give me any advice or pass on thoughts they would like me to convey to their counterparts in the U.S.? I knew, I said, that there were great difficulties on both sides in doing this officially at this time, and, that it might be easier to be frank on the unofficial side.

My words were met with an angry outburst from Zhurkin. "You!" he sputtered. "You! You are an honest woman, but you are being used as camouflage for evil men with sinister intent!"

I spoke of the president's speech of January 16, told him that I had had a meeting with him, and quoted his strong parting words about small steps toward better relations.

"Small steps will be deceiving!" exploded Zhurkin. "How to balance speech with American deployment of missiles! Empty words—substance, but bad substance!"

I waited for his temper to calm and asked, "What would you have him say? Would you rather he continue calling you the empire of evil? Why criticize him when he doesn't?" At this, Zhurkin quieted down and I was able to play my ace: "I am a writer," I said. "I have seen many powerful men. I have looked into the president's eyes. I believe he is genuine. This is a good moment. Seize it. Do not make the mistake of dismissing him and losing the chance, as you have in the past."

As it happens, there is almost exactly the same proverb in Russian as we have English, so in parting I threw out, "Don't look a gift horse in the mouth,"[6] and left.

This was the reaction I had foreseen and the reason I had insisted in Washington that I had to have time to walk away. I knew the Soviets would need time to digest this unlikely overture. After all, they had to decide what to make of me—a woman—and whether to believe that what seemed a highly unlikely emissary from the redoubtable Cold Warrior, Ronald Reagan, was for real. But I had faith in my instinct that they were anxious, that they needed an opening, and I was sure they would sort things out in their own time and their own way.

The next day, January 25, I met again with Warren Zimmerman in his large office in the American Embassy. He was polite, but not very helpful. He suggested I call MID (The Ministry of Foreign Affairs)[7] and try to reach Alexander Bessmertnykh[8] who, said Zimmerman, was an Americanist, head of the American Desk and among the most likely to be sympathetic. I went back to the hotel, put my feet up, checked my nails (still pink), placed a call, and then waited for the phone to ring. It finally did, but Bessmertnykh was distant and uncooperative. Clearly, despite McFarlane's call to Dobrynin, MID didn't want anything to do with the Reagan initiative. So now what?

Then the USA Institute rang again. Bogdanov was ready to receive me.

My initial surprise on learning that he was the man chosen to filter my mission was followed by a growing realization (which was to be supported many times later) that the KGB was calling the shots,[9] and was the real source of power, not the Party. At that time, it was thought by the Washington establishment that only high Party officials made decisions on policy questions, despite the fact that even many of these had close links with the KGB. I decided that, whatever the truth was, I knew the Russians well enough to know that there had to be a reason I had been presented with Bogdanov, and I decided to make the most of the chance that was offered to me.

It made sense. Yuri Andropov had headed the KGB before he became General Secretary of the Party. It was he who had carefully introduced Gorbachev into the higher ranks of power, acted as his protector, and thrust him, a country politician, onto the world stage. The top ranks of the KGB (I came to call them "the princes") were the best informed in the land about the problems of their decaying country. They spoke foreign languages, had access to books, to foreign newspapers, frequently traveled abroad, served in foreign embassies. This was in direct contrast to even high members of the Party, who rarely traveled abroad except to their satellites, and, as I had told President Reagan, "loved only their chairs, their privileges, and their positions." From my experience in Leningrad, I knew that the early initiatives of *glasnost* and *perestroika* there had originated from the KGB. It was they who supported perestroika in Moscow, and, when Gorbachev came to power became among his most powerful constituents. One thing that had seemed to prove this was in February 1986, when 113 members of the Central Committee resigned without a word of protest. Who, I wondered, could have accomplished this but the firm hand of the KGB?

Rodomir Bogdanov was a formidable opponent. He had a perfect command of English, a keen intelligence, a sophisticated and agile mind. Again he received me in his office that I always assumed was bugged. In the following days, we had meetings each lasting close to two hours. Bogdanov was completely informed as to why I was there and had read all my books. From the first and before every following meeting, he made it clear that he passed on our conversations "to the top." The opinions he expressed were frank and illuminating, sometimes conciliatory, other times angry and hostile.

He started off by announcing, "There is a complete lack of trust in this administration and a suspicion that the president's speech [on January 16], that he is doing this for election year."

I countered right away by asking about the possibilities of renewing the cultural exchange.

His answer was negative. "We are in a cycle of reaction now to your actions and this has become very hard. It would look silly for us now to resume contacts. We also have a public opinion and right now it is counter to the USA, which is perceived as Enemy Number One—out to destroy us."

He went on: "We are in different political cycles. There is the feeling that this administration wants to coerce the USSR into peace. We are concerned with how it [a cultural agreement] would be represented by the U.S.—that they would crow and claim victory."

I said that I was certain that official pronouncements could be sober and low-key, but I could not speak for our press.

I emphasized my belief that his analysis was incorrect, and that on the contrary there was a genuine desire for peace in the United States. I tried to explain why this was so now, and why I thought it was important for them to recognize the moment and act on it. I saw that he did not believe me. I knew the Russians well and I had expected this reaction. This was why in Washington I had said that it was vital that the President's words come directly from him, not from the president's men, not from me. I repeated the exact words of the question I had put to the president about his intention to pursue "small steps to better relations" and his final and definite statement, "If they want peace, they can have it!"

Bogdanov took this in but made no comment. Instead he veered onto a different subject. "There is a strong school of thought which has been growing stronger, that this administration does not wish to regard the USSR as a partner. All previous administrations always took the position that the Soviet Union was a partner in security, that we could work together. What is most dangerous now is that all of the dark forces have been strengthened. Our military now have a stronger voice thanks to this. We are not for disarming the United States. We respect a responsible defense posture of the USA. We recognize legitimate American interest in the Persian Gulf, Europe, and everywhere in the world. But what worries people is who really decides defense policy? Is it Perle or Burt? [Richard Perle, then Assistant Secretary of Defense, was a leading neoconservative hawk. Richard Burt, Assistant Secretary for European and Canadian Affairs in the State Department, had special expertise in nuclear weapons.] He [Perle] talks so arrogantly to our people that we assume he has instructions from above to talk to us in this way."[10]

It was an unfortunate tendency among both Soviets and Russians to think in a conspiratorial way and, despite all arguments, to never really believe in the freedom of our public officials to speak out and publicly hold contrary opinions. Tenaciously they held to their certainty that in the United States government as in theirs, everything was always controlled from above. Even sophisticated Bogdanov firmly held the mistaken assumption that if President Reagan didn't feel the same as Burt or Perle, he wouldn't have put these men in their positions—or kept them there. Americans found it impossible to fully understand how hard it was for even the most experienced Soviets to shake off this world view. They were capable of holding beliefs that were outrageously false and seemed to us incomprehensible.[11] One has to imagine being in a controlled environment where everything had to be censored and approved, where *no one* ever acted independently, and if they did, it was often at the risk of their lives, and how confusing the United States would sometimes seem. After all, the Russians had a constitution that promised free speech and religion and everyone knew it was a fraud, that they lived in a country where there was no relation between what was said publicly and what actually happened.

Although Bogdanov went on to state that officially they wanted to express disapproval of the Reagan administration and had refused "Guest of Embassy" status for me and insisted I come as a "tourist," they approved of the initiative of my visit because it allowed them to make definite pronouncements without an official change of policy. "If you had come as 'Guest of Embassy,' it would have been exactly as if we were talking with your Ambassador." This they were not ready to do. (*So*, I thought, *they had known about my coming, discussed it in advance, and decided to hear me out.* I took this as a modestly positive sign.)

"Hartman," he continued, "does not like Russians." (Our ambassador was very up-front with his support of dissidents, even to the point of having a notable dissident pianist play a concert and holding controversial movie nights in Spaso House.[12]) Bogdanov made it clear that they did not like him, didn't want to talk to him. He then inquired, "Is there any truth to the rumor that he might return in May to replace Eagleburger?[13] This would be a very good time to make a really fresh start. The ambassador has made enemies, the Church, the USA Institute," and repeated, "He does not like Russians."

Continuing: "We are in a world that needs stability, living with each other decently with a reasonable level of competition. This is good. Competition with you drives us to improve things—perhaps you, too. We have strong chauvinistic forces. So do you. Weinberger [Reagan's Secretary of Defense] is a 'cold wind.' Renewing exchange would be interpreted here as 'business as usual,' a deal that would paper over bitterness. We do not want to create troubles, but if you make troubles for us, we will make troubles for you in order to keep you busy."

Nevertheless, despite his tirades, I didn't give up, persistently insisting that it was essential to resume some kind of discussion with the United States. "Talk about anything," I urged, "talk for two years, but talk!" I brought up the KAL incident again, and how important it was to avoid such tragic mistakes.

This elicited a torrent of fury about the placement of U.S. Pershing missiles in Europe. "No cultural exchange until all the missiles are out of Europe!"

I threw back, "Those missiles will go in and you couldn't have done it better if you had done it yourselves! Arms control is the roof and we are now on the floor. We need to talk! Talk for two years, if necessary—but *talk*! It seems the only thing we can agree on is mothers and culture, and if we can't talk about mothers and culture, we're through."

"There is some logic in what you say," he said quietly.

It was a small crack in the wall, a tiny glimpse of light. It was then that I repeated the powerful words of Bishop Basil and his strong admonition: "Better for you to bring out the peacemaker rather than the crusader."

Bogdanov listened intently and then fell silent.

After all his negative talk during those first days, I didn't expect much success, but the next day I was surprised and gratified to find that his negative position had changed. He informed me that "the Minister of Culture's official position is that the USSR is ready to resume cultural talks, but the United States should take the initiative. Either Shultz or another person the U.S. feels is proper should discuss it with Ambassador Dobrynin and propose a date for the resumption of talks. The position of the Party is that they also agreed."

I left elated—only to find on the following day that his position had changed again. He was more equivocal, less positive. The thought came to me then that some change might be occurring with those "at the top." It was. Although it was unknown to the outside world at the time, the gravely ill Andropov, who had spent half of his fifteen-month term in hospitals, had only a few days left to live. He died on February 9, five days after I left the Soviet Union. The window of opportunity had been brief. An old Party hack, Konstantin Chernenko, took office as the General Secretary of the Communist Party and leader of the Soviet Union. He was so weak himself that he often had to be held up when he gave speeches, and he died in March 1985 after only thirteen months in office.

Yet to my great relief, despite the disturbing change of tone the day before, at our last meeting on February 3, exactly ten days after my arrival, Bogdanov made the official pronouncement I had been working for: the Soviet Union would agree to start talking again about a cultural agreement. He emphasized that this was official and made this statement: "We are always willing to talk about the reestablishment of cultural relations. The proposition should be made officially through Dobrynin right now. This is the moment. There is a precedent to do it this way. Every year we have talked about cultural relations. We are willing to resume these talks. This is fully the position of the Minister of Culture."

Then, to my surprise, he thanked me warmly and said, "A journey of a thousand days is not accomplished with one step, but you have made things clearer to us." Then he startled me with the question, "What do you want?"

I answered, "I am a writer. I just want to write my book, and I need to have permission to be able to come and work in Leningrad at the library and Pavlovsk Palace for at least two months." He said nothing.

As we shook hands in parting, he said, "Give my regards to Ray Benson."

When I communicated this to Ray who had not exchanged a word with Bogdanov for months, he understood the signal immediately and said, "Well, well. I will give him a call on Monday."

Both sides had agreed to pick up the phone again. It was the break in the ice that I had so hoped for. Still, I wasn't sure whether or not everything would go forward until I read in the newspaper that Vice President Bush, in his talks with the new Soviet leader, Konstantin Chernenko, at the funeral of Andropov had said to the press that "Chernenko had been remarkably forthcoming", that he had expressed the opinion that "our countries are not inherently enemies" and had shown an interest in going forward with discussions on cultural exchange. Only then did I know that my mission had succeeded. I was relieved and gratified. I had been convinced that, given the extreme mutual suspicions of both sides, renewed and hopefully expanded cultural relations could begin to melt the frosty and dangerous impasse that existed and become a first step toward a better relationship with Moscow. Those few meetings with Bogdanov had proved me right. I had cracked the ice.

A few months later, official discussions about resuming cultural relations began again and, after thirteen months of talk (less than two years!), resulted in the only agreement to be signed by Reagan and Gorbachev at their first meeting in Geneva in December 1985. Was I happy? Very.

I got home on February 5, exhausted and spent from my efforts. Knowing that President Reagan's birthday was the next day I wanted to tell him right away that I had good news, so I immediately placed a call to McFarlane at the White House. He was out, so I called Jack Matlock at his office in the Old Executive Office Building. When I started by saying that I had tried to call the White House, he angrily contradicted me saying, "This *is* the White House!"

I was startled by his response and didn't know what to say as it *wasn't* the White House I had called but the Old Executive Office building. I realized I must somehow have offended his *amour propre*, and shaken, made my remarks brief and quickly got off the phone. Bud later called me back from the White House, and I gave him a full account of my trip.

CHAPTER 7

LUNCH IN THE OVAL OFFICE
MARCH 1, 1984

On February 15, the President wrote me a letter saying, *"I waited to answer your letter until your return from the Soviet Union. In the meantime a great change occurred there. I dare to hope there might be a better chance for communication with the new leadership."*

Then, on February 28, just as I was preparing to leave for Washington where I was scheduled to give a talk the following day at the Sulgrave Club, followed by a lecture to the Ballet Committee at the Kennedy Center, I got an excited call from Wilma. "I want to extend an invitation to you to have lunch with the President tomorrow in the Oval Office. We are all very jealous because we only get to see him coming down the hall! I'm so glad! You know the President doesn't do this very often. He has lunch with the Vice President once a week in the Oval Office, but he really doesn't do this. It will just be you and Mr. McFarlane, from twelve to one." I told Wilma that this was just the time I was to talk at the Sulgrave Club, and she said, "Well, for the President, can't you fix it up?" and promised that they would speedily get me there afterwards in a White House car. I asked her what to wear and would my same old red jacket do? "Oh, yes," she reassured me, "red is the President's favorite color."

I called the club and the Ballet Committee and explained. "All right," they agreed. "That's the only excuse that will wash."

At 8:30 that morning, I was awakened by a cheery White House operator and asked, "What do you want for lunch?" (An unsettling question, as I thought that of course in the Oval Office I would eat whatever was set before me—even if it should be squid, which I hate.)

I didn't know what to answer so I asked, "What is the President going to have?"

She said, "Today is Mexican day."

"What does that mean?" I asked.

And she said, "Tacos, beans."

Thinking that would be a lot and might spill down my front, I thought I had better ask for something easier. "What else is there?"

She answered, "Everything. Omelet, cheeseburger, hamburger."

So again I asked, "What is the President going to have?"

She said, "I don't know. Do you want to take a chance?" She suggested consommé, shrimp, and green beans.

Fork food. That seemed safe. (I would have said baby food, but that wasn't on the list.) This seemingly benign choice turned out to be a near disaster.

At the White House, Bud McFarlane met me, and as we were walking up the stairs explained that although the president had been informed of the results of my mission to Moscow, he wanted to hear details from me personally. Unlike my first meeting, we didn't go in the ceremonial door that is reserved for formal meetings, but through a small private back door to the Oval Office, where I found four photographers at the ready. The President and Bud were both wearing their serious blue suits. (I hasten to add not for me, but for the prime minister of Morocco, whom they were to meet after lunch.) The President greeted me warmly, "I'm so glad to see you."

"I'm glad to see you, too, Mr. President," I replied. "You do me much honor."

"Let's go sit down," he said. "I'm glad to see you back. Thank you for your letter."

A small table for four, set with flowers and the presidential china (blue with the presidential seal in blue and white), had been placed between the two famous white couches. One chair was empty and I was told that Mike Deaver was delayed and would be coming later. The President gestured to the table suggesting, "Why don't you sit and look at the garden?" Knowing that if I were sitting there looking at the garden I would be blinking all the time because of the bright light, I excused myself saying, "My eyes aren't so good," and sat on his right. (I wish I had known what I learned later, before I asked to change my seat. President Reagan had lost hearing in his right ear in Hollywood due to an explosion on the set, and wore a hearing aid so preferred to have people seated on his left.)

Then the lunch came. I found that the President and Bud were on diets and they were served a cup of soup. I was presented with my consommé. I found the table too low and knew that in my nervous state bringing a spoon to my mouth risked spilling on my clothes so I didn't dare try. I waited politely, thinking the President and Bud would have something else but they had nothing more, so a solitary plate was put in front of me. To my horror, I found that the shrimp were still in their shells and the string beans so nouvelle cuisine that they were nearly raw and impossible to cut. Try wrestling delicately with a shrimp shell while trying to talk with the President! I attempted it only to have the first shrimp slide ignominiously across the table while I tried to retrieve it in a ladylike manner. After that I didn't dare risk negotiating with another shrimp and gave up on my lunch. The President noticed and asked solicitously, "Aren't you hungry? Wouldn't you like some fruit perhaps?" I eagerly agreed, and in short order a California-size bowl of fruit was placed in front of me that would have taken singular focus and a whole afternoon to tackle. So I ended up eating nothing. So much for my savoir faire.

When we initially sat down, the first thing the President said was, "I've just gotten a letter sent to me by someone who had received it from a Russian relative in Siberia. Of course, the censors cut out the bottom of the page so I couldn't see who it was, but this person wrote that the people of Russia were really praying for me. Do you think I dare hope that this may be possible?"

I could only answer truthfully, "I really don't know about this firsthand, Mr. President. I haven't myself personally met any Russian who has told me directly that they prayed for you. Propaganda against you, Mr. President, is very strong in the newspapers, but the Russians are very intelligent and used to reading between the lines, so I think it is very possible that there are some Russians praying for you, as many I know are praying for the United States."

Then I made the great mistake of adding that I knew they had for the Jackson amendment. He got a little testy about that. "Well, I don't believe in those things. I believe in quiet diplomacy."

Realizing I had better switch to another subject quickly, I went on to the Pentacostalist group who had taken refuge in the basement of the American Embassy for five years and had just recently been allowed to leave the country. I said that in that case, we had won. He then told me that no one had ever known that he had had a personal involvement in this. "But," he said, "I did."

I then began to report Soviet reactions from my recent mission and the Soviet concern that if we had a cultural agreement now, we would crow if they considered it and use it as a chance to say, "You see, they've come around." Firmly the president said, "No, that isn't necessary for us to do," again bringing up the Pentacostalists. "Nobody crowed," he said. "We made no fuss over it when they let them out." I told him that I had assured them that this would not be a difficult hurdle and that while I could not answer for our press, I was certain that officially this would be possible.

He then asked my opinion of the new leadership of Chernenko. I read him a number of quotes from Russians, adding my own opinion that Chernenko seemed to me very like the American TV character Archie Bunker, and that the two of them would get on very well. They had the same kinds of prejudices: the country was going to the dogs, discipline had broken down, the youth of the country didn't know how to work anymore and were into all these weird things—all the old values had been destroyed and the country was generally going to the dogs because of the youth, and he was racist.

Deaver joined us just as I was explaining the importance of ethnic identity in the Soviet Union—that it was a multinational state and that the term *Russian* represented a specific ethnic identity and none of the Soviet leaders had been ethnically Russian. For example, Chernenko was Ukrainian-Siberian, though Soviet media were now attempting to give him a Russian mother. He spoke Russian ungrammatically with a strong accent, as did Brezhnev, who was Byelorussian and was ridiculed in Russian jokes for his comical accent and bad command of Russian language. "They are not sweethearts, any of them," said I. "Sometimes I feel as though I have to protect you guys."

At this, all three men, including the President, laughed heartily. But incongruous as this might sound, I did have this feeling at that moment. In that august room—the Oval Office—suddenly I was acutely aware that the men present were decent men not dealing with other decent men, and it worried me. Russians had told me over and over about their leaders: "These men will do nothing but betray. Nothing, nothing, but betray. Anything. Any agreement. Anything, they will betray. They will destroy." They had even warned me that "they will try to kill you because you are trying to help us." By comparison, we in the United States went at things basically in a decent way. The President may have talked about the "empire of evil," but Ronald Reagan was a decent man, and no matter how our leadership might talk, they didn't have a real gut sense of how evil the men in the Kremlin really were—how they had lived with deception and killing. Gromyko and all his associates had cooperated with Stalin. Every one of those leaders had blood on his hands, not just a few power plays.

Before I had left for Moscow, feeling the need to know more about Soviet thinking and the men I was to meet, I had sought the advice of Bishop Rodzianko. I briefed the President on his remarks. The bishop had advised me that all the men I would meet would fall into three types. There would be the Russian nationalists who had some pride and patriotism in the country. There would be Party men who basically put the dictates of the Party first above all other things. Group two might have a little bit of group one in it, but basically they would be Party men. Then on either side there were those who were opportunistic, whichever way they chose to go, because they were not tied to either side completely. He had strongly counseled me to remember at all times who I was dealing with and that all of these categories were afraid of the Orthodox Church. He had advised me to "reach for the particle of humanity that there is in all men, although sometimes there's just a tiny little particle—even in Stalin—so try to reach for that. But always be aware of the demons that exist working in them at the same time." I worried about the decent men in our country dealing with these congenitally suspicious adversaries who always assumed bad motives from others and were looking for these all the time, and I did have a sense that I had to protect those men in the room from going too far with their basically decent intentions in dealing with such men.

Deaver asked if the Soviets were afraid of the Muslims, and how did they feel about their Asiatic peoples? I answered, "Of course, I cannot tell you authoritatively the official point of view, but I can tell you what Russians have told me and how very concerned they are about this problem." I had been told that the Muslim republics of the Soviet Union had put pressure on the government to go into Afghanistan because they were worried about Muslim fundamentalists on their borders. The government was aware that they couldn't risk sending Asiatic troops into Afghanistan. I gave them a general overview of that subject, as well as statistics about how many Asiatics were in the Soviet Army.

We talked about peace and about being careful about how to proceed. I told the President that I personally approved his firmness with the Soviet Union and thought that was a good thing, the only danger being that one had to be very careful that this firmness did not cross the line and become perceived as aggression—and, like the blade of a sword, careful that it didn't just slip.

Bud McFarlane had suggested that I tell the President about the circumstances of my trip, how I was received, how they had done it. So I explained their visa technicalities and how they had had some trouble in deciding the problem of how to receive me. Had I been received as Guest of Embassy, it would have made me official, so they decided to receive me ostensibly as a tourist. This, to indicate their official displeasure with the administration, that they were not quite ready to move officially, but also to express their interest and approval of the initiative. In the end, they had received me quite well, although I told him that at first Vitaly Zhurkin had accused me of being a "dupe, a camouflage for evil men with sinister intent." I explained, "Mr. President, you know I asked to see you before I left. This was not a personal or frivolous request. Knowing the Russians as I do, I felt sure that this might be the most important thing, and in the end it was. The fact that I was able to say that I had seen you personally made a great deal of difference to them. Zhurkin calmed down and grumpily said, 'Well, he may be trying to fool you by being nice.' At that point, Mr. President, I had to stand my ground. I told them that I was a writer and had seen many powerful men, that I had looked you in the eye and asked you a direct question, and that in my opinion you were genuinely interested in small steps toward new relations and that they would be very foolish if they dismissed it."

That day, I noticed that the President was wearing a hearing aid in his right ear and that he adjusted it now and then to hear better. Other than that, he showed no indication of his age. He looked ten years younger than he was. He was alert, eyes sharp, quick to pick up on everything I said. He seemed quite sure of his direction. I thought that this was not bad, as his mind was not closed but remained open, and he didn't shut his mind to a different perception someone might offer. The one thing that did surprise me, as it had the first time, was that, unlike many men in power, there was no arrogance in him. He was not devious in the least and was actually, it seemed to me, a bit shy. He did not come on forcefully but a little tentatively, and he was more gentle than he came across on the TV screen. In person, one could see that he came from a humble background, which one didn't notice on television because of the powerful image of his office and his famous face. He was very courteous, and no doubt this was why the people around him, and all the secretaries, liked him a lot; he was nice to everyone. For me it was quite surprising to see such a man as President of the United States.

I thought it important for the President to know how I had described him to the Soviets: "Perhaps it's difficult for you to understand being atheists, but Mr. Reagan our president, is a man of religious, Christian principles. He believes in these and sees himself as the defender of the principles on which our country is based. As you know, Christians have two sides, one side a pacifying, peacemaking side, but when these principles are threatened, Christians are capable of taking up the sword to defend them. It is more to your advantage to bring out the pacifier rather than the crusader."

When the president heard this he looked pleased. "I hope I did not take too many liberties," I said.

Smiling, he answered, "No."

I added that I thought this argument had sunk deep, because the last day I was in the Soviet Union when I reminded them of what I had said and urged, "Don't forget this," I observed the note-taker underline it three times. I spoke about their hostile feelings and the suspicions they had expressed about his January speech—that "it didn't mean anything" and was "without substance"—and I had answered, "All right. How would you like him to speak to you? Would you prefer him to continue calling you an empire of evil? His speech was carefully considered by President Reagan. Why don't you consider how else he could have said it, and all the other ways he could have spoken instead of this? Why criticize him for such an initiative? Only the strong can admit mistakes, the weak cannot." Again the President smiled his approval. "I went on to emphasize your genuine desire for peace, and pointed out to them that your constituency was the most likely to be against any conciliation with the Soviet Union, and that in our system a president could only begin to speak strongly of his desires after he had been in office for some time and was secure before he could bring them up, and that they should weigh your words very carefully, for if they consulted their own analyses, they could see how many times they had missed opportunities with us."

Reading from my notes, I touched on the information gaps and the difficulties they seemed to have about understanding the White House—about Clark leaving as National Security Advisor and McFarlane coming in. I explained how it seemed difficult for them to be on top of things that quickly, just as it is for us about them. Hearing that, the President gave a quick nod of agreement. I said, "One problem was that they had said, 'We are confused about who really makes defense policy.'" I didn't want to get into the individuals they had mentioned because I knew McFarlane could handle this better than I could so best to leave that to him. But I emphasized to the President that it was very hard for them to really comprehend the greater leeway of our officials to voice their own opinions publicly and their freedom to speak to the press in ways inconceivable for their officials and so make themselves seem more important than they actually were. I also told Bogdanov that I did not know exactly who made defense policy, but that it certainly wasn't just two people. I continued, "While that is obvious to you, Mr. President, it's not necessarily true that it is to them. They see things through eyes very different from ours, and it is their strongly held conviction that when they are spoken to harshly by a high American official it is as in the Soviet Union—that 'these officials have instructions specifically from the president to speak to us in this way.' A great concern is their feeling that all previous administrations had treated them as partners and now they feel as though they are being 'coerced' into peace, and they will not be coerced into anything! Mr. President, you kind of pushed them into a corner there with your strong words." I then suggested that perhaps he might consider soothing their ruffled feathers with something like, "'We need the strength of Russia in order to achieve peace and to build new foundations.' It would not cost us anything."

The President listened attentively to what I could see was new information for him, new perspectives that he was clearly not accustomed to. It was a lot to throw at him over lunch.

Later, McFarlane told me that he thought it would be wonderful if the President could use the kind of phrase I had suggested. And I told him that if he did, he should use Russia, not Soviet Union, because it will go right to the heart of Ustinov, (the Defense Minister—a Russian nationalist.)

I turned then to cultural exchange. "The Soviets told me that they are willing to restart negotiations. They have suggested that the next step come through Washington, from Shultz to Dobrynin. Is it possible for Dobrynin and our officials to do this? In my view, it is important for your credibility but also for my honesty to follow through now that the White House has made this initiative and the Russians have responded positively to it, so we should not wait too long. Otherwise, as Bogdanov warned, it will be like a soufflé that comes out of the oven and just falls flat. They couldn't get it up again if we did that. Of course, I'm not privy to all the information that is yours either domestically or internationally, but could I ask you what your feelings are about this?"

And he answered that yes, they wanted to go ahead with it and were going to be pursuing it in the next day, which, in fact I learned they did as part of the process of putting together a whole package of initiatives toward the Soviet Union, including the question of barring chemical warfare, something big on the Soviet agenda and on ours, too. I did point out to him something they had brought up, a phrase important to them: "No first strike, no use of force between our nations." But when they attempted to bring up the arms question I had cut them off and said it was not my place to discuss these.

Even after I had described the general atmosphere I had encountered in Moscow and the details of meetings and conversations with Bogdanov and others the President was eager to hear and to talk more. I knew that if the Soviets had agreed in principle to resume a cultural exchange, my task was now to convince him that resuming these discussions would serve the United States well and be a positive step forward for our nation. So I began by telling him again how important past American exhibitions had been for the Russian public, especially for the young people who flocked to see them, how much they meant to them, how eagerly they looked forward to these, and, in my view, how vital it was for the United States to keep these contacts alive and maintain a presence in the Soviet Union that would permit their people to see a truer picture of how Americans lived and thought. I suggested a number of possible ideas, among them an exhibit of Western art and artists—as the Russian people like those of many other countries, were attracted by the romance of our West and had never seen the work of Catlin and Remington and other fine Western landscape artists, let alone American Indian art. Then I suggested, "Why not send them a rodeo?"[1] saying that it would be a win-win situation—a great chance to show off the prowess of both sides, as the Russians had a tradition of magnificent horsemen and the Russian public loved stories of cowboys and the old American West. Along with the rodeo there might be the possibility of showing a series of Western films.

The President loved this idea, exclaiming enthusiastically, "That's a wonderful idea! A rodeo! Oh, that's a good idea. A rodeo!"

I stopped then and said, "After all, this is really the icing on the cake. There are plenty of ideas of what we can do, but first we have to have a cultural agreement because we can't even think about all these wonderful things we might like to do until we have one."

I emphasized once again how important—indeed, essential—were broader exchanges, as these had been too few, too elitist, and bureaucratic, and we got the same faces all the time from them and they from us. The Soviets would almost certainly object, as they had said "no jumbo jet exchanges," so it might be difficult to achieve but was something we should encourage and strongly push for, especially for younger people from both sides, college and high school students. I told the President that when I urged this on Bogdanov, he had answered poker-faced, "Well there are problems with exchanges that the Russians also recognize." The President sat back and waited. "Then he added, 'The difference between our two countries, you understand, is that you send us your best professors and we treat them as spies, and with us—it's the opposite.'"

It took the President a couple of seconds to get the joke; then he leaned back in his chair and laughed and laughed. "Did the Russians really tell you that joke? I like that! I'm going to put that in my joke file."

We discussed the question of his going to Moscow and inviting the Soviet leader to come to the United States. I told him, "You're a great communicator. I know if you went to the Soviet Union and knew even a little about their customs, I'm sure you could charm them, and I think you ought to invite them here."

Deaver and McFarlane jumped on that. They said, "Actually, it is our turn technically, because the last time, we went there, so now they should come here."

The President started reminiscing about the visit of the Chinese leader Deng Xiaoping and how much fun Deng had had horseback riding. "He really liked that. Deng was really knocked down when he saw how much we had here. He was really surprised how much we were able to do in the United States." Then he spoke as he had at our first meeting, about wanting to go up in a helicopter with a Soviet leader. "When I'm in that helicopter, I look down and see our little houses and all these nice little gardens, and some people even have swimming pools, and that's how our people are living. And I feel I would like to say to them, 'Look, you see? Look what we do for our people. Can you do as well for your people?'"

And at that point, I looked at my hands as demurely as I could and presumed to say, "Mr. President, I might suggest that there might be some advantage if you would ask them about their families and about themselves. Because it's pretty obvious to the Russians how much better we live than they do."

I reminded him that we were two of the three largest Christian countries on earth (the United States, Brazil, and the Soviet Union). He got a little testy again and said, "Well, I don't have any respect for that Orthodox Church because they're all infiltrated."

It's not easy to confront the prejudices and the suspicions of both sides, and I didn't want to give him a lecture, but I thought I'd better explain a few things. Looking straight at Deaver, who was across from me, I answered, "Well, you know the problem is that it's perhaps the most persecuted church in modern times and maybe ever. The first Five Year Plan in 1929 predicted that by the end of it, all vestiges of religion would be destroyed. Under Stalin and continuing nonstop, the Soviet regime destroyed eighty percent of the churches and massacred thousands of priests and believers. Yes, the remnants of the Church that have remained have been in a very difficult position. They have had to try to survive somehow. And they have. It's awfully hard to do that."

I quoted him the words of an Orthodox priest who told me, "For those of us who remained, it cost us real sacrificial suffering, but we decided in part to participate in this society, to serve it, to save it, and to redeem it. And now they cannot exist without us." I said that today there were KGB men who were religious and priests who were not, and the situation was amorphous. I felt that the United States should witness this—not necessarily make a lot of noise about it, but to be aware as I had been when I was told directly by a pious churchman that "the Church has never been stronger in Russia because it is very inconvenient and difficult for us and therefore we have gotten the strongest people. It is always good when the State opposes the Church. It makes it stronger." Reagan smiled.

I took the Polish example. Nobody had cared about the Polish Catholic Church. Our experts had declared that it was docile and regulated by the government and only permitted because it had to be. We were wrong. Also, in Iran we had underestimated the importance of religion. I told him about the Russian ideal of nonviolence begun by their first patron saints, Boris and Gleb, martyred in the 11th century, who counseled do not resist evil with evil. "So what looks like acceptance of the regime is not acceptance, but the Russian way. The Orthodox Church was going about its business quietly, trying to protect believers in whatever way they could." I think I convinced him.

I had brought to McFarlane the excellent book, *Lessons of Faith in Russia,* written by Michael Bourdeaux, an English Anglican priest and an expert on religion in the Soviet Union. When I had showed it to Bud in the anteroom, he recognized the name right away and said, "Oh, Mrs. Thatcher brought Bourdeaux to talk to Vice President Bush."

So I asked him, "Do you think the President would be interested in this? I brought it for you."

He said, "Give it to him."

And so I did. "Mr. President, this book can give you some information about all this."

McFarlane immediately stepped in and reminded him, "This is the man that Mrs. Thatcher introduced to the Vice President."

The lunch meeting had gone on for an hour and twenty minutes, very long and unusual for the President. I had thought that he would want to leave much earlier. He looked at his watch and said, "It's time," and got up. I quickly said goodbye and that I would send him my books as he had requested.

In such a unique situation, you never have the slightest idea how well you do. I was glad to have McFarlane there, a man I trusted and who was very supportive. I could feel him sending good vibes in my direction and that helped me a great deal, but I wished again that I'd been across from the President so I could have seen Bud's face and gotten some inkling of how it was going. So when we came out, I inquired anxiously, "Bud, I hope it was all right. I just hate it because I feel that I talk all the time and it bothers me very much."

And he said, "No, no, no. He needed to hear these things. It was just fine. That's what you were there for," and he thanked me very much for all I was doing. I asked him if I could talk about my visit with the President and he said, "Of course." I also asked if I could speak about what I had done. He answered again, "Of course. We appreciate what you have done for us. You should be recognized. And we want very much for you to help with this cultural thing." So we made an appointment to continue to talk. Except for the unruly shrimp and unyielding beans, it was a wonderful meeting. I left feeling happy and satisfied, along with the sense that I had accomplished what I had been asked to do and reported back. I had done my job and there was no reason to think that there would be further meetings with the President.

That day the President wrote in his diary, *"Had lunch with Bud & Mrs. Massie—just back from Russia. She's a remarkable woman with some great insight on the Russians. She reinforced my gut feeling that it's time for me to personally meet with Chernenko."* (He followed up with a letter to the new Soviet leader a few days later.)

I was whisked off in a White House limousine to the Sulgrave Club to give my talk, and then I went to the Kennedy Center to find the Ballet Committee ladies all in a flutter thinking the lunch had been a big White House affair and wanting to know who the other guests were. When I said, "No, it was just us," they asked incredulously, "What in the world did the President want to talk to you about?"

I answered, "I don't know; he just wanted to talk."

I had been invited to the dinner that followed the ballet performance that evening and found myself seated next to Ambassador Arthur Hartman, our current man in Moscow. He was the very model of a high State Department career official who had served as ambassador in Paris before going to Moscow, and was held in high esteem professionally by many of his State Department colleagues. He was not what was called by State a "Russia hand." I had met him briefly only twice. Before he had left for Moscow a few years earlier, he had made a quick visit to the Harvard Research Center and called to ask me to suggest books about Russia that he should read. Nothing else. He spent most of his time seeing those who were very much involved with the dissident and Jewish emigration issues. This of course was a very legitimate concern but not the only important one in the Soviet Union at that pivotal time. I had made a call on him when I was in Moscow in October of 1983, and from his remarks had gathered the impression that he was very cool toward

Russians. I had also written him two letters; both went unanswered.

His presence that evening was explained by news that had appeared in *The New York Times* that morning stating that the White House had summoned a roundup meeting of officials, including the ambassador, to discuss Soviet relations. Indeed, the first thing he announced at dinner was that he was here for three days to see the President. Realizing that somehow, for some reason, McFarlane had slipped me in first, my instincts warned me to say nothing about my lunch, so instead I asked innocently, "What are you going to talk to the President about?"

He answered, "Shultz and I. We're just going over the whole thing." Then, quite unexpectedly, he announced in a disapproving tone, "I heard Bud McFarlane had a *prayer* said for you!" (Evidently before I had left for my Moscow mission.)

I was completely taken by surprise, not only by the statement, but the disapproving tone in which he had said it that made me very uncomfortable. "Oh?" said I, "How did you hear that?"

"Bill Shinn told me." (Bill Shinn was a former U.S. consul general in Leningrad.) "He's at the same church."

"I didn't know," I said truthfully. And left it at that.

Because of course I assumed he was the man who would know, I asked how he generally felt about Chernenko, but, to my disappointment, he knew little. I knew that he had started showing American movies regularly at his residence, Spaso House, and inviting Russians to attend. So, lowering my eyes, I asked, "You know, I read about the *Ninotchka* incident and wondered what really happened, because the newspapers are so unfair."

"Well, I'd always heard about this film and I hadn't seen it for ages and thought it might be funny, so I ordered a copy and showed it to the foreign press corps. Of course, when I saw it, I realized that I couldn't show it to the Russians, so I called them up to tell them I wasn't going to show it—but of course the damage had been done."

Knowing this marvelously comic film, I certainly could understand why the super-touchy, paranoid Soviets would take umbrage at a U.S. ambassador showing a film that made them look foolish to the foreign press and members of the diplomatic corps. They took it as a deliberate insult, and in retaliation for the next screening of the film, sent the KGB to stop Russians from going in.

Then he added, "Well, you know, of course it was a little hard on my European colleagues, but even in bad times, of course, as American ambassador I always have much better access than anybody else. If I want to see Gromyko, I can see Gromyko. He'll always see me and he won't see the others."

"Is there any truth to the rumor that you may be coming back?" I asked.

He answered, "No. No, I haven't been there long enough. Not enough time." (For what? I wondered.)

Before I went to the Soviet Union in January, I knew that our Embassy had little if any contact with the Orthodox Church and thought that it wouldn't hurt to make some gesture, so I had suggested to Matlock that it might be diplomatic to make a call on a church hierarch. He had dismissed the idea with, "Oh well, if you do want to see the church, you do that on your own." I had been very well briefed on Metropolitan Philaret[2] personally and the situation of the Orthodox Church by Bishop Rodzianko and others, so I did go to call on him and had a formal meeting where we discussed in a general way how to improve relations between our countries—normal things you would discuss with the church. But to my surprise, in the middle of that conversation, as we were just talking very generally about how to improve relations, he suddenly burst out, "Of course, you understand that a great deal depends upon your representative."

And I said, "Our representative?"

"Yes," he replied.

"Oh? What is wrong?"

The Metropolitan then became quite upset and exclaimed, "Your ambassador speaks to us very harshly! He shook his fist at us!"

So that evening at dinner, I asked Hartman, "What happened between you and Philaret?"

Hartman snorted, "Oh, that man! He just represents the church. He's nothing but a KGB agent infiltrator!" confirming that indeed something had happened between them and the net result was that the church had absolutely nixed any relations with our Embassy. Then I understood better why Bogdanov had asked the question about the possibility of our ambassador being replaced, saying, "He doesn't like Russians. He is not popular. He has made enemies. The Church."

I was shaken by the conversation that evening, and when I happened to see Senator Bill Cohen a few days later, although I did not mention my conversation with Hartman, I said that I was having a very difficult problem about how to deal with embassy attitudes. I found that he shared my feeling. He told me that he had been in Moscow, had run into it himself, and had written a letter about it to Secretary Shultz.

I thought from Bill's remarks that perhaps this was why the Soviets were trying private channels—because they were not getting the kind of communication they needed through our embassy. I told Bill this concerned me, too, especially now that I had seen the President and realized that this was not the image he wished to present. I thought this might be one of the reasons the Soviets disbelieved the sincerity of the President's speeches because they saw our representative and thought, *That's what they really mean. The President is just saying those things for election purposes but doesn't mean them because we see what's happening here.* They had thought very carefully about the kind of image they wanted to present to important Americans. So their suspicions could be all the more possible because of the importance they placed on their ambassador Anatoly Dobrynin in Washington, an urbane, charming man who disarmed everybody, spoke perfect English, and gave Americans the idea that the Soviet Union was a reasonable, civilized, and knowledgeable place. He was the perfect person for the job. Instead, we often named representatives who couldn't speak their language. If Dobrynin couldn't speak English and could only

LUNCH IN THE OVAL OFFICE—MARCH 1, 1984   133

communicate through a translator, it would have been considered rather condescending of the Soviets. And if they showed a movie in their embassy in Washington that made fun of us, we would have been furious. So these were problems and things we needed to consider. Either there was a policy of better relations or there wasn't such a policy. If there was such a policy and a desire to build dialogue, we had to think very carefully about how to present ourselves in our best light to the other side.

After I became better known for my relationship with the President, in the years that followed and until he left in 1987, Ambassador Hartman and his wife, Donna, were extremely kind and hospitable toward me. I once stayed with them at Spaso House, their grand official residence. When I was in Moscow, they invited me to their receptions and once hosted a lunch for me, gathering Russian artists from the ballet, theater and music world of Moscow. At that lunch, I also met the very charming Guy de Muyser, Ambassador of Luxembourg, who graciously invited me to stay in his residence when I was in Moscow, an invitation that I gratefully took up on several other occasions, mindful of the fact that I wanted to make clear to the Soviets that I was an independent and private person, beholden to no one. I also made it a point to get to know the Swiss ambassador, as I was to find that a great deal passed through the more modest ears and eyes of the ambassadors of small and non-threatening countries.

CHAPTER 8

THE ACHILLES' HEEL

"There never was a nation founded and maintained without some kind of belief in something. Nobody knows what the outcome in Russia will be or how long this government will last. But if they do get by for a while on everything else, they picked the one thing I know of to suppress that is absolutely necessary to run a Country on and that is Religion. Never mind what kind; but it's got to be something or you will fail at the finish."
Will Rogers.[1]

I think that the one thing that startled me most about my first meeting with President Reagan was that the President of the United States did not know how important religion had been—and still was—to the Russians, or even it seems, that the Orthodox Church in Russia continued to exist. Evidently no one had ever told him. But how could this be, with the army of experts and specialists available to him in Washington? [2]

The moment impressed me so strongly, especially because when I met him in 1984, despite all the persecutions of their faith, some 55 million Russians were ready to state that they were Orthodox, more than three times the members of the Communist Party, which then numbered 18 million. This made Brazil, the United States, and the Soviet Union the three largest Christian countries in the world.

For me, this gap in the President's knowledge was striking because, of all the developments I witnessed between 1967 and 1991 announcing the end of the communist regime in the Soviet Union, none was more significant in that officially atheistic nation than the clear signs of a renewed search for faith and morality and the steady return of Russians to the Orthodox faith of their ancestors. Yet despite mountains of information and intelligence reports, nothing was more ignored, or, if noticed at all, dismissed by our Soviet specialists. Naturally, our establishment would not have heard much about this from the Soviet bureaucracy, with whom they dealt almost exclusively.

Although I did not know it at the time, this information, which, quite unknowingly, I was the first to provide to the President, turned out to be significant for him. His loathing of "godless communism" was a cornerstone of his political identity, but his mother had always told him that religion would sweep away communism, and in 1981 he had prophetically written to a friend, "religion might very well turn out to be their Achilles' heel."[3] So the subject was very much on his mind. During our meetings he came back to the subject often, and at his request, I was to be given the chance to tell him more about it.

There were reasons for our official blindness, among them that in the United States we have the tendency to see everything as a reflection of our own beliefs. Being "like us" is equivalent to being "right." We in America can choose our religion as if we were shopping for a new car, changing at will, and harbor thousands of offshoots and sects. Because our history is founded on personal choice for all religions we have no experience or understanding of a religion that represents a nation, and we find this somehow disturbing. The history of Russia is the opposite, and the communist regime of the Soviet Union always understood this fact completely.

Orthodoxy (*Pravoslavie*, the Russian word for Orthodoxy, means the "true worship") is inextricable from Russian history, and lies at the core of Russian identity. It was often said in the past that the Church was Russia and Russia was the Church. Indeed it is not too strong to say that, for most of its history, Orthodoxy defined what it was to be Russian. The ancient word for a Russian peasant is *krestyanin*—a cross-wearing person. From 988 A.D., when an early Russia adopted the Eastern Christianity of Byzantium, Orthodoxy became the most important cohesive force in the development of Russian culture and outlook on life. Russians once saw themselves as a clan linked by their faith. At the head of that clan was the patriarch and the tsar, chosen by God.

There have been only two attempts to tear Russians away from their

Church. The first was made by Peter the Great in the 18th century. In his youth, a xenophobic Church dominated everything in Russian life, and when he became tsar, Peter saw it as the greatest force against his determination to bring his country into the Western world and the center of attempts to stop his reforms. He approached the problem as he did everything, with titanic force, ridiculing the Church, separating its clerics into a caste, subordinating it to the power of the State. He removed the patriarch and created the Holy Synod, placing the tsar above all. But in the end, Peter was able to control only the upper level of the population over which he had power. Although the aristocracy took on many Western habits and in the 19th century the intelligentsia were to find another beacon in Western socialist ideas, the majority of Russians continued to believe as they had before. In the course of the century, Christian ideas found expression in the novels of Tolstoy and Dostoevsky and Orthodox philosophers whose books were banned or expurgated in Soviet times. By the turn of the century, there was a revival of Orthodoxy accompanied by reforms, and finally, in 1917 after the Revolution, the reinstatement and election of Patriarch Tikhon.[4]

Peter's attempts pale before those of the Soviet regime, which had the means to be far more thorough. Always recognizing the great power of the centuries-old Orthodox Church, in order to create a new Soviet man who would worship only the State and its leaders, it was vital to break its hold on the culture, minds, and souls of the Russian people by destroying it. From the time the Bolsheviks had taken power, all religion was considered Enemy Number One, but Orthodoxy the most dangerous, to be eradicated with all the ruthlessness they could command. They set out to commit what can only be called a genocide of the Church. In 1918, they began to wage what they called a "war on God." All manifestations of religion were prohibited as were all Church holidays, even Easter and Christmas. Liturgical music was banned until the mid-1980s. Sunday was made a compulsory working day and even the word was obliterated. (*Voskresenie*, the word for Sunday in Russian, is the same as the word for resurrection.) The word *god* was always to be spelled in lower case. Thousands of historic churches and all their treasures were destroyed outright. Scores were desecrated, turned into warehouses, movie theaters, swimming pools, and even public toilets. Millions of icons were destroyed, broken, or sold abroad along with other treasures of the Church. Melted down were the church bells that had for centuries regulated the life of the countryside.[5] Multitudes of priests and believers were murdered outright, more imprisoned or sent to labor camps. Confidently, the Party predicted that "all vestiges of religion will be destroyed by the end of the first Five Year Plan."

The mighty Church of the Savior, begun in 1839, consecrated in 1883 on the coronation day of Alexander III, was financed by the contributions of the Russian people in thanksgiving for the victory over Napoleon. As important an image as the Kremlin on the Moscow horizon, it was the largest Orthodox church in the world and contained the work of all the major artists of Russia of its time. On December 5, 1931, it was blown up by Stalin's bloody henchman Lazar Kaganovich who, as he pushed the dynamite lever, vulgarly chortled, "We'll blow up Mother Russia's skirts a little!"[6] Marble from the interior of the church was used to decorate some metro stations, these extravagantly admired as a sign of Soviet "progress" by thousands of unknowing foreign visitors. Some of the plaques, engraved with the names of the soldiers who had died in the Napoleonic battles, were turned over and used for steps to public lavatories. So viciously effective was this "war on God" that by the end of 1939, there were only four bishops left at liberty and only 100 churches in a country that once had many thousands.

Gruesome events, many that remained unknown in the West until recent years, took place between 1937 and 1950, one of these in a 39-acre field surrounded with barbed wire, called *Butovo Poligon* (Butovo Killing Field), in the suburbs of Moscow. "Enemies of the people," sometimes 500 a day and more than 20,175 in total (perhaps many more; the accurate figure cannot be determined), were gunned down and buried on the spot, among them uncounted numbers of clerics and believers.

Naturally, church attendance was prohibited for all members of the Communist Party, and for anyone known to be a "believer," their livelihood and often even their lives were threatened. (One of my early Russian teachers, a professor at Columbia University whose father had been a priest and had continued to bravely minister to his flock, was arrested and taken away. When her sixteen year old brother courageously went to the prison to inquire about his father, he was curtly told, "We have shot him.") When I first went to the Soviet Union in 1967, we were informed by our Intourist guide that there were only nineteen "functioning" churches in Leningrad (including the second largest synagogue in Europe). Brave couples who had the temerity to wish to be married in a church were required to sign a police register at the door. From the beginning, this concentrated onslaught against religion and the resistance to it on the part of the population was occasionally reported[7] in our country, but it merited little attention and was irrelevant to the formulation of policy on national security or defense. Considering this as well as the secular bent of many of our experts and our media, it was not entirely surprising that the regime succeeded almost completely in convincing the West that religion had ceased to exist in their new socialist society, or that in 1984 our president shared this view. Yet it was a lie.

Religion was not destroyed at the end of the first Five Year Plan, nor at any time after. Despite all their efforts the new regime was unable to entirely extinguish the Orthodox Church in Russia nor its influence on the Russian people. Indeed, when Stalin went into hiding for a week after the onset of the Nazi invasion on June 22nd of 1941, it fell to Metropolitan Sergei to announce the catastrophe to the Russian people.[8]

Although severely constricted and contained, the Orthodox Church would remain during the Soviet years the only non–Marxist-Leninist organization to exist at all, a tribute to its lasting hold on the hearts of the Russians. After World War II, there was a brief lull. Churches began to spring up again, but in 1959 Khrushchev mounted a renewed campaign against religion, and half of the churches that remained were destroyed.

Why were we so taken in by Soviet propaganda? We know that the United States considers itself a religious country and that no politician can afford to call himself an atheist. However, the ironbound American principle of separation of church and state is so ingrained that over time we officially developed a tin ear on the subject, and the effect of God and religion was banished from serious discussion of policy or relations between nations. Indeed, so secularized did our policy makers and media become that it was almost considered a mark of naiveté, lower class, or right wing to mention religion at all. I believe this to be one of the most important reasons that we completely missed the political importance of the Catholic revival in Poland when it began and the role of Orthodoxy in the fall of communism in the Soviet Union, as well as the fundamentalist movement in Iran. As it has throughout human history, religion remains one of the strongest forces in the world, a fact that we are facing again with the Taliban and the jihadist movement in the Muslim world today.

Throughout the Cold War, the common refrain in the United States establishment was that Orthodoxy was a dead religion in the Soviet Union, a dusty relic of the tsarist regime, and that the majority of the population was not interested. It was practiced, it was firmly stated, "only by old ladies" who attended the few "functioning" permitted churches that remained. All the priests were infiltrated and dominated by the KGB. As in everything connected with Russia, the truth was far more complex.

I often pointed out that it was important to note that these were *new* old ladies, not immortal leftovers from 1917, and that they were inexorably replacing themselves. (I should note here that the authorities early on also waged a war on the *babushkas,* trying in the first years after the Revolution to eliminate the Russian custom of having children cared for by grandmothers while their parents worked by instead putting children in State care centers. This didn't last long.) The combination of distraught mothers and *babushkas* won that one quickly, and throughout the Soviet years, the *babushkas* continued to take care of the children as they had from Russian time immemorial and were busy having them baptized—mostly in secret. These ever-renewing, indestructible old ladies kept the Church alive in its darkest years, then acted as stern nannies, instructing the young as they began coming back.

Gorbachev himself was one of these children and when he was asked at a press conference in Paris in the fall of 1985 whether he had been baptized, he answered calmly, "Yes. Isn't everybody?" This startling admission, the first ever from a communist leader, was not considered worthy of comment in *The New York Times*.

There are many remarkable stories about these secret baptisms. The famous writer, the late Vasily Aksyonov, told me that just before he was expelled from the Soviet Union, he was approached by an acquaintance who told him that he had to meet his baptismal sister before he left. When Aksyonov remonstrated, saying that he had never been baptized and so had no baptismal sister, it turned out he had. Although his mother was a committed communist and his father the communist boss of the city they lived in, his nurse, helped by his father's official driver would go off with babies and have them secretly baptized. Aksyonov had been one of these.[9]

As for the KGB. Well, yes. What did we in the United States expect? The KGB was present in every corner of Soviet life, another government employing many thousands of people. As the Orthodox Church, however strangled, was the only non–Marxist-Leninist institution permitted to exist at all, it was closely watched, infiltrated, and threatened. Of course there were some false priests, but an important fact to remember is that the Orthodox believer meets the Kingdom of God through the liturgy—the anchor, the rock, immutable and unchangeable through the centuries—not through the priest who celebrates it. However throttled, the Church fought fiercely to be able to continue to celebrate the liturgy in the few remaining "functioning" churches, and left it to their Maker to judge false priests.

In any case, I always thought that the KGB was much better off celebrating the liturgy than doing a lot of other things, and as Christian history teaches us, some who came to persecute stayed to pray, until, by the end of the Soviet years, it was becoming difficult to ascertain which tail was wagging the dog.

I told the President some of the stories about the many experiences and scenes I had witnessed over the years in that country of so-called "godless communism," a few of which I include here, revealing as they do how wide was the gap between the reality and the falsehoods of those days.

- For me, the first eye-opener was in 1967, during that first trip to the Soviet Union. After leaving Leningrad, my husband and I went to Livadia in the Crimea. It happened to be Maundy Thursday of Easter week. Passing a large church, we were surprised to see many people streaming in. Just behind the main crowd, I spied a grandmother hurrying along, firmly clasping her small grandson tightly by one hand, while the little boy was barely managing to hold onto a little red flag with the hammer and sickle in his other small fist. With steely determination, brooking no opposition, she steered him straight into the church. I had a sudden flash that I was glimpsing the future. Time was to prove that the communist regime was no match for the faith of the rugged, indomitable *babushkas* of Russia.

- Back in Moscow, we took the Intourist excursion to Zagorsk, 45 miles away from the city, to see the famed Trinity–St. Sergius Monastery (in Russian, *Troitse Sergeieva)*, founded by the holy monk St. Sergius (1314–92). This monastery grew from the 14th century to be the spiritual heart of the land. In the 15th century, Andrei Rublev, Russia's great icon painter and one of the world's great artists, entered the monastery as a monk. In the 16th century, Ivan the Terrible was christened there and his successor Boris Godunov lies buried there. By the 17th century, it had become an impressive walled citadel that contained a large monastery and several churches, one a massive cathedral crowned with gigantic blue cupolas dotted with gold stars and an interior entirely decorated with frescoes. So sacred was that monastery that even Stalin had hesitated to destroy it.

On the way, the Intourist guide, in an expressionless monotone, recited mechanically, "We are going to Zagorsk." (In 1991 restored to its former name, *Sergeiyev Posad*.) "It is named for Comrade Zagorsk, who invented the first subway car. There is also an old monastery which we shall visit." It was pouring rain. When we arrived, on the square in front of the monastery, loud jazz music was playing on a raucous loudspeaker to drown out the chants of the monks inside. Yet as we entered the monastery complex, I saw many people approaching the monks, kissing their hands and asking for their blessing. When we were taken to the 14th century Church of the Holy Trinity, which contained the relics of St. Sergius as well as icons painted by the great medieval artist Andrei Rublev, I witnessed a sad and poignant sight. The church was crowded with Russians, men in bedraggled wet coats, women with their heads covered in scarves, all valiantly trying to sing the service despite the deliberately loud disruptive voices of the Intourist guides accompanying foreign tourists.

We managed to stay inside when the others of the group went out to see a toy factory. Permeated with the smell of wet wool and beeswax candles, the church grew more and more crowded. I was so moved by the sight that I wanted to give some offering but the crowd was too great and the altar too far away, so I looked to find a woman about my age and tried to hand her some money. She was startled, frightened. It was prohibited to take any money from a foreigner. Then, looking into my eyes for a moment, she understood, quickly took my offering, and passed it up to the altar. (Later I visited the latrines and saw old women in rags sitting over the steaming holes trying to keep warm.)

In those days it seemed to me that Russians often behaved like an abused woman. Realizing that the superior strength that threatens coud kill her, keeping her silence, her head bowed, but never leaving. This was so with religion in the Soviet Union. The government was able to control the administrative hierarchy of the Church, to limit services and prevent all religious actions outside of a church building. But they could not control the minds of their people. Solzhenitsyn once wrote that when you take a culture away from a people, it is like committing a lobotomy on them. The Church remained the only unbroken link with Russia's past and ancient culture, and the Russian people refused to be lobotomized.

- Over the next twenty-two years, those first sights were followed by many powerful conclusive signs that, despite everything, the regime's relentless efforts to annihilate religion had failed. No doubt because of our American insistence on total separation of church and state, any contact with religious leaders in foreign countries had been strictly discouraged for our diplomats. During the Soviet years, our representatives attended church rarely, usually only for the Easter service and for less than an hour to view the *krestny khod* (the Easter religious procession) along with their guests.

Indeed, any official contacts with the Russian Church were avoided for so long that in Leningrad one of our consuls general, Richard Miles (1988–1991), noticing that because of our lack of interest the Orthodox Church had stopped inviting our representatives at all, made it a point to try to reconnect. A later consul general, John Evans (1994–97), kept up regular contacts with the Orthodox clerics of the city. Together we attended an Easter service in St. Petersburg at the St. Nicholas Cathedral. Immaculate in his blue suit and red, white, and blue tie, he stood stalwartly through the entire four-hour service. (There are no pews in Orthodox churches, as the Orthodox believe that they are in the presence of God and it would be unthinkable to sit in His presence.) Afterwards at the feast following the service the delighted priest warmly congratulated him, telling him that he was the only consul who had ever stayed for the whole service, and presented him with a huge red ostrich egg.

- From the beginning of my travels to the Soviet Union in 1967, I went to church often and stayed there, standing through the long services, watching the faces and the people. As a student of Russian history and culture, I knew the historical importance of Orthodoxy and had many contacts with Russian believers, both official and underground, with priests and Church hierarchs. As the only woman member, I participated for nine years in the official Dialogue of the Episcopal and Orthodox Churches, and so had an opportunity accorded to few Westerners to get to know many priests and princes of the Church. As a member of this delegation, I dined with Patriarch Alexey II (whom I had first met in Leningrad when he was the Metropolitan) in the company of his bishops and hierarchs, the only woman in a sea of bearded, cassock-clad men, some of whom seemed clearly unhappy about a woman's presence among them. I had met Bishop Kliment of Kaluga (today, Archbishop) when he was a priest in the New York Church of the Moscow Patriarchate and later when he was a member of the Russian delegation to our Dialogue. In a very unusual gesture, he invited me to his ornate 17th century home church in Kaluga, 93 miles from Moscow, for his Name Day (the day of his patron saint, as important a day in Russia as a birthday). I was, of course, accompanied by a woman chaperon from the Church office. At dinner, the bishop, who has a wonderful sense of humor, entertained us with stories of his years in America. I was taken to surrounding villages, where priests took us to visit orphanages and hospitals. There I saw heartbreaking suffering, illness, and need. At one orphanage an accompanying priest quietly hid a chocolate under the pillow of each child.

- In Leningrad, I attended the magnificent blue-and-white 18th century St. Nicholas Cathedral, dedicated to the Navy and especially revered in Leningrad because the city known as the "Venice of the North" had been built on piles sunk in the delta, and was crisscrossed with canals. I watched the long lines of people who waited for many hours on the Day of Epiphany to fill jars with holy water that priests distributed from huge copper kettles. These jars of water would be taken home and used through the year to protect against illness. In the nearby town of Pushkin, an especially active priest I knew fed up to 120 poor and hungry people every day, the food prepared by devoted women in the small kitchen of his home. He was in the daunting process of restoring a historic ruined church from Catherine the Great's time with the help of volunteers—among whom, to my surprise, I found the janitor of my apartment building in the city.

- As time passed, I observed the increasing crowds and, over the years, how their complexion changed. At first it was primarily the faithful old ladies, gradually joined by younger women carrying babies, then, old men, and then increasingly, young men, some in uniform, and finally, more and more rough-looking fellows wearing leather jackets. On the street, one could observe the growing number of crosses worn on the necks of young women. Ironically, in the late '70s and early '80s, the daughters of communist leaders were among the first to want to be married in white dresses and in church. (So much prettier than the uninspiring Soviet "marriage palaces.") In Moscow at dusk, I once watched as a young, well-dressed Russian businessman in an obvious hurry took time to stop and cross himself in front of a church. I talked to a maid in my hotel, who told me that, sadly, her grown children were not religious, but that she had had her grandson baptized and advised him not to wear his baptismal cross openly, but to keep it always in his pocket where he could touch it. A young soldier once approached me on the street and said haltingly, "Please tell your people we pray for you as we hope you will pray for us." I acted as a godmother at baptisms, was a witness at weddings, attended funerals, and was nearly crushed by the crowd at Easter services.

- One of the most startling sights happened in 1985 when I accompanied a young Russian mother to church in Moscow and saw a stream of people entering a side entrance with their children. When I went in, to my astonishment, I counted seventy-two babies and young children waiting in line to be baptized, the older children happily running around in their underwear, the babies held in the arms of their mothers and grandmothers. Two priests were busy crossing them all as fast as they could. Incredulous, I asked my friend, "Does this happen every day?"

She answered calmly, "Oh, no. Only on Sundays. During the week it is only five or six a day."[10]

Once, in 1985, a rumor was going around among our diplomats that one looking over the shoulder of an official at the theater had glimpsed a mysterious engraved invitation to a church in the Kremlin complex for Easter eve. Intrigued by this rumor, I was prompted to ask one of my Russian friends whether perhaps some of the communist leaders could be secret believers. "No," was the answer, "only their wives."[11]

EASTER AMONG THE "GODLESS"

During Soviet years, watching the long lines of Russians waiting patiently to get into museums, as well as the overflowing crowds in church, I realized how important the beauty so absent in their daily lives was to the Russian people. Russians believe that beauty and art are ways in which God manifests Himself to humankind.[12] Russian churches are called "the palaces of God," lavishly decorated with icons, frescoes, and glittering gold. Priests wear ornate and colorful robes of gold and silver brocade, swing censors of aromatic incense. Services are entirely sung a cappella by devoted and hardworking choirs who are regularly called on to sing for several hours. The resonant basso voices of Church deacons are famous. Russians respect the power of emotion and the mystical far more than we in the West, who worship the power of the rational and technological. Indeed, so deep-rooted are their beliefs and ancient customs that even Russians who do not attend church and are not official "believers," without even realizing it, think in an Orthodox way.

There is no better example of the power of Orthodoxy in the Russian spirit than the national celebration of Easter, which, by 1967 when I first saw it, was celebrated publicly again in the few permitted, packed-to-bursting, "functioning" churches. Unlike we in America, with our yearly Christmas shopping orgy and Easter marked by bunnies and chicks, Easter in Russia is the most important holy day of the Church, as well as the most festive celebration of the year. It is an extraordinary annual spiritual revival celebrated by the entire Orthodox population of the nation for a full two weeks following an eight-week Lenten fast observed sometimes strictly, sometimes less so, by millions of Russians. Not to understand its importance is not to understand the Russian psyche.

I. AT THE MONASTERY

I attended many Easter celebrations during the years of my travels—two during the Reagan years that remain fixed in my memory as poignant illustrations of the total lack of comprehension that existed at the time between official Washington and the Russian people.

One of these happened in 1985 with Ray Benson who was Cultural Attaché at the American Embassy in Moscow and one of the rare American officials at the Embassy who maintained a close connection with the Church. I was invited to celebrate the Easter vigil night with him at the Trinity-St. Sergius Monastery that I had first visited in 1967. The Easter vigil and liturgy began at 11 p.m. and the celebration that follows it ended at dawn the next morning. When we arrived, an unexpected and disquieting sight greeted us. In the darkness, silhouetted against the illuminated high walls and encircling the entrance to the monastery complex, stood armed soldiers, evidently there to discourage Russians from entering. Looming high above the walls shone the huge blue and gold starred cupolas of the main cathedral. Standing at the base of the high walls, the soldiers looked tiny and fragile. No sight has ever struck me as powerfully as this did of the pitiful uselessness of military power pitted against that of the Almighty. Despite their menacing presence outside there was a huge crowd inside the monastery. I wandered in the darkness, watching. There are several churches within the monastery complex, and in front of one of these, an old lady was trying with difficulty to make her way through a large crowd assembled before the entrance. Seeing her, the crowd parted respectfully to allow her to pass, but the guard in front of the entrance roughly tried to stop her. Cries of protest rose. "Let her through! She wants to pray! Do not stop her!" As the guard continued to hold her back, the cries of outrage from the crowd grew louder and angrier, to the extent that I thought for a moment they would attack the guard. Frightened by the growing hostility, the guard backed off and let her pass.

Standing in the night cold as midnight approached, we heard the first distant sound of the *trevzon*, the festive beginning of the first bells carried by the procession of monks and priests beginning the *krestny khod*, the symbolic circling of the church to seek the risen Christ. As they came closer, the *trevzon* grew louder, joined by the solemn tolling of all the church bells including the massive bells of the cathedral, rumbling like thunder. Priests and monks and the crowd that followed them, all holding lighted candles

that twinkled like stars in the night, made the symbolic three turns around the church while singing the solemn words of the traditional opening hymn of hope:
Thy resurrection, Christ our Savior,
The angels in Heaven sing.
Enable us on earth
To glorify Thee in purity of heart...
joined by the crowds of faithful that lined each side of the monastery paths.

The emotional power grew. But after the priests had entered the churches for the liturgy, a strange thing happened. All the soldiers began to filter into the monastery and the churches—so many that it looked for a moment as if the monastery was being invaded. Behind them came more throngs of people. I noticed that the *druzhinnki* (popular militia), men wearing red armbands there to prevent people from entering the churches, were all drunk and did nothing. All the churches were packed. The service I witnessed was particularly magnificent. Eighteen priests celebrated, bobbing and moving as gracefully as ballet dancers, changing their ornate robes four times during the long service in escalating colors: green to red to silver and finally to gold.

After the four hour service, Ray and I had been invited to join the monks, priests, and their families for the traditional *razgovlenie*, the breaking of the eight-week Lenten fast, an unusual honor. Long tables were decorated with flowers and colored eggs, with *paskha* and *kulich*,[13] the traditional Easter dishes. More lengthy prayers followed, and then everyone sat down to make merry, drink vodka toasts, and feast on ham and baskets of vegetables, tea, and sweets.

We drove back to Moscow as the first rays of dawn were breaking over the horizon. At the Bolshoi Theater that day, to compete with the religious services (one had to choose between staying up all night or attending the opera), they were presenting *Eugene Onegin* at noon. Along with a host of Russians, it is my favorite opera, Tchaikovsky's masterpiece, a musical encyclopedia of Russian ideas of love. I was determined, however exhausted, to attend. After the long Easter celebration, I was sleepy, yet uplifted. I was seated in the director's box directly over the stage. Hearing the first chords and knowing what was to follow, my tears began to flow. Leaning my weary head on the railing covered in deep-red velvet, I let myself float away to the immortal music of the great Russian composer.

II. THE SENATORS

The second Easter happened at the same monastery in 1988. The Energy and National Resources Committee of the Senate, chaired by Senator J. Bennett Johnston of Louisiana, had been invited by their counterparts in the Supreme Soviet to make a fact-finding trip to the Soviet Union and to meet with various communist bigwigs. James Billington, Librarian of Congress, whom I had known since he and my former husband, Bob Massie, had been Rhodes Scholars at Oxford, was academic consultant of choice on the Soviet Union for senators. I was invited by Senator Timothy Wirth of Colorado to accompany the trip as the other consultant.

We were all taken by bus to Andrews Air Force Base in Washington, where we boarded an impressive plane with the official seal of the United States: Air Force Two. It was comfortably configured with sofas and consulting rooms, all of the seats being assigned in order of importance, with the best, of course, going to the chairman. I suppose that what followed was common for such trips, but for me the experience was remarkable. As a writer I was fascinated; as a taxpayer—well, disturbed. Having never been on a senatorial junket, I was not accustomed to such luxurious treatment on the lowly commercial airliners I ordinarily frequented. It was, I thought, what it must have been like to travel as a member of the Raj at the height of the British Empire.

A crew of stewards, stewardesses, and military baggage carriers, in a ratio of two for every senator, were along to cater to the every need of the eleven senators, most of whom were accompanied by their wives. An official Air Force photographer went everywhere with us, recording our every move. For many of the senators, it was their first trip to the Soviet Union, and their knowledge about the country was almost nonexistent.

We traveled to several cities in the Soviet Union, where some of the senators took the opportunity to talk to waiting "refuseniks" (Jewish petitioners for emigration, a hot political issue in the U.S.). For me, who was used to facing hard-eyed Soviet customs officials, the experience was an eye-opener. We never had to handle a bag (carried for us by U.S. enlisted men, mostly corporals) or show a passport, and were greeted at every stop by flower-bearing officials. On the flights, we were treated to fine meals. The plane carried a full bar and even our own American ice to every location. In every hotel, a 24-hour Ready Room, well-equipped with liquor of every variety, was immediately set up by our attendants. In Moscow, in the Kremlin after the obligatory conferences, we were treated by our hosts to a banquet in the Palace of Congresses, complete with bowls of caviar, flowing vodka, and champagne.

Easter night was to be our last evening in Moscow, and I strongly suggested that it would perhaps be educational and useful for the senators to see how the Russians celebrated their most important holiday. There was reluctance on the part of the committee chairman as well as our communist hosts, but finally I prevailed and it was agreed that we would go to the Trinity-St. Sergius Monastery. The Church fathers were advised and stood ready to welcome this important delegation. However, on the way, our communist hosts, clearly unenthusiastic about the idea and wanting to delay the whole excursion, insisted that we stop at a roadhouse, where a copious meal awaited, along with floes of vodka and wine. Some of the administrative assistants grew ever more raucous, dancing to the loud orchestra and laughing uproariously at their own jokes. Jim Billington and I watching this, took a whirl around the dance floor looking at each other helplessly. When we were all finally poured back onto the bus, it was close to midnight.

We continued our trip with more boozy laughter and clinking of bottles. One of the senators asked me to give a little talk on the significance of the evening, but the noisy atmosphere was so obnoxious—especially considering where and why we were going—that at first I refused. Finally, after much persuasion, I stood up and said sternly, "This is the holiest night of the year for Russians. Many have been fasting for weeks. Out of respect, it is important that we behave with some dignity." Chastened, the bottle clanking and loud laughter quieted down.

When we arrived, we were greeted by an important bishop who courteously informed us that, in order not to be crushed in the crowds, it had been arranged that our entire group would stand immediately to the right of the altar in the space normally reserved for the choir. We had to wait outside for a time as the imposing procession of priests carrying candles circled the churches, accompanied by the tolling of the great bells. (I noticed that Senator Johnston who, tapping his feet impatiently and looking at his watch, asked repeatedly when it would be over.) Then we were taken inside and took our places in full view of an enormous crowd of devout Russian people who stood packed in the church. The bishop greeted our group warmly in English, welcoming us to the Easter service. The service was beautiful, the spectacle and the piety of the crowd deeply moving as they repeated over and over, "*Gospodin Pomilu*" (God have mercy on us).

Suddenly, Senator Johnston peremptorily insisted that we all leave. I was shocked as were several of the other senators, feeling that, after all the courtesy extended to us, to walk out abruptly in the middle of the service and in full view of the assembled crowd of devout believers was embarrassingly discourteous. However, we were hustled back to our bus, which roared off directly to the Moscow airfield, and around 2 a.m. we re-boarded the waiting Air Force Two, onto which our bags and liquor had already been loaded, and flew off.

Why was this haste and needless insult necessary? Perhaps an important vote in the Senate? No. I was informed on the plane that the committee chairman wanted to be back in Washington to play golf the next morning.

RELYING ON HIS INSTINCTS

It is a tribute to the intelligence and character of President Reagan and National Security Advisor Robert McFarlane that they were able to appreciate the implications of a growing religious revival in Russia to global affairs of peace, diplomacy, and safety.

I had no idea when I first met the President in January 1984 that he was a devoutly religious and spiritual man with a deep faith in God and Jesus Christ. This very private man did not wear his beliefs on his sleeve, but as I was to learn, the principles of faith developed from his early youth under the strong example and guidance of his beloved mother were a lifelong guiding force of his life. He faithfully read the Bible and prayed every day.

I met Reagan at a critical time in his presidency. It is well reported that Reagan's already strong faith grew even stronger after his brush with death on March 3, 1981, only two months after his inauguration. I was told by the late Michael Deaver, his close friend and Deputy Chief of Staff, that when he visited a recovering Reagan at the White House two weeks after the assassination attempt, finding him still in his pajamas, the President told him that he felt he had been spared by God, that his remaining years belonged to Him and that he had a mission.[14] He voiced the same thought to other close family and friends. Certainly, from that time on, Reagan began to reach out to Soviet leaders.

Deaver also told me that on that day Reagan showed him a four and a half page letter he had handwritten in black ink on the yellow legal pads he preferred. In it, he told Brezhnev how deeply he yearned for "a world without nuclear weapons." He had sent it to Alexander Haig, his first National Security Advisor, and the State Department, and it was returned to him totally rewritten. Disappointed to see his letter changed so completely, he showed it to Deaver saying, "Well, they are the experts. Maybe they know more about this than I do."

Mike told me that he protested vigorously: "You're the President! You can write anything you want! You were elected by a mandate. Nobody elected anybody to the State Department!"

The President thanked him, adding, "You know, since I've been shot, I think I'm going to rely more on my own instincts than other people's. There's a reason I've been saved."

In the end, with the strong insistence of his wife Nancy, two letters were sent, the President's original letter along with the State Department version.

(Alas, the answer he received in return was filled with Soviet venom).

"Reagan," said Edwin Meese, his Attorney General and close friend, "had a very personal faith, which came up as a natural thing in private conversations. The President was able to talk about religion in a comfortable way, better than almost any person I've ever met. He did not want to parade it before the public, where people would think he was using it for political purposes or to try and engender the idea that he was a religious man. He did not feel he should hold religious services in the White House as Nixon did. He felt that was ostentatious."[15]

Reagan did not make the obligatory appearance at church services expected of a president because he felt that his presence, with all the requisite security demands, would be disruptive. After his brush with death, he wrote in his diary that he was "indeed a risk to others." During his presidency, he continued making regular church contributions, and as soon as he left the presidency he became once again a regular churchgoer in California.

Bud McFarlane, himself a faithful and active member of his Presbyterian church in Washington, explained: "It is well known that the President was an optimist about life. Coming from a distressing childhood and an alcoholic father, some have been surprised that...he could be an optimist, but it was the love and attention he received from his mother, his neighbors, and the community in which he lived that lifted him up and gave him a sense of worth during his childhood. These expressions of love were extended to him from people who didn't have to—neighbors, friends—and by the time he reached early manhood, imbued him with a very strong conviction in the power of love.

On his own, and I have talked to him about this on the ranch more than once, in the early days, dating from the time when he was a broadcaster in Des Moines to his early days in Hollywood, he began to reason through the sources of love, and, as with many people, concluded that God in his wisdom created humanity with a very simple motive, and that was to test the ability of this elevated form of life to prosper and get along with each other. Could this genus as a form of life be wise enough to understand that our only purpose was to love each other? Reagan passed through that spiritual door and it became for him an anchor of his life.

In the optimism which grew from being raised by a devoted and loving mother, his only doubt was that a godless society could endure, and a fear that it created in him about the Soviet Union. His fear was that, without this governing principle of love for one another in a society like the Soviet Union, Russians, who are so bright and intellectually gifted, would channel this wealth of intellect into other pursuits and specifically into destruction. Predating back to his governorship, he feared, despite his optimism about life, that where love doesn't exist humankind could destroy itself—that this lack of spiritual influence among the leadership of the Soviet Union could lead to a distortion and a concentration of talent into destructive ends and imperial ambition. And that this could, in the nuclear age, present a risk of Armageddon. He was dramatically preoccupied with this fear."[16]

Not knowing about this thinking at the time, I was surprised to see how often the subject of religion came up in our meetings and how important it seemed to be to him. He was eager to know about what I had seen in Russia and the reaction of ordinary people. He wanted information and insights that he was clearly not getting from the bureaucrats. Little publicized during his presidency, he had five meetings and long discussions[17] with Pope John Paul II, not only in the Vatican but also in the United States. They held many views in common. John Paul II always maintained that communism and religion could not coexist, that one pushed the other out.

At the funeral of Leonid Brezhnev in 1982, the TV cameras had caught his wife quickly making the sign of the cross over his open coffin. This had impressed Reagan, and I was later told by members of the National Security Council that he came back to this fact several times.

My mission to Moscow took place only a few weeks before the death of Andropov on February 9, 1984. On February 10, in a letter at the time of the Andropov funeral, the President wrote me:

"Watching the scenes of the funeral on TV, I wondered what thoughts people must have at such a time when their belief in no God or immortality is faced with death. Like you, I continue to believe that the hunger for religion may yet be a major factor in bringing about a change in the present situation."

After attending the Andropov funeral, Vice President Bush emphatically reported that he had seen someone make the sign of the cross over Andropov. Bud McFarlane explained: "Up to that point, the President didn't have a lot of optimism about being able to engage with Russia and get somewhere, but then he had this brief window that maybe there is some hope there, that there may be some people in the leadership that are open to the idea of spiritual influence. It made him say, 'Well, God, it's worth it. Let's try to engage with these people and see if we can get somewhere.'" (When the ailing Chernenko died thirteen months later, before Reagan could get to him, the President famously quipped that he wanted to negotiate with the Soviet leaders but "they keep dying on me.") He was to get his chance with a new leader, Mikhail Sergeyevich Gorbachev.

When Gorbachev was first interviewed by *TIME* magazine on September 9, 1985, the press raved on about how "exact" he was, how he underlined every word with a different colored pencil. The only thing pronounced as unimportant was that Gorbachev twice used the word *God*. After all, said the press, it meant nothing. Russians, they said, often used the word *God* in casual conversation, and its use was irrelevant to important issues at hand like arms control or economics. But for Reagan, with his acute intuition for people, that word and its use by Gorbachev were not irrelevant. One of his first questions in a meeting with me after the Geneva Summit was, "Why does Gorbachev talk about God so much?" (At first, this worried me. I thought that perhaps Gorbachev, having learned that Reagan was a religious man, had done this deliberately. So, at this early juncture, I urged him to be wary.)

In an interview in Moscow a short time after his wife Raisa's death in 1999, I had the chance to ask Gorbachev Reagan's question myself. I was treated to a long answer about his respect for believers and how all his grandparents, for whom he had great affection, had been believers. He spoke of his favorite grandmother and how she had had to walk a long exhausting distance to attend church, and said that when he came to power he had had a church built in her village. He also spoke touchingly about Raisa, a dedicated communist, and how happy he was that she nevertheless had died as a believer in the Church. In his memoirs, published in 1996 he wrote, "Just like religious orders who zealously convert 'heretics' to their own faith, our [Communist] ideologues carried out a wholesale war on religion."[18] In a subsequent book published in 2000, he noted that the Bolsheviks, even during a time of "peace" after the civil war ended, "continued to tear down churches, arrest clergymen, and destroy them.[19] This was no longer understandable or justifiable. Atheism took rather savage forms in our country at that time."

Throughout his career, President Reagan had made it very clear that he understood perfectly the oppressive nature of the communist regime. According to Jack Matlock, "Ronald Reagan was intensely interested in the fate of individuals in trouble. He wanted to do everything in his power to help them. His harsh judgment of the Soviet leaders was based, more than any other single factor, not on the ideology he talked about so much, but on the perception of the way they treated their own people."

Reagan kept a list of human rights violations, and stubbornly brought up names one by one in all his meetings with Soviet officials. He announced in no uncertain terms his conviction that such a system could not, should not, would not endure. He always made it clear that religious freedom and the right to worship were essential human values—key points. This put him at odds with many of his advisors. Once he had learned that an aspiration for faith and religion was as strong in the Soviet Union as it was in the United States and, as he had said to Deaver, "relying more on his own instincts than other people's", his lifelong, deeply felt religious faith was to play a major role in guiding him in his peacemaking efforts with Gorbachev.

CHAPTER 9

MOSCOW INVITES AND WASHINGTON CALLS

MOSCOW INVITES

After our lunch in the Oval Office on March 1, it was many months before I was to see the President again. I had accomplished what I had been asked to do, reported back, and didn't think there would be another occasion to see him again. During the months that passed, I received two letters from him, and at his request sent him two of my books, and went back to my lectures and writing.

Despite my breakthrough in Moscow almost a year before, there was still no official cultural agreement between the United States and the Soviet Union, but I persistently continued my efforts to get permission to continue my research in Leningrad from the Soviet Writer's Union, the Ministry of Culture, and every other official avenue in the Soviet Union I could think of, with no luck. At the end of our discussions in January 1984, Bogdanov had asked me what I wanted. I had answered that I needed to have permission to spend two months in Leningrad to do research for my book *Pavlovsk*. At the time, he had said nothing. Then, in late March of 1985, I suddenly received a mysterious telegram from VAAP (Soviet Copyright Agency) inviting me to come to Moscow for two weeks. Moscow! I was furious. I didn't want to go to Moscow. I needed to go to Leningrad. What did it mean? What to do? That evening my eldest daughter, Susanna, happened to call. I talked to her about my dilemma and for no special reason said, "If only the Angel Gabriel would come down and tell me what to do!"

She laughed. "Mom, I think he would say, 'Have a cup of tea and go to bed,'" adding the old Russian proverb, "Morning is wiser than evening."

The next morning a very strange thing happened. As always before beginning to work, I turned on the radio. To my surprise, Glinka's "Valse Fantasie," originally called the "Pavlovsk Waltz," was playing. Then, with the waltz still playing, I realized that I had forgotten to turn my calendar to the current month. Flipping the page, I was confronted by an icon image of the Angel Gabriel holding the transparent globe of the world in his hand.[1] At that moment, my daughter called again. "Susanna," I said, "something odd is going on." I was so perplexed by this strange coincidence (where do these come from?) that after I hung up, I called Bishop Basil Rodzianko and asked, "Do you think this is a sign?"

"Yes, definitely," said he. "You should go."

I wired VAAP my acceptance of their strange invitation.

Upon my arrival at the Moscow airport, I was met ceremoniously as a VIP by the head of VAAP, whisked through customs, and put up at the famous old Hotel Ukraine.[2] I wondered what would happen next. I didn't have to wait long to find out. The next day I was informed that my visa had been extended for two months, and I was to go to Leningrad in two days!

I was accompanied on the train by a Moscow representative of VAAP, and we ended up talking most of the night and began a lasting friendship. On arrival, he introduced me to the waiting Leningrad head of VAAP. I was taken to the Hotel Europe and told that my accommodations had been paid for two weeks. After the two weeks passed, when I went out in the morning as usual to meet the waiting VAAP representative who, up to then had accompanied me everywhere, no one was there to meet me. The VAAP representatives had disappeared.

With a sudden rush of excitement, I realized what had happened. My two weeks of invitation were over; I was to be left alone. With no explanation from that morning through the remaining two months, I was left to work independently at the library and at Pavlovsk Palace. In this Byzantine manner, the fine hand of Bogdanov had honored my request. (On hearing about this strange turn of events, one of my friends, the great poet Victor Sosnora with his usual sardonic humor observed, "You are probably the only free person in the Soviet Union.")

Those two months were richly fulfilling, giving me a chance to do my first interviews with many survivors of the palace's destruction during World War II, including the rare opportunity of talking with a member of the military who had witnessed the burning of the palace, as well as with many skilled artisans who were working on the restoration. After my Moscow mission the year before, I had feared that my friends might be harassed by *them* and called in for interrogations. None of this occurred then or at any time after. Also, during those two months Georgy Arbatov called me to pass on a direct message from Gorbachev. During the time I had been trying so hard to get permission to work in Leningrad, I had sent Gorbachev two of my books thinking that most probably he would never receive them. But he had, and through Arbatov thanked me for them and for my "noble work." In response, I wrote him a letter of thanks.

Once the first two weeks were over, I was left to pay for my own accommodations. One of my friends, a writer who occupied a large apartment that had been given by the State to his late father, offered to put me up. I knew full well that it was forbidden for any foreigner to live in a Soviet apartment; nevertheless, there was Gorbachev's new initiative of *glasnost* and *perestroika*. I decided to test the boundaries. I boldly asked the VAAP representative if I might have permission to accept my friend's invitation. "You know," I said, "in every other country I visit, I always stay with friends. Why is it that Russia, the most hospitable country I know, is the only country where it is impossible to do this?" He looked extremely uncomfortable. He thought a while, and, in the end, left me to understand that, well, albeit unofficially, he would not object and I could do it. I moved in with my writer friend and nothing happened to me or to him.

WASHINGTON CALLS

August 5th, 1985, was one of those perfect sunny days in Maine when the sea is sparkling blue and the cool air smells of balsam fir. Around 4 p.m., my youngest daughter, Liz, and I were busy pounding the wall in our log cabin trying to put up a lamp in her bedroom when the phone rang. Liz ran to answer it and came back looking awed and a bit pale. "Mom," she said, "it's President Reagan." I thought she was joking, as she often did, but she insisted, "It is, *really!*"

After his operation for possible colon cancer, I had written the President a get-well note. I was certain there had been many thousands of such messages and never expected an answer. Nervously, I went and took the phone. I heard the cheery voice of a White House operator: "Hold on. I am connecting you with the President."

And then, on the end of the line, there was the familiar warm voice, a little hoarse and tired. "Oh," said he apologetically, "I must be interrupting you at your work."

I assured him quickly, "No, I was just putting up a lamp."

He had never called me before. Why in the world was he calling out of the blue now? I hadn't been able to follow his recovery here in the Maine woods with no TV or radio. I was so stunned that all I could find to say was, "How are you?"

"I'm fine, thank you very much," said he. "I had your letter and was going to answer it but I thought it would be nicer to talk to you."

I repeated again, "Well, how are you?"

"I'm fine, thank you very much."

Finally, the third time, I managed to blurt out, "Where are you?"

"Oh, I'm in my office, doing a little work," he answered.

I assumed the conversation would be short and that I should be prepared to stop momentarily with, "Thank you, Mr. President," but instead he went right on chatting. He told me he was reading Arkady Shevchenko's book[3] and asked, "Have you read Shevchenko?"

"Yes," said I.

He continued, "You know, I read in that book that in forty years, Gromyko hasn't put his feet on the streets of Moscow."

I said, "You know, Mr. President, it's funny you should mention that because it is exactly the phrase that struck me. I thought how much that fact explained because Gromyko is not the only Soviet in high position who is so isolated from the Russian population. Not only him, but western diplomats, too, who also have almost no contact with ordinary Russians. I don't think many of them have set foot in a regular market for years and live in such isolated, different conditions of life."

I had heard from some earlier White House conversations that the Summit was probably going to be held in Geneva, and that the President felt put out that Gorbachev might not have wanted to come to Washington. I didn't want the President to feel badly about that, so I urged him not to be concerned about Gorbachev not coming to Washington as soon as he (Reagan) had hoped. "I have just come back from two and a half months in Leningrad," said I. Then I told him about the enthusiastic popular reception I had witnessed a few months before when Gorbachev had come to Leningrad and, contrary to all previous practice of Communist leaders, had circulated among the people in the street, pressing the flesh and answering their questions.

"You know, he behaved a lot like you, going around shaking hands and talking to everybody. I can understand that it might not be so easy for him to come to Washington right now—perhaps it is not possible. In fact, it may not actually be safe for him to leave for that many days just now. Mr. Gorbachev is really freest in the Kremlin where he can order people around, and not among his striped-pants boys. And maybe he needs to get away from them. After all, if he came to Washington he would have to contend with Dobrynin, who has been here for years and knows everybody and would be running the whole show. He would have no independence."

The President only said, "Hmm."

He didn't have to say more—I could tell from his tone that he understood and that he would like to get away from *his* striped-pants boys, too.

I told him a bit more about my two-month stay in the Soviet Union, that I thought the atmosphere seemed a bit better. But he immediately brought up the fact that he had been hurt by TASS, the official Soviet news agency, writing that the United States had been dastardly for deploying the atom bomb. I said, "Forget what TASS says," and quoted the popular

Russian saying about their official newspapers: "There is no truth in *Pravda* (which means *truth*) and no news in *Izvestia* (*news*). The Russians are good at reading between the lines."

His mood brightening, he went on, "You know, I love Russian jokes, the kind they tell about their own government," and proceeded to tell me one. I laughed, but my mind was so befuddled, still wondering why he had called in the first place, that afterwards I could only remember the punch line. I responded with one of the latest Gorbachev jokes I had heard in Leningrad, which made fun of his youth and inexperience, that the President seemed to like. As the conversation continued, I remained stupefied and kept repeating at regular intervals, "How are you?" with him repeatedly answering, "I'm much better."

Being so out of things in Maine, I wanted to ask, "What's going on in the world?" But I knew I couldn't do that so I settled for, "What are your plans?"

"Well," said he, "I'm leaving for California tomorrow. But I've got this big scar. It's nearly eleven inches long, so I don't think I'm going to be able to cut any wood," adding firmly, "but I do plan to ride horseback. Pretty soon, Nancy's going to come in and make me take my rest."

And I said, "That's right. She's doing the right thing."

When we finally hung up, I just sat there dumbfounded. I called the White House to thank them, as I thought McFarlane or somebody might have said, "Do something nice for Suzanne." But when I spoke to Wilma, she told me, "We had nothing to do with it. The President just called up and said, 'Find her phone number.' We were going to call you and warn you that the President might call, but before we even had time to do that, he called us back and said, 'I've already talked to her.'"

So why had he called? Just being his usual courteous self? Or could it possibly have been because he was thinking hard about Russia?

My teenage nephew was strolling across the beach just then, and I excitedly called out, "Guess who just called—President Reagan!"

At that moment, the phone rang again, and he called out jokingly, "Maybe it's Gorbachev this time!"

The last word about the phone call came from a salty Maine old-timer I knew who, when I told him about the call, thought a while and said, "Well, I guess that's pretty unusual. I bet that doesn't happen to many people. I bet it has never happened to anybody in the state of Maine."

A few weeks after the President's phone call came another call from McFarlane's office, with Wilma on the line saying, "The President would like you to come down."

Washington was a long way off and it was expensive to get to there, plus it was very short notice. They wanted me to be there at 9:45 a.m. on September 3, the day after Labor Day, only a few days away. At first I resisted, asking, "Why? Is there anything special on the President's mind?"

Her answer: "Because he just likes to talk to you."

Still I resisted. "It's a long way to come," and said, "I have spruce needles in my hair."

"Bring him some," said she. "He'll be so happy."

"Who is going to be there? Are you going to throw all those guys at me again?"

"No," was Wilma's answer. "I think just the President. It might be just you and the President alone."

"All right," I finally agreed. "I'll be there."

So, putting aside my usual attire of worn blue jeans and sweatshirt, I searched through my minuscule wardrobe for a suitable dress, and then went out to find some spruce boughs with pine cones to give to the President. We were in the middle of a gale and I was blown all over the place. I couldn't find a bough with any pine cones, so I snipped some bits of aromatic balsam, then went to the shore and, feeling a little like a kindergartner preparing for show-and-tell day, gathered a bunch of sea heather. Going through Deer Isle village on my way out, I thought, *I've got to find something to put this in*, and stopped at the local gift shop. I found a small glass bottle weathered by the sea and bought it. Not until that evening did I notice, still faintly etched on that old bottle, the words "Davis O.K." (Nancy Reagan's maiden name) and then, "Aspirin."

As I drove down the Maine Turnpike for the five-hour drive to Boston to catch the Washington air shuttle, another thought suddenly popped into my head. When I had been in Moscow at Easter a few months earlier, I happened to pass a railroad station and saw a group of peasant women from the Volga city of Nizhny Novgorod (then called Gorky) selling painted wooden Easter eggs, a new sight at the time. Curious, I went to look, and among the many painted with flowers and the initials *XB*, (in Russian, *Khristos Voskrese: Christ is Risen)* I found an unusual one, primitively painted with an image of Mary, Mother of Christ, and the Christ Child along with these words written in Russian on the back: "We will not permit the world to be blown up." I had given it to my son, an Episcopal minister, who was not a Reagan fan and thought of him as a militarist. He had harrumphed, "You should give it to Reagan." I thought that this might be the time, so when I stopped in Boston, I asked him to give it back to me.

MEETING, SEPTEMBER 3, 1985

When I got to the White House for what was to be my third meeting, and was ushered into the Oval Office, I found that not only the President but Vice President Bush was also to be present along with Bud McFarlane and Jack Matlock. Before we even sat down, I said, "Excuse me, Mr. President, before we get started on business, I have some little gifts for you." I reached into my battered old briefcase (which, in those far-off innocent days, nobody had inspected) and out came the balsam boughs and the little vase with the sea heather. I presented it all to the President, turning to the Vice President and cheerily saying, "You should know what this is. You're from Maine!"

The Vice President looked completely blank, but the President was very interested, asking, "This is sea heather? Does it grow under water?"

I said, "No, it grows between the rocks near the water." (At this point, the Vice President decided he did know what it was.)

"Why, that's wonderful!" exclaimed the President, examining it in all different directions.

I pointed out, "There's something on the bottle," and as he started for his glasses, "I'll read it to you. It says: 'Davis O.K.'"

He laughed and seemed delighted with it.

Then I went on, "There's one more thing, Mr. President. I am really embarrassed to tell you that I was so startled when you called, I forgot your joke. Would you mind telling me the joke again?"

The President was relaxed and having a good time, and despite all those important gentlemen waiting stone-faced, he said, "The joke was that there were these two guys sitting in Red Square talking to each other about the future, and one of them says, 'Listen, do you think we're ever really going to get to communism?' The other guy says, 'Well, maybe; I don't know. But I can tell you one thing. It's going to get worse before it gets better.'"

The Vice President did not look amused.

The President went on, "George Montgomery just went over to Russia. You know, he's Dinah Shore's ex-husband. Well, he was over there making a movie, and it seems they didn't know he knew me or anything like that. He got them started talking about me and they all didn't like me. They hated me a lot. But he explained about me, and by the time he was through, they were all rather pro. They were all pleased."

I commented, "Mr. President, there are quite a few Russians who really like you."

I had thought a lot about what to say to him and had prepared some notes. I was getting opinions from all sides: "You have a historic mission. You can't talk to the President about this, or this…" But I had made up my own mind. The egg was one. Once again, I reached into my briefcase, pulled out the wooden egg, and said, "Mr. President, I thought you needed a talisman to take to the meeting. You should take something Russian with you."

He looked at it curiously, turned it over and over in his hand, and asked, "What is it?"

"Mr. President," I explained, "it's a Russian Easter egg with an image of the Mother of Christ and the Christ Child. On the back it says, 'We will not permit the world to be blown up.'"

"Did they do that?" he asked.

"Yes," I said, "there were no foreigners in that market, only Russians. It was painted by an unknown humble person from a town on the Volga River."

The President was so interested that I suddenly had an inspiration. Explaining that the egg was an ancient Russian symbol of new life, new beginnings, new hope, I suggested, "Why don't you give it to Mr. Gorbachev? It is from his own country, his own people, and I think he would be very surprised that you know that symbol."

"That's a good idea!" exclaimed the President.

"He will wonder, perhaps, where you got it," I said. "You can tell him where it came from so he doesn't think you got it from some American spy." Again, the President repeated, "That's a very good idea." And put it in his pocket.

Then we started to talk business. The Soviets often preferred to communicate messages through personal sources rather than official sources, trying out the ground without leaks and newspaper headlines, and they did this quite a lot. Since I knew they were aware that I knew the President, I expected such overtures but I was still surprised when one day I was asked to come to the office of the director of VAAP (ostensibly a man with no connection to *them*) to talk about "books." How odd, I thought, that the big man at the top of VAAP suddenly decided to see me to talk about "books." But I knew that everything in the Soviet Union was connected, and if the top man of that large organization suddenly wanted to talk to me, I had guessed that he was KGB.

He was a huge man, like Sidney Greenstreet, complete with sloping stomach. He talked about "books" for about two minutes and then sent everybody else away and immediately started laying out the Soviet agenda so specifically that it took me a few minutes to realize that any conversation that followed wouldn't have anything remotely to do with books, and I had better listen attentively and start taking notes. He proceeded to lay out a complete Soviet agenda for the prospective Summit. He began with Afghanistan and said the Soviets were ready to negotiate but that they would need our help—in other words, some way to discuss it. I emphasized the great importance the United States attached to human rights, and he said that they understood this and that there had to be some statement about that, and they were willing to say something supporting us, written in advance. He continued, saying that it was very important for them to have some words about trade, "nothing specific, of course," but some general statement about it that could also be written in advance, emphasizing that it was "very important for us to have something to sign—a cultural agreement." (I was, of course, happy to hear that.)

He also discussed the question of resuming direct Aeroflot flights to the U.S., which was, he said, "very important," a link that they had been fighting for. I was then informed about all of the negotiations of the cultural agreement, to which they had tried to link Aeroflot (something we objected to). He communicated this very strongly, emphasizing the symbolic nature of this for them, and that if we were going to have a cultural agreement, we should have a direct line between our two countries. He went right down a list of issues for the Summit, all the while saying to me, "Of course I'm nobody...." (my foot!) However, I knew he was serious, and, from my notes, I passed on all he had said to the President.

Presidential Oval Office meetings were always hard for me. I was expected to do most of the talking while silently looking on were the Vice President, Bud, and Jack (who I knew was not my best friend), none of them saying a word or cracking a smile. I felt like a fool in a vacuum, never knowing what they were going to say about me afterwards, plus having the big handicap of not being privy to their confidential briefing papers or their thinking. The other trouble was never knowing how long these meetings were actually going to last, so I couldn't very well plan what to say or how long to say it. I had been told that this meeting would be about fifteen minutes, but, as had happened in the past, the President stayed longer (in this case, for forty-five minutes).

I also found it extremely difficult because I didn't know what the President wanted. It wasn't an interview where I could ask, "Mr. President, how do you feel about such-and-such?" I felt it was rude, not going back and forth in conversation. But then I remembered that the President was not there to chat with me. It was not a give and take. I was there to give him something; he was there for information. It made me feel very strange, and always left me wondering if I was doing the right thing, but I came to realize that if he wanted to, he could ask specific questions and he sometimes did. In the case of the message I had just brought, I knew it was serious, and, as both sides were preparing for the Summit, it might possibly add an additional facet to help confirm a picture and round out purely official statements. So we went on from there.

One of the things I knew from our previous meetings was how concerned the President was about what the Russians were like as people. Of course he received a veritable snowstorm of position White Papers from his advisors and from think tank specialists. The word around the White House was that the President would not read more than one and a half pages of text, double-spaced. If true, having read some position papers myself, I could understand that. I knew they were pretty cold and dry—with not much life or juice in them. And Reagan was a people person. Indeed, he was the only politician I ever met (by then I knew dozens) who wanted to know not only what the Kremlin thought, but what the Russian people thought—what they laughed at, how they lived, their dreams and their fears.

As I got to know him better, I was beginning to understand that he was an actor after all and that actors think differently from political scientists. Reagan came to things in a much more intuitive way. He liked stories, learned from anecdotes and parables, and they stayed with him. I didn't realize this at first and always thought I was a flop in our meetings, but then in Moscow, to my surprise, our ambassador told me, "He really listens to you, remembers everything you say." I realized that it was perhaps because he learned best from stories. It was a big responsibility. Yes, I did know a lot about the Russians, but I always thought a lot about what to say and weighed it carefully, trying not to exaggerate in any way and to say only what I had experienced and witnessed personally. I wanted something to work out between our two countries and I wasn't only pushing Reagan, but the Russians, too, trying to move them toward each other, trying to explain things to the Russians that would help them understand Reagan—and vice versa—in a way that wasn't so blind and stereotyped.

In those days, our media was full of stories extolling Gorbachev, as if they were the cheerleaders and he the new football hero, never asking him a single difficult question, burbling on about how "young and vigorous" he was, how different from our "drowsy old President" who dozed in Cabinet meetings. I thought that no matter how good a sport Reagan was, it couldn't be pleasant to read all this. (I can't help inserting here a wonderful Reagan quip during that Gorbachev brouhaha time. He was in Florida when a high school student spoke up and asked, "How does it feel to be so OLD when Mr. Gorbachev is so young and vigorous?" Without missing a beat, the President answered cheerfully, "Well, I've had a lot of experience. I used to play second lead to Errol Flynn." Thereafter, the image of Gorbachev leaping about around the castle steps like Errol Flynn stayed with me.)

I had quite a different opinion from that of our media. I thought that if things were normal, Ronald Reagan was exactly the kind of iconic American that ordinary Russians would love: a "cowboy," informal, genuine, with a great sense of humor, easy with people, and, most important, very patriotic, a quality that Russians admire.

From my own experience, I knew that, although Soviet bureaucrats publicly fawned over our "peaceniks" and used them whenever it suited their purposes, in private they often expressed contempt for such people and did not respect their running down their own country. In Moscow, I once had a spirited argument with Georgy Arbatov. He complained to me about Reagan and his criticism of the Soviet Union. How shocking it was, said he, that Reagan had called the Soviet Union an "evil empire"—so insulting to the peace-loving Soviet Union. Clearly he was expecting me to agree with him. Such unctuous hypocrisy from this man, who had been so often in the United States and knew better, made me furious. I told him sharply that he knew full well that Soviet newspapers said far more poisonous things about our president and the United States every day, and that while they in the Soviet Union could stop malicious press reporting with a stroke of a pen, he also knew that our president couldn't do this in the United States. "So please, Georgy Arkadeyvich," I said, "enough."

He stopped and then said, "I admire you for your defense of your president."

Quite differently from some of Reagan's advisors, I thought that, precisely *because* of his personality and human qualities, the President would do just fine with Gorbachev, and I wanted in whatever way I could to reinforce his own instincts to be himself, not to be muted or formalized on the advice of the State Department and Kremlinology experts. I pointed out to him that the Soviet Union was far from being a monolith with everyone marching in lockstep toward a bright communist future, but a land of contradictions and problems. I reminded him that Gorbachev was still very new at his job, a younger man from a remote agricultural district in Russia, a product of the Khrushchev "thaw" generation who would no doubt be a bit different from the old Kremlin dinosaurs that preceded him, most of whom were more than a generation older and had been privileged and isolated from ordinary Russian life for years.

In my experience, the Russian character was not so inscrutable or difficult. If there was one key, it was that the Russians were much more spontaneously emotional than we in the West. This sounds simplistic, but it isn't. Our own language gives a clue to the difference. For us, the word *emotional* often has a disparaging sound. We say, "He behaved emotionally" or "She got emotional about it." But in Russian, the word *emotsionalno* has a positive ring and is considered a good thing to say about somebody. We in the United States are encouraged always to think and react first with our minds. A Russian is always affected first by his feelings (his instincts, more correctly), and then the head follows. This explains a lot of their negative behavior as well as their positive.

As an example, I told the President the story of General Nikolai Chervov, Gorbachev's military expert on SDI, who came to Washington with a high-level delegation for discussions, among these a congressional hearing on human rights that I attended. The head of the Soviet delegation was an arch-conservative Ukrainian Politburo member, Vladimir Scherbitsky, who presented the Soviet position in a thoroughly disgusting and shameful way. I was outraged, and scrutinized the delegation behind him to see if there was anyone in their group who looked embarrassed or ashamed. I saw two who obviously did. One of them was General Chervov and the other, Alexander Bessmertnykh, then head of the American Desk in the Foreign Ministry. So when afterwards we were all invited to the Kennan Institute for dinner, I made it my business to get there early to catch them both as we circulated at cocktail time.

I tackled Bessmertnykh first, who turned out to be a courteous, knowledgeable man open to a fair discussion of the issues. While we were talking, I spied General Chervov and said, "I have never met a Soviet general before, could you introduce me?"

"Oh, yes," said Bessmertnkyh, and took me over to him.

I spoke to the general in Russian, and in about two minutes, he was telling me all about his grandchildren and the American books he had read and how he loved Mark Twain. I asked him about his war record and where he had fought. He chuckled, telling me that he had been wounded so often and had so much metal in his body that he couldn't go through the airport metal detectors without setting off all the bells. As we parted for dinner, I said, "General Chervov, I want to tell you that although I know we have many differences, there is one thing that I think Americans do not appreciate enough and I do. I enormously respect the sacrifices, the great fight, and the courage of the Russian people during the last war."

At this, tears welled up in the general's eyes and he said emotionally, "So many kilometers to Berlin, and for every kilometer, ten thousand Russians fell."

Can you imagine an American general showing so much emotion in public? He might be sent for psychiatric observation for losing his cool. But for a Russian, tears are acceptable—even in public. The defense correspondent for *The Washington Post*, Walter Pincus, who observed this incident from a few feet away, was nonplussed. "What did you say to him? This is the toughest guy. Nobody can talk to him."

I told the President this story simply as an example of a different way of reacting, and that, despite the barriers between us, you could often get to a Russian in three or four sentences if you picked the right ones.

Then I also explained to him that in the Soviet Union people commonly referred to themselves not as "Soviet" citizens but by their nationality, and for them there is a very clear difference—not just like coming from Texas or Maryland. It was important to many Russians that Gorbachev was the first "Great Russian" to become the leader of Russia since Empress Elizabeth, the daughter of Peter the Great in the 18th century. "Great Russian" refers to an ethnic group in the Soviet Union different from Ukrainians, Armenians, Georgians, Moldavians, Byelorussians. All the tsars after Elizabeth were in some way German. Lenin was not Russian but a mixture of nationalities. Stalin was Georgian and did not even speak Russian very well. Khrushchev was Ukrainian; Brezhnev, Byelorussian. So the fact that Gorbachev was the first "Russian" meant a lot to his countrymen. I told the President that I was waiting to see whether Gorbachev would be more a patriot of his country or of the Communist Party. If his country, then he would have to take into consideration the real problems of his people, for the dismal fact was that the Russian people were committing suicide rather than bend. They were killing themselves with alcohol, they were killing themselves with despair, they were not reproducing themselves, and if Gorbachev was really Russian and a patriot of his country he had to pay attention to this. If he was a patriot primarily of the Party, that was a completely different thing. A patriot of the Party (as were all the Soviet leaders before him) was ready to sacrifice everything for the interest of the Party, including the people. If this should change with Gorbachev, it could be an important thing in dealing with him. We then talked a good deal about human rights and freedom of religion. I asked him to please say some words about the Russian Church if he could.

The President didn't seem to want to leave although the meeting had gone way over the allotted time. An aide came in and simply dropped a large leather bound volume in his lap saying, "Mr. President, here's your Cabinet meeting." But the President wanted to continue talking, asking questions. A few minutes later, the aide came in again and with some impatience said, "Mr. President, they are all still waiting," and pulled him up.

After that, the meeting broke up quickly. Keeping in mind our denigrating press calling our president "old" and "not able to remember facts," attempting to make him think that "young" Gorbachev was an iron man ten feet tall instead of a human being with emotions confronting multiple problems of his own, I wanted to leave the President with his confidence fully up, that his being older with a wider experience of life was an important advantage, as was being elected by popular majority while Gorbachev was only *trying* to be popular. So, as he got up to leave, I said to him gently, "Don't forget, Mr. President. You're older. You are wiser. You have been in power longer. You are secure in the affection of your people." And, looking at the Vice President, "As far as I know, nobody in your Cabinet wants to knife you. You are stronger. You can afford to be magnanimous." And then, "Remember, surprise him!" Giving me a big smile, off he went to his impatient Cabinet.[4]

CHAPTER 10

GENEVA: REAGAN AND GORBACHEV MEET

"Blessed are the peacemakers: for they shall be called the sons of God."
Matthew 5:9

Preparations for the Reagan-Gorbachev Summit dragged on for eight and a half months, fraught with back and forth internal arguments and disagreement between the State Department, the National Security Council, and White House advisors in the United States, and externally with their counterparts in the Soviet Union. There was wrangling about the location: the United States wanted Washington, the Soviet Union, Moscow. It was finally agreed that the meeting would take place in a "third" country—Switzerland, in Geneva, known as "the city of causes" on November 19 and 20, 1985. Considering the internecine fights among all the bureaucrats concerned, one can only marvel that it took place at all.

That it did in the end was because the President, firmly supported by his devoted Nancy, was determined to have it. What emerges clearly in reading the lengthy, sometimes self-serving official accounts is that, as he had said to Deaver after the assassination attempt on his life, he was going to trust more to his own instincts. President Reagan knew how he wished to proceed and exactly what he wanted, and insisted on getting it. Over and over he stuck to the position that he wanted to "get beyond the stereotypes" and conduct the first summit between a U.S. president and a Soviet leader in six and a half years in his own way. This distressed members of the State Department and the NSC, several of whom felt that Reagan was not "up to" conducting a face to face meeting with Gorbachev, not to speak of some in his Cabinet who were dead set against any overtures to the

Soviet Union whatsoever. Writes Shultz, "The word from the intelligence community and other Soviet specialists around the government was that the Soviet Union would never, indeed could never, change no matter how bad their problems were."[1] Managing right and left factions among his advisors and holding fast against the most hawkish ones, notably William Casey, head of the CIA, and Secretary of Defense Casper Weinberger, the President stuck to his own ideas with stubborn determination.

At a preparatory meeting, Secretary of State Shultz and Soviet Foreign Minister Shevardnadze had agreed that their staffs would work on a draft advance communiqué about the goals of the meeting, a normal procedure before earlier U.S. summit meetings. When Reagan saw the report of their meeting, he was annoyed by the idea of working on a joint communiqué in advance. He refused to have what he called a "precooked" summit.[2] He wanted Geneva to be *his meeting*, and insisted that any statement should be composed and written only after he met Gorbachev and not before, and any official discussion of a joint statement should cease immediately. This dismayed both the Americans and the Soviets who insisted that such advance communiqués had always been the practice in the past, and both sides had strict instructions to prepare such a document. Despite all appeals, Reagan stood his ground, and, contrary to all previous practice, insisted that there be no discussion of any "concluding document" until he and Gorbachev decided personally what to put in it. (Imagine! Reagan was insisting that they do what he and Gorbachev decided!) Bureaucrats on both sides thought that neither of them had the knowledge or experience to be trusted with decisions.[3]

Advance preparation for the agenda, both in Moscow and the United States, concentrated heavily on arms control issues. But Reagan had other ideas. Writes Shultz, "He insisted that human rights had to be on top of our agenda with the Soviets—only when they changed their human rights practices and recognized the importance of these rights to their own society could Soviet–American relations change at the deepest level."[4] In a four-and-a-half-page document dictated to the President's secretary outlining his ideas, Reagan devoted a full page to human rights.[5] Keeping his eye on the long view, he believed that improving the lot of Russians, including human rights and freedom of worship, was, in the long run, in the best interest of the United States. The President put new emphasis on a cultural agreement and the expansion of contacts between American and Soviet citizens—something we had talked about and I had strongly urged, both during our first meeting and also during our lunch in March following my trip to Moscow. Since my discussions in Moscow when I had told Bogdanov that because of Soviet behavior "the Pershing missiles would go in" and that "it seems the only thing we seem to be able to agree on is mothers and culture," I thought the Soviets would agree to talk, and happily, they did.

After my first mission to Moscow in January 1984, both sides had picked up the phone again. Official discussions about the resumption of cultural exchanges and other questions began again in August 1984. The culmination of a year and a half of talks had led to the first Reagan-Gorbachev meeting.[6] In early November 1985, by mutual agreement, proposals for cooperative projects and cultural educational contacts were put on the schedule. The proposed agreement was to cover not only traditional programs for the exchange of exhibits, performing artists, and graduate students, but a new wrinkle introduced by the United States—that large numbers (thousands or tens of thousands) of high school students and college undergraduates could spend time and go to school in the other country. Up to that time, the Soviet government had restricted high school and college students, sending only a few dozen Soviet "graduate students" (mostly middle-aged scientists in military related specialties). The Soviet government rarely allowed young people to study or make homestays outside the communist bloc. With intense concentration and attention put to a new and difficult script, Reagan prepared for the meeting.

According to McFarlane, Reagan had never pretended to have a great depth of knowledge of the Soviet Union. About communism, "He knew why it was bad and how misguided it was about the fundamental nature of human beings, but not a lot about the Communist Party or how it related to the decision-making role of the military in making Kremlin policy. "So," says McFarlane, "I decided that the President needed a much better foundation and knowledge of the several factors that influence Soviet leaders. I asked my deputy Don Fortier to task the preparation of short (up to 20 pages) papers. Each focused on a different dimension of Soviet governance or Russian history. I asked that he be sure to include the role of the Party, the history and role of the military, the relationship of the KGB to the government, Soviet negotiating practices, personal history of Gorbachev, Russian history, culture and art. I asked that these papers not all come from the government, but rather from outside authors. Don coordinated with Jack Matlock, who was asked to do a cover memo for each of about twenty papers that ultimately went to the President, one at a time, every Friday for his reading on successive weekends, starting with the summer of 1985 and running right up until we boarded Air Force One for Geneva in November. Reagan loved these papers, annotated them, and came in on Monday after a weekend spouting interesting factoids he had picked up in the paper he had just read. He thoroughly digested all of these two or three hundred very dense pages."[7]

In his book, *Reagan and Gorbachev*, Jack Matlock writes, "As far as specific talking points were concerned, Reagan needed little prompting by the time he left for Geneva, as he had firmly in mind what he wanted to say and how he wanted to say it."[8]

On September 5, following our meeting, I had sent the President directly an eleven-page paper with a number of details and stories from my most recent experiences in the Soviet Union. He also read a number of books, among them my *Land of the Firebird*, which he was still reading when he left for Geneva. I was told that in Geneva, at the three preparatory staff meetings held before the meetings with Gorbachev, the President would come down every morning with something gleaned from *Firebird*. He read the book so carefully that at one such meeting he interrupted his chief arms control negotiator, Paul Nitze, to ask, "I'm in the year 1830.

What happened to all these small shopkeepers in the year 1830 and to all that entrepreneurial talent in Russia? How can it just have disappeared?"[9]

President and Mrs. Reagan arrived in a wintry Geneva on November 16 and first went to their residence, La Maison de Sausure, lent by Prince Karim Aga Khan. Prince Karim's young son had left instructions for the President to please be sure to feed his goldfish while he was there. The President began immediately to follow instructions. Returning one evening after dinner Reagan saw that one fish was dead and writes "Maybe I hadn't fed the fish enough food, or maybe I had fed it too much. Whatever the reason, it had died on my watch and I felt responsible." Reagan asked the staff to put the dead fish in a box and take it to a pet store in Geneva to try and find one exactly like it. "Luckily they found two that matched and I put them in the tank and wrote a letter to the children to let them know what happened."[10]

Before I had left on that first trip to Moscow, I had asked the National Security Council for only one thing: that if I were successful, I wanted to be there to watch when they shook hands. It was agreed. But when it was finally to take place, my request was conveniently forgotten, so although there was a cast of hundreds who went to Geneva to participate, report, and watch, I was not among them. Instead, I was far from the action in Switzerland, miles away in cold and wintry Leningrad, trudging down the Nevsky Prospect to the gigantic (more than three million volumes) main public library, alternating days with the one-and-a-half-hour trip to Pavlovsk, 16 miles away from the city by subway, commuter train, and finally bus. I say alternately, because of the ponderous Soviet library system, which dictated that I had to search the voluminous files (many of the entries written in almost indecipherable Russian script) for the books I might want to consult, order them (requests limited to three), and then be forced to wait a full day before they would be delivered. If they turned out to be useless, or not the right ones, the tedious process and the forced wait had to be repeated again. No Xerox machines. These were kept under lock and key. Requests for copies had to be submitted in person and in writing to a special office, and the number of requests by foreign scholars was strictly limited. I had to wait until the day before I left to pick up the copies I had requested weeks before and had to fight to get even those. The Xerox office tried to tell me that they were "so busy" that they had not had a chance to do it in time, didn't know where they were, etc. Stubbornly, I stood my ground until finally they were miraculously "found" and given to me in a flimsy cardboard box tied with old string.

The best thing about the library was the *Garderobe* (cloak room). It was an ironclad custom in old Russia and maintained in the Soviet Union that everyone has to surrender all outer garments, coats, hats, and mittens to the cloak room upon entering any public building. In pre-revolutionary Russia, the job of attendant was traditionally reserved for retired veterans. At the library it was a gentle old man wearing a dark beret who tended the facility. At the end of a long day, as dusk was falling, I would wearily come get my coat. He would courteously help me on with it as he did with everybody, then gently say, "Congratulations, you worked well!" and slip me a hard candy. This I would happily munch in the darkness of early Russian winter as I made my way back to my room at the old Europe Hotel, in those days a shabby and run-down place, unrecognizable from the luxury hotel it has become today.

Because of the long trip back from Pavlovsk, sloshing through snow and slush, I always returned late, at about 9 p.m., cold and hungry. By then the hotel dining room was shut tight. I knew my friends were always willing to share whatever food they had with me however late it was, but I was usually too exhausted to brave another long, cold subway trip to get to their communal apartments. The few restaurants that then existed in the city were awful and mostly shuttered at that hour. So I would warm the *piroshki*, (small rolls filled with meat or cabbage which, as a precaution, I always filched and surreptitiously stuffed in my purse at breakfast), on my hotel radiator and use the metal coil I had bought to heat the packaged soups I had brought with me from the United States, difficult because the noodles always got tangled in the coils.

In those early days of November, there was tremendous anticipation and hope among all the Russians I knew about the first meeting between our two leaders. Many expressed their hopes to me—and yes, their prayers—for its success and for our president. As the date approached, I was still feeling pretty grumpy about being left out. Of course, I knew that the important thing was that the historic meeting was actually going to take place. Ashamed of my unworthy and petty thoughts, I decided to go to church to attend vespers, and made my way down to the Trinity Cathedral at the end of the Nevsky Prospect.

Russia is a mystical place where unexpected and mysterious things can and do happen. When I entered the darkened cathedral, full of the faithful lighting candles in front of icons, I suddenly saw a man about thirty years old sitting in an old battered wheelchair surrounded by a crowd of curious onlookers. As no wheelchairs were ever seen on the unfriendly city streets, where there were no ramps and multiple steep stairs to descend to the subway, and having had my son in a wheelchair in the United States, this unusual sight riveted my attention. I felt compelled to make my way through the crowd of onlookers to approach him. I started to say something to him, but the strange man did not wait for me to finish. Instead, he immediately reached out his hands to take mine in his. His hands were very warm, almost hot. As if he knew my thoughts, he fixed me with dark and compassionate eyes whose intense gaze seemed to look straight into my soul and said only, "*Budt'ye zdorovoy*" ("Be healthy").

Strangely moved and shaken by his words, I backed away to rejoin the crowd. The people around him remained silent, awed. One woman pushed her little daughter toward him to try and hand him some coins. But it was clear that he was not a beggar. An old woman whispered to me, "Who is he?" and I answered, "You know. He is holy." I had started to tell the unknown man that I often came to that church and would see him again, but somehow I knew that I never would, and no matter how many times I came back and looked for him, I never did. Yet after that inexplicable encounter, I felt strangely at peace, all unworthy thoughts banished.

Hearing all the good wishes for the success of the Summit extended to me by the Russians, I thought that perhaps the President might like to know about them. So I decided to send him a letter. Thinking that he was an actor, after all, I enclosed a postcard of beautiful Theater Street, one of the architectural wonders of the city. Designed by Carlo Rossi, the favorite architect of Emperor Alexander I, it was dominated at the end of the street by the Alexandrinsky Theater where Gogol's *Inspector General* had first been performed. In one of the other buildings on the right stood the former Imperial Ballet School[11] where George Balanchine, Rudolph Nureyev, and Mikhail Baryshnikov had been taught.

President Reagan had told me how to get in touch with him directly in a way that bypassed the hierarchy of the White House staff. Feeling as if I were throwing a message in a bottle into the ocean, I sent it. On November 15, three days before the Summit, I received an urgent phone call from our consulate. "We have a message for you!" said a slightly breathless secretary.

"Thanks," said I, "could you please send it over."

"No," continued the voice, almost stuttering with nervousness. "You must come over, it's from Washington!"

Thanks a bunch, I thought. *How will this sound to the listening ears that are always on the telephone lines?* It couldn't be good for me to be told that I was receiving messages from Washington.

So I went, to be met by the American consul, standing there holding a paper with his card clipped to it. This was a surprise. Up to then, no official from our consulate had ever bothered to greet us few exchange scholars from America, and I couldn't imagine why now. With a wan smile, he handed the paper to me. Direct as a lightning bolt, it was addressed simply "Suzanne Massie, Leningrad" and read:

Dear Suzanne,
Thank you very much for your letter and the picture of Theater Street. Believe it or not, I had just read about Architect Rossi designing the theater

and other buildings. Of course, I had read it in your magnificent book, which I'll have with me in Geneva because I'm only halfway through it. Thank you so much for sending it to me. I'm really enjoying it and it has also helped for the forthcoming meeting. I hope we can open a few doors and really get on with the business of a world at peace. I'm grateful for your good wishes and your prayers. Again, my heartfelt thanks.

Sincerely,
Ronald Reagan

I was, as you can imagine, astonished. The bureaucrats had shoved me under the rug, but not the President. After a pause to collect myself, I asked the now obsequious consul, "May I answer?"

"Oh, yes," he hurriedly agreed.

Probably because I was nonplussed, I couldn't resist joking, so I sent back a message that began, *"Dear Mr. President, Thank you so much for your kind message and warm words about my book,"* then added, tongue in cheek, *"Many people think the second half is better than the first!"* I added a few more sedate words about the fact that many people in Leningrad were expressing warm wishes for him and the success of the meeting. Afterwards, I was ashamed that I had been disrespectful in permitting myself to joke with the President across the ocean. But then, Ronald Reagan was the kind of approachable and human man that I thought wouldn't be offended and might even chuckle.

On November 19, the big day, I crowded around an old television set with a few Russian friends to watch Gorbachev's arrival at the Geneva estate where the Summit was to take place. It was the first time that ordinary Russians would see Reagan in person on television. Up to that time, he had only been seen caricatured in Soviet newspapers as a pistol-packing cowboy wearing a broad-brimmed Stetson decorated with a swastika. Anticipation that night was intense. All eyes were fixed on that flickering screen.

The meeting was to be full of surprises. At 10 a.m. on a bitter-cold day in Switzerland, Gorbachev arrived heavily bundled up in an overcoat, warm scarf, and brown fedora. Standing at the bottom of the stone steps that led up to the entrance of the mansion where the meeting was to take place, he hesitated slightly, looking up nervously. Then suddenly, hatless and coatless, Reagan bounded out into the cold and down the stairs to meet him. Gorbachev, who was a good twenty years younger, looked older than the President. Among the Russians in the room, Reagan's appearance had the effect of an electric shock. "Look at him!" exclaimed one incredulously. "In that cold! A seventy-four year old man not wearing a hat or coat! And ours, wrapped up like a bear! What a man is Reagan! What a country is America!"

Reagan greeted Gorbachev avuncularly, putting his arm around his shoulders, and with a broad smile ushered him into the house. It was a brilliant welcome, absolutely right. Remembering our pre-Gorbachev conversations, I was so proud of him, even more so when I was told later by those who were present that Reagan *had* been wearing a coat, but with an actor's sure instinct of the importance of a first entrance on stage, had thrown it off at the last minute and left it inside. The vigor and informality of that moment made an indelible impression and was never forgotten, not only by the Russians I was with that night, but by many others who had also seen it and expressed their admiration and amazement to me.

After that warm greeting, the President steered his guest into a side room for what was scheduled to be a meeting of twenty minutes with only interpreters present. The waiting bureaucrats stole nervous looks at their watches as the meeting continued for thirty, then forty minutes. Finally, after an hour and a quarter, the two leaders emerged smiling. The President said he had brought up the subject of human rights. He would later say, "As we shook hands for the first time, I had to admit... that there was something likable about Gorbachev. There was a warmth in his face and his style, not the coldness bordering on hatred I'd seen before in most senior officials I had met until then."

As for Gorbachev, he told me later in a long interview in Moscow, "I thought I was going to meet a dinosaur, but instead I met a *chelovek*" (a genuine human being).

At the corner near my hotel, there was a tiny kiosk where an old lady with the round proportions of a *Matriyoskha* doll polished boots and shoes. A short time after the appearance of Reagan on television, I chanced to bring my muddy boots to her. Affectionately known as *Tyotya* (Aunt) Tamara by all her customers, I found her listening to a Gorbachev speech on her old radio. "*Xoroshi paren*" (a good fellow), she announced, accompanying her rhythmic brush sweeps over my boots. "And that Reagan! So tall!" (More active brushing.) "Such a smile!" And then, finishing with a last emphatic sweep, "And he has a pretty wife, too!" Thus was expressed the judgment of the *vox populi*.

In an interview with me, McFarlane said that the effect of all the careful preparation by Reagan was palpable. "In Geneva he was more confident with a foreign leader than I had ever seen him before. You could see it in his body language. He was leaning forward, anxious to rebut each of Gorbachev's comments, animated, energetic, and absolutely focused." In his words, Reagan was "at the top of his game," "masterful." He added, "Here were perhaps the first leaders of the Soviet Union and the United States who were free from their pasts to engage without the baggage of history. Gorbachev was three generations from the Revolution. He didn't create it. He wasn't responsible for it and was able to think of how the welfare of the Soviet and Russian people could maybe be better off if they engaged with the United States. The reason I term the President 'masterful' is that on his insistence they would start with fundamentals: 'Why do Americans fear the Soviet Union? Why they should not fear us and what can you and I do to overcome these suspicions?' That is a pretty basic level of conversation. Nixon probably would have talked about Throw-Weight, MIRVS, and the arcana of nuclear deterrents. Not Reagan. He said we have to get to the fundamentals."[12]

Above all, Reagan wanted to convince Gorbachev that, as he had said so firmly to me at the conclusion of our first meeting in January 1984, "If they want peace, they can have it!"

Reagan and Gorbachev met in working sessions for almost eight hours of both days—half of that time alone with only interpreters present. They also had dinners together with their wives and senior members of both delegations. Reagan thought carefully about how to negotiate, considering the personality and political needs of his interlocutor, saying, "We must always remember our main goals, and Gorbachev's need to show his strength to the Soviet gang back in the Kremlin. Let's not limit the area where he can do that to those things that have to do with Soviet aggression. Let there be no talk of winners and losers. Even if we think we won, to say so would set us back in view of their inherent inferiority complex."[13] During the meetings when his speech writers (among them Pat Buchanan) wanted to use every possible occasion for verbal attacks on Soviet aggression, Reagan expunged the passages himself and told them, "Our main goal in this instance was helping people and not making propaganda points. This has been a good meeting—I can't keep poking him in the eye."[14]

During those two days, as he had in the past with every Soviet official he met, Reagan brought up human rights. He kept a list, which he brought up name by name. In Geneva, he broached the subject of human rights at every session both official and private. Gorbachev was sometimes annoyed and wanted to change the subject, but Reagan wouldn't drop it.

Reagan believed that the arms race could be ended and the stockpiles eliminated. His longstanding and overriding desire was to eliminate nuclear weapons (that Winston Churchill had once called "the balance of terror.") This fixed idea had its beginning in July 1979 when, as a candidate for the presidency, Reagan was taken for what was to be a definitive mind-changing visit to Colorado and the Cheyenne Mountain Headquarters of NORAD (North American Defense Command), a vast complex built into a mountain in the 1960s as the nerve center of a system of satellites and radar for monitoring against a nuclear attack. Given a full tour by Air Force General James Hill, he was deeply shocked when he was told that if a Soviet SS-18 missile were to fall within a few hundred yards "It would blow us away" and then, when he pressed the issue of what would happen if the Soviets were to fire just one nuclear missile at a U.S. city, General Hill replied "we would pick it up right after it was launched, but by the time the officials of the city knew it would hit them there would be only ten or fifteen minutes left. That is all we can do. We can't stop them." Reagan was deeply disturbed by these words, and afterwards expressed his distress saying "We have spent all that money and have all that equipment and there is nothing we can do to prevent a nuclear missile from hitting us … The only options we would have would be to press the button or do nothing. They're both bad."[15]

When, during his 1980 campaign Reagan first began to talk to his staff about his dream of living in world free of nuclear weapons, one remembered "well, we just smiled." But once elected he made it clear that in his view MAD (Mutual Assured Destruction) was a dangerous policy, and requested that these initials be stricken from any description of our defense policy. During his entire presidency Reagan was never to forget that visit to NORAD nor his essential dream that "it is better to protect people than avenge them" that led to his policy of SDI. Shultz writes that "From the beginning of his presidency and before, Reagan had spoken about this over and over, but the majority of his advisors pooh-poohed the idea as 'naive' and wishful thinking, remaining wedded to our longstanding nuclear deterrent policy and refusing to take him seriously."[16] In December 1983, Shultz writes "I found President Reagan thinking again about his desire to eliminate nuclear weapons. No one in the arms community shared his view." Shultz pointed out to them, "This is his instinct and his belief. The President has noticed that no one pays any attention to him in spite of the fact that he speaks about this idea publicly and privately."[17]

He continues, "For his January 16, 1984 speech, the President wanted to speak again about his hope for a non-nuclear world; the bureaucracy would not hear of it. Every meeting I go to, I told Rick Burt and Jon Howe, the President talks about abolishing nuclear weapons. I cannot get it through your heads that the man is serious. We have to convince him that he is barking up the wrong tree or reply to his interests with some specific suggestions." Shultz says that he gave the President a paper "with my line of reasoning" but it made "no real impact.... He stuck with his own deeply held view of where we should be heading."[18]

SDI was brought up immediately at the first meeting. Reagan and Gorbachev argued back and forth. Reagan's defense of SDI went far beyond the thinking of the Defense Department and NSC staff. He not only offered to share missile defenses, but was willing to formalize a commitment to do so by treaty to prevent and provide guarantees that no single country would have a monopoly of them. He offered to open U.S. laboratories to inspection by Soviet scientists and offered on-site inspection to verify that SDI research did not involve development of offensive weaponry. He did not demand a right to deploy missile defense systems but only to conduct research and testing to determine their feasibility. Although he would insist on a right to conduct some testing, he said nothing about testing components or developing weapons based on "other physical principles" cited in the ABM treaty. It was a sad and a great missed opportunity that the Soviets didn't see fit to accept.

McFarlane described their interchange in this way: "Reagan and Gorbachev argued for a while: 'We don't have to build it; you could reduce unilaterally,' said Reagan. Gorbachev said quite frankly, 'I can't do that right now; my military wouldn't let me do that. We have to find a way and keep this conflict out of the heavens.' At the second session, Reagan came back and presented many of the same arguments that he had in his one-to-one session, saying that Soviet actions left us no recourse but SDI. Gorbachev rebutted with four points why SDI was a misguided notion. Reagan came back with much of what he had said before. 'We will share it with you, you will protect yourselves, we will protect ourselves, and we will both reduce.' Gorbachev didn't find that possible. But there came a moment at the end of the first hour when Reagan was not only in command of the facts, he was leaning forward, eye contact was perfect. He was energized physically, well organized in his thoughts, eloquent. This was not what Gorbachev expected. I don't know if this is true but it seems to me, thinking back, sitting there, that about an hour and a half through the session you could see him arrive at a realization. But I do know that Reagan went there with 70% approval, after Congress had passed a joint resolution supporting his policy and after Margaret Thatcher and our allies at the UN together had stood up and given a press conference endorsing Reagan's position. The guy that Gorbachev had heard was a 74–75 year old guy, misguided and wrong-headed, who had a political power unmatched by any world leader, the public, Congress, and allies. Those three constituencies enable you to carry ideas into policy and get it funded. A dramatic moment followed. Gorbachev sat back in his chair and looked intently at Reagan and fell silent. Then, after a long pause, answered, 'Well, I disagree with just about everything that you have said. But I will think it over.' There was such weight in that sentence that I called it the end of the Cold War. It was the first time a Soviet leader had said or acknowledged that they had to respect an American political leader."[19]

The official accounts of the meetings between the two leaders and the details of what was discussed both leading up to and during the Summit meetings can be read in the published National Security Archives and also in George Shultz's massive *Turmoil and Triumph* (1,138 pages) and Jack Matlock's *Reagan and Gorbachev* (331pages). Speaking for myself, I can say that after reading these accounts that minutely describe the bureaucratic disagreements and the technical details of the discussions about arms, warheads, and missiles, they sometimes reminded me of the accounts of medieval discussions of how many angels could dance on the head of pin. In the end, no definitive arms agreements were concluded. But I was personally delighted that, as Matlock wrote, "The clearest success was in the area of cultural and other exchanges and cooperation on joint projects. All useful projects jettisoned by the Carter administration were restored. Airline service between the two countries would be restored, and cooperation to prevent another KAL disaster. Cultural, educational, and athletic exchanges would be expanded and include younger persons than before."[20]

But it was what happened personally between the two men in their private discussions, attended only by translators, that was the most important result of those two days. In 1983, Reagan had written, "I felt that if I could get in a room alone with one of the top Soviet leaders, there was a chance the two of us could make some progress in easing tensions between our two countries. I have always put a lot of faith in the simple power of human contact in solving problems. This was his chance."[21] The President knew what he was doing and set the stage carefully.

The Fleur d'Eau, the site selected for the meetings, was a stately home surrounded by several acres. He and Nancy had scouted the premises together. A gravel path wound down from the house to a cozy pool house. They both thought that it was a perfect place for the two leaders to meet alone. Nancy encouraged the idea of private meetings. "She knew that her husband was at his best in personal exchanges. He had a knack for making friends, a warm sense of human interaction and intimacy and in the process, sizing up the other guy." An advance team was ordered to keep a fire going in the fireplace. (Afterwards, Reagan told me with a mischievous smile, "There happened to be a fire going on in the pool house and I thought it would be nice if we just sat around the fireplace and talked.") There in that relaxed setting, sitting in comfortable chairs in front of a crackling fire, they gained a mutual understanding and were able to speak to each other in direct and positive terms, without the limiting presence of all their advisors. They got along well and agreed to meet again and continue their discussions in reciprocal visits to their respective countries, a major Reagan goal. In a letter to me on February 10, 1986, the President wrote:

> *I'm not going to let myself get euphoric, but still, I have a feeling that we might be at a point of beginning. There did seem to be something of a chemistry between the General Secretary and myself. Certainly it was different from talking to Gromyko. Incidentally, twice in our private conversation he invoked the name of God and once cited a Bible verse. This has stuck in my mind and stays a nagging question that won't go away. I hope nothing comes up to interfere with our next meeting which I hope will be in June.*

Reagan also told me when we met later that during one of the dinners Gorbachev had pointed to his wife, Raisa, and told him, "She's the atheist."

Coming back from Geneva in Air Force One, McFarlane said that Reagan told him that in one of his private conversations with Gorbachev on the way down to the pool house, he (Reagan) "brought up his long-held view that God's purpose and challenge was that the human race should seek to love each other; churches fostered this, so the way back is to build churches and teach these fundamental principles again. Gorbachev agreed," said Reagan, telling him that this was why he had built the cathedral (in the town of his grandmother), and continued, "We have to teach our children to love each other."

Reagan was impressed by this response and told McFarlane, "This is really quite inspiring. The guy means it. He is going to put his money where his mouth is."

Shortly after, in Moscow in December, Ambassador Arthur Hartman reported with some surprise that in a recent speech given by Gorbachev he had spoken "like a Baptist preacher" and talked about "spirituality" and the creation of a "new Soviet man".

The President's reliance on his own instincts and his personal diplomacy had been successful. It marked the beginning of relationship, not of agreement, but of trust between an American president and a Soviet leader. A historic first.

As for me, I got home from Leningrad in the first weeks of December and went back to work in my minuscule office under the stairs at the Harvard Russian Research Center. On my first day back, there was a call from the President. "Welcome home," said he. I was deeply touched. No one else had called me. How did he know? With everything that had happened to him, how could he have remembered?

With Dmitry Shagin, artist, and Boris Smelov, photographer, Leningrad, 1983.

In the apartment of Yuri Petrochenkov, artist, and wife, Nellie, surrounded by their collection of icons and work of unofficial artists, Leningrad, 1984.

Young poets listening to poetry readings in a communal apartment, Leningrad, 1972.

Three poets of Leningrad

Constantine Kuzminsky

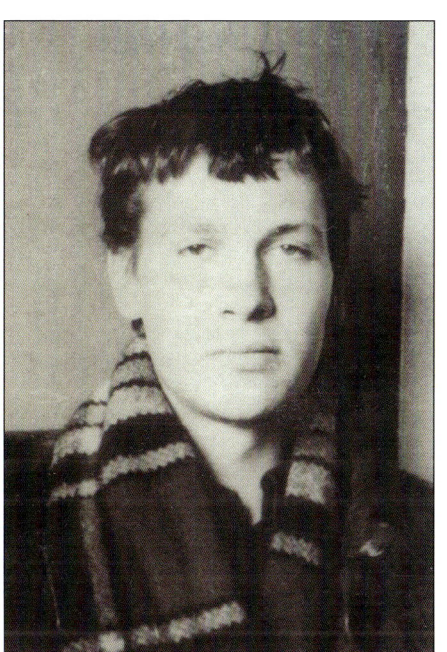

Oleg Okhapkin

Victor Sosnora

Crowds attending liturgy at Trinity-St. Sergius Monastery, Easter Night, 1988.

With Bishop Vasily Rodzianko and church-goers at restored chapel where Nicholas II and Empress Alexandra worshipped in Tsarskoe Selo.

President Reagan meeting with Pope John Paul II, in the Vizkaya Museum, Miami, Florida, September 10, 1987.

In a prophetic letter in 1981 Reagan wrote: "I have had a feeling...that in the Soviet Union religion may turn out to be their Achilles heel." He was right.

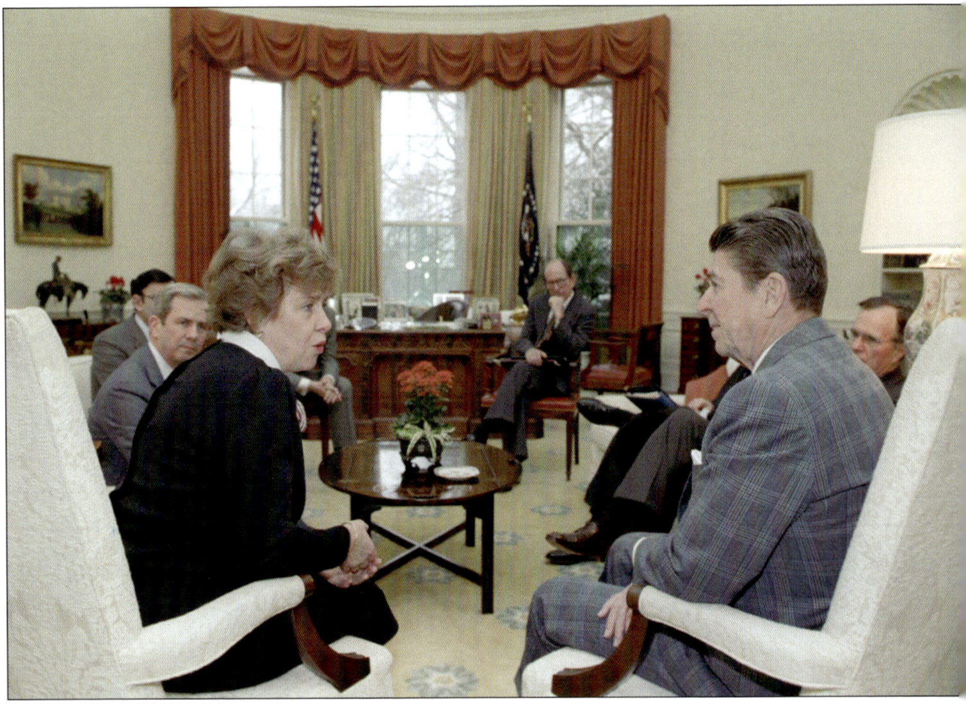

First meeting with President Reagan, Oval Office, January 17, 1984.

COURTESY OF THE REAGAN LIBRARY

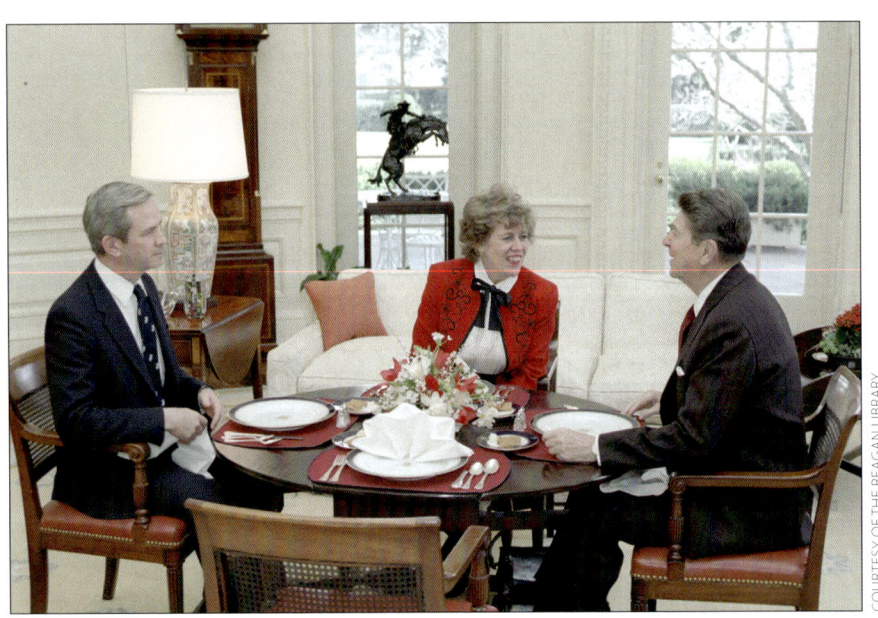

Lunch meeting with President Reagan and Robert McFarlane, Oval Office, March 1, 1984.

nch meeting with President and Mrs. Reagan on the patio designed by Mrs. Reagan outside
 Oval Office, June 2, 1986.

Attending meeting of Soviet scholars with President to give him advice, prior to his Moscow visit, Roosevelt Room, White House, March, 1988.

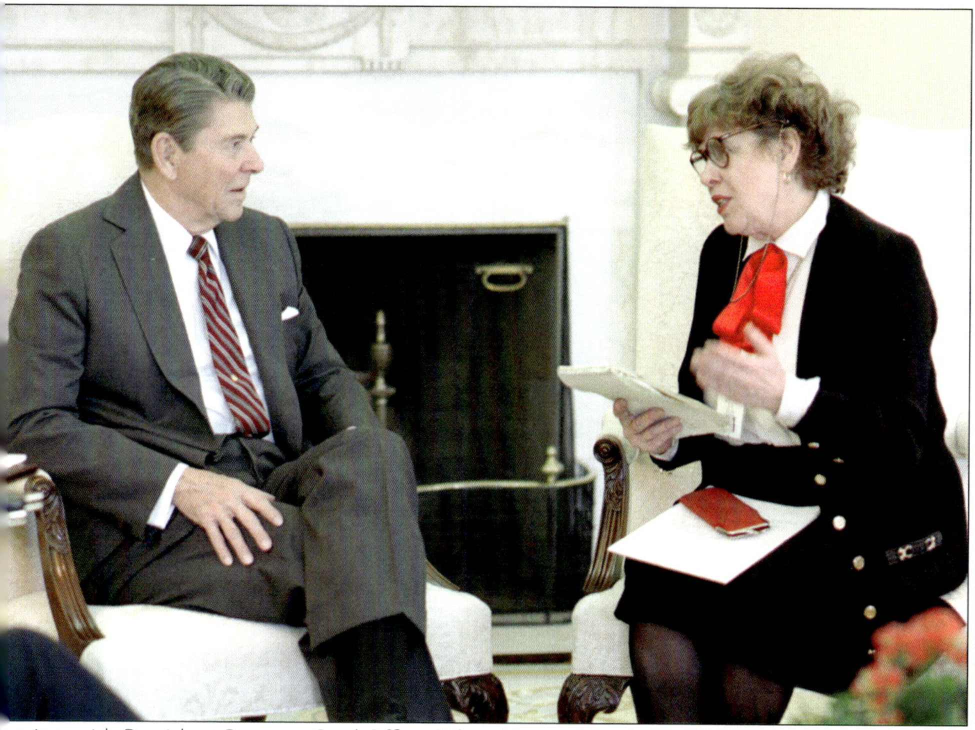

COURTESY OF THE REAGAN LIBRARY

·eting with President Reagan, Oval Office, White House, March 11, 1988.

COURTESY OF THE REAGAN LIBRARY

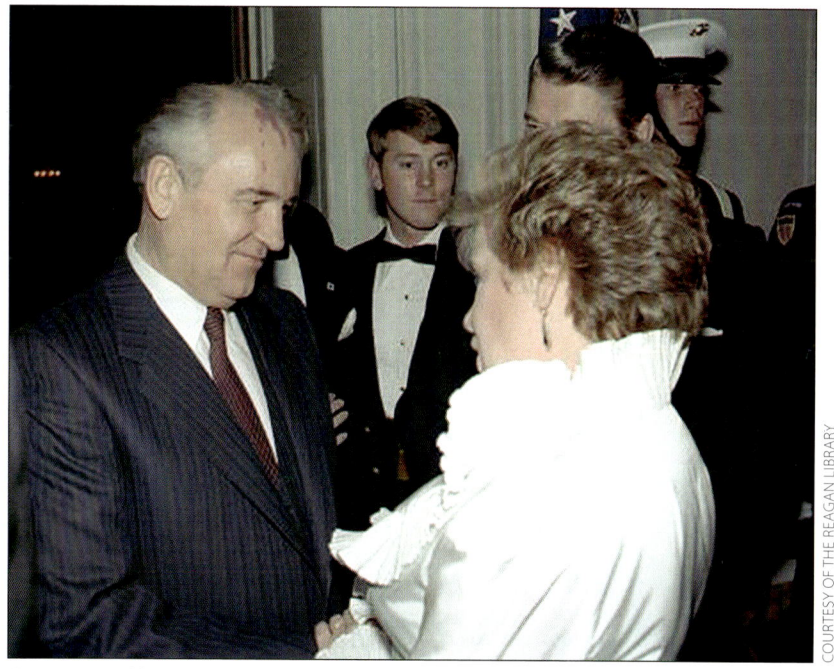

Greeting Mikhail Gorbachev at State Dinner, White House, December 8, 1987.

Igor Filin, KGB colonel and Executive Secretary of the Soviet Peace Committee, meeting Mother Teresa in Moscow, August, 1986.

Igor with me and my grandson Sam and his granddaughter Masha at Moscow book party celebrating Russian publication of *Land of the Firebird*, Moscow, 2000.

Alexander Bessmertnykh, former Soviet foreign minister under Gorbachev, with wife Marina, and son, Artyom.

Anatoly Sobchak, first democratically elected mayor of St. Petersburg, at my birthday party held at the residence of American Consul General John Evans, (visible in the background).

With my great friend, the late Anatoly Mikhailovich Kuchumov, chief curator of Pavlovsk Palace, in 1983.

A restorer of paintings at the Hermitage Museum introduces me to her grandson at Pavlovsk Palace, 1986.

Surrounded by four members of the Cossack choir in 1988 at the spring opening of the fountains of Peterhof, a great festival held annually on Peter the Great's birthday, May 26.

At the sensational opening of the first McDonald's in Moscow, 1990, mobbed by thousands of overjoyed Russian citizens.

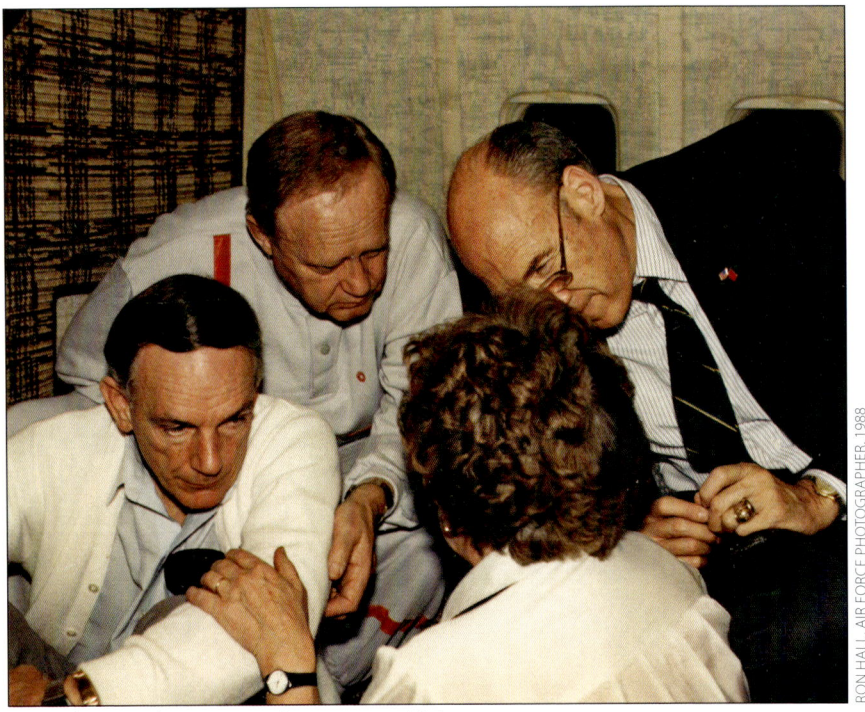
Consulting with senators, Simpson and Johnston.

Consultation with Senator Timothy Wirth aboard Air Force II.

Meeting in Kremlin conference room.

In the Kremlin complex with Senator Wirth and General Nikolai Chervov, Gorbachev's chief military advisor on SDI.

COURTESY OF THE REAGAN LIBRARY

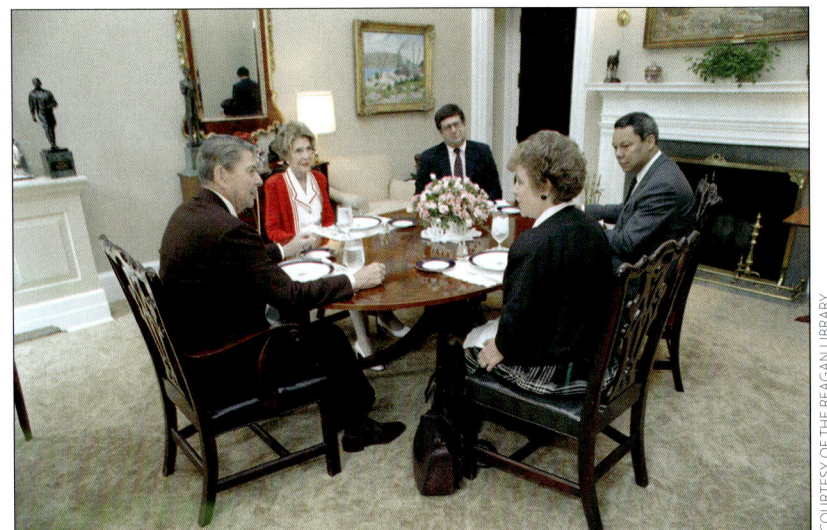

Last lunch with President and Mrs. Reagan in the Oval Office Study, White House, August 1,1988. Also present: Colin Powell, NSC Advisor, and Kenneth Duberstein, Chief of Staff.

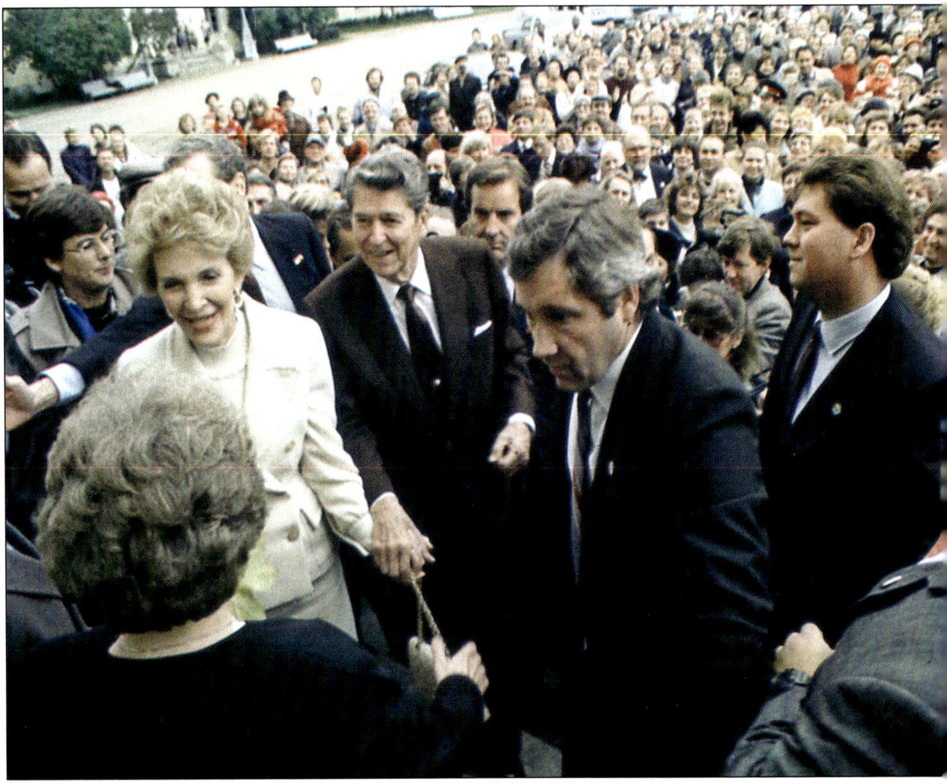

Former President and Mrs. Reagan arriving at Pavlovsk Palace and meeting me on the palac steps—looking on, a delighted crowd of Russians, September 10, 1990. This was the last tim I saw the president.

CHAPTER 11

LUNCH ON THE PATIO, JUNE 6, 1986

"She is the greatest student I know of the Russian people."
Ronald Reagan, diary entry May 20, 1986

After the Summit meeting in Geneva, I didn't see the President again until May 20, 1986, for a meeting in the Oval Office. That meeting lasted forty-three minutes. On that occasion, he mostly listened and I thought it was because I was such a chatterbox. I was embarrassed about what I felt was my rudeness, so when I was leaving, I said, "Mr. President, this is not a normal conversation! I want to know what you think!"

He laughed and said, "Come back again soon."

I was invited back two weeks later, on June 6, for what was to be my second private lunch with him. Given its importance in the life of our government and for such a powerful country as the United States, I was always impressed by the simplicity of the White House. It is more like a grand home, totally unlike the palaces and gilded halls of France's Élysée or the pomp and majesty of Buckingham Palace, let alone the overpowering size of the Kremlin. It is amazing how swiftly the extraordinary seems commonplace, how quickly one can get accustomed to the trappings of power. In those heady days, I thought nothing of popping in to the White House, acknowledging the crisp salute of the Marine guard at the door of the West Wing, greeting Dotty, the Bel Air elegant, white-haired receptionist, with a beautiful flower arrangement on her desk. Unlike the frenetic scenes of the popular television series *The West Wing*, the atmosphere was always subdued and quiet. I would help myself to a handful of the favorite Reagan jelly beans that were strategically placed everywhere, chat with the secretaries and the guards, and grew accustomed to referring to major government figures by their first names. I had entered a completely unreal world that I soon got to feel was perfectly natural.

On this day, I was met by Kathy Osborne, the President's personal secretary, and ushered into the Oval Office. I had been told that the new National Security Advisor, Admiral Poindexter, was going to be present, and I quickly looked around to see if the little table had been set up as it had been for our earlier lunch with McFarlane—but there was no table and Poindexter was not there. It was to be the President and Mrs. Reagan alone.

It was a broiling-hot day, 90 degrees, with oppressive humidity. The President was wearing the tan suit he seemed to especially like, and Mrs. Reagan, elegant as always, looked crisp and cool in a little white dress with red piping around the collar and sleeves. Cheerfully, the President announced, "Well, I thought it would be nice if we ate outdoors."

I happily agreed, "That would be wonderful."

They led me into a secluded private patio in a garden full of flowers right outside the Oval Office, enclosed by a low stone wall with a presidential seal on it. Just as if I were in someone's backyard, on the flagstone terrace was a cozy round metal garden table under a wide umbrella. I noticed that on the table stood what looked like a metronome with a presidential seal, and silver service with a large seal of the United States. I was so astonished at seeing this secret hideaway that I was sure the photographs would show me with my mouth open. The President sat down on my right and the First Lady on my left, and the photographer clicked away. As soon as he left, the President immediately took off his suit jacket and loosened his tie. (I thought, *If he does, it's all right if I do.*)

And there I was with the President, utterly, perfectly relaxed in shirtsleeves. Silent servitors came in and passed carrots and celery, then consommé, tiny croissants, avocado with crab meat and a little sauce, and, for dessert, a passion-fruit ice with strawberries, and iced tea. Given that the situation was absolutely extraordinary for me, I was at first so stunned with new impressions that I couldn't quite focus properly. All I could find to utter was, "This is so nice! So very nice!" They explained that the idea for this cozy and hidden patio had been Mrs. Reagan's, and she began telling me how it had been built and why she thought she would like to have it there. "I told the architects...." When the President broke in saying that the architects did so and so, she interrupted, "Not the architects, *me*!" and he agreed, "That's right. You did it!"

Then the President said jovially, "Well, you know, I just came from a big meeting with a lot of senators. Guess what we were talking about? You can't guess," he said. "Russia. Now tell me, how is it that *you* pronounce Gorbachev?" And proceeded to pronounce it incorrectly: "GorBAchev or GORbachev, or something like that."

I said, "Well, GArbachOV."

He said, "Hmm," and continued, "Because I was just talking about that and was telling them how to pronounce it, how you had told me, because I listened. But I thought you pronounced it another way."

"Mr. President, if you'll excuse me," I answered, "I'll give you a quick little Russian lesson. Russian is a very highly inflected language, and every word is pronounced with an accent on a particular syllable. So you see, the rule is that if the first O is not accented, it's pronounced almost as an A, and EV, when accented, as if it were OV. So it becomes GarbachOV. Another example is the word *khorosho*, which means 'fine, okay'—pronounced *harashO*, the last O accented." So as the President took all this in, I continued, "This is why English is difficult for Russians, because they pronounce every syllable and we don't, so they have a lot of trouble with English words like 'tough' and 'dough' because they're not pronounced the way they look." (All the while, I'm thinking incredulously, *Here I am giving a Russian lesson to the President of the United States. How can this be?*)

There had been a lot of meetings that day, and there were a lot of issues on his mind: Salt II, Managua, Nicaragua, a lot of different things. In an image I will carry to my death, quite suddenly the President of the United States, in shirt sleeves, like anyone else on their patio, leaned back and began rocking back and forth on his garden chair and, almost as if he were talking to himself, began roaming all over the world, talking about the situations in Nicaragua, Iran, Africa, Europe, country by country.

I was awed and listened spellbound, but he went so fast that I couldn't take it all in, and of course there was no way to take notes. Suddenly he was not the affable communicator with whom I had chatted as if he were an elder uncle, but an entirely different person. I saw the full stature and forcefulness of this President of the United States, the powerful leader of the free world. As he was speaking a strange thing happened to me—he seemed to be growing **bigger** and **bigger**—while I, like Alice in Wonderland was getting smaller and smaller. He gave off such vigor, such energy!

Reagan did not like flying and when I had seen him the week before, he had just come back from Tokyo and told me that he was tired and that night had really suffered from jet lag. This day he was absolutely in top form, in tough, rugged shape, moving like a man twenty years younger. His face, of course, was lined, but he didn't look old or show his age. That day, I realized that he was a very extraordinary personality, more complex than I had ever glimpsed before—complex and extremely determined, with his own vision, that he was not going to give up for anything. He might occasionally doze in his Cabinet meetings, but that was probably because he was resting or bored by what he was hearing. In the Oval Office, he was quite reserved and had never shown his power to me as he did that day on the patio. Only once, when he had said so definitely in our first meeting, "If they want peace, they can have it!" had I glimpsed his steely determination and eagle eye.

No doubt the reason he was so expansive, so relaxed, was because Nancy was there and he behaved as he did when he was alone with her. But I, who had no security clearance and had never been asked to sign any confidentiality promise, was astonished that he was so candid, so trusting in my presence, as though we knew each other well. It was clear that he had a plan, a strategy, tactics, and that he had thought these through carefully and in the most tenacious way had made up his mind.

"What are your goals?" I ventured.

"I want reduction of arms," he answered. "That's what I want. Dismantle those things. This is the only thing I want from them. No more treaties where people say, 'You get so many and we get so many. We go up and you go up.' Real cuts. ...and push as hard as possible to achieve these cuts from the Soviet Union."

The Reagan I saw that day made it clear to me that he was no sleepy "two-bit actor," as his detractors said; instead I saw exactly why he was president. If I had been a Soviet leader at that moment, I would have understood that he had his mind made up and would not be budged about his determination on the question of dismantling weapons. Then he repeated something that he had mentioned at our first meeting two years before: "Look, if we wanted to destroy them, we could have done that long ago. We could have done it when we had the bomb, for heaven's sake. We were the only ones who had the bomb. That was the time. If we had wanted to do that, we could have done it then. And what did we do? We didn't use the bomb against them at all. We turned it over. We actually suggested that it be administered by an international body like the UN. We actually did. But I'm glad it didn't happen. We have always used restraint with this. We have never wanted to use the bomb, therefore it's not us, it's not us, it's them."

And then he talked about Yalta. He seemed to have a bit fuzzy understanding about Yalta, but I decided it was not my place to contradict the President on this. He continued, saying that the problem had been that the Soviet Union simply didn't observe treaties and that there were so many treaties they hadn't observed. Interestingly, despite his strong words, he was not angry during his entire conversation, and was never aggressive about the Soviet Union at any time. He was, after all, in private and could have voiced any bile he had toward them, but he didn't. He was just absolutely determined to protect the United States and was so tenacious and tough that it was clear to me that no one was going to deter him. I had never heard him voice his desires in such definite terms. "That's it," said he. "I want to get rid of those weapons." No talk about changing their system, no business about collapsing their economy.

After those riveting moments, we talked about the bureaucratic problems on both sides that made candid discussions difficult. Both he and Mrs. Reagan agreed quite heartily that bureaucracy was a big problem for them. I told them that after returning from the Soviet Union, I had once jokingly told Bud McFarlane, "I have good news and bad news" and Bud had said anxiously, "Give me the bad news first." So I said, "The Soviets are ahead of us in one respect—bureaucracy. But the good news is that we are catching up very fast." The President really laughed at that and so did Nancy. I continued by saying that it seemed to me sometimes that the two bureaucracies were resembling each other more and more: they were wearing the same clothes and using the same acronyms, and that when I went to the State Department, I often felt I was in Moscow.

We started talking about Gorbachev. I asked, "You wrote me in your letter that you had a good impression, that there was good chemistry between you and Mr. Gorbachev. Would you care to tell me some more about this?"

He said, "Oh, yes, that's true. There was very good chemistry—just good chemistry between the two of us. And yes, of course he believes all that propaganda about us. He really believes that we're all run by big industrialists and all of that. He believes that. That's natural, that he should believe that, but he really isn't a bad sort except for that, and that's what he has been brought up with, so how else could he feel? But other than that it was just fine. He is nice."

Then he began to talk about Geneva, how Gorbachev was surrounded by his bureaucracy, too, and that when he had pulled Gorbachev away, he was happy. "At one point, you know, I got him aside and I said to him, 'Now listen, why don't we just go off by ourselves, just you and I, and talk this over? He agreed right away. Well, there was a pool there and a little house—of course there was a fire in the hearth." (The President was clearly pleased about this, and with a certain glee indicated that he had carefully planned it all.) "And I said to him, 'Here we are, you and I. We are just two...but in our hands we hold much of the fate of the world, and it's time for us to get together and get some talking done.'" (At this time, their advisors were in a twit that these two men had gone off alone, and they didn't know exactly what they had talked about.)

The President continued, "Yes, indeed, I want another summit absolutely, and Gorbachev wants this summit now, because Mrs. Thatcher saw him only a little while ago and Gorbachev told her, 'Yes, tell Reagan I want a summit.' (Mrs. Thatcher had passed this remark on to the President privately.) He continued "I wanted it in June. I wanted it really soon, but they didn't want it and now they've proposed September. But of course I'm going to be very busy running and campaigning for various candidates. It's going to be before the elections, so I'm going to be all over the country."

I suggested that perhaps another reason might be that they couldn't get their act together between February and June, which was the Party Congress, and that things moved very slowly in the Soviet Union. The President said that he now had his eyes set on November and felt that it would indeed take place because both he and Gorbachev wanted it.

(They did not meet in June of 1986 as Reagan had hoped, or in November. The President had to wait until December of 1987 for Gorbachev to come to Washington and then June of 1988 for his own visit to Moscow.)

What was most interesting for me was their unorthodox way of communication—completely outside their own bureaucracies. It was well known that President Reagan and Prime Minister Thatcher liked each other very much. But I saw now that there was an even closer relationship between us and the English than we knew.

So the conversation went back to how to get the summit on track since Gorbachev wanted it, too. I thought, *Let me see. Gorbachev has to tell Mrs. Thatcher alone, so obviously he has got plenty of problems with his bureaucracy too*, so I said, "All right, you both want it but how are you going to get that?" Bud had told me that I should bring up the idea that perhaps the President should have a trusted person, his own person, someone who's *known* as the President's person, who can go back and forth and exchange messages directly. The President answered that he had somebody. He had a contact (maybe Mrs. Thatcher?). "Fine," I said, "because it seems to me that the problem for Gorbachev at the moment might be that he feels he is communicating completely with headlines and bureaucracy and it is hard for him to know the real intentions of the president." So how to get the message to Gorbachev?

Then suddenly Mrs. Reagan exclaimed, "Oh! Oh! There is the wedding!"

And I said, "That's right, Prince Andrew's on July 23rd. Are you going to the wedding?"

She answered, "Oh, yes, I am. Actually we have gotten to be very good personal friends with the Royal Family, you see, and I like them very much. This isn't going to be a big, big wedding, but smaller, you know." Then she said to the President, "Ronnie, Mrs. Thatcher is going to be there. I could do it."

So they agreed on the spot that Mrs. Reagan would carry the message through the Royal Family to Mrs. Thatcher. Again, I was astonished that this exchange had happened in front of me.

At this point, I turned to Mrs. Reagan, who had been fairly quiet up to then, and asked, "You mentioned something about Raisa Gorbacheva at our last meeting. Would you care to tell me about that?" And she launched into a lengthy description, both tart and funny, that I have written about in detail in the chapter I have devoted to her (*Chapter 14: Nancy*).

She seemed to want to go on, but I saw that the President was anxious to speak again, and he started talking about how he felt about dealing with the Soviets and how he felt he *should* deal with them. He said he didn't like the Jackson-Vanick Amendment because "it was too precise, hemmed too much in and prohibited freedom of movement." I felt he was wrong about that, insufficiently informed about the ins and outs of the Jackson Amendment, and had somehow gotten it in his mind that it was very rigid. As a case in point of what he thought was the right way to proceed, he went on to talk again about the Pentacostalists who had lived in our embassy basement for five years. He told me again that it was *he* who had arranged their release. "Nobody wrote this. I didn't get any credit,¹ but I did it, and after they let the Pentacostalists out, you will notice, I lifted the grain embargo. Nobody knew this and it doesn't matter. But I got 'em out! Got 'em out!" (And I thought, if I were speaking frankly, I would have said, *"Mr. President, I think lifting the grain embargo was too much for the Pentacostalists."* But it was not my place to say that.) He was proud, was pleased with the result,² and it was a good model of the tit-for-tat way he wanted to do things in the future.

The President went on to talk about his concerns on human rights questions. I urged him to press for the reunification of 117 families—husbands and wives separated for one reason or another who could not get visas to join their loved ones. I briefed him on the conversation I had had with Alexander Bessmertnykh when I had met him in Washington, explaining that one of the very real problems we had with the Soviets on the question of human rights was that, in a very paranoid way, they were convinced that, in fact, we were not interested in human rights except as a political necessity because of the Jewish vote in this country and we were not really interested otherwise. This remained their cynical belief. I told him, "I have talked to the Soviets about this, argued with them, but I know they are still convinced that this is so."

I recounted the conversation I had had with Bessmertnykh on the subject, and that I had told him that their performance on human rights was outrageous. His answer was, "We would have no trouble if it weren't for 'the Zionists,'" I told him, "You are all wet. I'm not telling you what to do, but all right, if you don't want to deal immediately with Jewish questions, why don't you do something about reunification of families?"

He answered, "You're right, you're right. There is no reason not to do that."

"Well *now*," (sixty-four families had recently been reunited), I told the President, "they've done it in a bigger way than they have since 1953, and I think this may be a test to see if we react to something else. I would hope, if this should be the case, that you would take some notice of it. I don't believe in patting the Soviets on the back for doing what they should be doing anyway, but it might be a good thing perhaps, in some context or other, to take note of it presidentially. The State Department is making a big front-page story of it, but it would be nice if you could mention it, perhaps in this light: that you are gratified, that you are happy for these families, and that as soon as they have time to examine the remaining fifty-three cases bureaucratically, you are certain they will be resolved expeditiously in a positive manner."

He agreed with this and so did Mrs. Reagan, and she told me a bit later, "I will remind him. I will remind him to say something about that."

The President went on to talk about Afghanistan and the atrocities committed there, and said that some Russian prisoners in Afghanistan had now defected to us. "Those prisoners, you see, are telling about this." It seemed he had just had a new intelligence report about it and said, "Now those boys. They wanted to be free and they don't want to fight. They have been going over to the Afghans, to fight with the Afghans. The Russians have been going over."

Three years before, I had been told confidentially by Raymond Probst, the Swiss Foreign Minister, about Russian prisoners defecting and the Swiss intervention in these cases, which the President didn't seem to be aware of, so I suggested to him that the Swiss experience might be useful for us. Then he leaned back in his chair again, clasping his hand behind his neck, looked up to the sky, and exclaimed, "You know why our two countries should get along? Because we're *big*! We both have big spaces, and that makes a lot of difference in the way we think."

His remark struck me very strongly, as coincidentally, just a few weeks before I had heard the identical thought from the Soviet side: "We have *prostranstvo* (wide spaces) and so does the United States, and this make us think differently than small countries."

Finally, at the very end of the lunch and out of the blue, the President suddenly asked me, "What do you think about Hartman?"

I was unprepared for that. So I answered, "May I be candid?"

"Please do," they both replied, and both leaned forward.

I didn't want to say anything, but I knew I had to and tried to find a low key answer. I said that I felt there were areas where we could do better, that we should expand our public presence in the Soviet Union, as there were constituencies that we were not reaching, women particularly, and, finally, that our circle was too narrow and it was important to open it at this time. "You know that one of our problems with the Soviet Union and the Russians is that they firmly believe that our ambassador reflects in every way your point of view. And since they never do anything without instructions from above, they assume that your representative is having instructions whispered into his ear and that everything he does is really *you*, and what you say publicly is not the real you. So they tend to exaggerate and take seriously small asides. An example was their touchy feelings over the showing of the Hollywood film *Ninotchka* at the ambassador's residence because they thought Reagan would know the film and understand. I know this is really small change, but it made a great deal of difference and they took it as a deliberate insult. I think that if their Ambassador Dobrynin had done the same thing in our country, showing a film that ridiculed us, we would have considered it an unfriendly act."

They both agreed.

At this point, the president said, "Well look, between you and me, there's going to be a change." He did not explain, and I did not ask. The President looked at his watch and said it was time for him to leave for a signing ceremony. As we got up to leave, I thought to ask him whether he had actually given the Easter egg to Gorbachev and he answered, "Yes. I did give it to him."

He was in a hurry and didn't have time to elaborate, so when I asked, "What was his reaction?" he answered only, "He was surprised!"

After that, Mrs. Reagan and I were left alone and had a private talk of our own, which I have detailed in the chapter I have devoted to her.

CHAPTER 12

LONG LUNCH WITH THE PRESIDENT, SEPTEMBER 23, 1986

One thing that I was to discover early in my meetings with President Reagan is that presidents don't have the power people think they do, that they are often severely constrained by advisors, politics, and the media. Nothing demonstrated this to me as much as our conversation at that lunch.

It was always clear to me that there were forces on both sides that were not delighted by the successful results of the Geneva meeting and the growing friendship between Reagan and Gorbachev, and that there were attempts to sow doubt and slow down the process.

If one looks at some of the pivotal events in relations between the United States and the Soviet Union, one can see that many of these moments, perhaps coincidentally, seem to have happened at a time our diplomats call "the nightmare of summer"—when top leaders of both sides customarily took their vacations. Khrushchev was deposed at that time, KAL was shot down on September 1, 1983, when Reagan was on vacation and Andropov in the hospital. The Zaharov-Daniloff crisis happened in late August of 1986 when Reagan, Shultz, Gorbachev, and Shevardnadze were all away on vacation. Because of this, both leaders were caught unawares and left boxed in by their own services. Also perhaps by coincidence, it also happened just at the time when the first conference between Soviet and American scientists and scholars, organized by Susan Eisenhower, was scheduled to take place in Yermala, Latvia.

The stakes were high, as preliminary details were in the process of being worked out for a new meeting between Reagan and Gorbachev on arms reduction. In this delicate moment, for reasons still cloudy, the FBI took the initiative to set up and arrest Gennady Zaharov, a minor Soviet UN employee without diplomatic immunity, and, as could be expected, the Soviets angrily retaliated by arresting Nicholas Daniloff, a respected American journalist for *U.S. News and World Report*, falsely accusing him of espionage and imprisoning him. The whole affair was murky enough to lead me to the suspicion that somebody (or somebodies) in the U.S. or the Soviet Union might have decided it would be a great time to cause trouble. Daniloff's arrest caused a firestorm of indignation in the U.S. press and almost wrecked the Yermala Conference, as Jeane Kirkpatrick and Richard Perle, among other conservatives, dropped out in protest of Soviet actions, and, most importantly, threatened to poison all negotiations between the superpowers.

In the weeks preceding the crisis, I had gotten a lot of unusual attention from Washington. Jack Matlock had called me several times during the summer asking my advice about the Yermala Conference and asking me to edit his speech. While the foreign minister of the USSR, Eduard Shevardnadze, was in town in mid-September, the Protocol Office of the State Department had called and invited me to lunch with Mrs. Shultz and Mrs. Shevardnadze. Regretfully, I had to refuse because (although I couldn't say this), I didn't have the money for two visits to Washington in such a short time, and I knew that I was to meet with the President a week later.

I arrived on September 22, had lunch with George Cole, a top Russian analyst for the CIA, and saw Colonel Serge Cherney of the Air War College in Alabama, who had been involved in arms control negotiations and knew the archconservative Richard Perle well. He passed on the interesting detail that Richard had gone for his first visit to Moscow only a few weeks before and had seen his friend Nicholas Daniloff. I wondered whether the KGB had taken note of this.

When I saw Jack Matlock early that day, I tried to get to the bottom of the Daniloff affair and asked him some hard questions, the first being: "Who was behind the arrest of Zaharov, and who made the decision?" He seemed a bit nervous and explained to me in great detail why it was judged by the FBI to be very, very important to make an example for the Soviets—that they couldn't use the UN as a spymaster and use people who were in the diplomatic community in this manner, etcetera. But I remained skeptical, as I had been told in the White House that a lower-level official had approved it and from the State Department that they had sent an equivocal reply.

I told Jack that I frankly suspected more than this and was very disappointed in our press for not pushing harder and going more deeply into not only the Soviet actions, but into who exactly had decided ours in the United States. It was not Shultz and not the President, both of whom were on vacation. There was no way of knowing for sure whether the Soviets would have arrested Daniloff anyway without the Zaharov excuse, or had simply taken advantage of the situation we gave them—which, considering the timing, was a near disaster. I wondered, shouldn't the initial FBI action have been checked with Shultz or the President before they took the action they did? If indeed the decision was taken in the way it was, to show the Soviets that we were not going to accept their overblown number of personnel at the UN, why was it all over the front pages as it was? Jack answered, "I would have preferred that it wasn't."

"Then, Jack," I continued, "I have another question. Since it's perfectly obvious that we could have predicted that there would be some result, what about Moscow? Did our embassy move in any way to protect our people there by sending out some out sort of warning saying that the United States had done something ticklish and that American citizens were now going to have to be very careful for the next few weeks not to do anything out of the ordinary?"

"No," was his answer.

LUNCH WITH THE PRESIDENT

It was against this background that I met with President and Mrs. Reagan on September 23rd. It was my sixth conversation and third visit with the President in five months, half as many during that short period as I had

had in the previous two years. It turned out to be a very long meeting.

It was a sunny day, and I enjoyed the nice long walk from the front gate of the White House to the West Wing, passing the ever-present group of newsmen sitting around in their shirtsleeves with their cameras, patiently waiting for something to happen. The entrance to the West Wing is always striking because it's so small and modest for a place of such power. On the door hung yellow ribbons for the hostages in Iran, and, as always, a young, crisp Marine snapped to attention and saluted as I went in. The atmosphere inside was very cool and quiet. Standing around were two Secret Service men and an impressive guard, the biggest African-American man I had ever seen: 6'7" at least, huge with great big shoulders and legs longer than all of me. I was glad to think that the President was guarded by such a giant.

Frank Layman, the National Security Council coordinator, came to fetch me and we went down the hall to wait for the President in the small anteroom just outside the doors of the Oval Office. It was the first time I had heard the Secret Service men discussing the President's movements using his code name, "Rainbow." I waited for the summons from Rainbow himself, and when it came, as always, I said my prayers before I went in, preceded by a silent, very discreet photographer.

President and Mrs. Reagan were standing together by his desk to meet me. They greeted me warmly and the President announced, "Well, we're going to eat outside again!" The little door to the secluded patio in the Rose Garden was immediately to the right of his desk, and we went outside and sat down at the round metal table under the umbrella. It was another hot day, so after the photographer had left, the President took off his jacket and loosened his tie as he had done before. I now understood that the strange metronome sitting on the table was how the President summoned the waiters, who padded in noiselessly.

I saw right away that the President was a very different man from the one who had been so full of pep and exuberance on June 6th. He was deeply disturbed about the Daniloff affair and hurt because the American right wing had called him a "wimp" for negotiating to get him freed quickly. Anxiously, he asked me, "Do you think I'm a wimp? I haven't gone soft on communism."

I replied, "Mr. President, I know you haven't," and he repeated again, "I haven't."

He was eager to explain why it was so important for him to get Daniloff out of jail as soon as possible. Mortimer Zuckerman, owner and editor-in-chief of *U.S. News and World Report*, had reported to him that when he had seen Nicholas in jail, he was in such bad shape that Zuckerman thought perhaps the Soviets were feeding him drugs in his soup. And there was a feeling that there might be a forced confession and perhaps a show trial. "Nick was so confused and looked so strange," said the President.

It is not news to say that Reagan was a great and genuine patriot. I often had the impression that he might break into a chorus of "God Bless America" at any time. It is not so well known how much Reagan suffered personally when an American citizen was killed, imprisoned, or in trouble and that he was the one who moved most swiftly to cut the red tape to directly resolve the case. He was very apprehensive about what might happen to Daniloff and wanted to get him out, but didn't know quite how. I had an odd feeling that he seemed to be hoping that I might have a good answer or solution, something that of course I didn't have. The only word of comfort I could muster was, "Don't worry about being called a wimp by the press. You know it will pass. You know they will be onto something else next week. Don't worry. You're stronger and may be better able to take it than Gorbachev."

I asked if I might be able to read the Russian texts of Shevardnadze's and Gorbachev's statements as semantics were so important, but he did not have them. The President admitted that he hadn't known about the Zaharov arrest. He said simply, "I was on vacation. They didn't tell me." He didn't apologize or blame anybody. Despite the fact that he had been wounded by Gorbachev's harsh reply to the two personal letters he had sent him giving his word that Daniloff was not a spy, and that the Soviet press had called him "a liar," he was not angry. Instead he seemed grieved and self-doubting, saying, "You know, at Geneva we got on very well. The fact is, I mean, when I came in, well, I think he liked me," adding, a bit uncertainly, "and I don't think it was a snow job." It struck me then that the one thing that might save the situation was the good feeling that had developed between the two men, certainly from Reagan's side.

It was clear that he wanted to get Gorbachev off the hook and understood that he might be as hemmed in as he was. So, hoping to make him feel a bit better, I suggested, "We don't know what position Gorbachev is in or what his actions were or who may have forced him or didn't force him or where the decision came from on the Soviet side. After all, he was away on vacation, too. Nobody really knows. Our official guys are running around saying that this decision could not have been taken 'without Gorbachev and the Politburo,' but it can't be that simple. I wish I could help in some way, but of course I don't know the options. I am going to be seeing Secretary Shultz tomorrow. Do I have your permission to talk to him about this?"

The President said, "Yes."

Then he brought up his meeting with Soviet Foreign Minister Shevardnadze, who had brought him a five-page letter from Gorbachev on September 15th. (Mrs. Reagan interjected, "Oh, very good, that Shevardnadze," to which the President replied, "Well, that solves nothing with the congressmen.")

The Foreign Minister had also brought a message of good will for Mrs. Reagan from Raisa Gorbacheva. I told her, "Mrs. Reagan, since our last conversation, I did keep my ears open about what is said about her in the Soviet Union." I mentioned several things, but the one that seemed to impress Mrs. Reagan most was when I told her, "She has founded an independent Soviet cultural fund. Obviously, in that government there are no private funds, but this new foundation will for the first time be soliciting private funds for the arts."

"Well," said Mrs. Reagan, "that is interesting."

The majority of Gorbachev's letter for the President was devoted to a point-by-point reply to the arms control proposals that Reagan had made in a personal letter to him on July 25. Gorbachev's tone was impatient, frustrated, fed up with the slowness of diplomats working out agreements, accusing not only the U.S., but voicing his exasperation with his own bureaucrats as well.[1] Despite the ongoing Daniloff crisis, it was a measure of his desire to meet with Reagan again on the questions of arms reduction that in his last paragraph Gorbachev pressed the importance of having a quick meeting either in Iceland or Britain.

Reagan had refused to respond to that letter immediately. Instead, he recounted how he had delivered Shevardnadze a long, stern lecture about how important the Daniloff arrest was to the American people. Going on to explain his reaction, he told me, "I called in Shevardnadze and told him how I felt. I didn't make him feel at home," adding, "I didn't smile for an hour—and that's hard! I told him that the big difference between our countries is the importance of the individual. If we can't have that, we don't have anything. That is the difference between our systems and we cannot desert that position. He took a lot of notes." The President laughed when he said that Shevardnadze had told him that they had a free press.

I explained that however absurd it might seem to him, I thought that Shevardnadze might be trying to get off the hook by referring to the fact that, while the official Soviet press was often vitriolic about political matters, the domestic press was now so open that in the Soviet Union these days they were discussing everything and washing all the dirty linen on front pages. This was particularly apparent in the letters to the editor. So I suggested that someone on his staff should be giving him a digest of what else was in the Soviet press apart from the usual criticism and accusations against the United States.

At the end of his session, the President had told Shevardnadze that he would sleep on Gorbachev's proposal for a meeting, and the next day told Shultz to say yes—with one condition: no meeting until Daniloff was freed. This ultimatum proved to be a deal-maker and impelled a

LONG LUNCH WITH THE PRESIDENT 225

compromise on Daniloff. He was released in custody of the United States Embassy in Moscow on September 23 (the very day of our lunch) and was back home by September 29. Yet after Daniloff's return, American conservatives grumbled that the deal amounted to a swap of an innocent hostage for a real spy. Jack Kemp charged that the administration had set a "terrible precedent" and another critic that "this administration foreign policy has been to kiss the Russian bear's bottom."

"And now," said the President, upset, "they're saying that I'm doing this all because I want a summit. As a matter of fact, Gorbachev wants a summit more than I do."

One of the positives about Reagan was that he never lost his temper about the Soviets. Instead, he obviously had his mind on arms control and had never spent so much time as he did that day talking about this and how determined he was to get "real cuts." Nancy said, "We've just got to get this [the Daniloff matter] out of the way so we can go on with other things."

Voicing his view about how the Soviets negotiate, the President explained his feeling about zero options and no more missiles in Europe. "They're really funny. You know, we give them a position. Now they're taking that position—but it is *their* position. When they put out their position, they won't accept any of our positions. It's really strange. Of course, we talked about those missiles in Europe, and now they say yes but won't get out their missiles," explaining, "You understand, they have those missiles pointed at Asia, but all they have to do is turn them around and they're pointed at Europe again, so we want to get those out."

I could understand his confusion. It is hard for our Western mentality to understand the Soviet/Russian mindset. I responded by talking about the tenacity of the Russians and how very tough they can be, and told him that an experienced European diplomat had once explained to me that what the Soviets do is always ask for twice as much as they think they are going to get and then hang on, using tedium as a weapon, and that we in the West are not so good at patience.

Like the fair man that he was, the President talked about our way of compromising, how "we would come halfway, we'll meet them there." "Mr. President," I said, "the trouble is that they know this. It is a different way of arguing and if they ask for twice as much and we come halfway, they have already gotten more. It's not the kind of negotiation we are accustomed to. Our way of compromising is that we give a little, they give a little."

Ruefully, the President said, "Well, they give very little, very little."

I emphasized the state of flux I had observed in the Soviet Union. "Once you lift the lid, steam comes pouring out and it gets hard to control. It is a time of change and ferment, a time of imbalance, perhaps even dangerous, and we might expect some other unpleasant incidents. And think what a position Gorbachev is in, surrounded as he is with a vicious and even more entrenched bureaucracy than ours."

The President understood that immediately. At times, he seemed bewildered and let down by his staff and on guard with his own bureaucracy and seemed to want to deal with them as little as possible. We talked again about the question of our representation in Moscow. He looked wistful and said, "There's going to be a change there, but the wheels grind slowly."

I then passed on to him orally some messages from the VAAP director in Moscow. "Look, the man who gave me this information was KGB definitely. First he told me that '*personal* representation was better than letters.' My take on this was that they are even more scared about what gets put on paper that we are. After all, even in Washington now, people hesitate to put anything delicate on paper, and in the Soviet Union, even more so." I urged, "Mr. President, do take this seriously because you know that such remarks imply that Gorbachev can't trust anybody."

I continued, "After this preamble, minutes of a meeting between Felipe González, the Prime Minister of Spain, and Gorbachev in Moscow were read to me with the words, 'I have permission to share these minutes with you so that you would know them.' In these minutes, González was quoted as saying, 'Do you think Reagan wants nuclear disarmament?' Gorbachev answered, 'Yes, I think Reagan is willing, but there are some around him and some allies who will not permit it.' Then Gorbachev said—and this I was asked to take down—'I found Reagan to be a charming person and a statesman of wisdom.'" When I finished I told the President, "I don't know if all this is necessarily true, but if you want to, you can check it through the Spaniards."

As I knew the President liked to hear true stories about Russian behavior, I told him about something that had happened to me during my previous trip to Leningrad that I thought might amuse him and perhaps also have a slight bearing on the Daniloff case. I began, "One day I chanced to see a sign in the city that announced: 'FOREIGNERS: RENT ONE OF OUR FINE ZHIGULIS (a Russian made car)—9 RUBLES A DAY.' Thinking, well even I can afford that, I went to the Leningrad Hotel and ordered one. Sure enough, a mechanic appeared with a new car shortly after. We did a practice run and I heard an odd thumping noise and asked, 'What is that?' *Nichevo*' (don't worry about it), replied the mechanic, and so off I went, only to hear a few minutes later the thumping continue, and, as I was crossing the nearby bridge, grow louder and louder until suddenly a front tire blew off! Watching helplessly, I saw it roll down across the square at the end of the bridge and disappear into a nearby park, leaving me shaken and the car slumped on the busy bridge in the middle of traffic.

"My first thought was *'Defitsit!*' (that common Soviet word meaning lacking, scarce, unavailable). I had been warned that if I lost my windshield wipers it would be my nickel since in those days, because of the danger of theft, one commonly saw people removing their windshield wipers when they left their car. But a tire!! Then, in quick succession, thoughts followed: 'I could have been killed!' And then, 'This is a totalitarian country, where are the police?' Well, no police. So I stood helplessly beside the car waving my arms and crying, 'Help! I have lost a tire!'

"It was rush hour and cars just kept roaring by, ignoring me completely. Then I saw a passing car that had a driver and two military officers in uniform. I waved even harder. They, too, at first passed by, but a short time later I saw one of them, a captain, approaching me. In that short interval, they had managed to retrieve the tire, and as he approached, the captain asked me in Russian, 'Where are you from?' 'America,' I answered. Without missing a beat, he replied, 'Well, tell Reagan we aren't all bad!' Of course he didn't have an inkling that I knew you!"

The President laughed and laughed. He loved it and asked me what happened then.

So I continued, "Seems that the mechanic had forgotten to tighten the tire bolts, and the three men searched the road between passing cars to retrieve the tire bolts and replaced the tire. Then they drove me back to the hotel. All of this had happened so quickly that the mechanic was still there talking to the receptionist. They grabbed him by the neck and shook him. The two officers, full of grease stains from replacing the tire, then drove away with me effusively thanking them in the name of my friends, family, and country and leaving me with their driver. A husky, burly man, he proceeded to forcefully test drive the car around the parking lot, twisting the steering wheel hard over and over (explaining to me later that sometimes the steering wheel was known to fly off in a new car), and offered to drive me home.

"His name was Volodya (Vladimir). On the way, he confessed that although he was now retired and a car specialist for the military, he had once been a KGB foot soldier assigned to follow an American consul. At this confession, I couldn't help bursting out laughing and said, 'Well, I guess I really landed well!' Then, when he politely left me at my door, he said, 'If you have any problems, call me,' and gave me his number with the words, 'Don't give it to anyone. You know.' I thanked him, not being able to imagine any further car problems.

"But when I returned to the hotel to return the keys, the receptionist said that I was to be charged $150.00 for the tire!!! I protested angrily and uselessly, and decided to call Volodya. When I told him the sum, he said only, '*Eto mnogo* (that's a lot),' and told me, 'Don't worry, Suzanne, go to Moscow.'

"I was to leave the next day, so I did, and when I got back, went again to the hotel. To my surprise, I found the lady I had dealt with before all smiles. She told me that 'an honest mechanic' had come forth and told the truth about the accident and that of course I did not have to pay anything, but I would have to produce a paper signed by two witnesses. I thought that perhaps two Soviet military men might not want to sign a paper for an American, so again I called Volodya. Once more, he said, 'Don't worry.' He would ask them. Then he called back and said he would meet me and give me the necessary letter.

"When we met, I thanked him and told him how very warmly the lady had behaved and how very nice she had been. He fell quiet for a few moments and then admitted, 'Well, I did call my former (KGB) colleagues and they called the hotel and told them, 'We counsel you to look into this matter again. She is a writer. She could write about it. It would not look good for you. Look into it again.' Then, with the matter closed, he began to reminisce about the days he had been assigned to watch the American consul. I, in my naiveté, thinking of the Leningrad I knew as a place of museums and culture, said incredulously that I couldn't imagine what he would be spying on here. He answered, 'Kronstadt' (the Russian naval base on the Baltic, visible from the park at Peterhof Palace). He said, 'He was a nice guy (naming him). You have them, we have them. When yours are in our country, you call them 'observers,' and in your country, we call ours 'observers,' but they are spies. You can't tell if they have a hidden camera and you cannot touch them—if you do—*Mezhdunarodniye skandal* (international scandal)! So I would follow him and then would just nonchalantly move in front of him when he faced the base.'

"The moral of this tale," I told the President, "is that if even a rank and file, lower-level KGB foot soldier understood this clearly and had orders not to touch an American because of possible repercussions, it was proof that when they grabbed Daniloff in Moscow, they knew exactly what they were doing and what would happen when they did."

In all our meetings, I had never asked the President a direct question about his policy. I felt that that was a reporter's job and not what I was there for, but that day, he had been so fiercely adamant about his determination to get "real weapons cuts" that at the end of this long meeting, I timidly asked him, "Mr. President, what do you want from the Russians, anyway?"

Without a moment's hesitation, he turned and fixed me with the fierce eagle-eyed glance that I had seen in him only twice before, and with steely determination answered immediately and definitively, "I want to get rid of those atomic weapons, *every one!*"

It was then that I suddenly had an inspiration. "Mr. President, I've got something for you that might be useful in your discussions. Russians love to talk in proverbs, and there is one that might come in handy. It goes: '*doveryai no proveryai,*' which means 'trust but verify.' It's old Russian folk wisdom. You are an actor. You could learn it in Russian easily. Throw it into the conversation sometime. Just drop it in; it will have an effect."

I could see that this suggestion immediately resonated with both the President and his wife. "That's great!" she exclaimed. "Is there something we can write it on?" So at the end of lunch, before I left, the President, Mrs. Reagan, and I went into an adjoining office and I wrote it down for him and told him I would send it typed, which I did, with the accents emphasized. He was to adopt it as his own and to use it over and over.

The President then left and I had a few minutes more with Mrs. Reagan. That day had impressed me once more with how much the President sometimes felt himself a captive of his bureaucracy. I had already seen before how much on guard he was about them and how he wanted to deal with them as little as possible. It sadly reminded me of tales of Turkey under the sultan, when the ruler was contained in his palace surrounded by hordes of intriguing servitors. On this occasion I understood more than ever the important role of Nancy Reagan and her protectiveness, because the President really needed her. He was actually very gentle and idealistic. When he spoke so strongly about the importance of the individual, one could imagine he was there saluting the flag. I mused that he probably did not have too good a gut sense for intrigue, but Nancy did. She was very subtle and smart. She couldn't sit in on Cabinet meetings, although Rosalind Carter did and got criticized for it. This was one reason I always welcomed the times when she was present at our discussions, as her participation was important. As we parted that day, I said to her, "I do not think he was well served in this particular incident [Daniloff]," and she replied through clenched teeth, "I agree with you."

CHAPTER 13

TRUST BUT VERIFY— REYKJAVIK

"The most dramatic and controversial, the most productive and the most misunderstood of all U.S.–Soviet meetings."
George Shultz[1]

After our lunch on September 23, when I had taught President Reagan the Russian proverb *"doveryai no proveryai"*—"trust but verify"—the President followed up with a letter on October 3, in which he wrote:

We both enjoyed being with you and as always are grateful for the information you provide about the Russian people and their Soviet masters. Thanks too for the article, and the proverb. I shall have the latter with me in Iceland.

The President did not wait long to press the proverb into action. Only eight days later at Reykjavik, he used it for the first time in his initial one-on-one meeting with Gorbachev. Pointing first to the critical importance of human rights and regional issues, with respect to arms reductions he said, "There is a Russian saying, '*doveryai no proveryai*,'[2] which means 'trust but verify.' How will we know that you will get rid of your missiles as you say you will?" Gorbachev replied that he accepted strict verification, including on-site inspection.

This small nugget of Russian folk wisdom could have been the title of the meeting itself. *Verify* was a major issue, but sufficient *trust*, begun in Geneva, and only in its early fragile stages, was not strong enough to overcome the forty years of suspicion between the Soviet Union and the United States. After using the proverb that first time, Reagan would repeat it many times, so often, in fact, that it is now identified with him and has passed into the English lexicon. For me, it does not have a specific political meaning, but has always stood as a universal maxim for human relations. *Trust* has to come first—without it there can be no *verify*.[3]

The Reykjavik meeting (October 10–12, 1986), initially pronounced by the U.S. media as "a bust," now counts as one of the most important and historic meetings between the two men. The transcripts show that the actual positions and aspirations of the two leaders were very close. In fact, their mutual ultimate dream, the total elimination of nuclear weapons, was identical. They came heartbreakingly close to their goal, but, sadly, it remained elusive. As is so often the case, the devil was in the details.

What happened?

It may not seem important on the surface, but I couldn't escape the impression that the influence of the locale chosen and the climate that went with it was hardly conducive and couldn't help to have had some effect on the mood of the participants. Of course it made sense on paper. Iceland was a neutral place equidistant from both countries, one of the two locations suggested by Gorbachev (Britain was the other), but the reality was harsh. As I read and re-read the accounts, I was struck by how often everyone talked about the weather—particularly as I have read many accounts of other meetings and in none of them was the weather ever mentioned. This meeting took place in the bitter-cold and wintry landscape of Iceland, a tight little volcanic island set in the North Atlantic. I have been to Iceland in both spring and winter. In the spring it is sunny and covered by vast fields of lavender and purple lupines as far as the eye can see, but in the winter it is pitch-dark for most of the day, giving an overwhelming feeling of cold and the haunting unreal atmosphere of a lunar landscape.

The gloomy feeling engendered by the weather seems to have affected everybody. Reagan remembered an astronaut saying that "the moon was nicer than training in Iceland."

Gorbachev was shocked by his first sight of the country, writing, "We arrived in Iceland on the 10th of October. An unknown world opened before us—no trace of vegetation, nothing but rocks and boulders. And every half hour it would rain. Reykjavik means something like 'smoking place.' It appeared indeed as in a fog, which turned out to be steam produced by geysers."[4]

Secretary of State George Shultz, the ultimate experienced world traveler, took time to comment on how cold he was, writing that he had been in Iceland before and had found it comforting and exhilarating, but this time it was "foreboding, with endless hours of darkness."[5]

Then, too, accommodations were tight for all. President Reagan took over the modest residence of the American ambassador. Shultz was lodged in the small Holt Hotel that fronted on a narrow street far from the water. He describes rooms "small and taut as to give the cold, dark outside world as little space to penetrate as possible," and mentions a night when he was awakened by six members of the American delegation who crowded into his room at 2 a.m. for a rush meeting, saying that "an Icelandic chill penetrated the room," so much so that he had to put a sweater over his pajamas plus a bathrobe.[6]

As for the much larger Russian delegation, Gorbachev writes, "Our entire delegation stayed on the *George Otis*, an ocean liner which had sailed from Tallinn for this occasion." (Couldn't have been very comfortable, either, considering the turbulent sea.)

As if all that weren't enough, the meetings took place in a building, Hofdi House, that Shultz describes as "a grim structure set on a bare plain at the edge of the North Atlantic"[7] and Icelanders proclaimed to be haunted with gnomes and elves. Accommodations were so cramped that secretaries had to use the bathroom to do their secretarial work since there was no other space for the word processor and copier. Presidential meetings took place in a small room with not enough chairs and a view out to a gray and stormy sea. It rained so often that everyone arrived for meetings in dripping raincoats, blowing on their hands to warm them.

Once again, there were misunderstandings and miscalculations on both sides. While both leaders went to Reykjavik with hopes for starting on a path toward eliminating nuclear weapons, and the Soviet side considered Reykjavik vitally important, our side seems to have misread Gorbachev's intentions completely. From the beginning, wanting to emphasize that this was not a full-fledged "summit" but only "a meeting," both Shultz and Poindexter downplayed its importance, advising Reagan to proceed without permitting the impression that Reykjavik was a 'summit' or raising U.S. expectations for a future Summit III. In his briefing, Shultz advised Reagan that the Soviets were talking "from our script" when in fact they were about to present a new script.

In contrast to the extensive preparations for Reagan before Geneva, this time there was no real preparation for him and no new initiatives. On October 9, just before leaving for Iceland, the President wrote in his diary, *"I'm getting suspicious—here I am 12 hours away from leaving for Iceland and a half a dozen attempts are doing much to render me impotent and helpless in the face of Gorbachev."* He does not specify any details, but it is clear that from the first there were tensions and disagreements in the U.S. negotiating teams that continued during the meetings and made progress glacially slow. Gorbachev, too, was sharply critical of the Soviet bureaucracy.

Underlining our insistence that it was only "a meeting," our official delegation was small—only twelve people—and did not include any senior military officers, in contrast to the Soviets, who sent their top military man, Marshal Sergei Akhromeyev, Chief of the General Staff (comparable to the chairman of our Joint Chiefs of Staff), to serve as head negotiator. The U.S. chief negotiator was Paul Nitze,[8] considered the key architect of U.S. Cold War policy and the massive arms buildup under both Presidents Carter and Reagan. Nitze did not have authority to make a deal, but only to convene the meeting. Contrary to CIA advance reports that the Soviet military would be difficult and uncompromising, Akhromeyev turned out to be more reasonable than some Soviet Foreign Ministry delegates. In fact, Nitze was very impressed with Marshal Akhromeyev's "acuity of mind and command of the issues," declaring that in meetings "Akhromeyev is a first-class negotiator...a man of great courage and character."[9]

From the photographs, one is struck by the number of dark suits. Not a woman among them except for the ever-present and stern Rozanne Ridgway. Jack Matlock admits that he made a serious mistake in advising the President not to bring Mrs. Reagan along, and had assumed that "Gorbachev would do the same." In contrast, when the Soviet Foreign Ministry sent Gorbachev a draft schedule of activities that omitted any mention of his wife, he returned it saying, "You have reserved no time for me to consult my wife," and placed her number one on the list of delegates[10]—an insight into the difference between the American and Soviet approaches. Mrs. Reagan seems not to have been informed of the fact that it had been *our* side that decided she not come, and not that Raisa Gorbacheva had pushed her way in. Had Nancy known the facts, she could have insisted on the same responsibility for herself, The result was that she was furious and her husband annoyed. Why, I wondered, did we "assume"? Surely we must have received the list of Soviet delegates in advance. It seems a lack of human understanding about the talents of and the sometimes critical role that women can play, and, as it turned out, was a serious diplomatic error.

Human rights, regional issues, and communications were discussed, but the central issues were arms control and reductions—to which Reagan and Gorbachev returned over and over in intense discussions. There was stubbornness, suspicion, and acrimony on the part of Gorbachev. Gorbachev made the dramatic proposal that strategic missiles should be reduced by fifty percent,[11] along with the entire spectrum of arsenals. Reagan, while being generously and genuinely forthcoming, was unyielding in his conviction that only SDI, a space-based defense system, would eventually make possible the elimination of all nuclear ballistic missiles and shield America (and Russia as well) from potential atomic missile attack from each other and possible rogue states. Reagan presented a visionary, indeed, revolutionary, far-reaching concept. He proposed that testing of SDI would take place in the presence of Soviet observers who would inspect our research, progress, and results. If tests showed that the system worked, the U.S. would be obligated to share it with the Soviet Union.

Then an agreement could be negotiated on the elimination of all ballistic missiles and sharing SDI. But despite his efforts, he could not overcome Gorbachev's suspicions: "Excuse me, Mr. President, but I do not take your idea of sharing SDI seriously. You don't want to share even petroleum equipment, automatic machine tools, or equipment for dairies, while sharing SDI would be a second American Revolution. And revolutions don't occur that often."[12]

To which President Reagan replied, "If I thought that SDI could not be shared, I would have rejected it myself."

Nevertheless, despite Reagan's eloquent arguments and explanations, Gorbachev and the Soviets remained unswayed from their conviction that SDI, should it continue, would give the United States a permanent military advantage.

From our conversations at lunch on September 23, I knew how ardently the President wanted to accomplish reduction in weapons and move toward abolishing nuclear weapons, so I could in some small way appreciate his acute distress at the failure of his hopes. He had gone much further in his proposals than those of the U.S. defense establishment, and indeed, so much so that I couldn't help thinking that despite his popularity and great powers of persuasion, even he might have had a tough time getting his agenda approved in the U.S.

Both leaders had gone to Reykjavik with high hopes, and both were bitterly disappointed in the failure to reach agreement. In the famous photographs showing them leaving Hofdi House on the last day, their stricken faces show it. When the crestfallen Gorbachev asked Reagan, "I don't think you wanted an agreement. What else could I have done?" Reagan replied tersely, "You could have said 'yes.'"[13]

In studying the official accounts of that historic near-miss meeting, I had an overwhelming sense of the folly and aridity of the Cold War. Mutual arms buildup had become an uncontrollable monster with the dismal impossibility of ever toning it down. Over four decades, both sides had accumulated several mountains of ever more complicated and sophisticated weapons. A measure of the surreal situation into which we had fallen was demonstrated to me by the futile effort to compare apples (super bombers) with oranges (ballistic missiles) when it was impossible to equate all this deadly power in any way that could satisfy both sides. How could we all have gotten so completely focused on piling up weapon after weapon when it was obvious that we could annihilate each other—along with the world—with a *fraction* of these instruments of death? Madness.

Add to this the heaviness and mutual suspicion between the bureaucrats of both sides, coupled with their own internal disagreements and vying for position, and the multi-preparations limiting the President, one can only feel sympathy for the two hamstrung leaders. This was true of both sides. Gorbachev sternly criticized the sluggish Soviet bureaucracy. The Soviet side also complained that there was so much squabbling and disagreement among differing factions on their team at Reykjavik that progress made a snail look swift.

It was clear that Gorbachev had faced problems at home—as Reagan had also. Gorbachev was to write about the prelude to Reykjavik in Moscow: "Our generals and some people in the Foreign Ministry...were doubtful. They were firmly stuck in a logic of antagonism, and the military sought to protect their corporate interests. The existing state of affairs seemed to suit some of our negotiators in Geneva, who enjoyed having their wages paid in hard currency, thinking 'longer the negotiations, the better for us.'"[14]

No wonder all participants were exhausted with the Herculean effort of trying to reach any mutually acceptable final agreements, so that both leaders, although sharing the same goal, could find no way to untangle themselves—certainly not in the two short days allotted to the meeting. In the end, Reykjavik turned out to be perhaps the greatest *what-if* U.S.–Soviet meeting of the Cold War. Here are a few that occurred to me:

What if it had taken place in the sun, perhaps on an island in the Caribbean, the sunshine seasoned with good meals and a few vodka toasts?

What if Bud McFarlane had still been NSC advisor? Could he, an internationalist and supporter of the President's search for better relations while always protecting America's interests, have found a way to a compromise?

What if Nancy had been there to provide her advice, her support, and her acute judgment of those surrounding her husband? Everyone around the President knew how much he needed her and the strength and comfort she gave him. In that lonely and ghostly place, had she been there (as Matlock later wrote he regretted bitterly),[15] Reagan might have stayed the extra day the Soviets had asked for and might have reached some last-minute agreement with Gorbachev.

And most importantly, *what if* our side had been properly informed about Gorbachev's intentions and priorities, which instead came as a total surprise? What if we had been better prepared and had not insisted that it be regarded as only a "meeting" and "not a summit"? All the more so since, ironically, Shultz wrote afterwards that "in the eyes of the world, Reykjavik would become the epitome of the very word, 'summit.'"[16] It is chilling to read Shultz, who ends his account of Reykjavik: "I saw once again how poor the quality of our intelligence was about the Soviet Union. We had no accurate help from the intelligence community about what to expect; in fact, the message we received from the CIA about what to expect in Reykjavik was exactly contrary to what happened. The Soviet military was well represented, and, in the person of Marshal Akhromeyev, presented the most reasonable Soviet face."[17]

After the President got home, he faced acerbic comments from the U.S. right wing, among them that he had flopped the greatest chance to cash in on "star wars." There was a flurry of criticisms, including one from Admiral Bill Crowe on behalf of the military chiefs who were upset that they had not been there. They were alarmed at the idea of giving up ballistic missiles and felt that Reagan had gone too far.[18] Richard Burt and Rozanne Ridgway thought our policy would create a major danger to the alliance and were joined in this opinion by the old warhorse, Henry Kissinger. In the White House and the Pentagon, there was shock and negative opinions among many of the staff. Poindexter tried to talk the President out of his main idea, saying that it would be "disastrous to eliminate nuclear weapons."[19] For him, Weinberger, and many in the State Department, Reykjavik was seen as a blunder of the greatest magnitude.

Surprising to me is that the naysayers didn't seem to properly appreciate the President's clearly voiced goals and longtime fierce determination to find a way to rid the world of the fear of nuclear annihilation. I agreed with Shultz when he reminded them that "once the President has an idea in his head, it stays there." He writes, "Reagan had acted outside the boundaries and had attacked the accepted conventional wisdom. The world was not ready for Reagan's boldness."[20]

(Underscoring the opposition that Reagan faced, Roald Sagdeev, the Soviet Union's great physicist and advisor to Gorbachev on SDI, told me this shocking story: that one of the Soviet delegates returning to Moscow from Reykjavik had told him that one of the American delegates had approached him at the end of the meeting and said, "Thank you for stopping our crazy president.")

Sadly, Reagan would write, "At Reykjavik, my hopes for a nuclear-free world soared briefly, then fell, during the longest, most disappointing—and ultimately angriest—days of my presidency."[21]

But the initial judgment of the media, along with the popular opinion in Washington that Reykjavik was "a failure," was wrong. According to Shultz, "The achievements of the Reykjavik summit were greater than any U.S.–Soviet meeting before. Despite the failure to achieve agreement, the accomplishments were immense. We had arrived at an important turning point. Human rights became part of our permanent agenda.... Glimpsed was the possibility of diminished danger from possible nuclear devastation."[22]

They were joined in this opinion by Gorbachev, whose account[23] says that, as they stood by his car, Reagan reproached him saying, "You planned from the start to come here and put me in this situation." Writes

Gorbachev, "'No, Mr. President,' I replied. 'I'm ready to go right back in the house and sign a comprehensive document on all issues agreed if you drop your plans to militarize space.' 'I'm really sorry,' said Reagan. We made our farewells and he left in his car and did not wait for the final press conference."[24]

So Gorbachev was left to face a huge crowd of newsmen alone. He goes on to say that, although angered by the result and Reagan's parting words, as he walked down to the press conference, he decided that he should cool off and not gain propaganda advantage by blaming it all on U.S. recalcitrance. He gives this emotional account: "About a thousand journalists were waiting for us. When I came into the room, the merciless, often cynical and cheeky journalists stood up in silence. I sensed the anxiety in the air. I suddenly felt emotional, even shaken. Those people standing in front of me seemed to represent mankind waiting for its fate to be decided. At that moment, I realized the true meaning of Reykjavik and knew what further course to follow." The whole speech was published and commented on by journalists, scientists, and politicians, but *my* key phrase was: "Reykjavik is not a failure—it is a breakthrough which allowed us for the first time to look over the horizon."[25]

The audience gave him thunderous applause. A Soviet journalist wrote later that "When the General Secretary presented the failure of Reykjavik as strengthening our conviction that we had chosen the right course and that the Reykjavik meeting was a victory, Raisa Gorbacheva was sitting in the conference hall looking with awe at her husband with tears rolling down her face."[26]

Only two weeks later, Politburo notes show that Gorbachev had largely accepted Reagan's formulation and that he had come to accept the genuineness of Reagan's proposal, but it was too late. In the United States, Irangate exploded and Reagan's poll numbers dropped. He had lost the initiative. Yet many positive things had shifted the ground importantly, not the least of which was that the Soviets had for the first time accepted an American agenda as the base for their discussions. Both sides felt they had offered substantial concessions, but in the end remained deadlocked over a single word: "laboratories".

But perhaps the bottom line was expressed by Georgy Arbatov, whose final comment to Paul Nitze was, "Accepting your offer would require an exceptional level of *trust* (italics mine). We cannot accept your proposals."

And thus, tragically, a great historic possibility passed. I felt great sadness for both disappointed leaders and that my own efforts to try to promote that trust and understanding on both sides were not nearly enough to overcome the deeply ingrained suspicions that lingered. Still, I remained hopeful, and in the end, Reykjavik did turn out to be an important step forward.

CHAPTER 14

NANCY

During her husband's years in the White House, there was a lot of mean press and gossip about Nancy Reagan. There was clucking about Nancy's love for designer clothes (why not about Jackie's, which always won her extravagant praise?), her California society friends, and a lot about her powerful behind the scene influence and fierce protectiveness of her husband. She was sometimes caricatured, but the measure of a First Lady is not how popular she is with the press or the public,[1] but how much she helps the president, and in that role Nancy Reagan was an unquestioned success.

For me, it was only common sense that *of course* she had a powerful influence; she and the President were so obviously in love and so deeply attached to each other. No one was closer to him than his adored Nancy; there was no one he needed or trusted more. They shared everything. Over and over again, he stated how important she was to him and how passionately he loved her. Devoted wife that she was, he was always at the center of her radar screen, and she sought to protect her beloved man in any way she could. She was not like Jackie Kennedy, with her interest in the arts, or the retiring Bess Truman, or Mamie Eisenhower, the military wife, or Hillary Clinton with her personal career agenda, or the overwhelming and outspoken Barbara Bush who followed her. For Nancy, it was always clear that everything she did was for the good of her Ronnie, and for this I always sympathized with and respected her.

I did not get to know her as well as I got to know the President and I am sorry for that; I wish I could have known her better. I saw her close up only a few times. Early on, it occurred to me that if even a fraction of what was said in the press about their devotion to each other were true, then if

I were Nancy, I would want to take a look at *any* woman he was talking to about *anything*. So before our next meeting, in a letter to the President, I mentioned how much it would mean to me if Mrs. Reagan could find herself free to join us in the Oval Office, and I was very happy when she decided to come. She was very quiet, listened carefully, and seemed to me to be a bit overawed and unaccustomed to being in meetings in the Oval Office.

After that first meeting, I had three private lunches with her and the President and two meetings with her alone in the personal quarters of the White House. I saw her at a few formal occasions, including the State Dinner for Gorbachev. Over the years, I received some notes from her and had a handful of telephone conversations. She always impressed me as very feminine, the epitome of a romantic Hollywood heroine of the late '40s and early '50s. Exceptionally thin, she seemed as tiny and fragile as porcelain. She was always impeccably groomed and dressed in an elegant Bel Air, California, way[2]—not a wrinkle in her clothes or a speck of dirt on her shoes, not a hair out of place in her bouffant hairdo—and yet there was a touching air of vulnerability about her.

But when necessary, she could and did fight fiercely for her man, acting as a buffer against predators. It was said that she watched his advisors like a hawk and, in her own way, saw to their demise if she thought they were not loyal or supportive enough of her Ronnie. I can understand this and applaud her for it. She loved him, protected him, and kept him close, devotedly watching over and caring for him during the ten heart-shattering years when he disappeared from the world and from her with Alzheimer's.

Politically, she had a centrist agenda and an acute sense of public sentiment, as well as the worthy goal of keeping the President from being captured by the far right. Her instinct for moderation led her into White House controversies over everything from social policy (her "Just Say No" war against drugs) to U.S.–Soviet relations. (Reagan wrote that when she met Andrei Gromyko in 1984 and he asked her, "Does your husband believe in peace?" Nancy said, "Yes, of course." Then he said, "Whisper *peace* in his ear every night," and she responded, "I will, and I'll also whisper it in your ear." She leaned over and did so.)

In the time-tested feminine way of wives of kings and powerful leaders of history, she operated quietly by building coalitions of allies, maneuvering powerfully behind the scenes with the help of others, notably her chief surrogate and longtime friend, Michael Deaver. In her terrible grief and fear[3] after the attempt on Reagan's life in 1981, she turned to an astrologer and took a lot of cruel and unfeeling criticism from those who have never had to face such a wrenching tragedy. Having been the mother of a son with hemophilia and facing the unexpected near death of my second husband from a terrible accident, I knew firsthand how one can desperately seek any way to gain some control over the uncontrollable. It did no harm and gave her some peace. I thought such criticism also had the whiff of hypocrisy. She was hardly alone in consulting the stars. I have found over the years that just about anyone I meet, anywhere in the world, immediately knows their astrological sun sign, and few resist the temptation to turn to the horoscopes in the daily papers and magazines.

After the attempt on his life, she came to believe that her husband's destiny was to be a peacemaker and to end the Cold War. Although it had been more than six years since an American president had met with a Soviet leader, she lobbied constantly for him to meet face to face with one. A White House official remembered that "she would grab George Shultz and others and ask, 'What are we doing about this?'" When recovering from the assassination attack, Reagan's original handwritten letter to Brezhnev was returned to him rewritten by the administration's Soviet experts, who thought it naïve, but with Deaver's urging and hers, the President's original handwritten letter went to Brezhnev along with the official one from State Department.

The Secretary of State and some in the NSC, as well as other advisors, felt the President was not "up to"[4] meeting alone with Gorbachev and strongly opposed this idea, firm in their conviction that only the State Department and their experts knew what to do. Bud McFarlane, who supported the idea, sought Nancy's assistance and, strongly backed by her, in the end it was she who tipped the decision that resulted in the Geneva meeting.

Astute woman that she was, she always knew that although anticommunism was popular, peace was more popular. Always mindful of Reagan's potential legacy, she encouraged her husband to quiet his anti-Soviet rhetoric and wanted him to hear other points of view. I was one of these, and was told by McFarlane and also by Michael Beschloss, the presidential historian, that she and Deaver were pleased by my first visit and urged that there be additional meetings. Given her strong sense of protectiveness, I can only surmise that my subsequent meetings with the President might not have continued as they did if she had been against them.

Typical of the often nasty press notices, it was cattily intimated in the newspapers that when she received Frank Sinatra to tea, she left orders not to be disturbed—as if there were something suspicious in that! Well, I can report that even though I was not a longtime friend like Frank Sinatra, when in early 1987 Mrs. Reagan invited me to tea in the lovely living room of the family quarters of the White House, she also left strict orders that she was not to be disturbed, evidently her common practice. Nevertheless, during our tea the phone rang. Answering, she reiterated that she was *not* to be disturbed. A short time later, it rang again and her tone was chilly when she repeated this. When it rang a third time, she looked prepared to explode. But when she impatiently picked up the phone, she looked up at me and in a soft voice that held the delight and joy of a teenage girl, she covered the receiver and said happily, "It's my husband!"

At first, we talked generally about how relations with the Soviet Union were progressing, and she told me that Jack Matlock had been appointed to be the new ambassador to Moscow. Given his experience, she said, she was sure I would approve.

But that was not the only thing on her agenda that day; there was something else bothering her. I certainly didn't expect what followed and was shocked when she angrily exclaimed, "The Soviets have refused my son, Ron Junior, a visa!" and, very agitated, continued, "How could Mr. Gorbachev do that!" This could indeed be viewed as an underhanded slap, especially considering the fact that since their Geneva meeting, Reagan and Gorbachev had been exchanging regular letters and Reagan had invited Gorbachev to Washington. Still, having had plenty of experience with the Soviet bureaucracy and knowing how often the right hand didn't seem to know what the left hand was doing, I hastened to reassure her, saying that I was *sure* that Mr. Gorbachev knew nothing about it and would never have done *that*. As I was about to go to the USSR again, I tried to calm her and offered to try to clear up the matter.

Thinking it over afterwards, I realized what might have happened. ABC television had hired young Ron to make some commentaries for a TV program during a trip they were planning to make to the Soviet Union. It had also been announced that the network was planning to show a film titled *Amerika* that showed the Soviet Union in an extremely unfavorable light. The Soviets protested shrilly, but when ABC went ahead and aired the film anyway, in clumsy retaliation the heavy-handed Soviet bureaucracy decreed that every employee of ABC was to be refused a visa. I figured that young Ron might have fallen into that collective basket.[5]

When I arrived in Moscow a short time later, I called Bogdanov who took the matter very seriously. I was told to come to the USA Institute immediately. Always wary of what he might have up his sleeve, I didn't want to go there alone without anyone knowing my whereabouts. Once again, the military came to my aid. Colonel John Concannon, a friend from Odom's West Point instructor group who was then Military Attaché at our embassy, offered to drive me there. One of those sinister black limousines was waiting under the portico. Telling John that I would check with him when I got back, I walked to meet it and got in. Bogdanov was inside, and we were immediately driven to the inner sanctum building that was the Central Committee headquarters. It was a formidably guarded place, soldiers in front and inside. One opened a locked elevator and accompanied us going up and another when we left going down.

Bogdanov took me to an office on the same floor and a few doors away from that of Gorbachev himself where I confronted a man named Vitaly Gussenko, one of Gorbachev's two personal advisors, sitting in a spacious office behind a very large desk. He was a courteous, very intelligent man who spoke perfect French.

Even though I was fluent in Russian, I remembered again the astute counsel I had received from the friend of my father, Raymond Probst, former Swiss Ambassador in the United States and later Secretary of State in the Swiss Foreign Ministry. Probst's father was Swiss, his mother Russian. He spoke Russian fluently and had given me some precious advice: "Never speak Russian in official meetings. They will always speak it better than you do. Instead," he said, "listen carefully to the speaker and then use the additional time taken by the translator to think over what you have heard before you answer. Then, after six, in social occasions, speak Russian." The astute advice of this experienced diplomat had served me well in other official meetings and, on this occasion, as French was my native language, I decided to use it. First I delivered the President's message that cordially invited Gorbachev to come to Washington. Thus positively begun, I then took the opportunity to mention the question of the refusal of a visa to Ron Jr. Gussenko looked genuinely startled to learn of this and indicated that Mr. Gorbachev did not know of this either. (Just as I had suspected, those on high knew nothing about what the lower-level drones might have done.) He explained apologetically that what had occurred was that personnel of ABC had been refused as an expression of disapproval of their series *Amerika*, but **not** Ron individually. About ABC he asked me "What would you have done?" I answered, "I would have let them come." He said "This was not possible" and went on to say that they had received a great deal of mail from offended Soviet citizens demanding some kind of governmental reaction to what was seen as an affront to their country. When I went on to describe my conversation with Mrs. Reagan, her consternation and annoyance with Mr. Gorbachev he looked aghast, realizing immediately that in a delicate period when there was a fragile warming of superpower relations, relatively small personal matters could sometimes affect larger ones, and that, indeed, this action might have seemed a premeditated insult. Very concerned about what might be its potential effect, he asked me apprehensively, "Surely this will not affect our ongoing relations with the President?"

"No," I answered soothingly, "I can't imagine that it would, but you know that the feelings of a mother can be very strong."

"Yes, yes," he agreed hurriedly. "Of course. Please tell Mrs. Reagan that her son will be welcome in the Soviet Union whenever he would like to come. Please assure her of this."

When we left, accompanied by a soldier all the way out until we got back in the black car, Bogdanov paid me a rare compliment: "My congratulations," said he. "You handled that with brilliant diplomacy." (Gussenko called me back the next day with the personal response of General Secretary Gorbachev and expressed feelings of gratitude from them both for the invitation.)

It is no secret that from the time they first met at the Geneva Summit, Mrs. Reagan did not get on well with Mrs. Gorbachev, and their tiffs were eagerly exploited and exaggerated by the press. It always seemed to me that some of their differences could have been smoothed over with a little explanation,[6] and I often wondered where our diplomats were—or theirs, for that matter. Too occupied with arms control, I guess, to bother with the ladies. No one seemed to have prepared either of them for their first encounter.

No two women could have been more different. Nancy was Big City elegant, sophisticated and tart. Born in New York, gently raised in Chicago where her father was Professor of Surgery at Northwestern University, she had graduated from prestigious Smith College, where she studied drama, and later became an actress in New York and Hollywood. Raisa was a provincial Soviet woman, of working class parents, her father a train engineer, born in a small town in the sparsely populated region of Altai, a remote mountainous area in Siberia bordering China, Mongolia, and Kazakhstan.

Ambitious and hardworking, she tenaciously worked her way up from the provinces to earn an advanced degree at Moscow State Pedagogical Institute and taught briefly at Moscow State University, and, knowing no other, was committed, indeed imbued, with the pedantic and verbose communist style and point of view.

Nancy was eighteen years older, with years of experience in society and the glare of public life as the wife of a famous actor, important governor, and President of the United States. Raisa Maximova had met her husband at a ballroom dancing class when he, the son of an agricultural mechanic on a collective farm, was a law student at Moscow University. She married him at age twenty-one in 1953 and spent the next twenty-three years living in the small city of Stavropol in a mountainous region of southern Russia near Georgia. It was 800 miles from Moscow, light years away from sophistication and savoir faire, a town that one Soviet émigré described as "an overgrown village whose life centered on a single street." There she taught Marxist-Leninist philosophy in a local school, worked on her dissertation, and received the equivalent of a Ph.D. in sociology in 1967 while her husband worked his way up the Party ladder. Attractive and ideologically correct, she helped him entertain important Soviet higher-ups who came for vacations at nearby spas, the most important among them Yuri Andropov, head of the KGB. (When Raisa saw a picture of Andropov in Washington, she exclaimed, "We owe him everything.")

Then, in 1985, she was abruptly metamorphosed into the only real "First Lady" of the Soviet Union in history, a role for which there was no previous model and no accumulated feminine experience in the finer points of international social protocol or diplomacy. When she met Mrs. Reagan, her husband had been in power for only nine short months. So it is no surprise that the relations of two such different women with such diametrically opposite backgrounds and styles got off on a very wrong foot.

Their first meeting in Geneva was disastrous. At my first private lunch with the President and Mrs. Reagan, in June 1986 out on the secluded patio behind the Oval Office, I asked her about her impressions of Raisa.

There was no doubt that she had made a terrible first impression, and Mrs. Reagan needed no urging to talk openly about it. Hearing her unsparing description, I could certainly understand why she felt so strongly. She began by telling me that when Raisa came to call on her, the first thing she said was that the chair offered for her was "not right" and asked that another be brought, and then, still not satisfied, yet another. "Something I would *never* do!" said Mrs. Reagan. "She talked nonstop, and there was no way to stop her unless you pressed in."

Mrs. Reagan had noticed that her guest was wearing a tie and wondered, "Why in the world is she dressed like that?" When she discovered later that Raisa was the only one shown in the picture that appeared in the Soviet press, and that she was dressed in the style of a Soviet professor, Mrs. Reagan realized, "She wanted to show herself in that get-up!" Later, when Mrs. Reagan made a reciprocal visit to Raisa Maximova at the Soviet headquarters, she found a table groaning "with pies and so much food!" (I tried to explain that this is a Russian custom for honored guests, but it was obviously overkill in this case.) Raisa shocked Mrs. Reagan with her nouveau important manner, "throwing her weight around," imperiously "ordering her servants about with a snap of her fingers," and saying, "It is so difficult for someone in my position, with all the demands of my position. It is so difficult. I am so busy."

"We all are, dear," commented Mrs. Reagan dryly.

I asked, "What did she talk about?"

"She kept pointing out missiles," continued Mrs. Reagan. "A book of children's photographs and weapons was brought out, and she kept pointing out children and the missiles and the weapons." Over and over until fed up, Mrs. Reagan said tartly, "I can tell a missile all by myself." To top this off, "She talked on and on about Russia and how wonderful Russia was, and I don't know what. There was no way to talk except to just break in!"

(As I listened to all this, I thought it sounded a lot like the old Russian fairy tale about a poor fisherman who caught a golden carp and was granted three wishes. He got rich and his wife grew more and more puffed up, asking for more and more. When she finally asked for the sun, the fairies got furious and reduced her husband back to a poor fisherman. Some Russians I knew had a word for Raisa: "She is a Russian *baba*,"—a colloquial expression with several meanings, in this case, an uncultured woman.)

At a later encounter, Mrs. Reagan, who always stood by gazing adoringly at her husband, found it unthinkable "that when the press asked Raisa's husband a question, she contradicted him!"

"Well, how did he react?" I asked.

"He just looked at her."

I volunteered that possibly Raisa's toughness was something he needed, as Russians like strong women. At this, Mrs. Reagan paused thoughtfully for a moment, but went on, "She played to the press. She loved to be photographed, loved to be in the limelight, and sometimes even flirted with the press."

At dinner with the Reagans and other official guests, Raisa Maximova inappropriately launched into a lengthy and pedantic dialogue on Soviet policy, and after the Gorbachevs had left, Nancy fumed within the hearing of the other guests, "Who does that dame think she is?" (Secretary Shultz, who was present, later described Raisa to me more diplomatically: "Well, she is quite attractive, quite intelligent, but I wouldn't want her as a cruise companion.")

But then, hearing all this and knowing the Soviet Union as well as I did, Raisa's heavy-handedness was a little more understandable. At home, she came as shock to the entire Soviet system and she was much criticized. In the Soviet Union, it was said that "she wears the pants in the family and doesn't know her place," and, wearing furs when she went to visit a factory, was accused of "showing off." A Soviet translator commented sourly, "She shouldn't lecture everyone she meets."

Previous wives of Soviet leaders had barely been glimpsed. Raisa was a new phenomenon, the first wife of a Soviet leader to be young, with a red-hennaed, saucy haircut and a blinding smile, stylishly dressed and attractive, the first to be seen publicly and, contrary to customary Soviet practice, to accompany her husband on foreign trips. Indeed, on her initial trip to France in 1985, she confided privately to Madame Mitterrand, "Give me some tips. I'm new at this job." A neophyte with no experience on the world stage, over-puffed with new importance, a professor of Marxism trained in the pedantic Soviet academic style, no doubt overanxious to represent her country and describe what she thought were its merits, it was pretty obvious that, as the French expression goes, she "didn't know which leg to dance on" and certainly picked the wrong leg.

(It was easy to trip up. Mrs. Gromyko, who was rarely seen in public, was once attending a diplomatic reception in Moscow. Anxious to demonstrate her knowledge of English, she brightly responded to a toast by exclaiming, "Up bottoms!" Raisa, too, knowing a handful of English expressions, some totally inappropriate, once startled reporters by saying knowingly, "See you later, alligator.")

After the Geneva debacle, another slap followed. It had been decided officially (by the U.S. side) that no wives would come to the Reykjavik meeting in October 1986, so Mrs. Reagan was outraged when she heard that Raisa was going anyway. In Boston, while dining at the venerable Chilton Club with Muffie Brandon, who had been a member of the First Lady's social staff told me about Mrs. Reagan's annoyance and urged me to call her. I hesitated, but at Muffie's insistence, I placed the call from the club's old-fashioned wooden phone booth. I was immediately put through to Mrs. Reagan, who angrily sputtered, "*That* woman! I don't know what she is trying to do! It was decided that there would be no women, and I am *not* going, no matter what she does!"

I did my best to try to soothe her, but I am sure it couldn't have helped things much when a complete press blackout imposed by the American side during the Reykjavik conference left the press photographers with little to do. So they flocked to photograph Raisa wearing a flirtatious fox-fur jacket as if she were a new starlet. (When Mrs. Gorbachev arrived in Washington with her husband in 1987 and cheerfully said, "I missed you in Reykjavik," Mrs. Reagan, still miffed, icily replied, "I was told women weren't invited.")

The faux pas continued. As protocol dictated, Mrs. Reagan immediately invited Mrs. Gorbachev to lunch. No reply. Finally the First Lady's office was notified that Mrs. Gorbachev could not make lunch. Mrs. Reagan then invited her to tea instead. With her office impatiently holding her schedule open, again the answer was long in coming, and when finally one did, it was that Mrs. Gorbachev couldn't come for tea, but would come for coffee. To which Mrs. Reagan angrily remarked, "When one asks someone to tea it is *not* for coffee!" Then, to top it off, came the news that Mrs. Gorbachev had accepted an invitation to lunch from Pamela Harriman—a major donor and supporter of the Democratic Party. There Raisa discussed the U.S. Supreme Court and the inner workings of Congress with Barbara Mikulski, who said, "She talks in paragraphs like an Eastern Europe professor." However educational that lunch might have been for Raisa, it remains incomprehensible to me how the suave and experienced former Soviet Ambassador Anatoly Dobrynin, who knew Washington backwards and forwards, could ever have permitted such snubs of the First Lady.

Then there was Raisa's much-publicized visit to the White House. In Russia, when one is invited to see an important place, it is considered courteous to bone up as much as possible in advance as a compliment to the host. So when Mrs. Gorbachev came to the White House, in front of the press she, (I believe unknowingly), thought she was doing the customary thing in exhibiting her knowledge. Instead, she deeply embarrassed Mrs. Reagan—who was recovering from breast cancer surgery and mourning the recent death of her mother—by relentlessly questioning her and seeming to know more about the White House portraits and art collections than she did. This onslaught left Mrs. Reagan to say lamely, "I'm afraid I'm not much help."

A witness to this commented, "Their face-off was extraordinary. They didn't seem to understand each other." Why not? Again I wondered where all the diplomats were. It would have been easy to explain this Russian custom to Mrs. Reagan in advance, thus saving her from painful embarrassment and allowing her to take the high road by graciously complimenting Mrs. Gorbachev on being so knowledgeable about our country's historic building.

All of this was too bad—a debacle of diplomacy on both sides. For despite their very different backgrounds and Raisa's unschooled and sometimes crude behavior, the ladies had some important things in common. Both enjoyed unusually happy and close marriages and played an influential role in their husband's political life as close friend and advisor. In Paris, Raisa had once confided to a dinner companion about her relationship with her husband saying, "We are really friends, or, if you prefer, we have a great rapport."

Her husband seemed to enjoy her feistiness, saying on one occasion, "My wife is a very independent lady." In a TV interview with Tom Brokaw, when Gorbachev was asked if he discussed "Soviet affairs at the highest level" with his wife, he answered, "We discuss everything."[7]

Who knows; if the two ladies had developed a better connection, they might have been able to coordinate their efforts to whisper "peace" into their respective husbands' ears. Then too, both ladies worked hard on worthy independent projects of their own, to which they devoted much energy and time and which they could have fruitfully discussed. Nancy became a champion of the pioneering Foster Grandparents Program and authored a book, *To Love a Child*, on the subject. In connection with her "Just Say No" campaign against drug and alcohol abuse, Nancy traveled to forty-seven cities in thirty-five states as well as abroad, and lectured on the subject at the UN. In a Soviet Union rife with alcoholism and beginning to cope with drug addiction brought home by veterans of Afghanistan, Raisa might have profited from Nancy's experience.

On her side, Raisa was a founder of the Russian Cultural Foundation (where I once gave a lecture), dedicated to preserving Russian culture, the first such effort independent of the Ministry of Culture. She actively supported the Russian charity "From the Hematologists of the World to Children," she and her husband making generous contributions to buy equipment for blood banks and train Russian doctors abroad, resulting in improved surgical success rates and blood-cancer treatment for children nationwide in Russia. Ironically, Raisa herself died of leukemia in 1999 at the early age of 67, leaving her husband disconsolate.

These were missed opportunities. Something that often seems to be forgotten in modern diplomacy is that diplomacy is not only about position papers and conferences, but is above all, about relations between people—something that President Reagan understood perfectly.

As for me, there was one important missed opportunity, which I attribute to my false sense of propriety. At that memorable June lunch, I had a very interesting conversation with the President, which I have detailed in an earlier chapter. But after the President left for a signing ceremony, Mrs. Reagan and I were left alone to talk privately for a while. We continued the topic of problems of representation, a subject that the President had brought up. I told her, as I had told the President, that I felt there were constituencies we had not touched—notably women—that our circles were too narrow and needed to be opened out. I expressed my thanks to her, saying that her presence at our morning meeting had been a great help to me, bringing as she did, a different sensitivity, which I appreciated.

I mentioned that I had noticed a tremendous calm and strength in the President, and felt that she must be a great source of this inner calm and strength and that this realization had touched me very much. I said I would write a letter of thanks for our lunch, but she said, "No, please don't write just for that, but I do hope you will give your ideas." And again, "Please do write your ideas."

Her unexpected request came as a surprise for which I was totally unprepared. I considered that my meetings with the President were as a private citizen, not an official advisor, and not knowing quite how to answer, I responded reluctantly, "Well, I wouldn't presume to just volunteer my ideas."

"Please do," she urged again. I asked her where she would be. She said, "Sometimes in California, but of course everything always reaches us wherever we are," and again urged, "Please write your ideas." Then she added, "And if you find it uncomfortable to write to him, write to me."

Without saying it, both of us knew what she meant—any letter I would write to the President was seen by many eyes in the National Security Council and elsewhere, but if I were to write to her, it wouldn't be seen at all. I didn't realize then what a tremendous offer that was and never implemented it, foolishly hesitating and thinking it an imposition for me to do so. I wish I had taken her advice. Not to have done so was a big mistake on my part. The only time I did send a few of my ideas to her was more than a year later, when in 1987 I sent Mrs. Reagan a short paper about social problems in the Soviet Union and possible discussion points for a conversation with Mrs. Gorbachev. I never knew if she received it.

I will always remember the many gracious attentions that came from Nancy Reagan during those Washington years, I received some very nice notes from her, one thanking me for a small icon from a young Russian who had asked me to give it to her with his warm wishes. She invited me to the Senate wives' luncheon at the White House and to the small star-studded breakfast for special guests that preceded the historic moment when the Gorbachevs arrived on the White House lawn for the official greeting ceremony. She included me among the guests of the super-exclusive State Dinner that evening, thoughtfully arranging to send one of the military aides in a White House limousine to fetch me so I wouldn't have to arrive at the dinner alone. These were all things that she absolutely didn't have to do, and I remain always grateful to her for according me these precious memories.

CHAPTER 15

GORBACHEV COMES TO WASHINGTON
DECEMBER 7, 1987

In March of 1987 the President Reagan had asked me to carry an invitation to Moscow for Gorbachev. He had spoken to him directly in Geneva and had made clear his desire to receive him in Washington, but there had been no definite reply through official channels, so the President asked me to deliver his invitation once more which I did through Vitaly Gussenko, one of Gorbachev's two personal advisors, when I had seen him in Moscow. The message read:

> *The First Lady and I are still very much looking forward to the opportunity to welcome you and Mrs. Gorbachev to the United States in 1987, with my coming to the USSR in the following year. There is much to discuss in our continuing face-to-face dialogue, and I would hope to hear from you at an early date.*

Despite the disappointment of the Reykjavik meeting, the back-and-forth false starts, the long hoped for, long awaited visit of Gorbachev to our capital finally took place in early December 1987. It sent shock waves through the small southern city, stifling hot in the summer, panicked by an inch of snow in the winter, hermetically sealed from the outside world, that is Washington.

Like any small town, Washington's lifeblood is intrigue, nourished by gossip. Every day, there are cocktail parties and receptions taking place all over the city where deals are made, positions sought, and eyes dart about to see who might be more important than the person they happen to be talking to. Small, intimate Georgetown parties are given by ambitious, well-heeled society hostesses vying for influence. All those cocktail parties and dinners have only one goal in mind: power. Mecca is the White House, which looks more like the mansion of a plantation owner of the Old South than the heart of the most powerful nation in the world. Combining as it does the trinity that drives Washington—politics, policy, and society—an invitation to a State dinner at the White House is the pinnacle, the ne plus ultra test of status.

I had only been to a State dinner once before, in 1968 after the publication of *Nicholas and Alexandra*. My first husband, Robert Massie, and I were invited by President Lyndon Johnson and his wife, Lady Bird. The President greeted me with a Texas style bear hug, and I met Anatoly Dobrynin, then Soviet Ambassador in Washington, who, said the President when he introduced me, had liked our book.[1] That was a memorable occasion, but even in blasé Washington, accustomed to the visits of foreign potentates, the first visit of the Gorbachevs was, reported *The Washington Post*, "like Christmas, New Year's, and July 4th rolled into one." It was a historic trip from start to finish.

From the time Gorbachev stepped out of his plane, the press breathlessly covered every moment. Upon his arrival, Gorbachev made news immediately, announcing in friendly but forceful tones, "The visit has begun. Let us hope. May God help us." (Reagan later remarked on hearing this, "I have to believe that if he is talking to God we ought to get along, because so am I.")

Security surrounding the entire visit was unusually intensive, demonstrating to me that a warning I had gotten earlier from Bogdanov had been taken seriously. Kornilov, the translator, was amazed to see the formidable security preparations. "It was an immense, impressive caravan, fifty vehicles. Gorbachev's Zil limousine flanked by about a dozen motorcycles and protected from behind by a Secret Service armor-plated pickup with its tail apart showing Secret Service agents armed to the teeth with submachine guns, grenades, and pistols, and all wearing bulletproof vests. This was followed by Soviet security agents. The route had been cleared of traffic, helicopters whirred overhead. When the next day they were driven to the White House, both sides of the terrace were lined with American and Soviet Security guards and packed with black jeeps with SWAT teams with heavy Uzi submachine guns. The security precautions were extraordinary."[2]

According to habitués, the State dinner to be given for the Gorbachevs was the most exciting social event in Washington since Prince Charles and the glamorous Princess Di had come to town, outdoing even the visit of Queen Elizabeth herself. Wrote the *Washington Post*, "Weeks before the dates were even announced, people all over town were preparing stories as to why they hadn't been invited to the dinner or making plane reservations to explain why they couldn't go to what was, all agreed, the hottest ticket in town. …. Whining and crying, people vied for invitations through lobbyists, public relations firms, influential friends."

State dinners are usually announced months in advance, but in this case the vying process was made all the more complicated because the White House did not know the exact date of the dinner until the last minute, and invitations were sent only five weeks before. At last, the long-awaited date for the dinner, December 8, 1987, was finally announced. Yet, as the White House does not release the final guest list until just before the dinner, a lengthy guessing game was set off about who might be the lucky ones to make the cut.

The State Dining Room seats 130. Mrs. Reagan was said to favor a maximum of 96 guests and finally agreed to 126. The Soviet delegation numbered twelve to sixteen, with an equal number of American officials automatically invited as counterparts, plus a few other essential U.S. government dignitaries.[3] Members of Congress, normally six, are always included (in this case, given the importance of the event, mostly members of the leadership).

The decision process was ferocious. A dizzying number of people were involved. In fact, there were far more people deciding to whom those precious seats were to be given than the number of actual guests. Each governmental group had its own priorities. The State Department Soviet Desk compiled a long list of suitable candidates, basing their decision on who might make some contacts or conduct useful business for them. The West Wing of the White House made lists of possible guests compiled by the offices of Public Liaison, Intergovernmental Affairs, Legislative Affairs, Media Relations, Military and Political Affairs. The President's Press Office considered media, industrialists, and Soviet scholars. Then there was the National Security Council, where names were checked for possible faux pas. The First Lady's East Wing staff provided finishing touches, but the final word on the guest list was decided by Nancy Reagan alone. Little did I know about all the scrutiny, not being among the cognoscenti, but when the final list was done, somehow I was on it.

I arrived two days before the main event, in time to attend the Prayer Vigil service for the U.S.–Soviet Summit sponsored by the National Council of Churches at the Washington Cathedral for representatives of both Orthodox and Protestant churches of the U.S. and the USSR. I did interviews for ABC, CNN, and Michael Dobbs of *The Washington Post*, saw Michael Beschloss, the presidential historian, Bishop Basil Rodzianko, and Bud McFarlane. I stayed with my friends Teresa Heinz and Senator John Heinz in their splendid Georgetown home, which had once been the Imperial Russian Embassy and home of the first Russian Ambassador, Baron Alexander de Bodisco.[4]

The big day, December 8, started off for me with an invitation from Mrs. Reagan to attend a small breakfast at 9 a.m. in the East Wing Reception Room before the arrival of the Gorbachevs on the South Lawn. An eye-opening breakfast it was. I had no idea who would be there. My only clue was that I stood in line behind George Will, the columnist, as the guards checked our invitations. When we got inside, there was a long table with orange juice, assorted Danish pastries and muffins, tea and coffee. When I turned around, coffee cup in hand, I found myself face to face with a shy, quiet fellow that I suddenly recognized as baseball legend Joe DiMaggio. (In my confusion, all I could think of was "he was married to Marilyn Monroe!") Behind me, I heard the inimitable voice etched in my memory by countless movies: Jimmy Stewart. On the couch were two gray-haired gentlemen engrossed in deep discussion, who turned out to be Edward Teller, the father of the H-Bomb, and jazz luminary Dave Brubeck. A skyscraper-tall fellow towered over the crowd: Meadowlark Lemon of the Harlem Globetrotters. Picking out a Danish was the pint-sized Olympic gymnast Mary Lou Retton.

I ogled them all, but didn't have time to make a full appraisal of the guests, as we were all quickly summoned, marched out, and lined up like ducks in a row on the South Lawn. (Across the lawn, where the high Soviet officials were standing, to my surprise I spied Mr. Gussenko, who was listed in the program as "advisor to Mrs. Gorbachev." If he really was, I could not imagine this courteous man allowing the gauche social missteps in Mrs. Gorbachev's schedule.) I stood to watch next to New York Philharmonic conductor Zubin Mehta and his statuesque blonde wife as the famous visitors appeared on the lawn at 10 a.m. to be greeted with full military honors. Our printed directions stated that, after the playing of honors for the President and his guests, we were to stand at attention during the playing of "Ruffles and Flourishes" and then, during the playing of "Hail to the Chief" and our national anthem, to place our right hand over our hearts. This was followed by the Soviet national anthem. The Fife and Drum Corps played, troops passed in review, cannons boomed, and after short welcoming speeches, the President and Secretary Gorbachev went into the White House for a ninety minute meeting.

The big political event took place in the East Room of the White House at noon, where Reagan and Gorbachev signed the INF (Intermediate Range Nuclear Forces) Treaty, which was to eliminate an entire class of atomic weapons, a historic first. During the pre-signing remarks in the East Room, Reagan again used the Russian proverb *doveryai no proveryai*—trust but verify—that had become a favorite of his. Hearing this once again, Gorbachev good-naturedly shook his head and chided the President, "You repeat that at every meeting."[5]

To which Reagan smiled and cheerfully replied, "I like it," and continued with his talk.

It gives an idea of the holiday atmosphere that the CBS correspondent broadcasting from a square in Moscow over which a giant TV screen loomed, reported that crowds watching the live transmission from Washington broke into spontaneous applause. The people of Moscow were so delighted by the two leaders meeting that one U.S. newsman said that he risked getting bear hugs on the street from Soviet citizens.

I spent the rest of my day at a fancy Washington hairdresser getting properly coiffed and made up, and back at the Heinzes' ironed the ruffled white taffeta top and black taffeta skirt I was to wear. The State dinner had been scaled down to emphasize that this was a serious business meeting. The dinner was to begin at 7 p.m., half an hour earlier than usual, because the Gorbachevs had requested an earlier start so they could retire early. As I was coming alone without an escort, Mrs. Reagan arranged that one of the White House military aides, Lieutenant Commander Philip Matyas of the United States Coast Guard, in full dress uniform, would come to fetch me at 6:30 in a White House limousine.[6] (The rule was that the officer escort could pick you up—but not take you home.) Filing down the long White House halls for such an occasion is a pretty impressive business, and it was definitely comforting to have an aide at my side.

Making our way down the halls lit with sparkling chandeliers and candlelight, we were greeted with harp and flute music. As it was just before Christmas, the halls of the White House were splendidly decorated with white azalea trees and a bank of scarlet poinsettias massed on the stairs. The tall White House Christmas tree, beautifully decorated, stood in the Blue Room. My military escort stayed discreetly at my elbow during the cocktail hour, got my drink, took it away when empty, and held my bag while I was dancing.

A sartorial tempest in a teapot had developed that caused much clucking in the press. Dress for State dinners is always formal: black tie for gentlemen and for ladies a marvelous opportunity to show off their best gowns. Contrary to accepted Washington practice, the Soviets had requested business dress, black tie, being considered by them as "un-proletarian" (my, how this has changed since then!), and specified stuffily that the Gorbachevs did not plan to wear formal dress. Nevertheless, the White House invitations stuck to established protocol and specified black tie. Although in the end the President and the American guests wore black tie, the masculine members of the Soviet delegation insisted on coming in business dress anyway.

"Hail to the Chief" announced President and Mrs. Reagan, who entered the East Room with General Secretary Gorbachev and his wife. National anthems followed. Gorbachev came dressed in an elegant three-piece dark-blue shadow-striped Italian suit, a wine and dark-blue striped tie, and shiny new shoes. The President wore black tie. Naturally there was intense journalistic curiosity about what the ladies would wear. Mrs. Gorbachev chose a formal black taffeta dress with a long skirt and a matching peplum, black jacket, and pearls. Mrs. Reagan, slim and elegant, wearing diamond drop earrings, sparkled as she walked in a beaded black gown with long red-and-white-flowered sleeves, by the American designer Galanos.

As the receiving line was being formed, I chanced to walk by the Gorbachevs, who were walking arm in arm. Raisa turned to look at me, and I was surprised to overhear her say to her husband, *"Eto ona!"* (It is she!). When it was my turn to go through the line, Gorbachev took my hands in his and greeted me warmly, with Reagan looking on like a benign uncle—one of my favorite White House photos. To my surprise, Raisa Gorbacheva held my hand tightly and, holding up the line, did not seem to want to let it go. In Russian, she said enthusiastically, "It is a wonderful book!"(speaking of *Firebird*) and bid me get in touch with her when I was next in Moscow. Evidently, she was so eager to greet guests that the receiving line took an extra twenty-five minutes. Joe DiMaggio brought along a baseball for Gorbachev to sign (which he did the next day).

At cocktail time, guests milled about the East Room greeting each other, and I had a good chance to look them over. The elegant crowd comprised a crème de la crème of Washington, the highest government figures (among them some well-known hardliners), along with a Reaganesque mix of a colorful cross section of America: prominent journalists Hedrick Smith, Robert Kaiser and George Will, along with Billy Graham, David Rockefeller, Chris Evert, Van Cliburn, Mstislav Rostropovich, Zubin Mehta, Jimmy Stewart, Saul Bellow, and Claudette Colbert. I spied the fox-like face of Zbigniew Brzezinski. I spoke to some of the guests I knew: Richard Perle, from Scoop Jackson days, my old friend Hedrick Smith, and Jim Billington Librarian of Congress, whom I had known since his Rhodes Scholar days at Oxford.

I noticed that the members of the Soviet contingent were looking ill at ease and quite lost. Somehow, they were without a translator, so, as I spoke Russian, I decided to make it my business to greet them personally. I first tackled Alexander Yakovlev, who at the time was considered to be a tough nut, a totally committed Soviet and fiercely anti-American.[7] He was, however (or so I had heard), reported to be a great fan of Canada, having served there for ten years as ambassador. He was standing all alone, wearing a rumpled brown suit and a sour expression. So I went up to him, introduced myself, and shook his hand warmly. His only response was to answer gruffly, "Yakovlev," blowing a whiff of very bad breath in my face.

"Oh," I continued cheerfully, "I know that you know a great deal about one of my favorite countries—Canada."

I could see that he had not expected this. He smiled and warmed up. On the basis of this very brief encounter, he was to receive me later in Moscow for some very substantive meetings when he was the head of the Commission on the Rehabilitation of Soviet Repression Victims.

Marshal Sergei Akromeyev, Chief of the General Staff of Soviet Armed Forces and Deputy Minister of Defense, was standing bewildered and alone in the middle of the room looking at the extraordinary crowd. Somehow, he, too, was without an interpreter, so I went up to him and asked, "Sergei Feodorovich, would you like to know who some of these people are?"

"Oh, *da!*" he answered, much relieved. So, linking my arm under his, we made a circle of the room. I pointed out Pearl Bailey (who insisted that everyone simply call her Pearl), and other luminaries of screen, sports and journalism as well as some of the distinguished government figures. During our stroll, we had a good conversation during which he told me (to my delight) that Gorbachev had had a copy of my book *Land of the Firebird* with him on the plane coming over and had spent a long time consulting it.

At dinner, I was at a table hosted by Mrs. James Baker III, with General Colin Powell, who that day had replaced Admiral Poindexter as National Security Advisor, Deputy Foreign Minister of the Soviet Union, Alexander Bessmertnykh, Henry Kissinger, Richard Helms, ambassador and former head of CIA and Archibald Roosevelt, also a former head of CIA and husband of Chief of Protocol Selwa Roosevelt, Senator Tom Stevens and a frail, mute Mrs. Armand Hammer.[8] I was seated to the right of Colin, resplendent in his dress uniform with a dazzling multicolored row of ribbons on his chest. I didn't know him well then and had never really talked to him, so I asked him politely to tell me about his career. This set off a monologue that lasted more than twenty minutes without his taking a breath or asking me a question. When he finally stopped, I breathed sweetly, "There is only one word I can think of, General—amazing!"

Across the table, Henry Kissinger, with his heavy German accent, dominated the conversation. Bessmertnykh, a courteous man considered the top Americanist in the Soviet Foreign Ministry, whom I had met earlier in the United States, timidly tried to interpose a few remarks but was regularly cut off by Kissinger's pontificating before he could finish a sentence.

The tables were beautifully decorated in dark green and gleaming white, set with the Reagan's new White House china, vermeil candlesticks, and vermeil bowls filled with white freesia, amaryllis, and dark-green galax leaves. Needless to say, it was an elaborate dinner. We dined grandly on Columbia River salmon with lobster medallions and caviar sauce, loin of veal with wild mushrooms and champagne sauce, tarragon tomatoes and corn turban, this followed by a medley of garden greens and brie cheese with crushed walnuts, topped off with a dessert of tea sorbet and honey ice cream. All this was washed down with an All-American choice of wines: Jordan Chardonnay, Stag's Leaf Cabernet Sauvignon 1978, and finally Iron Horse Brut Summit Cuvée 1984. This last, a rare vintage sparkling wine, came from a small family-owned winery near the Russian River in Sonoma County, California, a place where many Russians had first settled in the early 1800s. It was a special choice of the Reagans, as it had been served at the United States dinner at the Geneva Summit, and they requested that it be served again at this symbolic occasion.

The President's toast and short speech was judged by the press as the most gracious and deftly delivered of his presidency (which is saying a lot). He ended with, "So I offer a toast, a commitment on behalf of the American people, of seriousness, goodwill, and hope for the future," concluding with the Russian toast, "*za Vashe Zdorovye*" ("to your health"), a gesture that met with happy applause from the Soviet party.

In his speech and toast, Gorbachev responded with warm words: "Today, following Reykjavik and the extensive preparatory work that has made our meeting in Washington possible, it can be said that winter is on the wane," and ended, "May I wish good health to you, President Reagan and Mrs. Reagan, happiness and well-being to all those present here tonight, peace and prosperity to the peoples of our two countries."

I had another surprise when, in the course of the evening, Vice President Bush came over to me and said, "I need help, too. Would you call me?" and gave me his direct number. I did as he asked but he never called me back. Years later I realized what had happened. Lt. General Brent Scowcroft, a man of decidedly Cold War bent, former National Security Advisor to Gerald Ford, was named NSC advisor by his long-time friend George H. W. Bush. Scowcroft introduced into the National Security staff a young ambitious academic named Condoleeza Rice, who brought a more palatable "realistic" view of Soviet–American relations. My help was no longer needed.

In another departure from tradition, instead of gathering for coffee and conversation in the Blue, Red, and Green Rooms as is usually done after White House dinners, we went directly to the East Room to hear Van Cliburn's program so that the Gorbachevs could depart at 10:00 p.m. (They wound up staying until 10:50.)

The late Van Cliburn, the Louisiana-born pianist, had been the first American to win the prestigious Tchaikovsky Competition in Moscow in 1958, becoming a hero to the Russians and a cult figure in the Soviet Union, was the perfect choice to perform that evening. I had known Van, a gracious Southern gentleman and a warm and generous person, and his mother, Rilda Bee, to whom he was devoted and who accompanied him everywhere, for many years. He was a great fan of our book *Nicholas and Alexandra*, and our family always looked forward to the magnificent poinsettia plant he sent us every Christmas. I was lucky to be seated on the end of the first row left of the podium, next to David Rockefeller and his wife, a spot that offered me a direct view of Gorbachev and his Raisa, who were sitting diagonally across from me in the first row in front of the podium. As Van started to play, I saw her snuggle close to her husband, and during Van's entire program of Brahms, Rachmaninoff, Schumann, Liszt, and Debussy, they cozily held hands. Afterwards, a delighted Raisa rushed up to Van and exclaimed, "What a pity you don't have an orchestra and you could play Tchaikovsky!"

He said that, with her help, he could provide an encore and sat down again to play the popular Russian song "Moscow Nights." As soon as Van started to play, Gorbachev happily started to sing along. Sitting behind their leader, the Soviet delegation at first shifted nervously on their chairs, not knowing exactly what to do, but as Gorbachev continued to sing, by the second verse they all joined in lustily. Afterwards, Van came down and enthusiastically gave the Soviet leader the traditional Russian three cheek kisses.[9] (Speaking of Gorbachev's singing, Reagan was reported to have joked, "Tell him to stay around. I can get him some bookings!")

After the performance, the Marine Band struck up for the usual dancing, and although the evening was cut short earlier than usual, I managed to get in a few turns with Georgy Arbatov and Van. Then my Cinderella evening was over and it was home to the Heinzes, not in a carriage, but alone in a White House limousine.

CHAPTER 16

KGB "PRINCES"

Of course I was afraid of them. Just like the Russians, I feared the sinister "Organs" who could threaten, ruin, or end lives for no reason and with no warning. From the onset of the communist regime, the mere initials KGB[1] and their bloody predecessors, the CHEKA, OGPU, of Bolshevik days the NKVD of Stalin's time, were synonyms for terror. This gigantic shadow government numbered in the hundreds of thousands. They had many faces and occupations, and no one could ever be sure who they were or when they might strike. I had heard one story after another of what *they* did—and could do. As a foreigner, often alone with no protection, I knew that as soon as I entered the Soviet Union the door clanged shut behind me and Western laws no longer applied. I was always on guard. Intourist guides had to report to *them*, as did all employees who worked in hotels for foreigners. Anyone could be called in for little chats in their forbidding buildings in Moscow and Leningrad with their menacing steel doors and shaded windows where electric lights burned all night. Once inside, you never knew what might happen—or when or whether you would come out.

The ones who made the lurid newspaper accounts abroad were the notorious "wet affairs" specialists who poked people with poisoned umbrellas or, as in the famous Litvienko affair, dropped polonium-210 in his tea. Then there were the brutal goons at home who tossed dissident poets and artists into insane asylums for the weekend—or longer.

But Russia remains ultimately a country of contradictions. By Gorbachev's time, among the elite of the KGB were also numbered the most intelligent and sophisticated minds in the Soviet Union. This new face of the KGB was the brainchild of Yuri Andropov, who headed the KGB from

1967–1982. In 1973, he was granted full membership in the Politburo, the Central Committee's ruling inner circle, and in 1983 became the leader of the Soviet Union.

According to French Sovietologist Hélène Carrère d'Encausse, "Andropov came to the KGB with a double mission: first, to rebuild an efficient police apparatus, and second, to transform it into a modern, efficient instrument of the Party. He succeeded on both counts. What the security operation lost in brute force it more than made up in political power."[2]

To help build the new KGB, Andropov encouraged recruiters to go after the best and the brightest in the Soviet academic world (as in the U.S. of the '50s and '60s, when the CIA actively recruited students from Ivy League colleges). Leonard Shapiro, a Soviet specialist at the London School of Economics, in 1983 said, "In the 1930s the KGB was full of thugs. Now it has become an elite that skims the cream from the universities."[3]

In the early 80's, a campaign in books, movies, and TV was mounted for the Russian public showing KGB men not as brutes, but as heroes who foiled their enemies with their superior intellect rather than their pistols. Recruiters looked to enlist youths who spoke foreign languages for possible assignment abroad, with students from Moscow's prestigious Institute of International Relations in particular demand. For many youths, the appeal of a KGB job combined patriotic impulse with shrewd calculation. A post in the KGB conjured up the sugarplums that came with it: higher pay, larger apartments, foreign travel. As the regime grew increasingly moribund, there were very few such good opportunities. One could try to work one's way up in the deadly dull Party apparatus or drop out entirely and take State-assigned jobs to stay alive. But for the ambitious and talented, eager to speak foreign languages, travel abroad, land a job in a foreign embassy, read forbidden books and newspapers, joining the KGB was the way to go. One of our top American diplomats called it "the Harvard of the Soviet Union."

Those at the top I called the "princes" of the KGB, and, during the

Reagan years, I got to know two—Rodomir Bogdanov and Igor Filin. I always told President Reagan who I was seeing, what I knew about them, and what I suspected. Dealing with them, I never had any misconceptions. Always, I had the feeling that I was in a cage with two seemingly amiable but potentially deadly tigers. But as I got to know them both, I could hardly believe what I was seeing. Astonishingly, springing as they did from the Andropov era, it began to look very much as if they were part of a group of high-ranking KGB officers who were pressing for change, and a powerful and important constituency supporting Gorbachev's policy of *perestroika*. Privately, I came to refer to them as "the Decembrists."[4] (Shortly after Gorbachev came to power, I often wondered why 113 members of the Central Committee resigned without a peep.[5] Who could have accomplished this but the fine hand of the KGB?)

Of course, in a way, it made perfect sense. It was always thought in the West that the most sophisticated and intelligent members (and often the most charming) of the Soviet Embassy had to be KGB. From my friends in the Soviet Union I knew how much Communist Party members high and low were held in contempt, how increasingly the Party became thought of mainly as a boring place for second-raters who couldn't or wouldn't do anything else, who landed comfortable jobs in organizations and institutes, thanks to their connections, and were content with their privileges. The KGB elite were different, the only ones in a position to know the true situation of their country, and their behavior was often very curious.

I was not completely surprised to encounter paradoxical figures like Rodomir and Igor, whom I got to know in 1984 and 1985 in Moscow because of what I had witnessed in Leningrad in 1983 and 1984. Beginning after Brezhnev's death, there had been some strange straws in the wind. Discontent with the regime was rampant, especially among the young, who, restless and bored, were chafing to express themselves, to explore, to know. Anything connected with the West had the attraction of forbidden fruit, and adopting the customs and habits of pre-revolution Russia was a mark of protest. There were no Western movies shown publicly, no rock music, no foreign magazines. Beards and blue jeans (that became as precious as jewels) were the badges of nonconformism, and religion was called "internal emigration." Nonconforming poets became the prophets of this young generation, recipients of the kind of adulation reserved in the West for rock stars. The threat of secret terror was always there, a fact of life in the Soviet Union, but it became more erratic, encouraging bolder souls to push the boundaries.[6]

In 1983 and 1984, when Andropov came to power, the KGB, those stern guardians of State security, recognized this and the need to lift the lid to let some steam escape. In Leningrad, there was a popular movement to create a Dostoevsky museum in the basement of a house where he had lived. It became a cause célèbre in the city. Communist Party bureaucrats became so nervous about this independent initiative that even the benign effort to produce and sell facsimiles of Dostoevsky's calling card was summarily forbidden, treated almost as treason. Then, suddenly, it became acceptable for nonconformist poets to hold regular readings in the fledgling museum, and even though it was widely said that this was a KGB initiative, people went to hear them anyway. After years of battling with city officials, it also became possible for nonconformist painters to hold a huge show in a city exhibition building. Who else but the KGB could have made this possible? In literature, too, in the fall of 1985, an unknown publishing firm brought out an almanac of the work of unofficial writers and poets. A tiny printing—only a few hundred copies—but nevertheless a milestone, impossible without KGB knowledge and permission.

I have already written about how I first met Rodomir Bogdanov, First Deputy Director of the USA Institute, of having been sent to him by Lt. Colonel Tyrus Cobb of West Point and the National Security Council, so from the first, I knew quite a bit about him. He was well known in the West as a high-ranking First Chief Directorate KGB officer. One American Embassy official told me authoritatively that he was believed to be a general in the GRU (Soviet Military Intelligence), others that he was a general in the KGB. He had been Resident[7] in New Delhi, supervising all activities in India. I once met a psychologist who had come to know Bogdanov who told me that he had gypsy origins, a fact that seemed extraordinary. (Gypsies were considered "enemies of the people" and routinely exterminated in the Stalin years.) If true, how had he gotten to his high position?

As I got to know Bogdanov better, I saw that he was indeed a complicated man and not a rubber stamp mouthing the usual knee-jerk Soviet phrases. We had many substantive discussions and arguments about U.S.–USSR relations that were completely devoid of the usual Soviet doublespeak. There were many mysterious things about him: the unusual etymology of his name, which in Russian is derived from "root of peace" (Rodomir) and "given by God" (Bogdanov)—a last name that I was told was often given to foundling children. A veil always existed between us. The simplest details about his personal life remained completely unknown to me. He never invited me to his home. He never mentioned his wife or family. Over the four years that I knew him, I saw him mainly in his office, where I always assumed our conversations were recorded. But when we were alone, walking on the street or lunching in a restaurant, he was much more outspoken—sometimes startlingly so.

In the winter of 1985, after having worked for three months on my book *Pavlovsk* on a U.S. IREX grant in Leningrad, I was on my way back to America. Before leaving, I stopped in to see Rodomir in Moscow and he asked me pleasantly, "How is your work going?"

After my cold months in Leningrad, making my way with difficulty through snow, slush, and three changes of public transportation to get to Pavlovsk Palace, 16 miles away from the city, I answered grumpily, "It's going all right, but if I were doing a book about a castle in France, I would live near the castle so I could do my research more easily. That's what I would do if this were a normal country—which it isn't!" And I stamped out.

The next spring, when I was back, he announced genially, "We have found you a *garçonnière*." (a charming French word that translates roughly to "bachelorette pad.") I thought then Rodomir was joking. Turned out, he wasn't. Once, in 1986 while were we eating lunch, he suddenly told me quietly, "I am a communist, but I believe in God." Nothing more, immediately continuing with another subject.

So when I left to go back to America and came to say goodbye, I looked him straight in the eye and said, "Rodomir, I have a favor to ask of you. Please do what you can to protect believers. They do no harm. They are good citizens who love their country and want to stay. Russia needs them."

"Anyone special?" he asked.

I said, "No. In general," and he just nodded his head.

On the basis of his admission that he believed in God, when next I was in Moscow in early January 1987, I decided to give him a piece of scented cotton that had been given to me from a famous miracle-working "weeping" icon, [8] along with a picture of the icon and an explanation. "Rodomir, I know you are not a Church believer but here it is. There has been a miracle and it might help your health."

He appeared very touched and said, "I will keep it with me always. I will put it in my wallet," which he proceeded to do.

I admonished him, "Of course, you know, Rodomir, that you have to be very reverent toward it for it to work."

Emotionally, he said, "I am. I will be."

After I went with him to the Central Committee on January 28 to take up the question of Ron Jr.'s visa, we came back to the USA Institute and his office. There he announced, "We have an important message for you from the highest level."

"Gorbachev?" I asked.

"Yes. Can you take it to the President? Perhaps you can go through Mrs. Reagan."

I said, "I don't have to do that. I can get it to him directly."

"Without Carlucci [Reagan's current NSC advisor] and all that?" he asked.

"Without Carlucci and all that," I confirmed.

"Tomorrow we will give it to you. We want you to take notes."

Instead, the next day when we were again lunching in the Praga Restaurant alone, he brought the message with him and gave it to me. It was a handwritten penciled note in English on plain white paper that read:

> *U.S. assistance in national reconciliation in Afghanistan would be very positively regarded in Moscow. The Soviet side in that case might be of help in* (here the word "unloading" had been crossed out, replaced by the word "untangling") *some other regional conflicts that would also facilitate reaching compromises on problems of arms reduction."*

Orally, he explained the Soviet position, which was that all members of the conflict, including the former king, Zahir Shah (who had been in exile), and all warring parties inside and outside Afghanistan as well as the communist leader then in power, would hold a conference under the supervision of the United Nations in an effort to reach a government of law. He asked me, "Do you understand everything?"

I said, "Yes, I do. I understand."

I tried to get him to be more specific about the message, but he would go no further. "No. Just leave it the way it is, what we have said."

So I went on to ask him, "What are the chances of Gorbachev coming to the United States?"

"He's not going to come."

"Why is that?"

I expected Rodomir to say something along the lines of, "There is no point in his going to Washington now because there can be no substantive agreements," which was, in fact, the official Soviet line. Instead I heard this: "He's not going to come. No. Because he would be killed."

Shocked, I asked, "Rodomir, are you serious? Really *serious*?"

He said, "I am. He is too important to us."

I saw he was in dead earnest, and my strong feeling was that, although he did not say it, he was not so much worried about our side but about some in theirs—who might use the occasion to kill him in the United States—and that it was something Rodomir was in a position to know. It was a lot to take in.

Then I had another surprise of a quite different sort. Just as we were about to leave the restaurant, he asked, "I wonder. I have a question for you. It seems to be losing its scent. Does that mean something?"

I answered, "Well, show it to me." He carefully took the small piece of cotton out of his wallet and handed it to me to smell. "No, Rodomir," I reassured him, "it's not losing its scent. It's perfectly all right. The Mother of God loves us all. So don't worry."

Then to top off that eventful day, back in his office after lunch, with no preamble, he suddenly asked, "What is your financial situation?" (*Was this to be the dreaded moment I had always feared?*)

There was no point in pretending, so I laughed and said, "Well, Rodomir, since you know everything, you know it is not good."

"Well," he continued, "you know you are being helped. Don't you think we should help, too?"

I answered firmly, "No, I am not being 'helped' by anyone and really don't need any help. I have applied for a grant, so really, I don't need anything, but thank you, it is kind of you to be concerned."

After that chilling exchange, I did not sleep at all that night, and in those dark, sleepless hours, I got what I still consider a flash from heaven. So the next day, I went in and said cheerfully, "Rodomir, I have thought about how you could help me. The best help would be to see that one of my books is published in the Soviet Union. That would really help me and make me very happy as well—for instance, *Journey* (my former husband's and my book about our son and his hemophilia). Why not? Or perhaps one or two chapters of *Firebird* could be printed in *Novaya Gazeta*. I would get some royalties, make some money, and that would be wonderful!"

At that he fell silent. That was the perfect answer for me and I felt very comfortable with it because I knew full well that even the KGB couldn't have any of my books published then, and he knew it, too. After that he never mentioned the matter again or made any other such proposition.

IGOR APPEARS

One day in 1986, walking along a Moscow street with Bogdanov, I had asked, "Rodomir, when I can't reach you, is there someone else I can call?"

He thought for a while before he answered, and then said, "Yes. It's time for you to meet someone."

He told me to come to the USA Institute the next morning, and when I arrived, he informed me that I was to have lunch with this unknown person. It was not an invitation.

As I sat waiting apprehensively in his office, the door suddenly opened and in came a tall, very fit-looking man (already a dead giveaway that he was KGB, since ordinary Russians never looked that fit). He was blond, handsome, wearing a well tailored Western three-piece brown tweed suit. As he stood in the doorway, he scrutinized me intently as if he knew all about me and was curious about seeing me in the flesh.

The late Max Hayward, my great and lamented friend, brilliant Oxford scholar and translator of Soviet literature with whom I had worked on *The Living Mirror*, had once told me that if *they* wanted to scare me, I would see them, but if *they* really wanted to shadow me, I would never know it. I had seen the first category in Leningrad, following me in their black cars, and searching me at the Moscow airport, but when this mysterious stranger appeared in the door and looked at me so quizzically, I understood that the curtain had parted, and that he was a person from Max's second category, the one who, unknown and unseen, had been shadowing me for a long time. When he sat down, I was much relieved that it was *his* penetrating blue eyes that were facing the window and the bright sun, not mine. I was very nervous, all the more so when I was told that this was the man with whom I was to have lunch. He was clearly a high KGB man. I was terrified that now would be the time when *they* would make some kind of proposition to me. What if he were to ask me to become a double agent? What would I do?

We went to the National Hotel, directly across from the Kremlin, at that time the most elegant hotel in Moscow, where I had stayed occasionally in the days before I lost my visa. He spoke good vernacular English, and not knowing what to do to protect myself, I did what I often do to keep people away: talked nonstop, not letting him get a word in edgewise. I chatted on about my family, my children, the scenery of the state of Maine. When I eventually took a breath, I asked him if he had ever been to the United States. He told me that he had spent several years in Washington as First Secretary of the Soviet Embassy. "Do you have a family?" I asked. He said that he had a daughter married to a Soviet diplomat then serving in Rangoon, and that she was expecting his first grandchild. Relieved to get him off my case, I trilled, "How wonderful! What a coincidence! I am expecting my first grandchild, too!"

"When?" he asked.

"This summer," said I.

"Same for me," said he.

During the meal, he suggested helpfully (!) that I allow them to deliver the books[9] I had brought to those I had wanted to give them to. I quickly thanked him, assuring him that it was absolutely not necessary for *them* to go to the trouble. He didn't pursue it. Other than this, the meal passed without incident, and, to my vast relief, there were no other propositions of any kind. Relieved and emboldened, as we were getting our coats I finally said, "You seem to know a lot about my projects, but I don't know anything about yours. Tell me, what do you want for your country?"

As he was putting on his hat, he turned and, to my astonishment, quickly answered, "I want free speech and a convertible ruble."

That is how I first met Igor Petrovich Filin.

He had all the signs of a ranking KGB officer—but who was he really? I was staying with friends in the American Embassy compound where many of our embassy staff lived (still do) behind brick walls and high, guarded gates. I immediately told the then DCM[10] about my experience and asked him to help me find out who Igor was. He did check, and told me he could find nothing, but that they really didn't know much about who the high KGB officials were. I wasn't satisfied with that and once again turned to our military, the Air Force attaché, an American colonel that I knew. I told him about my worries and apprehension and asked him whether he and the military could help me find out about Igor and what he did. A few months later, they had the answer: Igor was indeed a high KGB official, a colonel in charge of foreign visitors, the Executive Secretary of the Peace Committee—a notorious organization, known to be run by the KGB, in charge of giving permissions and monitoring all international groups that came to the Soviet Union for any reason. I asked what I should do and was advised by the American colonel that I should continue to behave as always. So I did, but I was always wary, always on guard, always worried how I would parry if and when he confronted me with treasonous propositions.

But as things developed, relations with Igor took a very different turn because of a coincidence that could only have happened in that country of supreme contradictions. Some months after our first lunch, I was again in the Soviet Union serving as a personal guide for Texas millionaire Anne Bass and a few of her friends. I had just arrived in my hotel room when the phone rang. It was Igor. Keeping up the façade that I didn't know full well who he was as I had been advised to do, I said innocently, "Oh, Igor! How did you know I was here?"

Right away, he happily announced that his first grandchild—a girl—had been born.

"What a coincidence! I just had my first grandchild—a boy!"

He asked when and I answered, "August 5th."

"The same day!" he exclaimed, then continued, "What time?" I told him "2.22 AM" "Oh!" he jokingly exclaimed, "Americans, always ahead!" He said he would like to drop over to see me later and I agreed.

I met him in front of the hotel. He was still in his exercise sweat suit, and as he approached me, he greeted me happily. "*Babushka!*" (Grandmother), and I answered, "*Dyedushka!*" (Grandfather).

I must explain that in Russia when two people have a first grandchild on the same day, it is considered extremely important, linking the two grandparents almost as relatives. Suffice it to say that from that moment, our relationship, in his eyes at least, changed. He asked for a photograph of our little Sam and subsequently put it up in his family apartment. Thereafter, every year we got a telegram of birthday wishes on Sam's birthday and I sent back good wishes for his grandchild, Masha. Whenever I was in Moscow, Igor invited me to his apartment for dinner, to his *dacha* (country house) outside the city in a gated forest compound for KGB officers, I got to know his wife, Maya, his daughter, Marina, and his granddaughter, Masha.

In Moscow one night, he took me to meet the famous Georgian "faith" healer that Brezhnev had consulted. Her studio on the Arbat, where she painted strange surrealistic paintings, was overflowing with a crowd of suppliants for her "healing" help.

We never talked about President Reagan and he never asked me. Among the things he did tell me was that, assigned to my case by Andropov himself, he had investigated me for two years. (This is no doubt why, after I did finally meet him in 1986, he always made the mistake of thinking we had met earlier.) After Andropov's death, he told me, "He wanted to meet you. Didn't you know?" (How could I?) I have often mused on that one.

He had started his surveillance job by going to Leningrad to search all the files and reports he could find about me. Laughing he said "You talked to everybody!" but he reported back to his superiors that he had found nothing against the State. Once, when I said that U.S. Soviet specialists believed Bogdanov to be a KGB general, he firmly corrected me saying, "No; colonel." In Leningrad he warned me, "Be very careful. They are very bad here. Don't take out any manuscripts." (I had done that only once, in 1972, when I had taken out some of Joseph Brodsky's unpublished poems for *The Living Mirror*. I had been searched at the Moscow airport and the poems had been taken. Although that incident had happened fourteen years before, he knew about it.)

When I got to Pavlovsk in the spring of 1986 and made my obligatory first visit to the director (a staunch Party member), she made me a surprising proposal: Her aunt, said she, had a small apartment within walking distance of the palace and was willing to rent it to me for two rubles a day. (A pittance, even at the official inflated rate of $2.00!) This unexpected offer, the *garconniere* that Bogdanov had so coyly referred to, was made clearer when I learned a year later that prior to my arrival the director had had a visit from Igor.

The apartment was in a typical Soviet building, a short walking distance from the palace park gates. To say that it was Spartan is an understatement. It was basically empty except for a rickety bed, a table, and wooden chair. In the tiny bathroom, the tub was so small I had to sit upright in it, and the ancient gas hot water heater gave off a frightening *whoosh* when I gingerly touched a match to light it. One of my friends, the archivist of manuscripts and books at the palace, took one horrified look at the place and exclaimed, "You can't live here!" I thought to myself, *It's a test, and I can*. She and her friends generously lent me dishes, glasses, and cooking pots, put up rudimentary curtains, and even gave me some pictures to hang on the wall. I remember distinctly the strange feeing I had when suddenly I realized that I was no longer looking *into* one of those Soviet buildings but looking *out*!

Those few weeks were among the happiest and most contented of my life. In the spring sunshine, I walked through the vast park to the palace, worked peacefully in the archives, lunched on a palace terrace drinking tea with my friends the curators, who always shared their lunches with me. I was able to see and do all the work I needed for my book. I spent long hours with my old friend Anatoly Mikhailovich Kuchumov, the former chief curator, who, retired and confined to a wheelchair, lived with his ailing wife in a small apartment in the town. There I recorded his reminiscences of the war years and the palace restoration on thirty-five tapes, each an hour and a half long. The archives of the palace were opened to me as well as the photographic files, where I went through several thousand photos and chose the ones that were eventually used in my book. I lived as a Soviet citizen, rode the bus, and did my own shopping—and also, from time to time, the Kuchumovs'—in the local markets. No one suspected that I was a foreigner, since no foreigner had been permitted to live in the town of Pavlovsk since the Revolution. Perhaps most important is that neither I, nor any of my friends were ever bothered or questioned by the Leningrad KGB. In short, those two Moscow "princes" had created a *cordon sanitaire* (a protective barrier) around me.

An interesting story about the paradoxical Igor took place in August 1986, when Mother Teresa made her first visit to the Soviet Union, invited by the Soviet Committee for the Defense of Peace. She had come with the hope that the Soviet government would let her set up a charity mission near Chernobyl. *The New York Times* reported, "If she receives permission to bring her sisters of the Missionaries of Charity, it would represent a significant shift in official attitude toward religious activity in the Soviet Union," adding: "The official in charge was a certain Igor P. Filin, who was quoted as saying noncommittally that the government was interested in 'joint projects' with the nun, but that the 'nature of these ventures' had not been worked out."[11]

Just before her arrival, Igor learned that somehow no one had been assigned to meet her at the airport. As executive secretary of the Peace Committee, he would not have gone himself, but he decided that it was improper for no one to be there when she arrived, so he went. He told me of his astonishment when the first thing she did on approaching him was to lay her hand on his arm and say, "I will pray for you and your family." This surprising greeting unsettled him so much and left him so deeply perturbed that he brought up the incident to me not once but several times. "Why?" he asked me. "Why would she say that?"

"Well," said I, "she just said she wanted to pray for you. What's wrong with that?"

Still baffled and upset by her words, two weeks later, when we were in

Leningrad, he repeated this same question again. That evening, I chanced to pass the hotel dining room and spied him sitting alone at a table nervously downing vodka shots. The next morning I wickedly asked him, "Igor, are you by chance a believer?"

"No!" he exclaimed defiantly. "We are taught that Lenin is a god!"

Soothingly, I continued, "Igor, you know that no man is a god. The Bible says, 'Render unto Caesar the things which are Caesar's, and unto God the things that are God's.'"[12]

At that he fell silent and said nothing more about it. But a few days later, embarrassed and hesitant, he confessed to me that he had come to feel it was his responsibility to see that Mother Teresa would be able to bring her nuns and work in the Soviet Union. Although at the time, Soviet law barred religious organizations from charity work on the grounds that this could become a way of winning converts, thanks to Igor, her request was granted. Six nuns were permitted to come and work in Chernobyl and later in Moscow. Mother Teresa was indeed powerful.

My relationship with these two paradoxical men was certainly highly unusual, and it is not surprising that there have been incorrect media reports implying that I was bouncing back and forth to Bogdanov carrying multiple missives. The fact is that over four years of seeing President Reagan, I carried only a very few messages. The first, which I have written about earlier, was initiated by the White House to investigate the possibility of resuming a U.S.–Soviet cultural agreement, when I first met Bogdanov. In 1987, the Afghanistan message was passed directly to me through Bogdanov. The last was the invitation for Gorbachev from President Reagan.

END OF AN ERA

Both Rodomir's and Igor's behavior toward me had been, as the French would put it, "correct." Bogdanov had kept his word, whether about the cultural agreement or my work. The last time I saw him was in 1988. After that, I heard from Igor that his heart condition had grown worse and that he was often ill. He officially retired from the USA Institute in 1989 and died before my book *Pavlovsk* was published in the United States in 1990. I had been grateful for his help in early 1985 when he had managed to arrange my first permissions to work in the archives and the library when there was no cultural exchange between the U.S. and the Soviet Union and all the Party functionaries I had petitioned had refused me. I was so discouraged then that I was close to giving up entirely and *Pavlovsk* would never have been written. I regretted that I was not able to give Rodomir a finished book.

After the fall of the Soviet Union in 1991, the Soviet Peace Committee ceased to exist and Igor was out of a job. KGB veterans like him fell into what can only be called a psychological crisis. What were they to do? I saw him from time to time over coffee or a drink when I was in Moscow at one of the city's fancy new hotels. (He commented dryly on the inflated price they were charging for a drink, remarking that one could buy a whole bottle of scotch whiskey for that price). The tiger who had once held such power was downcast and depressed, looking for work and finding only a series of temporary jobs with the fledgling businesses just starting up in the new Russia. He once proposed that we write a book together. I refused. I had no desire to get into that kind of material, and certainly had no way to accurately check his facts.

Nevertheless, his opinions were interesting. He was most definitely an admirer of Andropov. He said he knew that the West considered Andropov brutal because of his crackdown on dissent and saw him as a policeman, but that he was a "wise politician" who "wrote poetry." According to Igor, Andropov was so shaken by the Soviet violence in Hungary that he felt a change was needed. According to Igor, Andropov gathered a group of "intellectuals" whom he liked to meet with, naming the head of IMEMO (The Institute of World Economy and International Relations), Alexander Yakovlev, along with Yevgeny Primakov and Georgy Arbatov.[13] Igor criticized Gorbachev because he had been, in his view, indecisive, and because when he came to power he did not give enough credit to Andropov, who, he said, had "laid the stones" that Gorbachev walked on. (This seemed to be supported when in 1987, Raisa, seeing a picture of Andropov during their State visit to Washington in December, had exclaimed, "We owe him everything.") Andropov, Igor said, needed someone from the younger generation in a sufficiently high position to follow him, so he had Gorbachev appointed to the Politburo. When Andropov died, Igor went on, the old Brezhnev faction took over again and named Chernenko General Secretary, but when Chernenko died, the Andropov group was able to get Gorbachev elected. I asked him once how afraid the KGB was of the American threat. "Not very," he said. "It was the military who blew it up because they wanted more money for the defense budget."

In 1999, Igor wanted me to meet Krychkov, the KGB chief who followed Andropov, and had been the leader of the revolt against Gorbachev. I declined. In 2000, he accepted my invitation to the book party that was held in Moscow for the Russian language publication of *Land of the Firebird*, which had been financed by an independent Russian businessman and his friend, an Indian businessman. Igor brought Masha with him, and as Sam had come from the United States for the occasion, the two teenagers with the same birthday finally met and one night went to the Moscow circus together. Igor was still a good-looking man, and one of the American wives present whispered to me, "Well, if someone had to follow me, I would have liked it to be him!"

I did not see him during the years that followed, and only when I called in 2010 did I learn from his wife that a few months before, at the age of 67, while sitting on a park bench in front of his apartment Igor had died suddenly of a heart attack He is still often in my thoughts. With him, an era passed.

Masha is married and an airline flight attendant in Russia. Sam graduated from Yale as a Chinese scholar. He speaks Mandarin and Cantonese fluently and, as the only foreigner, worked for two years in Quangzhou (formerly Canton) in the office of the Chinese CEO of a large electronics company employing 8,000 people.

CHAPTER 17

THE AMBASSADOR FLAP

The most startling event that occurred during the years I met with President Reagan was the one I call the "ambassador flap." It happened in December 1986.

It was a grim time in my life, when I was virtually penniless and involved in a painful divorce. I had barely enough to live on and was forced to occupy furnished rooms, moving my meager possessions around from one storage facility to another, sometimes finding them gnawed on by insects. The worst was a former armory that was like a prison with its great steel doors. I was terrified that I would somehow be locked in there, and still today when I see its looming silhouette in Boston, it gives me the shivers. During this gloomy time in my life, I was desperately trying to finish my book and sometimes going down to Washington to talk to the President. Often, despite the honor he paid me, I was reluctant to go because I didn't have money for my shuttle fare and didn't think it appropriate to ask for reimbursement.

The "flap" began on December 19, 1986 a gray day of pouring rain in Cambridge. I arrived dripping wet at the Harvard Russian Research Center (today renamed the Davis Center)[1] and was shaking out my hat and soaked umbrella when I was greeted by excited secretaries announcing that I was in *The New York Times*! Eagerly, they showed me an article on the front page headlined, "Arthur Hartman Planning to Quit as Envoy to Moscow in Early '87." The article that followed read: "The spokesman said no successor had been chosen. One reported possibility is Jack F. Matlock, Jr., Soviet specialist on NSC staff in the White House." Then, to my utter astonishment, it went on to state, "Another possibility put forward by a White House official was *Suzanne Massie* [italics mine] an American author and lecturer on Russian history. She is said to have impressed President Reagan in briefing sessions she held with him before his first meeting with Mikhail Gorbachev in November 1985."

I was stunned. I had no idea where this had come from or the identity of the anonymous "White House official" quoted. To say I was a dark horse is a gross understatement. The few women ambassadors we had had up to then were usually named to countries like Luxembourg and Austria, never Moscow, the coveted pinnacle appointment for male State Department heavies. Shaken by this unexpected news, I went upstairs to the room where all of us scholars at the Harvard Russian Research Center met every day for coffee and discussions of world news. An eminent professor emeritus was the first to arrive, and, scrutinizing the paper, mused out loud, "Well, there might be some truth in it. I hear they are having a lot of troubles with the help over there."

I couldn't help saying a bit acidly, "Well actually, of course, I do iron and know how to cook well and am probably better at those things than Jack Matlock."

It is true that by then I had attracted some attention during those two years. Articles had appeared about me and my meetings in the press, among these *The New York Daily News*, *The New York Times*, and *The Boston Globe*. I was asked from time to time to comment on Russian relations on WGBH news programs in Boston. I had been giving a lot of lectures all over the United States, including several in Washington, two of these in the spring of 1986 before the annual assembly of the constituents of Senator Timothy Wirth of Colorado and then those of Senator John Heinz of Pennsylvania. After these appearances, Wirth and Heinz and other friends in government began suggesting to me that I ought to have some official designation, and on June 3, 1986, in a letter I learned about for the first time in James Mann's book, two respected Republican senators, William Cohen and John Heinz, had written to the President about me saying, "Her presence in the USSR in an official capacity for your administration could provide a two-way conduit for promoting understanding and better relations."[2]

In the early fall of 1986, Senator Wirth had mentioned the ambassador idea to me but apprehensively asked, "Would the Soviet Union accept a woman?" So when I was next in Moscow, I asked his question at an informal lunch with Bogdanov, telling him that in Washington there was the feeling that the Soviet Union might have objections to a woman ambassador. "Why?" he answered. "We had Kollontai."[3] He followed it up the next day in a formal meeting in his office, (where I knew everything was listened to, and told me, "I wish to inform you officially, and this comes from the very top—I repeat, the very top—that the Soviet Union would have no objection to a woman. This comes from the highest source."

Then, on December 30, 1986, just ten days after the *Times* article, another appeared in a small newspaper, *The New York City Times*, titled "Our Man in Moscow Should Be Mrs. Massie" written by the noted Russian-American journalist, the late Peter Klebnikov.[4] After both of those articles, experienced Washington hands, including senators, asked me if I had ever spoken to the President about this. I said no. They insisted that I *had* to tell the President that I was interested. This, they said, was common Washington procedure. One couldn't just wait in the plantation for the messenger to come. How else would he ever know?

The President had once said that I was the only person who had never asked him for anything. I was proud of that, and I was not about to start then. But the Washington hands were so insistent that I thought that, however far-fetched it seemed, they knew much more about these things than I did. If it really was what was expected in Washington, reluctantly, I finally gave in. On January 4, 1987, I wrote to the President and sent him the newspaper articles—very late in the game as it was already a done deal. As although it had not yet been officially announced, Carlucci, in a memo to the President, had written that the decision to name Matlock had already been communicated to the Soviets on December 25.

I was not surprised that the President was dumbfounded by my letter. However, he responded with a long, warm letter on January 13 saying that he had *no idea that you wanted to be our man in Moscow* at the end, adding in his own hand: *You are a trusted advisor and I hope you will remain so.* But forever after, I remained deeply embarrassed that I had broken my rule of never asking him for anything.

It was, of course, an extraordinary act of optimism from the unknown Washington official who had floated the idea to think that anyone as unconventional as I was had any chance to be considered at all over the fierce determination of the State Department to have one of their own. It was common knowledge that Jack Matlock desperately wanted the job. I knew him well, had met with him repeatedly, and once spent the night at his Washington home. After dinner that night over coffee, with what very much looked like a tear glistening in his eye, he defiantly told me that becoming ambassador was something that "I have worked for all my life." Indeed he had. Having climbed the State Department ladder rung by rung, he was a thoroughly qualified foreign service career professional.

As for me, I certainly had no such credentials, but then again, not all of our former ambassadors had come from that State Department background. Some did, but others did not even speak Russian. I certainly did not qualify as a wealthy political donor. I did come from a diplomatic family. I had a wide knowledge of Russian history and culture, spoke Russian fluently, and, in those Cold War days, had unique connections and the experience of knowing and dealing with a wide variety of Russians, both good and bad, high and low—and they trusted me. At that juncture in our relations, with the help of an experienced State Department DCM, my knowledge might have been useful and I might have been able to offer a diplomacy and style that was different from the usual at that pivotal time when America's image and relations with the Soviet Union were so important.

It also probably didn't help that I was a woman. There was only one woman involved in high-level diplomacy between the U.S. and USSR: Rozanne Ridgway, a quintessential, totally committed State Department employee who, since the age of twenty-two, had spent her entire career of twenty-nine years making her way up to what was then the highest position occupied at State by a woman. It would be ten years in the future before anyone, even in their wildest dreams, could conceive that a woman would actually be named Secretary of State (let alone three of them) so it was not surprising that a number of State Department heavies were adamantly determined to have one of their own and were bitterly opposed to me for a position they always considered was theirs.

Although Secretary Shultz was always very popular among ladies, I had been told he was never particularly supportive when it came to women for high diplomatic positions. True or not, when my name was rumored as a possible choice for ambassador, the State Department panicked and flew to their battle stations. I was told by a witness who wishes to remain anonymous that, when learning the news, Mark Parris, a career State Department officer, then Director of Soviet Affairs (1985–88), immediately rushed out of his office to find Rozanne Ridgway, and together they went to Shultz's office to protest. Some years after "the flap," it was explained to me by a high member of the government that in the end it was Shultz (so friendly and even complimentary to me in our meetings), who had vetoed it because "he wanted someone he could control." (Actually, if he had ever asked, as the daughter of an experienced diplomatic family, I didn't think I was that "uncontrollable," but I couldn't change my sex.) In January 1987, Jack Matlock, a State Department and White House insider, achieved his dream, was named ambassador, and quickly confirmed.

POSTSCRIPT

It didn't entirely end there. By the time Bill Clinton became president, I had received some awards from women's organizations and learned a good deal more from them about what the political reality for the selection of women actually involved. Powerful women's organizations that raised considerable funds for Clinton's election kept lists of women they wanted to have named to high government positions. Madeleine Albright, a friend of Hillary Clinton had reached the top of such a list, and with some effort, female fans of mine had also gotten me on the list for ambassador.

Representatives of those women's organizations told me that knowing him from White House days when he was Reagan's last NSC advisor, I should get in touch with Colin Powell. I had gotten to know him quite well and thought he was my friend, as when we met at one occasion or another he always greeted me with warm words, a hug and a kiss. So I thought it might be alright to call him to ask for his support only to find that, when I did, his voice turned cold. He curtly refused saying, "It doesn't make sense politically."

After Ambassador Matlock's four years (1987–1991), President Bush immediately appointed Robert Strauss as Ambassador to Moscow. He spoke no Russian and had no State Department experience, but he was a respected and influential Washington insider, former chairman of the Democratic Party, a stupendous fund raiser and donor, head of a prestigious mega-law firm, and very experienced in international trade relations. After the fall of Gorbachev, President Clinton reappointed Strauss as Ambassador to the new Russia under Boris Yeltsin, where he remained until 1992.

At the time of the fall of the Soviet Union in 1991, Patriarch Alexey II and the first democratically elected mayor of Leningrad, Anatoly Sobchak, had warned us that "It is not economics that is the most important problem in Russia, but morality." The U.S. government ignored their knowledgeable and prescient warning. Knowing the facts of daily life on the ground in the Soviet Union as well as I did, I knew they were right. I did not believe that "business" American style would be the panacea that would swiftly bring utopia to Russia after seventy-five years of a totalitarian and corrupt regime. I tried my best without success to argue in Washington that "business" alone was not enough and that we needed to make some gesture that could be interpreted as purely altruistic toward the suffering Russian population. I had done some serious investigation in Leningrad and had some suggestions. I went to see Vice President Al Gore to plead my case. He was sympathetic and sent me to his chief deputy and USIA, where I learned that the funds Congress had designated to help Russia had all gone to

Los Angeles, which had suffered an earthquake. Instead, we continued our relentless one-note emphasis on "business" that ended up helping not the Russian people or the rise of "democracy," but instead the rapacious oligarchs (most of them former members of the Communist Party). The result was the discrediting of the word *democracy* American style to this day in the minds of much of the Russian population.

Twenty-seven years later, we still have never had a woman ambassador in Moscow, although by now there have been two women consul generals in St. Petersburg and a DCM in Moscow. This still seems a bit strange to me in a country where the majority of the population over fifteen years of age are women, who are now fifty-two percent of the labor force. However, I am happy to say that we were represented in Russia from 2008–2010 by a brilliant and effective American ambassador, John Beyrle, an experienced State Department appointee. A warm and approachable man who studied Russian in Leningrad as a student and traveled to many parts of the Soviet Union as a guide for those American exhibitions that I had so strongly urged President Reagan to support. His command of Russian is astonishing. He speaks the language as easily and flowingly as a waterfall. While ambassador, he began a blog where he personally answered Russian people's questions in Russian. To top it all off he was ably supported by his wife, Jocelyn, also a Russian scholar. How can you beat that? I can only say that in my opinion there has never been an ambassador (I have known twelve) as popular or effective with the Russian people as he was. Given his multiple talents, I had hoped we would have the good sense, as the Russians do in the United States with their ambassadors, of keeping him in place for many years. The obligatory short (three-to four-year) merry-go-round of our diplomats in foreign countries may fit the capitals of Western Europe, but not Russia, a country where it takes a long time to gain the in-depth knowledge, confidence, and trust of both leaders and people. To move our ambassadors in and out so quickly does not help our national interests.

In June of 2011, after having just been extended to serve for an additional year by the State Department, John Beyrle was abruptly replaced by President Obama, who named his NSC Russian advisor, forty-nine year old Michael McFaul, an academic, previously a professor at Stanford and Fellow at the conservative Hoover Institute and CNN commentator. Only the second ambassador to be named to the post in 30 years with no foreign diplomatic experience, McFaul was confirmed in December 2011 and is now in Moscow.

CHAPTER 18

CROCODILES IN WASHINGTON

"The smylere with the knyf under the cloke."
(The smiler with the knife under the cloak.)
Chaucer: *The Knight's Tale*

Just after the "ambassador flap" in early 1987, and continuing into 1988, unknown to me, opposition to my meetings with the President among some of his close new advisors grew nastier. Neophyte that I was, I had naively assumed that the President of the United States, elected twice by popular mandate, had the right to consult with any person he chose without interference. I had a lot to learn about our government.

It is the nature of establishment bureaucracy that it must at all costs preserve itself. This was as true of the United States as it was of the Soviet Union; indeed we had become mirror images of each other. The prevailing view of our Soviet policy was founded on the basic assumption that the communist regime was firmly in place, immutable, and that we had no course but to adapt to it, attempt to contain it, but never change it. Reagan proposed a revolutionary new idea: our system was better. Communism would inevitably fail. This idea was deeply upsetting to many of the champions of the status quo, particularly the national security establishment, heavily invested in military superiority and Cold War policies. Since all bureaucratic careers were based on managing this status quo and keeping their positions, anyone from the outside who had different views was, by their very nature, suspicious, threatening, and, like a virus, to be excluded or neutralized. I was unconventional in both my career path and approach and so was the President. Maybe that was one reason we got along.

When in January, 1984 I was sent by the NSC on a back channel mission to Moscow to explore the attitudes of the Soviet Union about the possibility of resuming the cultural exchange, Bishop Rodzianko had warned me that "You will be like Daniel in the lion's den. A hundred pairs of eyes will be watching you," and advised, "Reach for the particle of good that exists in every human person, but always remember that the demons exist side by side." This was excellent advice for the Soviet Union, but I never suspected it would be just as useful in the United States. Washington was indeed a lion's den where there were a lot more than a hundred pairs of eyes watching. The big difference was that I never had the chance to reach for the "particle of good" because I never knew who my adversaries were.

The fact is, I knew much more about Moscow than I did about Washington. I never had any illusions about the nature of the Soviet Union. I knew what to expect, was always on guard and prepared for the worst. Ironically, dealing with Soviet hostility and the "princes" of the KGB turned out to be a lot easier than coping with the false smiles and seeming friendliness of some of their counterparts in the U.S. In the Soviet Union, suspicions and hostility were open. You could look your adversaries in the eyes, meet them head on, argue. Not so in Washington. There I was never confronted openly. It was done in secret, behind my back.

From the first, I had realized that there might be jealousy among the men who surrounded the President, and also, of course, within the State Department. The bureaucrats and academics of Washington looked largely for those who echoed and supported their views and their "truth" about Russia/Soviet Union. I was not a member of this tight club and they were suspicious of me. Behind their apparent friendliness, I could often sense this, and, knowing the importance of discretion, I tried to disarm it by doing my best not to be threatening.

Although I was sometimes besieged by the press[1] during the years that these meetings were taking place, not a word of what we talked about did I ever leak to the media. Instead, I deliberately trivialized myself by answering their insistent question, "What do you talk about with the President?" by answering sweetly, "Culture." (Culture is permitted to a woman, after all.) Then, adding in my best innocent Judy Holliday voice, "Of course, I'm not privy to the President's schedule and I'm sure he talks to lots of people!" (If I had said, "Afghanistan and throw weight!" I would perhaps have found myself in the Potomac. When I told McFarlane this some years later, he chuckled and said, "It was a great cover." But none of my efforts at discretion did any good.[2]

The fact is that the president of our republic has become more like an emperor, isolated and insulated from the outside world, surrounded with guards and courtiers. Among the president's advisors and executive staff, just as in royal courts of the past, there is jealousy, infighting, intrigue, a competition for power and influence, and a desire to limit the president's access to themselves alone. I was totally unprepared for its intensity.

We are told these days that we have a problem with obesity in the United States, and nowhere is this more apparent than in our swollen bureaucracy and the executive staff of our president, whose number has increased exponentially since the founding of the republic. George Washington had only a single clerk who he paid himself. Thomas Jefferson had one messenger and one secretary, both of whom were paid by him personally. It was not until 1857 that Congress appropriated money ($2,500) for the hiring of one clerk. How things have changed since then! The 40th president, Ronald Reagan, had an executive staff of 1,683, and today Obama, the 44th, has an estimated 2,000–3,000. (It is a fair assumption that neither has paid any of these personally.)[3] Today when our president travels, it is on a gigantic plane accompanied by an entourage that rivals that of the most powerful potentates of history. Six presidents, of which Reagan was the last, used a relatively modest Boeing 707, which, when I visited it at the Reagan Library, now looks small compared to the imperial Boeing 747 (not even one, but two!) required for the humongous presidential entourages of today.[4]

McFarlane had once told me, "Knowledge is power. Access is power and you have both." I did not realize it when it was happening, but I had an access to the President that most of them could only envy. Wilma Hall told me that there were no meetings like the ones I had with Reagan, "an outsider, someone from the private sector, not one of their own," said she. "Staff people did not want any views other than their own to penetrate to the President." It had begun early on. Wilma told me that one high White House official used to storm into the office angrily asking, "*Who authorized this meeting?*" "Bud used to ignore him," said Wilma. I had some champions among the senators, but in the White House and the NSC, Bud McFarlane was the only one. (Perhaps also Ty Cobb, but to date he has always declined to give any details.) There was also Mike Deaver, Nancy Reagan's close friend and champion, and, indirectly, Nancy Reagan herself, who, always mindful of the Reagan legacy, had the worthy goal of keeping the President out of the hands of the hardliners.

As a rare woman in that virtually all-male world, I grew used to being trivialized. At first, the presidential establishment was satisfied with characterizing me as "a romantic" with "no serious credentials" and unlimited faith in the "Russian soul," and although this often made me hopping mad, I had learned to swallow it. After all, I was in good company, as some of Reagan's official entourage didn't much like his ideas either. Behind his back, they trivialized him. He was a "Hollywood"—perish the thought—"actor"(!), a "romantic," "not too intelligent." What did he know about important things? Some called him "a loose cannon" who needed to be contained, watched, and "controlled."

As our meetings continued, things got nastier. In 1984, Admiral Inman had warned me that there were "a lot of crocodiles down there." He certainly was right. During the brouhaha of the Iran-Contra investigations, Bud McFarlane and Admiral Poindexter, who had followed him as NSC advisor, had both resigned. Reagan named Frank Carlucci[5] as new National Security Advisor with Colin Powell as his deputy. Carlucci was a defense establishment man who had served as deputy secretary to Casper Weinberger, the most hawkish member of Reagan's Cabinet, and in 1987, Carlucci was named Secretary of Defense. During his short tenure as National Security Advisor, he and Powell tightened their control over the

NSC by changing most of the personnel and issuing strict new orders that everything was to be done "above board and by the book. No secret operations and no freelancing."[6] A conservative and committed Cold Warrior, CIA veteran Fritz Ermarth replaced Jack Matlock as NSC Soviet specialist.

Despite the fact that Reagan had insisted on continuing SDI research, the Reykjavik meeting in October 1986 had produced the stunning assertion that he would be willing to move toward his long-held and cherished dream of the elimination of nuclear weapons. The CIA, the Pentagon, and the national security agencies establishment, permeated with decades of Cold War paranoia and suspicion, panicked at the thought of what Reagan might do in his future dealings with Gorbachev. There was so much concern that, according to Nelson Ledsky, who served on Reagan's National Security Council in 1987 and 1988, "After Reykjavik, Reagan was watched by someone during all the rest of his term in office." (*And we were worried about the Kremlin!*) "He was surrounded with people like Carlucci, Powell, and Howard Baker."[7]

As I had been named in the media as Reagan's "influential advisor" their anxiety about the President turning "dove-ish" spilled over onto me. In 1987 and 1988, trivialization turned to attack. High-level crocodiles, lurking unseen under the water, began a treacherous whispering campaign against me, waged under the cover of secret classified documents labeled "NSC Intelligence Document." At the time, I knew nothing about this campaign, and only learned about it in 2010 reading James Mann's book. Their goal was to discredit me and keep me away from the President, who, in their eyes, I was turning "soft." These secret memos (which to date remain classified), with no concrete evidence whatsoever, attempted to discredit me by insinuating that I was being used as an unwitting dupe by the KGB as a conduit to influence Reagan, and ludicrously tried to link me with a sensational spy case dominating the headlines at the time. As another old Russian saying goes, "It would have been funny if it weren't so sad."

How wrong they were about me! How little faith they had in the

President! The thought that I might change this "susceptible," not very "astute" President with my "romanticized" view of the "Russian soul" was pure hogwash, not only condescending and deprecating toward me, but even more toward the President. Ronald Reagan was unshakable in his basic principles, one of which was that our relations with the Soviet Union would never change until they changed the way they treated their own people. Détente had indeed, as he had often stated, been a one-way street. I agreed with him on both counts.

From the beginning, my position had always been crystal clear and unwavering: fiercely anti-Soviet–pro-Russian people—a position which did not endear me to either side. I never saw the Soviet Union through rose-colored glasses. I had seen too much there toward people I cared for and had experienced personally the hypocrisy and repression of the regime. I had also observed how often and easily the Soviets had hornswoggled our "specialists" with their propaganda. I always said that every Soviet citizen wore a mask and the higher the person, the tighter the mask. Paradoxically, in the Soviet Union it was always clear that there were hidden anti-communist sympathizers at the very highest level. This was not so in the United States' high levels, so totally imbued with Cold War mentality that they remained lost in their fixed ideas, convinced that nothing could ever change, blinded to the last from the fact that it was changing before their very eyes. Only the President, supported by his wife, from the beginning, kept his eyes open to the possibility of change and maintained the conviction that he, with his great instinct for people and talent for engaging with them, could do something about it. In 1983, he wrote, "I have always put a lot of faith in the power of human contact in solving problems."[8]

In 1986, after the Chernobyl catastrophe, Fritz Ermarth, the new Soviet specialist in the NSC, wrote a positive memo to Carlucci: "I just had a long telephone conversation with Suzanne Massie. She has been in the Soviet Union several times since Chernobyl and is keenly attentive to the popular reaction.... She is indeed a fascinating window on the USSR." However, by early 1987, he seems to have changed his mind and decided that I was a dangerous influence on the President, and on April 23, 1987, anxious to keep me away and "cool the relationship," drafted a letter he sent to Carlucci along with a memo saying that "it was designed to discourage future visits." Purportedly from the President, it read:

> *Dear Suzanne,*
> *Thank you very much for your letter of April 13. I am delighted that your trip to the Soviet Union went well. As you can imagine, the pace around here has become pretty tempestuous* [A very un-Reagan-like expression]. *It is for this reason that I was unable to take your call* [I hadn't called, I had written] *and won't be able to visit with you around May 1. I would very much appreciate it, however, if you would brief Frank Carlucci or key members of his staff on your impressions of the current Soviet scene, or perhaps send him a more detailed report of your impressions.*
> *Nancy and I send our best regards.*
>
> *Sincerely,*
> *(Ronald Reagan)*[9]

Evidently, the President did not agree. He never signed the letter and it was never sent. Our correspondence and meetings continued until the end of his presidency.

But the effort to cut me off from Reagan continued. Although he had no in-depth knowledge of my views, or, for that matter, of Russia, and relying on secondhand information and stereotypes, Carlucci sent a memo to Reagan, Vice President Bush, and Chief of Staff Howard Baker on April 30 casting doubts about my views on Russia/Soviet Union. Considering that I had only met him briefly once or twice when he sat in on my meetings with the President (as the NSC advisor always did) and never had a direct conversation with him, this struck me as just one more oblique dig at Reagan's judgment.

The only glimpse of Carlucci's views I ever had was from an interview[10] where he was quoted as saying, "When I became National Security Advisor

I found that she was the only person he would meet with alone. [*He was dead wrong about that.*] I finally said, 'Look, I can't be your National Security Advisor if you're talking about the Soviet Union alone with Suzanne Massie.' He said that would be okay. So I attended the meetings. They were harmless enough. She would talk about social developments and culture, human rights, and religion in the Soviet Union and he was fascinated by that. Arms control bored him to tears. Bored me to tears, too. But he had this thing about atomic weapons."

For the record, I never once used the expression "the Russian soul" in my discussions with the President. As commonly used in government circles, it is a meaningless, denigrating cliché in the category of another I often heard in Paris, where I lived for four years. At elegant dinners there, someone caressing one of the several wine glasses before them would sigh knowingly, "Ah, the Slavic soul. They love to suffer." (When I mentioned this in the Soviet Union to Russian friends, one of them commented dryly, "*Loving* to suffer and *having* to suffer are two different things.")

The Russians have a word for the mishmash that usually passes for information about them in the West. The word is *klukva*, which translated means "cranberries."[11] In that category, they often joked that the only thing the U.S. seemed to know about Russia was, in their mocking word, *Tolstoyevsky*, an accusation which seemed all too true when Condoleezza Rice, a "realistic" Russian "expert," was famously reported to have advised George W. Bush that Dostoevsky summed up "the Russian soul." (It is a matter of fact that the Russians have always felt that if anyone captured their soul, it was not Feodor Dostoevsky but Alexander Pushkin, the single writer they most revere, often referred to by them as "our all.")

Although I knew four NSC advisors (McFarlane, Poindexter, Carlucci, Powell), I met few Cabinet members. I met Edwin Meese and his wife, Ursula, at the West Point graduation of their son. I ran into William Casey for the first time at a Washington cocktail party when he stopped me and growled suspiciously, "I hear you are meeting with the President and that he listens to you." Later, he invited me to CIA headquarters at Langley to meet with him and a group of his top analysts. Several were very experienced and informed, although one later told me in private that their analyses did not reach the top in their original form, but were edited as they went up the ladder to the President to frame the policy views of higher-ups, an unsettling bit of information. So in fact the only Cabinet member I got to know at all was Secretary of State George Shultz.

CHAPTER 19

SECRETARY SHULTZ

Secretary of State George Shultz was a formidable figure, the quintessential Washington insider. An economist before entering government, he had been a professor at the Sloan School of Business at MIT and dean of the Graduate Business Schools at both the University of Chicago and later Stanford. He was named Secretary of Labor and then Secretary of the Treasury under Nixon, and by Reagan, Secretary of State, a post he occupied for six and a half years (1982–89), one of the longest terms of any Secretary of State.[1]

Given the fact that his background was heavily in business with no background in foreign diplomacy, languages, or cultures, as Secretary of State, Shultz relied primarily on the State Department to formulate and implement Reagan's foreign policy. In true corporate style, by the summer of 1985, he had personally selected most of the senior officials in the Department, emphasizing professional over political credentials, which made him extremely popular in the Foreign Service, who responded in kind by giving Shultz complete support. It was widely said in Washington that Shultz was uncomfortable with anything not directed and handled by the State Department, and that he made his disdain for anything else, including the "confusion of unprofessional contacts" and "back channels" that he could not control, well known.

In his book, Shultz wrote that every time I saw the President "he would send her over to me."[2] This statement came as a surprise to me. I had met the President in January 1984 and had had five meetings with him before I ever met Shultz (and many after), and only three meetings in all with Shultz, two in 1986 and one in early 1987.

The fact is that at first I was too intimidated to ask to see Shultz.

When I finally did, it was thanks to Wilma and McFarlane, not the President. One day, Wilma cheerfully told me, "He will love you. You're going to really like each other."

I answered, "Do you really think so? I think he's scary."

"Oh, he's not scary at all," she said. "He's adorable. He's really sweet. He's just nice."

But still I hesitated. "Well, I wouldn't dare. How could I see him?"

"Oh, Bud can do that for you," said Wilma. "You just ask Bud and tell him you want to see him."

I would never have had the courage to do this without Wilma's encouragement, but I trusted her, so I went in to see Bud and asked, "Bud, you know, I'd like to see Secretary Shultz."

"I should have thought of it myself," he said, picking up the phone.

I was summoned to Shultz's office at the State Department for that first meeting in the spring of 1986, a short time after the Chernobyl catastrophe in the Soviet Union that had occurred on April 26. Still, despite Wilma's warm words, given his heavy establishment background, I was even more intimidated at the prospect of meeting him than meeting the President.

The 7th floor of the State Department, where the Secretary of State has his office, is dramatically different from the anonymous blue halls of the beehive below where the drones toil. I emerged from the large, silent elevator onto mirror-polished floors into a hushed atmosphere exuding power. The wide entrance to the Secretary's suite is flanked by a uniformed guard and large American flags in shining brass stands. After checking my credentials, the guard ushered me through luxurious suites of waiting rooms with Oriental rugs, Federal reproduction antiques, large couches and settees, and imposing portraits of former Secretaries of State looking down from the walls. It was all intended to be impressive—indeed, overwhelming—and it was. So much so, that as I waited nervously for my audience on one of those large couches, I did yoga breathing exercises to still my beating heart. Deep breath, inhale, slowly exhale one…two…three. Over and over. It does calm the pulse rate.

When I was at last ushered in for my meeting, I found Shultz in his small private office sitting at his desk wearing an informal blue and white Norwegian-patterned cardigan sweater. Improbably, my first impression was his strong resemblance to Bert Lahr, the Hollywood actor who had played the lovable lion in *The Wizard of Oz*. Directly behind him on the bookcase was a row of pictures of his grandchildren, and, like any proud grandparent, he showed them to me one by one.

I described for him what I had previously told the President about the popular reactions that I had witnessed to the catastrophe in the Soviet Union. Since the Soviet government had given no information to their population about the accident, fear and rumors swirled among the people in Leningrad, where I had just been for Easter. These were intensified by the fact that it had happened during Orthodox Holy Week, which, for the first time in many years had coincided with communist May Day. Ordinary people, indeed, the country as a whole, had immediately associated the ominous Biblical significance of the word *Chernobyl*—(which means "wormwood" in Ukrainian)—evoked in Revelations' description of the Apocalypse, and felt the disaster to be God's punishment or warning.

This psychological fallout from Chernobyl continued all the time I was in the Soviet Union and would do so for a long time after. I told Shultz how I had been approached by several terrified and anxious young mothers in Leningrad who begged me to see if I could get milk for their children from diplomats who, it was said, were now getting their milk from outside the country, while they had no recourse but to obtain it from State stores they did not trust. During our conversation, Shultz was clearly worried and fell silent often, turning to look thoughtfully out the window at the Washington Monument in the distance. At one point, he burst out impatiently with the emphatic declaration, "I get nothing from my intelligence reports! I have been trying, trying to find out how much force was in that explosion!"[3]

In the Soviet Union, May 1 is a huge holiday when there are parades, and thousands of people were on the street a few days after the explosion.

It rained that day in 1986, and unknown to the population, all out celebrating was that a radioactive cloud had drifted over Leningrad. When this became known later, it was widely believed to have caused people to fall ill with a vitriolic and swift-acting cancer that killed many of those who had been exposed. Among these was the former naval captain husband of one of my close friends, who had been out gardening that day and died of cancer a short time after. Statistics recorded and kept secret by devoted doctors in laboratories in the city, shown to me surreptitiously, reflected that birth defects in the city had increased dramatically after the catastrophe.

I found that day and subsequently, that talking with Shultz was very different from talking with the President. Shultz is an academic and thinks like a professor. He is much more analytical—a person with whom one can really get into the meat of a discussion—which you couldn't with the President. The President's greatness was actually an intuition and openness that was very pure. He had a fresh eye and was informed not just by intellect but by a combination of rational and artistic sensibilities that could grasp some meanings too subtle to be expressed in purely rational terms and that could not be analyzed in that way. He came to his decisions, and quite a few complicated ones, without a whole lot of intellectual cogitation. Shultz is different, an intellectual. He knew the world much more than the President did, and confronted with many diverse problems, thought like an academic and a businessman in solving them.

After that, I saw Shultz only twice more. The second time was six months later, on September 24, in the middle of the brouhaha of the Daniloff "spy" crisis when the Secretary was in New York conducting meetings with Soviet Foreign Minister Eduard Shevardnadze. This time, Shultz asked me to come and seemed anxious to see me. The day before, I had seen the President, Admiral Poindexter, and Jack Matlock in Washington and had to get myself back to New York in a hurry to meet with Shultz. I was late for the New York shuttle and facing the problem of any ordinary citizen preparing to try to get a taxi at rush hour in Washington. Again

Wilma stepped in and sent me off to the airport in Admiral Poindexter's official car so I could make my flight, only to find after boarding that I and the 5 o'clock shuttle were still on the ground at 7 o'clock.

A measure of how tired I was is that, by the time I got to New York, I grabbed the first taxi I could, only to realize halfway to the city that I had left my car at the airport and had to go back to retrieve it. Then I had to circle the city blocks to find a parking place on the street. The result was that I didn't get any dinner and got to bed at 3 a.m. I woke up with a start at eight. No time for breakfast. I had to rush to Secretary Shultz.

Getting from West 67th Street to the extreme East 42nd Street UN Plaza Hotel felt almost as far as going to Washington. I tried to get a taxi. Rush hour. No taxi. It was very hot. I had no cool summer power clothes, so was wearing hot power clothes. Realizing that I couldn't be late for the Secretary of State, I started to run, huffing and puffing, desperately still searching for a cab. None anywhere. Finally, in desperation, I had to find a subway to get there.

In front of the hotel was a big blue limousine waiting patiently, and in the lobby, a crowd of reporters was keeping a permanent vigil, waiting to catch the Secretary when he left. None of them turned a head in my direction. Completely unnoticed, sweating and breathless, I made it to the 37th floor of the UN Plaza Hotel where Shultz had his office, a kind of mini State Department that he used when he was at the UN, complete with Marine guards. Luckily, the Secretary of State was a little late, and his minions, seeing my unstrung state, did send a waiter with some very welcome coffee and juice.

The Secretary arrived accompanied by his deputy, Charlie Hill, who was always there, a silent presence taking notes. The Secretary started right off by asking me, "How are we going to handle this Daniloff case? There are so many ins and outs to it." He proceeded to outline some of these, talking about what kind of deal they could reach, adding gloomily, "They've got a lot on Nick."

I replied, "I'm not surprised. They wouldn't do this if they didn't think they had something they could make stick. The line between permissible behavior and spying is very, very thin in the Soviet Union. Let's face it, you can't walk down the street in the Soviet Union without breaking some law. There are so many laws, any Russian or anyone else can be nabbed for breaking one. The government can dredge up convenient ones anytime they want or need to."

"Yes," he repeated, "they've got a lot on him."

The U.S. and the President had absolutely denied that Daniloff was a spy, and, standing firm on that assurance, Shultz had worked out a delicate deal that would not involve an official U.S. tit-for-tat spy exchange with Zaharov. Daniloff had been released to the custody of the American Embassy in Moscow on September 23rd (the day of my lunch with the President). I absolutely assured the Secretary of State, as I had the President, that in my view they certainly weren't "wimps" for making a deal to have Daniloff freed. "Mr. Secretary, I am mad at the press. They screamed and yelled and carried on about getting him out. When you tried, they screamed and yelled that you were wimps. Think how the media would have gone on if he had continued to be imprisoned and Ruth Daniloff was crying in front of the jail every night!"

Then I gave both Shultz and Hill my impression of the atmosphere in the Soviet Union at the time this happened, and how important it seemed to me that it had occurred when none of our top embassy officials were in town. A sleepy, slow summer period when many people, including Russians, were away, and that Nick Daniloff was neither watched nor warned by our side. I told them that I had asked Jack Matlock whether anybody in our embassy had been alerted that we were planning to do something ticklish and that it might be a sensitive time and had been told, in fact, no. The Secretary of State asked me, "Would you have arrested this guy [meaning the Soviet, Zaharov] at the time?"

I said, "No."

I asked whether it was possible for me to read the Gorbachev and Shevardnadze statements in Russian to check what they had said myself, although perhaps these were already obsolete. He said, "Oh no, it's not obsolete, it's still really open." Adding, "We just can't change our position on this, but we're both trying really hard."

Speculating about the conspiracy theory…who, where, I said, "It seems quite possible to me, in the Soviet Union certainly, that there were those who were so opposed to Gorbachev initiatives that they wanted to cause trouble and seized the occasion we gave them as an excuse to act. We don't know and there is no point in pretending we do."

I felt it important to emphasize that the Soviet Union was in a period of flux, as I was not absolutely sure that our people were sufficiently aware of this, and that there might be no one on the spot to explain that the Soviet Union was not a monolith, not a country that was now acting in unison. In my judgment, given this period of imbalance, I felt we could expect a few more troublesome things to happen. They did. The affair escalated into a big expulsion of Soviet personnel from the UN and massive retaliation on the U.S. Embassy by the Soviets. I gave him all the information I had heard about people's attitudes toward Gorbachev and what he'd done, how Russians were saying, "Oh, look at poor Misha! Poor Misha, his hair has turned to gray, or white." Shultz asked curiously, "Is that a Russian nickname?" (That our Secretary of State, who dealt with the Russians, didn't seem to know the most common of Russian customs, that of nicknaming everybody, came as a surprise.)

Charlie Hill took notes all the time. I briefly told them the story I had told the President about losing my tire on the bridge in Leningrad. They loved it, but I emphasized that I hadn't told that story just because it was funny but because it revealed the matter-of-fact attitude of even a lowly rank-and-file KGB man toward spying: "You call them 'observers,' we call them 'observers.' You have them, we have them, but they are spies." Which is, in a way, the attitude the Soviets had been taking with Daniloff. So perhaps it might be useful to note this thinking and the fact that, if they put a hand on an American, they were fully aware that it would cause an international scandal, knew exactly what they were doing and the result it would have. So then it becomes not just a question of nobody at home, but a calculated action. Of course, we don't know whether they might or might not have made such a move, even without our arresting a spy, because of unknown intrigues.

Shultz told me that he had made a great effort in his relationship with Soviet Foreign Minister Shevardnadze and how he and his wife had worked hard to become personal friends with the Shevardnadzes. He said that was working well now, and, basically, that he and Shevardnadze were having very good talks, on a good level.[4] We discussed the whole win-win factor. He told me straight out, "Now we're just in the position where neither side can blink," and that he was trying hard to straighten out the messy matter.

I suggested that perhaps he ought to take the initiative, because maybe in the end we could afford to take it better than Gorbachev.

I told him what I knew about Gorbachev and passed on that I had been told in the Soviet Union that it was not Gorbachev who had ordered Daniloff picked up, but the hardliners (always referred to as the shadowy "they" of the regime). This pressure on him, I was told, "was intense and his room for maneuvering narrow." Based on this possibility, I had urged the President not to push Gorbachev too far on the Daniloff matter as I believed that what I had heard was accurate and that pressure would primarily serve those in the USSR who, I was told, wanted to "stop the process of improvement."

At one point, Shultz said to me, "You know, I just love to talk to you because you've got these wonderful insights. I don't get this from the CIA. I just don't get this in any of my reports." And he reeled off a standard, stereotypical, academico, journalistico, reaction to Gorbachev. Then he added, "I don't know. I don't necessarily believe that. I've told those boys that I know more than they do because I know the guys."

And I agreed: "You're right, Mr. Secretary. Trust your instincts. Don't trust anybody who says they *know*. I like to think I know a lot about the Soviet Union, but nobody knows for sure what's going on with Gorbachev.

Of course, one of the key things here is when and if Mr. Gorbachev knew in advance and did he order it? I think we have to give Mr. Gorbachev as much of a doubt as we gave Mr. Reagan. Since our president didn't know, it is not absolutely certain that Gorbachev knew. Our ambassador wasn't even in the Soviet Union for the last three months, and I've heard that he is saying authoritatively that 'this could never have been done with the agreement of the Politburo. This could never have been done without Gorbachev.' How do we know for sure? It's true that once it was done, just as Reagan had to take a hand, Gorbachev had to take a hand. Basically, they got mouse-trapped and hemmed in by their own services. It's all educated guesses.

And as far as our 'experts'—if there's anybody who's writing who hasn't been there on the streets of Moscow in the last few months, just throw them out entirely. Think of it: If any Russian was purported to be writing authoritatively about the American political scene and political mood who hadn't been here for a long time, we would laugh him out of town."

As I was leaving, I got a big laugh out of them by saying jokingly, "Use me. A woman is very useful. We have a lot of advantages because everybody knows women don't know anything and it's very easy to avoid the press."

Shultz laughed heartily and so did Charlie. And Shultz said, "We will. We will use you again."

He thanked me a lot and gave me a big hug.

On the way home, I thought of a couple of other things, so I wrote him a memo that they sent a messenger to get. I don't know if these ideas were useful or not. What I wrote seemed awfully obvious to me, but you can never assume that the obvious has been covered. I asked these questions:

"Do you think that since the Soviets never consider the effect on their own public opinion, that they really understand the enormous effect this incident has had on the congressional and American public opinion? They say they do, but I think they don't. Do they understand how this has boxed in Reagan with his right wing and the forthcoming congressional elections? Again, they say they do, but do they?

"How much do they point to this as a 'conspiracy'? They have been extremely insistent on this, even for them. Is it just rhetoric, or more? Have they come forward with any concrete evidence of any kind in private? Maybe they're not so wrong. Perhaps it was a conspiracy, or something at least that could be interpreted as conspiracy. At the very least, it was people operating on standard operating procedure. Someone in the U.S. or the FBI gave the order to find a spy, so they set out, nabbed someone as he was accepting a bribe from an FBI plant, and arrested him. As could be expected, the Soviets retaliated.

"I'm sure you've already done this, but as you were asking me to express an opinion, I would certainly emphasize in the strongest terms to Mr. Shevardnadze that they were playing a very dangerous game with this kind of action at this time and that public opinion in the United States is not as easily controllable as it is in the Soviet Union and can't be turned on and off like a spigot, and that ours can have ramifications that are very long-lasting and are not controllable by Reagan or anyone else." (I felt sure that Shultz had done this, but then, you can't be sure.)

At the end, I suggested, if he thought it appropriate and since Gorbachev had personally congratulated me on my "noble work" in writing about Pavlovsk, when he saw Shevardnadze, that he pass on my personal regards to Mikhail Sergeyevich and extend my hope that the Soviet Union in this very important moment would exhibit the wisdom, foresight, and generosity of which they are so fully capable. Maybe it wouldn't do any good, but I didn't think it would hurt. I have no idea whether Shultz ever took me up on this suggestion.

In early January 1987, a scant forty-five minutes before I left for the airport to go back to the Soviet Union, I got a breathless call from Shultz's secretary, who exclaimed, "Oh, I'm so glad to have caught you before you left!" and then Shultz immediately got on the line.

"Now tell me, what are the three most important things going on in that country?"

I answered, "Mr. Secretary, I can't tell you. You know I'm just leaving for that country and it's my considered opinion that so many things have been happening during the past six months since I have been there that I wouldn't presume to pronounce myself. But I'll let you know when I get back."

"Will you come to Washington?" he asked.

"I doubt it, but do you want me to call you?"

"Please," he said.

After I returned on Saturday, January 31, I called Jack Matlock the next day, but hesitated to try and get in touch with Shultz until Monday. But Jack said, "No. Just pick up the phone and call the White House." So at 9:30 on a Sunday morning I did, thinking I would be leaving a message, but only a minute went by and Secretary Shultz was on the phone. We made a date to get together on Tuesday, February 3. I did not tell either Shultz or Jack that I had a message for the President.

I then called Mrs. Reagan, chatted a bit, and made a date for Tuesday morning for coffee, and did tell her that I had an important message for her husband and would be in touch with his private secretary, Kathy Osborne. I called Kathy, telling her that I needed to see the President right away. "I'll get you in," she said. I assured her that I only needed a few minutes. "Come at 11 a.m. I'll get you in somehow."

When I got to the White House that Tuesday morning, I had to wait around a bit and began to worry about being late for Mrs. Reagan, whom I was scheduled to see at 11:30, and I asked the White House receptionist what I should do. Firmly, but with a smile, she told me, "*He* always comes first."

Deftly, Kathy slipped me in through her private door immediately outside the Oval Office, where I found the President all alone working at his desk. He was wearing his good blue suit and looked wonderful. His constitution, as always, amazed me. He invited me to come sit next to him at his desk, and I said, "Mr. President, I have a message for you. Here it is."

As I always did, I told him immediately who had given it to me and pulled out the little handwritten note that Bogdanov had given me at lunch only a few days before. The President asked me to read it to him, put in his hearing aid, and listened intently as I did so:

> *U.S. assistance in national reconciliation in Afghanistan would be very positively regarded in Moscow. The Soviet side in that case might be of help in untangling some other regional conflicts that would also facilitate reaching compromises on problems of arms reduction.*

He seemed pleased at the content and said, "Secretary Shultz should see this right away." I told him I had an appointment with the Secretary at six. "I'll be seeing Secretary Shultz at five," he said. "I'll be seeing him before you, and I will tell him that we have gotten this."

I told him that the Soviets had said that they did not want to risk a public rejection on this message and that if, in fact, the United States had any desire to pursue it, I was to let them know and they would pursue it through official channels.

The President said, "We'll think it over."

I gave the original note back to him, saying, "I wanted to put it first into your hands alone."

He seemed quite glad about that and put it right on top of the pile of papers on his desk. He wanted to talk some more, but an aide was pacing about with a paper in hand and the First Lady's secretary was there impatiently waiting for me to go up to see Mrs. Reagan.

Shultz's account of this message in his book is quite different: "Suzanne Massie had come to the State Department on February 3rd carrying a handwritten message that she said was from Gorbachev to Reagan." (Incorrect. I never gave this handwritten message to the State Department, but only to the President.) He continues, "I was skeptical that the message came from Gorbachev. It had been given to Suzanne by Rodomir Bogdanov, Deputy Director of the USA Institute and KGB officer. I welcomed any indication that the Soviets felt they needed to get out of Afghanistan, but I could see they were pairing Afghanistan implicitly with Nicaragua. The Soviets also seemed to condition progress on arms control upon our letting the Soviets depart on their own terms. This was yet another instance of the confusion that multiple, unofficial channels create."[5]

Since then I have wondered, although the message carried no signature, wouldn't it have been relatively easy for the State Department to have checked the handwriting? It is understandable that Secretary Shultz was uncomfortable with anything not directed and handled by the State Department, but in my view it was a limiting strategy, particularly since the Soviets often found their proposals leaked and appearing in headlines in our press and therefore favored unleaked personal messages. Such interchanges have been part of diplomacy between nations from time immemorial.

Shultz's account further states that "The President had sent the content over to me with his own comment on top: 'I know you are seeing Suzanne Massie this evening. She delivered this handwritten message from Gorbachev. He asked her to deliver it to me personally,'" and goes on to quote the President as saying, "They don't want to go public with this proposal if we are going to say no. I don't think we can say yes if they plan to withdraw troops but leave a Communist government." Shultz continues, "The President was right."

This account confused me, as the message itself said nothing about withdrawing troops and leaving a communist government, which made me wonder what advice about this the President was receiving. I was not aware at that time, but the message I had brought that day was not the first but the third overture (or perhaps even more that I don't know about) that the Soviets had made about resolving the Afghanistan quagmire. In the official accounts I read for the preparation of this book, I learned that Gorbachev himself had brought up the subject at his first Summit meeting with Reagan in Geneva in December 1985. In the spring of 1985, it had been brought up to me orally by the director of VAAP (KGB man, no doubt). In 1986 Shultz wrote that "Art Hartman had informed me that they wanted to talk about Afghanistan. They were ready to discuss a timetable for Soviet withdrawal and a government of national unity that would include the Afghan freedom fighters and even leaders of armed Afghan groups outside Afghanistan." He continues with his own assessment, "We would be premature to engage in the agenda as they stated it. We would not accept a government broadened out of the present regime. Nevertheless, it was an important blink…" (If it was, as he says, "an important blink," why did we not pursue it? I guess the answer is that we were too firmly wedded to a policy of helping the mujahideen harass the Soviets.)

Shultz's reaction can perhaps be explained by what I was later told by a high CIA official—that the stonewalling policy in Afghanistan was masterminded, supported, and directed by the late William Casey, who had been Reagan's campaign manager in 1980 and became Director of the CIA. Casey played a large part in shaping Reagan's foreign policy, particularly the President's approach to Soviet international activity. He had served in the OSS (predecessor to the CIA) during WW II and became head of its Secret Branch. A lifelong dedicated hawk, Casey was convinced that the Soviets could never be trusted and could only be dealt with by force, repulsed, pushed back, and destroyed at any cost. During his tenure, Casey oversaw the re-expansion of the intelligence community, in particular the CIA, and encouraged and oversaw covert assistance to the mujahideen in Afghanistan with a breathtaking budget of over $1 billion of taxpayers' money. (!)[6] (In 1985, I chanced to see two of these "freedom fighters" in full battle uniform [without rifles] in the White House mess with two White House officials.)

Shultz wrote triumphantly, "Our policy of aid to the Afghan

mujahideen who were fighting fiercely against Soviet occupiers and their Afghan collaborators was paying off."

What a payoff, considering the tragic events and the continuous bloodshed and slaughter on all sides that have followed to this day without respite in that unhappy land. Of course, I am not privy to the behind the scenes facts, but I have often wondered what might have happened had we taken these multiple Soviet overtures a little more seriously and been willing to at least explore them further, instead of dismissing them outright and continuing our misguided policy of arming the Taliban "freedom fighters" and Osama bin Laden, who eventually turned our own weapons on us.

After my quick meeting with the President, I immediately went up to the living room of the family quarters of the White House to see Mrs. Reagan. When I had met with her there on the Friday before I left for the Soviet Union a month before, we had almond tea, but this day it was coffee and cinnamon toast. We talked about Ron's visa, and I was able to assure her that this was no longer a problem. We also talked again about the forthcoming Wyeth exhibition in Leningrad and my suggestion that she consider going and opening the exhibition. She had seemed very excited when we had first discussed it, and I had advised her that I would check the plans and get back to her right away when I returned.

As we were talking, once again the phone rang a couple of times, one time with a regular sound and the other with a very funny ring. It was the President. She said, "Hello, honey. Look, I'm having a very nice meeting with Suzanne Massie, so can you call me back? I would like to read the letter; why don't you call me back later?" He must have agreed, because she hung up and turned back to me.

We spent an hour or so together. I offered to help her if she did decide to come for the Wyeth exhibition, and I told her about Pavlovsk. I said that if she were to come and see it, I would explain it to her and give her some ideas for a speech. She said, "Speak to Secretary Shultz."

That day, Mrs. Reagan was most eager to talk about her desire to have Gorbachev come to Washington. As my meeting with the President had been cut short that morning, I had not had a chance to tell him the disturbing reason Rodomir had expressed about why Gorbachev would not be coming right away, so I told her. She dismissed it. "Oh pooh, we're all afraid of being killed. He goes to other countries." (*They are not the United States*, I thought.)

I was not able to tell the President personally about Bogdanov's warning until February 25, when I had a chance to talk to him alone after a meeting in the Oval Office with him and several members of the NSC. His reaction was very different from his wife's (as was that of Secretary Shultz when he learned about it). That night Reagan wrote in his diary: *"A fine meeting with Suzanne Massie. Very interesting—she suggests maybe I should go to Moscow instead of Gorbachev coming here. Then she dropped a bomb. A top Soviet official told her Gorbachev might well be killed if he came here. There is so much opposition to what he's trying to do in Russia—they could murder him here & then pin the whole thing on us. I don't find the warning at all outlandish. The KGB is capable of doing just that."* [7]

That long day of February 3rd, after my morning coffee with Mrs. Reagan, I had been told to appear at the State Department at 6 p.m. for what was to be my third and last meeting with Secretary Shultz. I spent a good part of the afternoon briefing a group of senators: Wirth of Colorado, Heinz of Pennsylvania, Nunn of Georgia, Rudman of New Hampshire, Stevens of Alaska, Quayle of Indiana, and five foreign policy advisors sent by Dole and Warner, who couldn't come because they were hearing testimony.

My basic message was that something important was happening in the Soviet Union. I had seen a new chance for dialogue and possibilities for us because they were much more open, and I felt that our government would be wrong to dismiss it. It appeared to me a little like the Prague spring—a time of much greater willingness to discuss various ideas and an opportunity to make some inroads internally, and that we might express an interest in this opportunity to discuss bolder ideas—for instance, media reciprocity of all kinds, including printing some articles from our press. It was my opinion that this openness was not just a political maneuver aimed at the United States, but a movement of fundamental changes to improve their productivity and get their creative juices flowing.

I believed that Gorbachev was really trying to do something and that we could make some progress on human rights. I passed on the cynical comment from Bogdanov, who expressed the opinion about Reagan and Irangate: "They will leave him in his chair but will suck him dry," and that at one point he had talked about our relations saying, "Well, it's good if you leave us alone—you need us."

"How's that?" I had asked, and he continued, "Because we are the Demon. You need us." (*Alas, he's right*, I had thought.) It was easier to dismiss the Soviet Union as being a demon than to face the possibility of change and what, on many levels, that change might mean for the United States.

Yet some of the senators had begun thinking about the question, "If the Demon is undemonized, what kinds of policies will be our response?" (The next day, when I saw Senator Nunn alone, he told me he had read one of my recent speeches carefully and asked me to formulate some questions on basic American foreign policy which he would like to present to the Senate.)

I also told the assembled group of senators that despite his cynical comment, Bogdanov had hinted that there would be some more moves in human rights and emigration, and expressed the opinion that it would be useful if U.S. public statements would stop being so dismissive of everything they were doing as "insignificant." In particular, he objected to our always saying that there was "no fundamental change" because obviously Gorbachev would get his ass kicked off and wouldn't be there, but instead, it would be helpful if we could say things like, "Our government is watching with great interest and great hope as the Gorbachev leadership moves to change its society into a more productive life for Russians and relations in general," rather than always being negative.

I then explained that Secretary Shultz had asked me before my recent trip, "What are the three most important things going on in that country?" and thanks to his question I had asked a number of people of different backgrounds and specialties what they would name. An economist who was working with a group of economists to figure out a way to make the Soviet film industry become independent of government subsidies immediately named "decentralization of industry." As he explained, "I am working without pay because it is so important! We are awakening! We are coming into our spirit. We have been asleep and now we are awake and we must do it now, because if we don't, it's all finished."

Another thing, which probably would not get much notice in the United States, were Gorbachev's efforts to revive Russian villages, to grant larger plots to cultivate and pay more attention to the miserable situation of the village as an entity that had once been the backbone of the nation and had fallen into almost total destruction.[8] Also, he wanted to reverse the regime policy that routinely sent criminals, drunks, and murderers released from Gulag camps into remote villages where they bullied and terrified the few remaining inhabitants.

At the USA Institute, Rodomir Bogdanov gave me his list, the most important being democratization, the new openness, the right to appeal to the court, and the proposal to have elections by secret ballot, the decentralization of industry to give more independence and rule the economy by economic, not political, criteria. He also named the victories of the environmentalists: the North Rivers projects of Lake Baikal, and even Chernobyl, and their outspokenness about trying to get atomic plants decommissioned. Another was the increased printing of books, and articles now being printed in *Pravda*, that only a few years before people would have been sent to prison for, such as strong criticism of the emigration policy and how unfair it was for people to have to wait so long.

But most surprising for me, and something few Americans had heard about, was that many people cited as one of the most important things then happening in the Soviet Union was the release and public showing of

Repentance, the last film in a trilogy by the famed Georgian director Tenghiz Abuladze (1924–87). This film, a complex metaphor about the evils of tyranny, was the first Soviet film to openly denounce the ramifications of Stalinism. It was a powerful political parable on the evils of eliminating the intelligentsia and the Church, and was built on values that Soviet citizens acquired through the Orthodox Church. Although made in 1984, it was prohibited until 1987, and its release caused a sensation among the Soviet population.[9]

I saw the film at the Dom Kino in Leningrad. It was also widely shown in Moscow and Georgia and on television. It contains all the clichés and phrases that were used to justify brutal rule—persecution, torture, mass expulsion of people to labor camps—and was an entire reexamination of Soviet history. After all the cruelty and horrors, its unexpected final scene is unforgettable. The plot concerns a little girl whose parents were unjustly and brutally stripped away, and who, now grown up, works in a bakery situated on a street named after the dictator and bakes cakes with church steeples and symbols on them. An old woman looks in the window and asks, "Dearie, tell me, where does this road lead to? Does it lead to the *khram* (church)?" The woman answers, "No, there is no church at the end of the street." The old woman looks up and says, "Well, if it doesn't lead to the church, then what good is it?" Curtain.

This senatorial briefing went on much longer than I had thought, and I worried that I would be late for my appointment at the State Department. But, told by the senators that the Secretary of State was just at the end of the hall still testifying, the Wirth staff took me down and pushed me through to his Secret Service men. Looking at their list they confirmed, "Yes. Appointment with Mrs. Massie. Six o'clock," and offered, "You can ride with us in our Secret Service car."

I said, "That will be a treat!"

And at that moment, Secretary Shultz in his formal blue suit and blue television shirt, looking very natty and a lot thinner than the last time I had seen him, emerged and said, "Come on, you're going to come with me."

In very courtly fashion, telling me to hold onto the railing so I wouldn't slip on the marble steps, he took my arm and led me out through the assembled television cameras with his Secret Service men buzzing all about him. (And they do buzz, too. They're very intent and, like bees, keep moving constantly around the person they are protecting.)

We were quickly escorted into his enormous limo, and a Secret Service man jumped in the front seat. In motorcade style, in front of the limo was a motorcycle cop and a jeep with a revolving light, while close behind us was the Secret Service car. Comfortably settled in the soft blue seats of the limo, riding down Constitution Avenue, I looked at the illuminated Capitol building and thought, *The President and Mrs. Reagan this morning; the Secretary of State now! Incredible!*

Right away, I suggested, "Mr. Secretary, you must be awfully tired. Wouldn't you rather not talk now and just relax until we get to your office?"

He said, "Oh boy, no! This is my dessert, having you." Then, "Would you like a cup of tea?"

"Of course," I said, "that would be very nice."

"All right," he said, picking up his car telephone (in that ancient time before cell phones). First the phone didn't work at all and then he got a mechanical, nasal telephonic voice that announced, "The number you have dialed is not in service. Please check the number and call again." He tried again several times, always with the same answer, so got on his intercom to the Secret Service man. "You try it. Call my secretary and ask her to put the kettle on for tea." So he tried, too. Still no luck. "Try again!" ordered the Secretary.

He did, over and over, and got very perturbed, fussed with the power source and everything else, and finally from the front seat came his apologetic voice, "Sorry sir, we can't get through to the State Department."

I remember thinking at the time, *Wow! If the Secretary of State can't reach his office from Constitution Avenue, our communications aren't that good!*

At one point during the ride, I told the Secretary that Teresa Heinz (where I was staying) had suggested that she would love to have him and his wife for dinner if they were free.

Without hesitation, he responded, "I'd love to come to dinner."

Finally, just before we arrived, the front seat managed to connect Shultz with his secretary in the State Department, and he said, "Now listen, Laura, would you like to make us a cup of tea?"

A few moments after, the limo glided smoothly into the special entrance for the Secretary of State in the basement. As we got out, pistol-packing Secret Service men hurriedly pushed us into the Secretary's private elevator, and in what seemed like one second, we were whisked up to the 7th floor.

As soon as we arrived, the ever-present Charlie Hill was there to take notes. I came again into Shultz's private office and saw his favorite Norwegian-patterned sweater hanging on the back of his chair. We sat down and started to talk. We talked about Mrs. Reagan going to open the Wyeth exhibition in Leningrad. Secretary Shulz thought it was a good idea, too, and said he would call me in Maine and we could talk about it. (In the end, she didn't go because the President did not want her so far away. I thought this too bad, as it would have been a great diplomatic gesture both toward the Russians and AT&T, and good for the President.) Shultz then asked me about my impression of our embassy in Moscow and our present Consul General in Leningrad.

I told him that I didn't have a very good one and that I was upset about this. "He is strange man who stays mostly isolated in his residence and rarely goes out, which in a city like Leningrad matters terribly. He very rarely makes any speeches to the people and is very negative. First of all, putting all else aside, the man is supposed to be a diplomat. I am an American citizen and AT&T has given me the responsibility of organizing this unique exhibit of the work of three of our most famous artists. AT&T is important and this exhibition on March eleventh is the biggest American art exhibition that has come to the Soviet Union for twenty-five years and the first time there's ever been such an important opening in Leningrad. That by itself, as far as I'm concerned, should obligatorily have ensured a little extra help and effort on our side. But our consul general never asked me about it, never said, 'How glad we are to have you here. What can we do to help you?' Instead, all he said about the exhibition when I asked was, 'Nobody will come,' then adding, 'Well, the opening should be at two o'clock in the afternoon because then the bureaucrats can take off time at work, and they like to do that. It counts for their work.'

"I objected, 'Those are not the only people we want to have come to see this exhibit. Ordinary Russians can't get off until after six.'

"Instead, all he wanted was to show off his residence to me. I was ashamed for our country. So instead, being convinced that the exhibition was important for the United States, and using every bit of the experience, connections, and ingenuity that I had accumulated about the city, its officials, and its citizens, I masterminded the entire occasion with no help from our side—with the exception of the cultural affairs officer at the consulate who helped to distribute the invitations. It happily turned out to be a great success, attended by the greatest number of Soviet citizens ever to come to any American exhibition in Leningrad. AT&T was delighted and so were Jamie Wyeth and his wife, Phyllis, who were present.

"How do these things happen? Obviously I don't understand anything about our process of selection for these posts. It looks to me like insensitivity or worse—arrogance—that we don't take personality more into consideration when we appoint people to foreign countries, certainly the Soviet Union, as it is such an important country for the United States. It's uncomfortable for me to say these things, especially as my name came up for a post, but I really found that a good deal of the trouble I have had with cultural and other initiatives is the negativism of our side. The Russians are mainly very cooperative. Of course, I know that in our embassies and consulates over there are many good individuals who work hard and do their best, but basically the problem with our embassy, I think, is that those at the top are looking back over their shoulders at the past instead of the future. And if that is the case, Mr. Secretary, then the fact is that this is something one has to take into account."

We had a substantive, hour-long talk. First, we discussed the Afghanistan message. Shultz did not tell me that he had talked to the President about it that day and said only that he was interested, but would be back to me so I could be back to them, and he would call me. (He never did.)

Talk then turned to the fallout from the Daniloff matter. Daniloff had returned to the United States on September 29. The United States then expelled one hundred Soviet personnel and the Soviets retaliated by pulling out the entire Moscow embassy Russian support staff (drivers, maids, cleaners, etc.). Shultz writes that, as reported by Michael Armacost, state department official, "The situation at the American Embassy in Moscow was terrible. The place looked shabby and dispirited. Our personnel, short-handed, forced to do all the work previously done by 260 Soviet nationals as well as their own jobs, were exhausted. The embassy building was a drab and dusty rabbit warren."[10]

This extreme inconvenience for our embassy resulted in such detrimental results as, on the day the Plenum[11] opened, our one and only expert on the Plenum couldn't go because it was his day to clean the courtyard. The embassy personnel were in disarray and furious at the new ambassador who was seen, rightly or wrongly, as a "captive" of the CIA and the FBI and the architect of the decision to pull out the UN Soviet diplomats in order to placate U.S. hardliners.

In my talks with him, Rodomir Bogdanov had expressed the pessimistic view that our new ambassador "was a great disappointment to the Soviet Union… He is arrogant and he will want to throw his weight around. We will work with him in general, of course, but are quite pessimistic about Reagan right now," adding sadly, "He was a great president. He was."

Shultz was silent but Charlie busily took notes.

Then, looking at his watch, Shultz slipped out to change, as he was expected at a function at the Australian Embassy to make a speech, and when he came back, he asked Charlie and me, "Do you think I could try this out on you?" and proceeded to read us his speech. I only remember the part where he joked saying that he was wondering "if there was anything left of Australian relations because we were beating the pants off them in the America's Cup." When he left he suggested, "If you want to stay here, I'll come back in a minute and get you and O'bie [his wife]."

So I sat there waiting and talking to Charlie Hill about Russia as another hour slipped away. Then the Secretary was back and I was treated to another ride in the marvelous limo.

The Secret Service had cordoned off the Heinz house entirely and stood waiting in the street. The jeep with its revolving light was placed right in front of the front door. Waiting for Senator Heinz to return from the Senate, Teresa, Shultz, and his warm and friendly wife O'bie[12] (to whom he had been happily married for forty-one years), had cocktails and fresh caviar I had brought back from the Soviet Union. Teresa called him "Shultzie" and had told me when we were alone that he was "very sexy and had a wonderful twinkle," which he demonstrated during the cocktail hour, telling us a comical story of how he had met O'bie that could have come out of the play *Mr. Roberts*. It seems that in WW II, when Shultz was a captain in the Marines in Hawaii, liquor was scarce, but somehow he had gotten a bottle of gin and a bottle of whiskey. "We heard there were some nurses over there in the hospital." So, he said, "What I did, I got up there and waved a bottle of whiskey and a bottle of gin in the air and she flew right into my arms!"

Teresa is an outstanding hostess, so followed one of her impeccable dinners. I had agreed with the Secretary of State earlier that I would do the confidential part with him but the assessment of the talk to the senators later. So after our drinks and chitchat, the Secretary of State announced, "Well, I wanted to hear this assessment, so I want Suzanne to make a report." So I did it again. At dinner then, political talk whirled. Shultz and Senator Heinz discussed important and subtle Senate maneuvers. The major subject among the guests was Don Regan, the irascible and unpopular White House Chief of Staff. All were dying to get him out and discussed all the other possible candidates. (They got their wish; Regan handed in his resignation three days later.)

Shultz stayed until quarter of twelve. I had spent from 6 p.m. to midnight with the Secretary of State, and that memorable day and evening were the last time I saw Secretary Shultz and his wonderful wife.[13]

When in 1986 and again in 1987 Secretary Shultz made his critical remarks to me about the CIA intelligence he was receiving, I was startled until I read his account of a meeting with Frank Carlucci on January 4, 1987. In *Turmoil and Triumph* (p. 865) Shultz writes that he told Carlucci sternly that "I had no confidence in the intelligence community, that I had been misled, lied to, cut out", that CIA analysis "was distorted by strong views about policy", were completely wrong about Gorbachev, refusing to accept Gorbachev's changes, and when it became evident that changes were happening, dismissing these saying "they would make no difference." This account made abundantly clear what had made me uneasy after my visit to Langley when one analyst told me privately that views were modified as they went up the ladder to the president.

Other disquieting evidence has strongly supported this conclusion.

In 1991, testifying before a Senate committee considering the nomination of Robert Gates to head the CIA, former CIA analysts testified that in the 1980s the CIA was so politicized that estimates were slanted and false information presented to the White House to match the policy objectives of William Casey, the agency's director, and tailored to Casey's objectives.

Makes you wonder about today.

CHAPTER 20

REAGAN WOWS MOSCOW

"Systems might be brutish, bureaucrats might fail. But men could sometimes transcend all that, even the forces of history that seem destined to keep them apart."
Ronald Reagan, May 31, 1988, speech at Moscow University

PREAMBLE

On May 5, 1988, as part of the preparation for President Reagan's first trip to Moscow, I was among a group of nongovernmental Soviet specialists who were called together for a lunch at the White House with the President. We were advised that each of us would have three minutes (!) to give the President our advice for his forthcoming trip. I was the only woman among the male academic heavies that included Seweryn Bialer of Columbia University; James Billington, Library of Congress; Murray Feshbach, Georgetown University; Maurice Friedburg, University of Illinois; Mark Garrison from Brown University; Frederick Starr, Oberlin College; and my old friend Adam Ulam of Harvard University. The meeting took place in the White House Roosevelt Room, where we were seated around a long oval table, diplomatically, in strict alphabetical order, to avoid any academic faux pas, with Bialer on the right and Ulam on the left of the President. As my last name started with M, the official photo comically shows only a bit of my profile and nose sticking out at the curve of the long table.

This was such a grand occasion for pontification that, totally ignoring the three-minute rule, several of these erudite gentlemen pulled out long and dense papers which they proceeded to read. The President made no comments and began to look a little drowsy. I had planned and prepared something else to say, but by the time it got around to me, remaining time was short so I decided to ad lib: "Mr. President, I would like to speak up for another constituency: women. If I were a politician, I would say something about the contribution of Soviet women. After all, fifty-one percent of the workforce are women, and *perestroika* can't succeed without fifty-one percent of the labor force. Even generals have mothers, and who do you think takes care of the drunks? The fact is that Russia is a matriarchy ruled by men."

The President perked up, and, his mood livening, chuckled and said, "Well, I agree, I've always said we would be in skins if it weren't for women, but I get in trouble when I say that!"

Little did I guess how much he would take my unconventional bit of advice to heart when he got to Moscow.

At a prior private meeting with the President, when, as usual, I had briefed him on the human side of things in Russia, I had strongly advised him that when he went to Moscow he should be sure to make some gesture toward the Russian Orthodox Church and Russian believers, and urged him to call on the Patriarch Pimen and to visit the Danilovsky Monastery—a place that held a revered place in Moscow history and in the heart of its people. The first monastery in Moscow, that was then a small isolated northern settlement, was built in 1282 by Moscow's founder, Prince Danil, son of Alexander Nevsky. I told him about its history. The Danilovsky had been closed in 1929–30 and, in Stalin's time, gruesomely turned into a prison for the Children of Enemies of the State. In 1982, Brezhnev, on his deathbed and visited by Metropolitan Alexey,[1] returned the monastery to the Church in his dying moments. The monastery was then in ruins in a degraded Moscow neighborhood among junkyards of old cars. A statue of Lenin stood abandoned in its dilapidated courtyard and its tall bell tower was empty.

I explained to the President how important bells were to Russians. Each bell in every church had its own name, tone, and message, and, in that vast land, regulated the life of the countryside. They were, in a way, the voice of Russia, and so vital a part of Russian life that the communist regime had also waged a war on them. They too had to be silenced and destroyed. The Danilovsky's famed set of bells, some from the 16th century, were seized and melted down, with the sole exception of eighteen. These were saved by Charles R. Crane, a wealthy American businessman who, in 1930, seeing them being melted on the banks of the Moscow River, bought them from the Soviet government and donated them to Harvard.[2] Among these was the prized Mother Earth bell, nine feet across and weighing thirteen tons with a clapper that weighed 700 pounds. They were hung in a newly-built tower of Lowell House, where their sound was heard in Cambridge every Sunday at 1 p.m. (and at other times to announce Harvard football victories).

In 1983, the statue of Lenin was quietly removed from the monastery courtyard and full reconstruction began in 1985. The return of this monastery to the Church was so important to the Russian population that as soon as it was announced, people came from all over Russia to volunteer their time and talents to its restoration. I visited the monastery several times while it was being rebuilt, and it was always a moving experience. One evening in 1985, I arrived at dusk and saw dark silhouettes of workmen still toiling on the high walls. The courtyard buzzed with the sounds of people hard at work. I was with a monk and a woman approached him saying, "Father, my husband and I will have a few weeks off this summer and we want to help. He is a carpenter. I can work, too."

"My child," he answered quietly, "we would be grateful, but can offer you only simple meals."

She kissed his hand in thanks.

There were two former cathedrals in the complex, one built in 16th century and the other in the 19th century. Curious, although it was past 8 o'clock at night, I walked into the 16th century church, which was fully under construction, and happened upon two workers still working. They were from Kiev in the Ukraine, and had come to work on the church. Seeing the bare walls and scaffolding, I incredulously asked one, "Do you think you will be able to finish by the Millennium (of Russian Christianity)?"

He stood straight and tall and in a strong voice answered confidently, "With God's help, we will!"

I asked his companion the same question and again came the same strong answer, "We will! With God's help, we will!"

And they did. In an extraordinary burst of energy, they and the beehive of volunteers restored the entire complex, including both cathedrals, in less than five years, and it was ready by June 1988, in time for the Millennium celebration. The most gifted icon painter in Russia, the monk Father Zenon, had painted all the icons for the 16th century church as well as for a chapel. Surrounded today by its high white walls and including a new administrative building for the Patriarch, the Danilovsky is now the headquarters of the Moscow Patriarchate.

REAGAN ARRIVES IN MOSCOW

From May 29–June 1 of 1988, Ronald Reagan finally made his long-desired trip to Moscow, the first visit of an American president in fourteen years. He was personally so successful that had *Variety* covered it, they would have called his performance "boffo."

President and Mrs. Reagan landed in Moscow on a bright sunny day at an airport decorated with banners and U.S. and Soviet flags, where a flock of U.S. and Soviet dignitaries were waiting to greet them. They were officially welcomed by stone-faced Andrei Gromyko, titular head of the Soviet Union (whom Reagan had once described as "a frosty old Stalinist" and whom Russians called "the old Kremlin wolf") and his wife, Lydia. "*Velcom*, Mr. President," said Gromyko stiffly, managing a thin smile.

After this greeting, Reagan turned and saw Igor Korchilov, the translator, whom he had met in Washington, and said warmly, "Nice to see you again."

Reagan's greeting impressed Korchilov deeply, and he wrote, "I understood why he was the Great Communicator. It was the way he conducted himself toward people whatever their station in life…his warmth, friendliness and affability…the way he looked you straight in the eye…he was tremendously likable."[3]

Beginning from that first moment with the translator, Reagan was a hit with the Russian people, confirming my certainty that Russians, if given the chance, would warm to our President, just as Gorbachev had from their first meeting in 1985. After a review of troops and the playing of national anthems, a short meeting was held in the VIP lounge with the Gromykos, where, according to Korchilov's hilarious account of those moments, Mrs. Gromyko, a far warmer person than her husband, eagerly broke into her husband's official greetings and insisted on trying out her broken English in welcome. Then, in their presidential Lincoln limousine, which had been flown over from Washington, and accompanied by a phalanx of helmeted Soviet motorcyclists, the President and Mrs. Reagan were driven to the city along a wide boulevard decorated with Soviet and American flags. Entering the Kremlin grounds, they were met by the Commandant of the Kremlin and the Chief of Protocol, another review of troops and another playing of national anthems.

The Moscow visit was to be the high point of Reagan's emphasis on human rights, and especially freedom of religion in Russia—a subject he had brought up at Geneva at his first meeting with Gorbachev and continued to press persistently during their talks throughout the next three years. For a full month before leaving for Moscow, Reagan had brought up the subject in his United States speeches and in his departure statement on May 25, promising that he would press the Soviet leadership to increase religious freedom for all faiths. Stopping in Helsinki on the 27th, in a speech there, he repeated his intention and spoke of Russia's religious past, noting that Moscow had once been called "the city of 'forty times forty' churches," and saying that "the world welcomes the return of some churches to worship, but there are still very few functioning churches and almost no bells." The Soviet press growled with displeasure about his statements and mocked his referral to "forty times forty." Unperturbed, on May 28, the evening before his arrival in Moscow, Reagan wrote in his diary, *"I'm going to tackle him [Gorbachev] on religious freedom—not as a deal with us, but as a suggestion to him as an answer to some of his problems."* And so he did from the first day.

Escorted by the Commandant of the Kremlin and a large delegation of officials, he and Nancy mounted the sixty long steps of the impressive red-carpeted Grand Kremlin Staircase to face at the top a huge fifteen-foot painting of Lenin exhorting a Komsomol crowd in 1920. Knowing Reagan's very public feelings about Lenin, his reaction was closely watched by the group of Soviet officials, who expected some kind of strong statement, but Reagan only commented calmly, "I sort of expected him to be here. I knew I was going to see a lot of Lenin."[4]

The Reagans were escorted into the 200-foot-long St. George (Georgievsky) Hall, the largest hall in the Kremlin, where the most important ceremonies are held. It is an impressive place with a sixty-seven-foot-high vaulted ceiling and walls decorated with insignia of thousands of celebrated soldiers and military units of Tsarist Russia. The Reagans entered from one end of this vast hall and the Gorbachevs from the opposite end, meeting on a red carpet in the center. In his greeting, Gorbachev remarked that he knew Reagan liked Russian proverbs and taught him a new one: "Better to see once than to hear a hundred times."[5]

Reagan tried to respond in Russian with another: "*Rodilsya nye toropilsya*" (roughly, "He was born but not hurried"), which nonplussed all the translators, who had never heard it before, and concluded his remarks with "Thank you and God bless you."

Korchilov writes that these ending words sounded "like blasphemy to some of the ears of the Soviet officials present" and "the heretofore impregnable edifice of communist atheism was being assaulted before their very eyes."

Reagan was to end every speech in Moscow with that same farewell, and it had the same shock effect on many Soviet officials.

Then the ladies went off to make a tour of the Kremlin grounds while Gorbachev escorted Reagan down the stairs of the 700-room Grand Kremlin Palace, built by Nicholas I, to the St. Catherine's Hall, a sumptuous chamber hung with pink silk and adorned with malachite pilasters, where they were to conduct their first meeting. On the way, Gorbachev asked Reagan about his first impressions of the Kremlin. Reagan jokingly replied, "I like everything that's older than me." And then he made a suggestion that was not on his official schedule but turned out to be the most symbolic happening of his visit. He asked Gorbachev if it was possible to see Red Square, about which he had heard so much from George Shultz. Gorbachev instantly agreed. "We'll go together," said Reagan, diplomatically adding that Shultz had recommended him as a great guide.[6]

So much for friendly chat. As soon as their first one-to-one meeting began, Reagan, just as he had promised, immediately raised the subject of freedom of religion and human rights in Russia. Gorbachev, irritated, responded by claiming that there was no problem with religion in Russia, but acknowledged that there had been "excesses." Reagan suggested that Gorbachev read the U.S. Constitution. Their debate on the subject of religion continued so long that it comprised two and a half pages of the official notes taken by the American note-takers.

Finally, after the meeting was over and the ladies were back, the Reagans went to Spaso House, where the spacious Presidential Suite awaited them.[7] The U.S. ambassador's grand residence is a vast yellow-and-white colonnaded former mansion of a wealthy 19th century Moscow merchant, with a rotunda that looks out onto a wide green lawn bordered with trees, flower beds, and a mass of magnificent lilac bushes.

In order to put the best possible face on their capital, the Soviet advance teams had outdone themselves. The streets leading to Spaso House had been repaved, and chipping facades of old buildings where they were to pass had been repainted and whitewashed. (Moscow inhabitants were delighted with the improvements and voiced the hope that more American presidents would come and visit.) Prostitutes had been cleared out of all hotels where the more than 700 members of the American delegation and the 3,300 journalists were to stay. The city authorities had boasted that the famous masses of lilacs in the Russian capital would be in bloom to greet him and the sun would shine—and both performed on schedule.

Despite the sunshine, the lilacs, and the warm welcome, that first afternoon marked an incident when Reagan saw for himself the rougher side of life in the Soviet Union about which I had often told him. He and Nancy decided to take a short stroll along the Arbat, a pedestrian street lined with shops and vendors not far from Spaso House. Being a warm Sunday afternoon, it was packed with people. As soon as the word got around that the Reagans were there, they were mobbed by an enthusiastic and friendly crowd, all wanting to glimpse him, greet him, shake hands. Suddenly, without warning, KGB security forces charged the crowd, fists flying, throwing people aside with such fierce intensity that reporters and the President were shocked, and he exclaimed, "This is still a police state!"

That night, the President, writing about the events of that crowded day in his diary, ended his entry with: *"It was amazing how quickly the street was jammed curb to curb with people, warm, friendly people who couldn't have been more affectionate. In addition to our Secret Service, the KGB was on hand and I've never seen such brutal manhandling as they did on their own people, who were in no way getting out of hand."*[8]

POTHOLES AGAIN

There were three official plenary meetings (May 30, 31, and June 1), these far less successful than Reagan himself. For each of these meetings, the President was surrounded by his high-level eight-member official advisory team. The warm temperature dropped several degrees when these officials stepped in. Once again the superpowers were out of sync. As it had in Reykjavik, the devil remained in the details of "trust but verify." In Reykjavik, the Soviet officials and Gorbachev had not sufficiently trusted Reagan's initiatives and passionate desire to eliminate nuclear weapons, and the meeting ended in a stalemate. In Moscow it was the opposite. In the year and a half since that meeting, Gorbachev and the Soviet position had moved closer to Reagan's, but this time it was the American side that hung back.

Even before the Moscow visit, there had been several indications of the go-slower views of Reagan's new National Security team,[9] headed by Defense Secretary Frank Carlucci and NSC Advisor Colin Powell, both of whom remained deeply skeptical of Gorbachev's intentions. The April 26, 1988, National Security Decision Directive (No. 305) darkly warns against "exaggerated expectations on the future pace and achievement of U.S.–Soviet relations or the reform process underway in the Soviet Union." This was in stark contrast to the possibilities envisioned by Gorbachev and even Reagan himself at the Reykjavik Summit, demonstrating "how profoundly U.S.–Soviet relations had changed since the time when both sides seemed ready to work together on the issues where differences had previously been thought to be irreconcilable."[10]

The Soviets were anxious to conclude further concrete steps toward the elimination of weapons, especially nuclear weapons, and hoped to advance these goals at the Moscow meeting. But the American side dragged its feet, insisting on a more purely ceremonial visit, refusing ratification of the START treaty as well as the more inclusive verification that the Soviets proposed, and in general taking a more rigid position, a shift that both surprised and dismayed Shultz and undercut his efforts. New documents now available from the Gorbachev Foundation state simply that "Gorbachev was thwarted in his efforts for rapid arms control progress by lack of trust on the U.S. side."[11] Korchilov, who was translating, writes that there were misunderstandings on both sides during the sessions. Gorbachev was still grounded in Soviet thinking, convinced, as most Soviets, that real power in America flowed from Wall Street and that the military–industrial complex dominated the American political process. The American side clung to suspicions of Soviet motives, continuing cautious, ostrich-like views and Cold War skepticism. But although Gorbachev had many changes of mood during the sessions and sometimes even lost his temper during the discussions, Reagan did not.

I will mention just a few highlights of these ponderous talks. At the first plenary session, a veritable alphabet soup of acronyms of arms control limits—START, ABN, ACLMs, SLCMS, and ICBM (to name but a few)—were brought up in the two hour meeting. The results were nil.

At the second meeting, Gorbachev brought up the issue of "verify." In this, the Soviet side wanted to move much further than the Americans, and Gorbachev challenged them to abide by their earlier statements, saying, "You always said that you are for the strictest verification, that you are ready for any kind of verification. And now we are persuading you to agree to this kind of verification."[12] No luck. The American side, finding it too intrusive, turned down his proposal. So much for "verify."

But the coup de grâce happened at the last meeting. At the first one-to-one meeting on the day of Reagan's arrival, Gorbachev had proposed a paragraph be included in the final communiqué:

Proceeding from their understanding of the realities that have taken shape in the world today, the two leaders believe that no problem in dispute can be resolved, nor should it be resolved, by military means. They regard peaceful coexistence as a universal principle of international relations. Equality of all states, noninterference in internal affairs, and freedom of socio-political choice must be regarded as inalienable and mandatory standards of international relations.

That first time, there had been no response from the American side, although President Reagan, looking over the statement quickly, found nothing difficult in it, and said he "liked it" but would consult with his advisors. They didn't like it at all. The official advisors (notably Rozanne Ridgway) emphasized, with justification, that some of the statements, like "peaceful coexistence" and "noninterference in internal affairs," anathema to American conservatives, sounded too Soviet and vague. Gorbachev offered to change the language and the statement was rewritten by Bessmertnykh and Ridgway.

This statement was clearly of vital importance to Gorbachev, who was facing the all-important 19th CPSU Party Conference a short time after Reagan's visit and perhaps needed to have some progress to show to conservatives, and in one of his many changes of mood during that last meeting, angry and irritated, he threw it on the table again, passionately pleading that the Americans sign on. Shultz asked for a short break to caucus with the advisors, who, after only sixteen minutes of consultation, still remained adamantly opposed to the paragraph and persuaded the President not to agree. Bowing to his advisors, clearly with reluctance, Reagan went back to Gorbachev and, according to Korchilov's account, said softly, "I'm sorry, this language is not acceptable."

"Why not?" asked Gorbachev.

"We can't accept it," said Reagan and fell silent.

(In his book, Shultz reports Reagan's words differently as: "I'm very reluctant to put this in. I don't want to do it.")

Gorbachev sighed, "All right. I see I can't change your mind."[13]

Korchilov writes, "I had the distinct impression that Reagan would have agreed if it had not been for Shultz and Carlucci."

Gorbachev, bitterly disappointed, gave up. Then, without rancor, putting his arm around Reagan, they walked out together to the final ceremony of ratification of the INF Treaty they had signed in December 1987. U.S. Ambassador Matlock voices the dissenting view that "Gorbachev seemed to need Reagan's agreement to some sort of language to convince wavering Politburo members. If so, we should have been sympathetic and tried to find words that could serve his purpose and that the language could have been adjusted so long as they did no violence to our positions. What he gave us could have been fixed with small alterations."[14]

In the end, no arms agreements were signed.[15] The National Security Archive synopsis ends with the statement, "Just as Gorbachev's lack of trust in Reagan led the Soviet leader to miss the Reykjavik opportunity for nuclear abolition…so too the misguided assessment of Gorbachev's intentions created another missed opportunity for reducing the nuclear threat."[16]

This is sad. How often have we been locked in our own stereotypes? If only our side had been able to read Korchilov's description of the importance of the Gorbachev changes from a Russian point of view. He marvels how in the Soviet Union in the few short months since the Washington Summit (December 1987), "The ferment of *glasnost* had become unmistakable. Changes were visible in political and spiritual spheres."[17] To him, these were astonishing, indeed, almost unbelievable for a Soviet citizen. "The gradual weakening of censorship of the press, literature, theater, the movies, the increasing criticism of the Soviet past, the present, and even the Soviet leadership, which was not only tolerated but actually encouraged. The emergence of so-called cooperatives, food stores, restaurants, including the first McDonald's in Moscow, possibilities to buy at major newsstands foreign newspapers—*The New York Times*, *The Washington Post*, *Figaro* and *Le Monde*, *Der Spiegel*. All this and much more were unmistakable signs of the transformation of Soviet society."[18] Traveling as often as I did to the Soviet Union, I can support his comments, as these changes were obvious to me as well as to anyone on the street in Moscow. I was present at the gala opening of that first McDonald's in Russia. It was an extraordinary, surreal happening that assumed an almost cataclysmic importance for the Moscow population. That evening was a gala occasion, a celebration, complete with klieg lights, eager movie and television photographers, and joyous mobs of people clamoring to get in to buy hamburgers. Inside the packed restaurant, the most startling sight for me was the young Russian waiters, both girls and boys, wearing the familiar McDonald's outfits and sporting badges with the greeting (in Russian): "My name is Sasha (Vanya, Tanya). How can I help you?" All these happenings and many others that I had observed and talked about in my lectures in the United States were milestones, inconceivable only a short time before.

Of course, these might not have not seemed like much to Americans, but they were important and concrete changes in Soviet life and entirely underrated, if noticed at all, by the American officials in their Moscow sessions. (After all, they traveled in limousines and rarely walked the streets.) Instead, they remained steeped in outworn Cold War doubts about whether

Gorbachev was "for real" or his reforms "far-reaching." They were both. As I read about those futile plenary discussions, I couldn't help wondering where our Kremlinology "specialists" and the small army of intelligence analysts were when we needed them, especially when these dramatic changes were in no way secret but visible to the naked eye. But alas, it seems our officials in Moscow took no note of these, perhaps in their eyes small, but nevertheless important, changes in Soviet society brought about by Gorbachev's policies. If they had, perhaps they might have exhibited a bit more boldness and confidence in their sessions.

As for Gorbachev's insistence on that all-important statement he was so anxious to have, in hindsight he did need help, as Matlock had correctly sensed. Korchilov, who later was privy to reading the proposals put before the Party Congress, found that Gorbachev had been striving toward even more radical changes. "Far-reaching proposals had been completed under the supervision of A. Yakovlev for discussion at the all-important Party Congress," says Korchilov. "When I read them I couldn't believe my eyes. These included provisions on freedom of speech, press, and assembly, multiple choice elections and secret ballots, rights of citizens, separation of powers, and independence of the judicial branch."[19] They were voted down by the entire Politburo except for Yakovlev and Shevardnadze. Yes, Gorbachev was "for real," and, as Matlock noted, could have used our help at that critical juncture.

Although the plenary sessions were disappointingly inconclusive, Reagan more than made up for them. In every one of his encounters with the Russian people, he was always diplomatic, never missing a beat, his charm and personality winning over the Russians as it had the Americans. He came, he saw, he conquered, wherever he appeared.

MAY 30

In the morning of the first full day of his visit, despite the fact that before leaving, in the United States he had been criticized for his plan to do so as being a bow to the Soviets, Reagan nevertheless immediately made a visit to the Danilovsky Monastery as I had urged him to do. He also tried to meet with Patriarch Pimen, an ailing and feeble man, broken by years of coercion from the Soviet authorities, but was frustrated in his desire when the Patriarch made it a condition of receiving him that Reagan would not meet with any independent-minded priests.

But at the newly reconstructed Danilovsky Monastery, our President and his wife were warmly welcomed by two Metropolitans (equal to Cardinals in the Catholic Church), as well as a large group of monks and priests, and taken to visit the monastery complex. The President made an eloquent speech—almost a religious sermon—that deeply impressed all present. Opening his remarks with, "It's a very good pleasure to visit this monastery and to have a chance to meet some of the people who have helped make its return to the Russian Orthodox Church a reality. I am also addressing in spirit the thirty-five million believers whose personal contributions made this magnificent restoration possible."

He spoke of the power of icons: "One cannot look at the magnificent icons created and recreated here under the direction of Father Zenon without experiencing the deep faith that lives in the hearts of the people of this land. Like the saints and martyrs depicted in these icons, the faith of your people has been tested and tempered in the crucible of hardship. But in that suffering, it has grown strong, ready now to embrace with new hope the beginnings of a second Christian millennium." He spoke not only of the Russian Orthodox Church, but expressed the hope that "Soon all religious communities that are now prevented from registering or are banned altogether, including the Ukrainian Catholic and Orthodox Churches, will soon be able to practice their religion freely."

He called the restoration of the monastery a "first" and hoped it would be followed by a "religious spring of religious liberty." He finished with a long quote from Solzhenitsyn about the pacifying sight of churches in the Russian countryside, saying, "In our prayers we may keep that image in mind, the thought that the bells may ring again, sounding through Moscow and across the countryside, clamoring for joy in their newfound freedom." [20]

It was a milestone. No American president had ever spoken to the Russians in this way, and those present were deeply moved, so much so that although the official Soviet press, not surprisingly, stridently criticized his visit and his remarks, they are remembered so fondly at the monastery that a photograph of the Reagans is proudly displayed in their administration building to this day.

Later that day, the American ambassador hosted a reception at Spaso House for a group of 98 dissidents. Among the guests was Father Gleb Yakunin, one of the courageous outspoken Orthodox priests that the Patriarch had objected to Reagan meeting. In his speech, Reagan offered his and United States support for their concerns and, sometimes to their bemusement—although it was largely a secular audience—once again brought up the subject of religion. The Soviet press turned from critical to vitriolic about this gathering and the President's speech, calling it "anti-Soviet," but none of the attendees were harassed by the KGB afterwards—a big leap for Soviet society.

That evening, the Gorbachevs hosted a dinner in the Granovitaya Palace of the Kremlin. This, the oldest public building in Moscow, built in the 14th century, is a historic place where, in the 16th century on his high-backed throne, Ivan the Terrible, surrounded by his *boyars* (noblemen) received the hardy Tudor British mariners, the first Englishmen to see him and Moscow, an unknown place in the West at the time. In this grand hall known as "the holy of holies," under an ornate painted ceiling and surrounded by images of saints, Reagan presented Gorbachev with a copy of the American film *Friendly Persuasion*, starring Gary Cooper, about a group of pacifist Quakers during the American Civil War. In his toast, the President called it "an American classic" and stated that the movie showed "not just the tragedy of civil war, but the problems of pacifism, the nobility of patriotism, as well as the love of peace," and raised his glass "to the art of friendly persuasion." It was a jolly dinner accompanied by numerous warm toasts, much laughter and talk, so friendly that Korchilov, who translated, marveled that it was like seeing the ice of the Cold War melting before his eyes.

MAY 31

At their first one-to-one meeting, Reagan had asked Gorbachev to show him Red Square, although it was not on his official schedule. So on May 31, the two of them took a historic twenty-minute stroll, resulting in a photo of the two leaders happily chatting in front of St. Basil's Cathedral that sent a shock of delight throughout the world. As a curious crowd looked on, Gorbachev gave Reagan a little lesson in Russian, explaining that the word *krasnaya*—"red"—in olden days also meant "beautiful," and that it remains the root of the modern Russian word for beautiful, *krasivaya*. He tried to steer Reagan toward Lenin's tomb. But Reagan quietly said, "Let's not go too far," and, putting his arm around Gorbachev, turned him gently away. (Later, when Reagan was asked why he didn't go see the body of Lenin, he diplomatically replied, "The tomb is only open four days, and the line was so long we didn't want to interrupt it.")

The most dramatic moment occurred when a reporter asked Reagan whether he still considered the USSR an "evil empire." Reagan answered, "No. That was another time, another era,"[21] which delighted Gorbachev, who wrote in his diary that he considered this remark the most important occurrence of the visit, equal to a proclamation of the end of the Cold War. (To keep things in ironic perspective, just out of range of the famous official photographs stands U.S. Navy Lt. Commander Woody Lee, carrying the "football" briefcase containing U.S. nuclear war plan options and launch codes for missiles targeting Moscow and Red Square.)

This was followed by another meeting not on his official schedule, again suggested by Reagan himself. He went to the Central House of Writers to meet with a group of writers, artists, filmmakers, architects, and actors. There he made another eloquent speech (no doubt helped by well informed speech writers, identity unknown), impressing his audience with many allusions to Russian literature, including quotes from Boris Pasternak, Anna Akmatova, Nikolai Gumilev, and others—and above all, Alexander Solzhenitsyn, whom he said he admired, personally voicing the hope that he would soon be published. His audience of the cultural elite of

Moscow warmly applauded his words, and afterwards, one of the attendees asked an American official to tell Reagan that his wish would soon be granted.

Second only to the President's memorable walk in Red Square was the success of his talk at Moscow State University in front of a packed audience of students. Reagan had hoped to have his address broadcast live or at least in its entirety to the whole Russian population, but to his keen disappointment, despite *glasnost* and Gorbachev's earlier agreement, this didn't happen. Only excerpts were shown on *Vremya*, the nightly news program. He delivered this speech standing before a wall of mosaics with red flags and a huge marble bust of Lenin looking down disapprovingly behind him. Although the American side had tried mightily to have the statue moved, the Soviets had refused.

It made no difference in the end. Unruffled, Reagan carried on calmly, speaking like a professor giving the students an impressive basic lesson in American civics and the four freedoms (thought, speech, information, and communication) that are cornerstones of our nation, as well as the virtues of democracy. He called for the removal of the Berlin Wall—"that sad reminder of a divided world." He reached out to the Soviet people, expressing his support for Gorbachev's encouraging the forces of change and new policies, but avoided direct criticism of the Soviet system (although he took a shot at the bureaucracy, which he termed "a problem around the world.") Instead, using examples from the American experience, he voiced his hopes for the new Russian generation, urging them to bring a new freedom to Russia. Korchilov declared it "one of the finest displays of oratory I had ever heard." When he finished, Reagan received prolonged wild applause and a standing ovation so warm and enthusiastic that one observer noted that he thought it greater even than his convention nomination.

That evening, there was an official dinner at Spaso House where jazz luminary Dave Brubeck entertained. It was attended by the highest Soviet and American officials, along with Senators Bob Dole and Robert Byrd, diplomats and the military, artists and athletes, and perhaps most importantly, Andrei Sakharov, who had recently been released by Gorbachev from his exile in the city of Gorky, along with his wife, the feisty Elena Bonner. For the high members of the Politburo to sit down at dinner with them was something inconceivable before Gorbachev. Definitely, times were changing.

As for talking about the contribution of Soviet women, talented politician that he was, President Reagan took me up on this idea not once but three times. The first occasion was an interview on Soviet television when Reagan said he wanted to speak about the great contribution of Soviet women. His remarks took the Soviet interviewer by surprise, throwing him so off balance that he burbled weakly, "We like our women, too." Reagan's remarks caused a small sensation among the ladies, even as far away as the city of Perm in the Urals on the border of Asia and Europe. A close friend of mine, a movie director from Leningrad, was shooting a film in Perm and reported that, while having her hair done in a beauty salon, she heard all the ladies chattering happily, "Did you hear what Reagan said about Soviet women?" I was also told by a Russian friend who attended his Moscow University speech that after Reagan had finished and left the stage, he came back to add, "I forgot to say…" and once again paid tribute to the contribution of Soviet women. At his last press conference before leaving Moscow, he was asked what he had learned in the Soviet Union, and, to the surprise of his interviewer, replied, "I am going to give this one answer because I have wanted to say this and I say it every chance I get. I think that one of the most wonderful sources of stability and good that I have seen are the Russian women" (leaving his audience "somewhat mystified" says Korchilov).

In the three days that he had been in Moscow, Reagan had scored a triumph in the Soviet Union greater than any American president. Jack Matlock wrote that "Reagan exhibited a remarkable degree of cultural empathy. While he concentrated on important themes on the American agenda, he did so with the sensitivity to the concerns of ordinary Soviet citizens and praise for the country's cultural values."[22] With his warmth and wit, he had captured the imagination of the Russian population. The Russians loved him. Lou Cannon, who was there as a journalist, reported that "eager crowds lined the streets wherever his motorcade passed, cheering and waving."

Reagan, too, was touched by what he had seen and the warm reception of the Russian population, proving the truth of the proverb "Better to see once than to hear a hundred times" that Gorbachev had quoted when he first arrived. Although the official Soviet government press was hostile and attacked him for his revolutionary remarks and references to religion, Gorbachev's biographer wrote, "The speeches he delivered to the students… and to the Soviet writers were perhaps his most spectacular performances and touched the deepest chords of the Russian psyche."[23]

As I was not an "official" of any kind, I was not there to witness all this in person, but I was there in spirit. *TIME* magazine on June 6 reported, "The President's visit to what he had once called the 'evil empire' marks the end of an intellectual odyssey…the culmination a result of responding to advisors far more pragmatic than the hardliners of his first term. The new counselors include author Suzanne Massie, who has tutored Reagan in Russian culture; among other things, she has persuaded him that the Soviet Union is on the verge of a religious revival." Continuing, "She has become Reagan's chief guide to the human aspect of Soviet affairs…. She has even taught him what is now his favorite proverb, *Doveryai no proveryai*. (Trust but verify)." For me, following the President's success in Moscow seemed the culmination of our meetings during the previous four years—a little like watching a gifted and brilliant pupil pass the final exam with flying colors. As I studied his schedule and read his speeches, I could see that, as on previous occasions, he had internalized what was useful for him and, in his own inimitable manner, used it masterfully. Matlock, who had been present at two or three of our sessions in Washington, wrote about the Moscow visit that "His [Reagan's] admiration for Soviet women, accustomed to holding full-time jobs while maintaining a household in the midst of scarcity, his love for Russian literature and music, his sympathy for the terrible human losses during World War II and to Stalin's terror, his sensitivity to Gorbachev, and his refusal to take credit for changes in the Soviet Union"[24] could almost have been a synopsis of the content of some of our meetings.

Although Gorbachev was disappointed about what he publicly called "missed opportunities" and took some sharp digs at the President and his advisors during his final press conference, privately he called it "another milestone to better relations." He was delighted at Reagan's press conference when the President was asked, "Who deserves the credit for the changes in the Soviet Union, you or Gorbachev?"

Reagan graciously responded, "Mr. Gorbachev deserves most of the credit as the leader of this country."[25]

He and Gorbachev parted as good friends, and Matlock writes that "Reagan's popularity was probably greater in the Soviet Union than in any other country including the United States—except, perhaps, in some of the captive nations of Eastern Europe."[26] No small achievement. In the end, everyone agreed that the "human factor" had been the most important result of the visit and an important step forward in U.S.–Soviet relations. I was very happy to read this and, I admit, a little bit proud.

CHAPTER 21

MILLENNIUM OF RUSSIAN CHRISTIANITY, JUNE 4–16, 1988 AND LAST LUNCH, AUGUST 1, 1988

Only three days after President Reagan left Moscow, the Millennium of the Russian Orthodox Church was celebrated in the Soviet Union, marking the year 988 when Prince Vladimir of Kiev Rus,[1] then a pagan country, ordered that his nation be baptized into the Eastern faith of the Christianity of Byzantium. The prince ordered mass baptisms in the Dnieper River, along with the destruction of all statues and images of Perun, the Slavic god of thunder. Since the bear was the totem of that ancient pagan god, throughout the centuries after the baptism, the Orthodox Church opposed bear handling at fairs or anywhere else, but despite their disapproval these continued. (I even once saw an icon in which, from behind a bush, a little bear could be seen peeking out, and to this day the bear remains a symbol of Russia.)

In the U.S., our media and Soviet experts paid little attention to the Millennium celebration, calling it unimportant and dismissing it as "the last vestiges of an outworn and discredited religion." I knew differently. For the millions of Orthodox believers in Russia, the celebration of 1,000 years of Russian Orthodox Christianity was an event of the greatest national and historical importance, and for any student of Russian culture, it was a must. As I surely wasn't going to be around to see the next one, I was determined to find a way to be invited to witness it. I had good connections with the Church, and many months before, I had expressed to several Church fathers my great desire as a historian to be there for this event. I had been assured by an important hierarch, Metropolitan Philaret in Moscow, that I would indeed be invited. I scanned the mailbox everyday as the date approached, but no invitation came. It became increasingly obvious to me that being a woman, a secular historian and not a Church official, I was not considered important enough by the high Church authorities to receive one. Crestfallen, I thought I would have to give up.

In Moscow some months before, I had seen my former watchdog, Igor Filin, the KGB colonel who had been assigned to investigate me six years earlier, now the Executive Secretary of the Peace Committee, the powerful organization in charge of all official foreign visitors, and had told him how much I, as a historian, was hoping to attend the Millennium celebrations. He said nothing at the time. Then one day, when I had given up all hope, the much-desired invitation finally arrived in the mail. It was only when I got to Moscow that I learned how this had happened. The Church was obliged to secure the approval of the Peace Committee for all invitations, and as the date grew closer, Metropolitan Philaret had begged Igor for permission to issue 200 additional invitations in order to be able to invite more international religious personalities. Igor agreed, with one condition: "that the first invitation go to Suzanne Massie." So it was thanks to Igor that I was able to witness it all and to be, to my knowledge, the only foreign secular historian present.

From the beginning, the Communist Party had been entirely opposed to holding the Millennium celebrations in Moscow, insisting that these be held in some more distant city. But I was told by a high Church official that at a large reception in the Kremlin, Patriarch Pimen had been approached by Gorbachev, who asked him, "How are the preparations for the Millennium coming along?"

Too cowed to say how much opposition the Church was facing, the ailing Patriarch answered timidly that they were "going well."

Then Gorbachev told him definitively, "If you have any trouble, come to me." The celebrations were held in Moscow.

Clerics from all over the world had been invited. To house their small army of guests, the Church had entirely taken over the thirty-story Ukraine Hotel that contains more than a thousand rooms, one of the four skyscraper-tall Stalin "wedding cakes" that dominate the city's landscape. When I arrived, the vast lobbies of the hotel were overflowing with a kaleidoscopic array of church dignitaries of every Christian denomination in the world, all wearing resplendent vestments—the flowing cassocks, purple and black headdresses, and veils of the Orthodox; the severe black suits and white neck ruffs of the Danish Lutherans; Episcopalian and Anglican bishops in bright fuchsia; Copts from Ethiopia, wrapped in their black capes, their faces almost covered under dark hoods; Roman Catholic Cardinals in red robes, flanked by their monsignors in black cassocks and scarlet sashes. Upon arrival, each guest was handed a briefcase containing descriptive literature, a medal, and invitations for major events of each day each in a different color according to importance of the event: green, blue, yellow, and white, all engraved in gold.

Every need and expense of the guests was taken care of by the Church, including hairdressers and laundry. Outside, 150 chauffeured cars and a fleet of buses waited to transport us to all events. The two huge dining rooms of the hotel were divided between those who were fasting or had special dietary needs and those who did not. Waiters, who in Soviet times were primarily distinguished by their soiled uniforms and sullen and lethargic service, were for this occasion spic-and-span neat, smiling, running speedily to take orders and serve. Most startling for me was a special room where Church representatives were empowered to issue visas for their guests to go anywhere they wished in the Soviet Union. In a land where 75% of the country was closed to foreigners, this was amazing.

As we traveled in buses or cars on our way to various events throughout the city, crowds of people lined the streets to watch us pass, the men respectfully removing their caps and the women in head scarves, all bowing and crossing themselves.

The first gala reception was held in the Kremlin. I vividly remember the stunning impression of following behind several hundred black-cassocked

Orthodox priests with their black headdress veils flowing behind them as we mounted the long red-carpeted Grand State Kremlin staircase that President and Mrs. Reagan had climbed only a few days before, crowned at its summit by the enormous painting of Lenin. While the most important church visitors were officially greeted and welcomed by Andrei Gromyko himself (not a man generally assumed to have religious inclinations) I sat in a huge anteroom (everything in the Kremlin is huge) along with the covey of silent priests, waiting to be summoned to the reception.

It was a reception worthy of the tsars of history, in the magnificent gold-and-white St. George (Georgievsky) Hall with its six enormous crystal chandeliers, where President Reagan had been greeted by Gorbachev. Rows of long tables stretched from one end of the two-hundred-foot hall to the other, crowned with elaborate flower arrangements and large pastry swans, and laden with enormous silver platters of intricately decorated hors d'oeuvres, long Siberian crab legs, large silver bowls overflowing with caviar black and red, and sweet pastries of every sort, along with a forest of champagne bottles, and, of course, vodka. As I looked incredulously over this extraordinary scene and the crowd of clerics, I happened to overhear behind me two Orthodox bishops speaking of the Kremlin, one saying only half jokingly to the other, "If we can hold it for the night, it's ours."

On the following days, a dazzling scenario of events unfolded. Every day, huge meetings were held in the Bolshoi Theater, attended by the clerics of the world as well as many Russian scholars. I noted that Raisa Maximova (although not Gorbachev himself) was present at every one of these, sitting quietly in the second row of the orchestra. When I saw her after one of these sessions, she greeted me warmly and enthusiastically told me how successful Reagan's visit had been and what a wonderful impression he had made on the Russian people.

In the ancient council room of the St. Sergius Monastery, hundreds of assembled Orthodox priests held their conference. In their cassocks and headdresses, they looked exactly like the 17th century gravures of such councils of the past that I had seen in museums—as if nothing had changed since. I remember being struck by the contrast between the lonely and totally abandoned statue of Lenin in the town square while hundreds of townsfolk, all of them bowing reverently and making the sign of the cross, waited in the streets as the priests passed in their buses.

At the Danilovsky Monastery, I witnessed yet another historic event: the formal ceremony of the official return of the Patriarch to Moscow. During the Soviet regime, the Patriarch and his official headquarters had been isolated forty five miles away from the capital at the St. Sergius Monastery, but that day, in the courtyard overflowing with people, the Patriarch was returned to Moscow and the new headquarters that had been built for him at Danilovsky Monastery. For any Russian historian, this was a significant event. Since 1325 the official seat of the Russian Orthodox Church was in Moscow but during the Soviet years the Patriarch had been kept away from the capital, exiled and isolated. Hearing the enthusiastic applause, seeing the joy and excitement of the huge crowd that day when the Patriarch arrived was a clear sign that the communist regime, not being able to destroy the Church, had bowed to it.

After the Danilovsky ceremony, I went to the monastery's newly built hotel, where a portrait of the Patriarch hung on every floor and the dining room served the most authentic and delicious Russian food in the city. There I ran into Igor sitting in the lobby. He was uncharacteristically pensive and quiet and looked so melancholy that I felt sorry for him, so to cheer him I was prompted to say, "Igor, I think you were trying to do some good things."

"Yes," he answered enigmatically, "but we failed."

What did he mean? I don't know.

There were lighter moments as well. I saw my friend Bishop Kliment of Kaluga (now Archbishop) and met the young and dynamic Metropolitan Kiril of Smolensk, who would be elected as the present Patriarch Kirill I in 2009. In the dining room of the hotel, as we sat informally at any free seat, I met clerics from many countries. One morning, the only place open was next to New York's popular and active Cardinal O'Connor, who was finishing his breakfast along with several of his monsignors. I was a bit overwhelmed by that company and not sure how to act, but he turned out to be a friendly and informal man who welcomed me heartily. We had a short conversation and when he got up, shaking the crumbs of his breakfast toast from his scarlet vestments, he cheerfully said, "Well, I've got to get dressed in my ball gown now."

I saw him again at yet another milestone—the blessing of the cornerstone for the first new church to be built in Moscow since the Revolution. Behind us towered newly-built Soviet apartment houses that stood at the edge of a large empty field. Police cars were massed at the entrance to the field. When Patriarch Pimen arrived in his black Zil limousine, he was driven over the waving grass to a red carpet that had been laid for him leading to the site where a large inscribed rock stood, the cornerstone of the future church. Again, there was a large crowd. I stood next to Cardinal O'Connor in his formal red cassock and white lace vestments and South Africa's Bishop Desmond Tutu in his fuchsia cassock, their robes fluttering in the brisk wind. Prayers were said and the Chairman of the Soviet Council on Church Affairs, Konstantin Kharchev, read a special message from Gorbachev himself in which he proclaimed that this new church was to be "the symbol of perestroika" for all, "believers or nonbelievers—one country, one people, one history."

The most spectacular evening was a festive concert held at the Bolshoi at 10 p.m. on June 10. It was the most elegant evening in that ornate gold-and-red theater that I had ever seen. Every seat was filled, clerics in their best vestments, along with what appeared to be every important communist personality, all in formal clothes. Patriarch Pimen was seated in a box of honor. Astonishingly, a huge medallion of St. Vladimir holding up the cross was hung above the stage. Up to that time, liturgical music had been banned in all public theaters, but that evening there was a concert by the best of Moscow's religious and monastery choirs, who performed magnificent Russian religious music. Strikingly, when each choir finished their splendid program, they turned and bowed deeply, not to Raisa Gorbacheva, who was sitting in the first row, but to Patriarch Pimen sitting in a box, stage right. At intermission, I mingled in the crowd, where I spotted Foreign Minister Shevardnadze, the head of the Church Council Kharchev, and other top government officials, also the painter Ilya Glazunov, ballerina Maya Plisetskaya, and other leading artists and Moscow personalities.

On June 12, there was a formal gold-engraved invitation from His Holiness Patriarch Pimen for the final reception. For this, the Church had entirely taken over the four floors of what was then one of the elite restaurants of Moscow—the Praga on the Arbat. Elegant food and drink overflowed, musicians played on every floor, and once again all sorts of well-known regime faces and Moscow personalities appeared.

For those twelve spectacular days, the Church had taken over the city. It was a time when the Orthodox Church, so long denigrated and persecuted by the Soviet regime, came into the open and demonstrated its enormous and—up to then—largely hidden power. Seeing what occurred during those days remains among the most extraordinary experiences of my life, and for me, it was crystal clear that I was witnessing the end of communist rule and that it would soon be on its way out, as indeed, just three years later, it was.

So, when I look at those gold-engraved invitations today, it is as if I were looking at the end of communism. After seeing what I had, it did not take a sage to know that the State had run aground on the immovable rock of the nation—Orthodoxy—and that things would never be the same again.

Rather than attend all of the lengthy Church conference sessions and meetings that continued to take place in the final two days, I decided to take advantage of the opportunity to travel to places in Russia that had previously been prohibited to foreigners. I went off with my friend, the late Dmitry (Dima) Pokrovsky, a great music scholar, the Alan Lomax of Russia. With great difficulty under the communist regime, Dima had managed to travel all over the land visiting distant villages in Russia to copy, preserve, and record traditional native music that was fast disappearing. He had formed a singing group that performed this native music in authentic traditional Russian garb, concerts so eagerly awaited by the public that, although hardly publicized, they were mobbed whenever they occurred.

Amazingly, we simply bought plane tickets. No watchdogs, no questions, no papers to show, and flew down to Rostov-on-the-Don. From there, we boarded a venerable riverboat up the Don River and spent three memorable days on the former island stronghold of the Don Cossacks, staying in the humble dwelling of three church restorers who were Dima's friends, dining on salted fish and strawberries from their garden, and drinking homemade *samagon* (Russian moonshine).

One morning, I went for a walk and lay on the sand on the banks of the Don, peacefully soaking up the sun, watching the cranes flying, and marveling at where I was. An old lady appeared out of the woods and scolded me ferociously for being provocative, lying on the sand like that! I fled. The next day, cossack families from the collective farm across the river came over and sang and danced on the village green. Providing a pair of their soft boots (which they later gave me), they invited me to join them and I did, wishing with all my heart that my family could have seen me!

Back in Rostov before we left, I was taken to a horse farm and saw the most splendid horses I had ever seen. There I was lucky enough to be taken by an elderly coachman for a troika ride on the turf of the race track. Galloping at a breakneck speed that took my breath away, I exclaimed about his skill, but he told me sadly that none of the young people of the present day wanted to learn his craft. They don't know what they're missing!

Thanks to the Church, to Igor, to Dima, I was blessed with unforgettable days that showed me that the Russian past, despite everything, had never really disappeared.

POSTSCRIPT

Although some of his entourage snickered behind his back about Reagan's "hang-up" on religion and Colin Posell once told him sarcastically that he should not get carried away and "think that Gorbachev was going to get down on his knees in front of him"[2] Reagan stubbornly stuck to his bedrock principles, trusting his instincts and deep conviction about the importance and impact of the religious revival in Russia that I had told him about. After my return from the Soviet Union in early 1986, although less stringent than Powell, Shultz was dubious about what he judged to be my "buoyant enthusiasm for what I saw as "a renascence of Russian spirituality" writing: "I was not swept up by her rhetoric... Suzanne Massie gave a different glimpse of a different Soviet reality from the one I read about in my secret briefing papers... There might well be a vast historic transformation developing I felt, but the dimensions went well beyond religion and reached into the realm of economics, politics and the changes wrought by the information revolution as well."[3]

Of course he was not wrong. There were many currents at work and economics were to play a large role in the end of Communism, but in the Soviet Union of 1986, when Shultz wrote, the influence of the information revolution was not one of them. Although already an established factor in the West, it was still years away there and not a significant element of change. At the time, xerox machines were still kept under lock and key and computers so rare and expensive that no ordinary Russian citizen could even dream of owning one, let alone know how to use it. I continued to believe, as the President did, that the rise of religion in Russia was a critical dimension, just as it had been in Poland. My conviction was reinforced by what I had witnessed at the Millennium.

LAST LUNCH WITH THE PRESIDENT

After my return to the United States, I was invited to have lunch at the White House with President and Mrs. Reagan in the Oval Office Study, where I had never been before. Present also were NSC Advisor Colin Powell and Chief of Staff Ken Duberstein.

I had always tried to report to the President the good things I had heard said about him in the Soviet Union, so I related that, when I had seen Raisa Gorbacheva at the Bolshoi Theater she had made it a point to tell me enthusiastically how successful the recent visit of President and Mrs.

Reagan had been and how glad the Russian people had been to greet them. I then added that it seemed to me that despite her sometimes unschooled behavior, Raisa was somewhat insecure and shy. To which Mrs. Reagan interjected indignantly, "*Shy* is not the word I would apply to that woman!"

I did not contradict her and neither did the President, but he very quietly said to me, "I think you may be right." He spoke happily about how impressed he had been with his visit to Moscow, how unexpected and heartwarming the reaction of the Russian crowds had been for him, and how much it had meant to him.

This lunch was quite a different meeting than the others. We didn't discuss Soviet–American relations as we had usually done before, mainly my impressions of the Millennium, the enthusiasm of the Russian crowds, and the overwhelming reception of the Church to all the international clerics. I also told them about my unexpected visit to Rostov-on-the-Don and the cossack island—events that I considered landmarks of changes in Soviet society. Both Colin and Ken were quiet and never asked any questions.

In his diary that night, the President, sounding a bit disappointed, wrote, *Back to a lunch with Suzanne Massie (just back from Russia). Nancy, Colin, & Ken D. on hand. It was a strange one. We expected her usual insider type of information but instead it was almost like a travelogue. She did say the Russians have a real feeling of friendship for Nancy & me.*

Guess he was right. My trip to Russia for the Millennium had been a purely personal one. I had seen a lot that was startling, but had not had any unusual conversations with government figures to report, nor any "insider" information. Although actually, it was "inside information" since I was the only secular foreign historian invited, and witnessed what I was convinced was a pivotal turning point in Russia. I guess I hadn't made that as clear as I should have.

When we parted, the President gave me a hug and Mrs. Reagan thanked

MILLENNIUM OF RUSSIAN CHRISTIANITY AND LAST LUNCH

me and said warmly, "Come see us in California." After those four years and all that had happened, certain it would be the last time I would see them, I left feeling wistful and sad. Afterwards I exchanged a few cards and notes with them and when I was in Washington, Michael Deaver gave me news.

―――

But it was not to be the last. Although I never did see them in California, I was to see them together again once more two years later on September 16, 1990 when, on their way to Moscow to bid farewell to Gorbachev they took time to make an unpublicized stop in Leningrad and came to visit Pavlovsk palace, the subject of my book, which Reagan had read. This palace, a work of art executed by some of Russia's greatest architects and artists of the late 18th and early 19th centuries had been burned and virtually completely destroyed by fleeing Nazi armies in World War II. Since 1944, miraculously risen from the ashes of war, Pavlovsk was the first palace to be rebuilt and is especially dear to the citizens of Leningrad. Thanks to the work of a host of devoted Russian artists and artisans, the palace and grounds have been painstakingly restored—and the work continues still. So, this unexpected visit by a former president of the United Sates was a fantastic event and he and his wife were greeted by cheers of delight from the crowd of surprised and delighted Russians who happened to be visiting the palace that day. As Leningrad Documentary films were making a film about me at the time, they were the only photographers present and captured the joyous arrival of the former president and his wife as they made their way through the throngs of people to where I was waiting for them on the palace steps, where both greeted me with a kiss Then along with the overjoyed senior palace curators, I took them through the palace. I noticed that throughout our tour Nancy held her husband's hand especially protectively and that he seemed a little more vague than usual. When the visit was ended the gracious palace curators gave me the pen with which Reagan had signed their guest book.

There was to be a comical finish to the visit. As the Reagans left, I was whisked into a car with our consul general and his wife to join their motorcade that swept out at top speed to return to Leningrad—only to have the entire motorcade brought abruptly to a complete stop at a nearby railroad crossing by the waving hands of a determined old babushka, responsible for the opening and closing of the barrier fence well in advance of the scheduled train. Nervously fingering their pistols, KGB and U.S. security men exploded out of their cars. Doggedly, they tried to convince the old lady that given the importance of the motorcade she MUST signal the train to stop and lift the barrier. Arms folded stubbornly over her chest, she refused. No argument or threat could persuade her. No matter that the former president of the United States, the American consul general, Soviet and American security details had to wait. For her, one of Russia's indomitable and fearless grandmothers, that barrier was a sacred duty, and she would not be budged. We were forced to wait, interminably, it seemed, until the long commuter train with all its cars had passed. Only then, in her own time, with no apologies, she walked at a snail's pace to the barrier and calmly lifted it. I didn't have a chance to ask the President what he thought of her performance or even say thank you and goodbye to him, as because of the delay, he and Mrs. Reagan were whisked directly to their plane for Moscow.

That was the last time I saw them together. It had been a memorably happy day. But when in 1994, we learned from the president's fine and courageous letter that he had been stricken with Alzheimer's, it came back to me how unusually tightly and protectively Nancy had held his hand as we went through the palace that day.[4]

CHAPTER 22

A FEW LAST WORDS

I never expected to be seeing the President on any kind of a regular basis, but he kept the relationship going with the result that, even while they were taking place, I thought each meeting would be the last and was not aware at first that I was having any influence on him. Indeed, I knew less about Ronald Reagan and the details of the contentious White House background of the events he was facing during those four years than I do now. I think my full realization of how extraordinary these many meetings actually were came when I was told by a senior archivist at the Reagan Library after the President's death, that I had had more "face time" with President Reagan on the subject of the Soviet Union/Russia than anyone but his closest advisors.

The past four years of studying my own notes and tapes, and the extensive research I have done in the preparation of this book, have considerably deepened my understanding of those days. One thing that continues to surprise me is how much my experience with the 40th President of the United States has continued to excite so much curiosity and questioning from people all over the world, even though many years have passed since it all happened. Persistently, I am asked: "What was Reagan really like? What did you spend all that time talking about? Why did you get along? What did you both learn?"

So, fully aware that there are many who knew him far better than I did and have had their own impressions, here are a few of mine.

From the very first time I saw him, I was struck by the fact that the President in person always gave the impression of being physically very big. He was 6'1", rangy, broad-shouldered, but perhaps because of his always erect bearing, he projected the impression of being even taller. Michael Deaver observed that he had "a presence that dominated the room." People often whispered that he dyed his hair, but the President himself always swore he didn't. In a letter to his friend, the singer Rudy Vallee, he wrote that "No, the truth is the color is my own—no dye. My older brother has hair about the same color as mine. It must be genes or we are just lucky I guess."[1] He said he never used makeup even when he was in the movies in Hollywood. His face looked his age, with some nice laugh wrinkles, but because I had known so many dancers, what impressed me most was how gracefully he moved, effortlessly rising from his chair with the ease of a man decades younger.

I wondered how could he be in such good shape? We never saw him huffing and puffing, running in his exercise shorts like Clinton, or bicycling with a helmet on like Bush (the younger). This was no accident. The fact was that he exercised faithfully every day in the White House gym, working out with weights and developing terrific biceps. He even did so on the road, but we never saw him doing it.[2] He was photographed riding, which he loved, and cutting brush at the modest ranch that he adored, but never sweating. Reagan was always conscious of how people expected a president to behave and look, and he did so with grace, dignity, and respect for the office, along with the actor's sure sense of what was right, and privately paid close attention to the small details of his public appearance.[3]

Reagan was always proud of the fact that he had been an actor, and was hurt when some meanly called him a "two-bit actor." All one needs to do is take a look at the film *Kings Row* to know that he was a good one. Those who sneeringly underestimated him and denigrated him for being "only an actor" forgot, I think, how much an actor needs to know and how useful such training can be to a politician. Actors are first and foremost, students of human behavior and emotions. To be good at their profession, they need to develop the intuition to understand and depict character, the sensitivity to get under the skin of another, to discern how and why a person entirely different from themselves may think and behave. They do not look for mirror images. I have known several actors and have found that they are often shy and reserved and live most vividly on stage. They learn best not from position papers, or the abstract ideas of geopolitics, but from watching and listening. Good actors are sensitive, observant, and emotional. Reagan was all three. Gorbachev himself told me how struck he was by Reagan's "sensitivity to people," saying "that's an actor's talent."[4]

Actors also need to be able to speak well and convincingly, and President Reagan was confident of his ability to touch people. He did not need any image-makers. What you saw was what you got, a quality that has all but vanished today with spin doctors and touched-up photographs.

He was accused of sometimes seeing things in a "romantic" Hollywood way. For me, the opposite of "romantic" is "prosaic," and he certainly was not that. Reagan was an artist, not a bureaucrat, an idealist, and yes, a dreamer who believed in happy endings and the American dream as shown in the movies. I could understand this. I like movies and the old Hollywood, too. As a teenager, I collected movie magazines and cut out pictures of stars to make scrapbooks. If my mother had not thrown out all those magazines after I went to college, I would be a lot richer today. If I could have, I would have liked to be in the movies myself, and I don't know how I would have survived in the most difficult times of my life without movies to take me away from times of worries and despair. So I could sympathize with Reagan and understand why he preferred to watch mostly "old movies" when he was in the White House. I watch them all the time. In the best ones, the women are not victims, they are strong, elegant, witty, resourceful, independent, and intelligent—Bette Davis, Rosalind Russell, Katherine Hepburn, Jean Arthur, Barbara Stanwyck. Men respect them and are delighted by them. I feel sorry for the young women of today who, obligatorily, it now seems, are treated to endless repetitive scenes of naked bodies breathing hard and writhing in bed, plus bloody violence and fiery explosions. The President loved to tell stories about his movie days. The fact is that the Hollywood he knew and loved did, and still does, continue to inspire millions of people all over the world and make them dream.

Yes, he was polite and courteous, an "old-fashioned" kind of guy in the leading man Hollywood mode of his friends Jimmy Stewart and Spencer Tracy, all gentlemen from a more polite era. Courtly and gallant, he liked and respected women and told me more than once how proud he was that he had been the first president to name a woman to the Supreme Court (Sandra Day O'Connor in 1981). He adored his wife and treated her like a princess. His beloved mother, Nelle, was an outstanding woman of great accomplishments, compassion and principles whose example and Christian life inspired him and remained a guiding example all his life. Michael Beschloss, the noted presidential historian, told me that, in the course of preparing his book, *Presidential Decisions*, he had seen "somewhere, perhaps in the President's personal papers," that Reagan had written that I "reminded him of his mother." If true, it is the greatest compliment he could have paid me.

He was unshakable in his belief that America was a beacon of light for the rest of the world—not because of its wealth or military power, but because of the ideals it stood for. People sensed his sincerity and respected it even when they disagreed with him on many things. Today, in our age of unprincipled vitriol and innuendo, he looks like an Eagle Scout, and I believe that historians will look back on the Reagan years as the end of an era for America—a better, less cynical era.

If there is one thing mentioned in the mountain of books about President Reagan, it is that despite his famed affability, people often found him mysterious, elusive, opaque. It unnerved many that he did not talk much in meetings and mostly remained silent. Many found this upsetting. Some even took it as a personal affront. Edmund Morris, his official biographer, seemingly frustrated when confronted by his silence, finally had to resort to fictionalizing him. Others, even his nearest and dearest, his beloved wife and his son, Ron Jr., referred to a "veil" that remained between him and others. (Michael Deaver told me that even Nancy was not sure how he made his decisions.)

His fourth National Security Advisor, Admiral John Poindexter, once told me how surprised he was when, after he was finished his daily briefing of the President, in the short time it took Reagan to get up and go to the door of the Oval Office, he would change from attentive seriousness into the affable personality of the "Great Communicator." I, too, was surprised to find that he was among the most reserved and interior men I had ever met. When, in our first meetings, I, too, ran into his silence, I thought it was my fault. I know I talk a lot, and although I rap myself on the knuckles mentally, I can't seem to change.[5] Ashamed that I had done most of the talking, as we were winding up our fifth Oval Office meeting, I blurted out, "Mr. President, this is not a normal conversation! I want to know what you think!" He laughed, and I found that when we were lunching together with Mrs. Reagan later, he was relaxed and talked freely.

As a writer, I found this disparity between the so-called "Great Communicator" and the extremely reserved and complex man who kept his inner thoughts private and played his cards close to his chest, fascinating, contrasting as it did so dramatically with his well-known public persona. In our meetings in the Oval Office with his advisors present, except for a few memorable times, I rarely knew exactly what he was thinking. He mostly listened and I could sometimes discern no obvious reaction. Though this unnerved me at first, I always felt that I was at his service and that whatever he wanted to hear about, I should tell him. I had no axes to grind. I wanted things to be equalized, and for that you need a win-win situation—people can't lose face. It was only as time passed, when I saw that he acted on information I had given him that I realized how carefully he had listened and internalized the information that was most useful to him.

I did sometimes wonder whether his silence might be a tool that gave him the chance to closely observe the person talking to him, giving him the time to judge and decide whether he trusted them with his thoughts. He was wary of "intellectuals" and "experts," and distrusted bureaucrats. He often had totally different ideas than did the conventional wisdom of a Washington establishment that felt that some of his ideas could not possibly succeed, but he often proved that conventional wisdom wrong. Since many of his advisors were opposed to some of his most cherished ideas, perhaps his fabled "impenetrability" and "opaqueness" stemmed in part from the fact that he had learned that he could not come right out and express his deepest thoughts and aspirations, and shrewdly understood that his opaqueness gave him the chance to make his own judgments, to say only what would serve his ends but not limit him until he was ready to act. I wondered, too: could the fact that he was the son of an alcoholic possibly play any role in his famous silence? Doctors say that children of alcoholics are often opaque and tread carefully to avoid painful confrontations.

The quality that impressed me most was his modesty, and modesty is the beginning of wisdom. As a reporter and writer, I have met many powerful men in many countries. Reagan was different. He was comfortable with himself. He had his ego firmly under control, a rare thing in any man and especially one with such power. I was often struck when entering a room that the men around him were tense and exuded ambition. But not him. He was calm, and the first message he gave to anyone was "Relax." It seemed to me that he quietly accepted the fact that he was "not brilliant," not an "intellectual" (whatever that is). He never tried to be anything but himself, and was firmly centered in a set of values from which he would not deviate. He often corrected those who called him the "Great Communicator", saying that he was not that, but that there were "great ideas to communicate." George Shultz wrote, "He was very content with himself. That was one of his great strengths. He had an inner peace—as contrasted with inner turmoil we have witnessed in other presidents before and since. He had a strong value system that was unshakable."[6]

Perhaps it was this modesty that was at the core of his famed sense of humor. I noted how well he used jokes didactically, understanding perfectly a fact that I had learned myself in my lectures—that what people laugh at, they often remember more clearly than long and dry analyses. Reagan's public jokes were never mean or cynical and were often directed at himself. Jokes and humor can also be a protection, a way to hide, to cover up one's own hurt or anxiety, defuse tense situations, and put people at ease, as I know from my own experience. A prime example in President Reagan's case is when, after his near-fatal assassination, he managed a joke to comfort his terrified Nancy, saying, "Honey, I forgot to duck!" When going into the operating room full of anxious doctors, he famously said, "Hope all you guys are Republicans!" After his surgery, with a breathing tube down his throat and unable to speak, he managed to scratch out with a pencil the jocular message, "If I had gotten so much attention in Hollywood I would have stayed there." And only then did he follow with his anxious personal questions: "Can I chop wood? Will I be able to ride?"[7]

How important jokes were to him was recently revealed once again when a box containing thousands of jokes in his handwriting on 3 x 5 index cards were found. He loved and collected jokes that Russian people told about themselves, and always wanted to know the latest jokes I had heard in the Soviet Union. I read that he also had a great supply of off-color jokes, but I never heard him tell one—at least not in front of me.

As I've said before, he was often denigrated. Among the enduring myths about him is that he did not work much. Wrong. Many witnesses report that he worked all the time, often until late in the night. It was also said that he did not read much. Wrong again. From his early youth, he was a broad and eclectic reader, and continued to be so during his presidency. (For my part, I know he read my books.) Nancy said that he read every night before going to sleep.

He was a tremendous writer and wrote easily and well. For me nothing demonstrates better his talents as a great communicator than this. As governor of California and in his early presidential campaigns, he wrote his own speeches. As president, he rewrote large sections of the speeches and proposals that were given to him. He jotted down observations on almost everything in life from the joy of a starry night to executive imaginings of missile defense. He dictated 265 letters during his presidency and discontinued this in 1982 because he preferred writing by hand. He wrote upwards of 10,000 letters in his lifetime, making notes for many of them in black ink on the yellow legal pads he preferred before they were typed.[8] He faithfully kept a daily journal. Much of this can now be read and seen in the Reagan Library and in the fat volumes of his published letters and journals. I treasure the ten letters he wrote me and the many comments and mentions of our meetings in his journal.

He was a good listener, asked succinct and often unexpected questions, not rooted in a career of study but an understanding of human nature. He was interested in motives and attitudes and always seemed to know exactly what he needed to hear and to absorb the essentials, including small details, very quickly, yet never losing sight of the big picture. I never knew what he would find useful and only later, when I saw how he acted in a given situation, was I able to see what he had absorbed. People said he drifted off all the time, but one observer commented, "He drifted off after he heard what you had to say, when he became convinced you had nothing further to say to him."[9] I am proud of the fact that he never drifted off in our meetings, not once.

As I got to know him, my respect for him not only as president, but even more as a human being, grew. I found him to be more a man of the heart, not logic, and, as the French say, "the heart has reasons that reason cannot know." I don't know why we got along so well. We just did. It was a kind of miracle. No one has described our connection better than Bud McFarlane, who, in a January 8, 1992, interview with Chris Lydon, who was writing an article about me for *The Atlantic Monthly*, said:

> "I introduced her to Reagan for two reasons: First she has a profound knowledge of Russian history and culture that I thought would be educative for Reagan, who had a superficial knowledge of other countries and cultures. Second, knowing that Reagan thought more in terms of his role as a historic figure, a person who by dint of persuasive ability could influence the thinking of a foreign counterpart, as opposed to an analytical geopolitical approach, he was a human-to-human thinker, and I thought Suzanne's approach would ground him in who Gorbachev was as an individual. And finally she's a realist not a romantic. She has a passionate love for the Russian people but no illusions about the damage done by the Marxist–Leninist authoritarian political system and the demonic history the Russians had confronted in the 20th century.

So she had a depth of knowledge, realism, and the ability to relate to this more humanly rounded policy. I think it worked. In her sessions, she educated Reagan on the difference between the Russian people and the Soviet government—and the fact that they weren't to be held responsible for the policies and goals of this government.

Before she arrived, he was disdaining the whole problem—in effect, why should he bother with a lot of Commies? But to get him interested in the human dimensions of the Russians was to engage him. Human beings he related to. One way to motivate him was to paint for him this stunning mass of humanity and convince him he could do something about it. You could tell that in his body chemistry it was working. Her language is salty, she can be severe in her criticism. Reagan began to lean forward.... She's a bit of a performer, and they related that way. Their personalities are similar...She was talking his wavelength about people.... I would say it was dangerous to bring somebody in with this humanistic turn of mind if they brought also a lot of illusions. You wouldn't have brought an art scholar into the Oval Office for the romanticism of it. Suzanne is a realist about Communism. And she had been recommended by Scoop Jackson and Bill Cohen, whom I respected a lot."

I think I was simply in the right place at the right time to communicate what I had learned for his use, and that I was able to give him some tools in dealing with Russians that fortified the President's own instincts and perhaps in a small way increased his confidence to use his instincts and human approach as only he could do. I do not really know why the information and the stories I told him played a role in reshaping his thinking, but I am grateful that I was able to communicate my personal passion and experiences to him. It was a great privilege and a gift for which I can only be grateful to God, as it seems now that this proved of benefit not only to him, but ultimately to the people of the United States and the people of the Soviet Union.

CHAPTER 23

THE PRESIDENT LEAVES

I was at home in Maine on June 5, 2004. It had been a long week. I had been ill, trying with difficulty to work my way through a pile of boring correspondence and queries, which had finally come to an end. Each of the myriad details of leaving for a long trip that would take me to St. Petersburg, Russia, London, Istanbul, and the Black Sea had been checked off meticulously. My husband, Seymour Papert, was already on a plane that was winging him from Australia to Heathrow airport, where somehow we were to connect. I was finally packed and could at last sit down and catch my breath before tucking in early.

I turned on the TV and got the Belmont Race Track, where the wonder horse that had won everybody's heart, Smarty Jones, was to try for the Triple Crown. The huge crowd was joyous, excited. More small bets had been placed on him than any other horse in history. He was a horse that had come out of nowhere, it seemed, sprung not from a multimillionaire's fancy stables, but from a modest owner in a wheelchair, a down-to-earth trainer and jockey from Philadelphia, where even nuns had been praying for him. The hopes and hearts of thousands of ordinary folk all over America were with Smarty Jones, and as the wonder horse and his jockey slowly walked through the crowds, people tried to reach him and held up signs of encouragement. Their enthusiasm was catching, and, as the beautiful animal began to run, I found myself, alone in my living room, cheering along with them, happy, smiling, hoping. Heartbreakingly, he lost by a short length, and even the winning jockey was sad.

Then I switched channels and learned the news. At ninety-three, after his ten-year struggle against the disease that had taken him into the shadows, President Reagan had died. Somehow for me the two images were joined—that marvelous horse who had won the hearts of ordinary folk and the president who had given Americans a joy, a pride of nation, and an optimism that had since been taken away from them. The parade of pictures, the many commentaries I heard and saw, came through a haze of memories along with a great sense of loss and the strong feeling that with his death had come the end of an epoch of the America he liked to call "that shining city on a hill." Exhausted as I was, instead of being able to go to bed, I sat down and tried to write a letter of condolence to Nancy Reagan, but, full of emotion, my words were woefully inadequate for what I felt. I wrote that letter with no expectation of attending the funeral.

In sadness, I left for Russia but I was in St. Petersburg barely three days when, to my astonishment, I was called by the State Department. The National Security Council had gotten in touch with them and was looking for me on behalf of Mrs. Reagan, who wanted to invite me to the President's state funeral. I was deeply touched that she, burdened by her grief, had thought to remember me.

But how to do this? By the time Washington had found me, it was 4 p.m. on Wednesday afternoon Russian time (8 a.m. U.S. time). The funeral was to be on Friday morning, less than two days later. What to do? To get there in time, I would have to be on a plane the next morning. My husband urged me to try, saying that I would regret it all my life if I didn't make it. In those days in Russia, all offices closed down tight at 5 p.m. No way to call an airline or book a plane ticket after that, and no way to do so at the airport, where, before even being admitted to the departure area where the airline representatives worked, one had to show one's ticket.

Blessedly, I can say that I have countless friends in St. Petersburg. I called one of them, a private travel agent, who somehow managed after closing hours to not only get me a reservation but to produce a ticket and have it delivered to me in the space of an hour. In hurried phone calls in the United States, my assistant in Maine managed to find my old friend

Marilyn in Washington, who offered to pick me up at the airport, and had just time to catch FedEx to send an appropriate dress.

Hurriedly, complicated arrangements were made for me to be able to get my official invitation to the ceremony—no easy matter, as the strict rule that I was required to do this personally had to be waived.

I left St. Petersburg early the next morning, Thursday, to catch my plane in Helsinki, and found that I was traveling on the same plane as the former president of Finland. There were delays in Finland and in New York, but I managed to get to Washington by 9:30 p.m. Thursday night.

In California, over 100,000 people had snaked for hours through roads clogged with traffic to pay their respects at the Reagan Library, where the President's coffin lay before being flown to Washington. In Washington, another 104,184 people had waited for three hours in line in the beating heat of summer to view the coffin lying in state in the Capitol Rotunda, and when I arrived, despite the late hour the lines were still long, many still waiting patiently to pay their respects—people of all ages, some pushing strollers and baby carriages. It was as if all felt they had lost a member of their own family, which indeed, in a real sense, they had, for Ronald Reagan loved people, connected with them, and always knew how to make them feel as if he were talking to each one individually. It certainly was so with me.

On June 11, the day of the State funeral, the gigantic Washington Cathedral, with its tall stone towers, soaring Gothic arches, and stained glass windows, was packed with over 4,000 people. Members of Congress and the Senate, Supreme Court Justices, political candidates and world leaders. Dame Margaret Thatcher, former Prime Minister of Great Britain and Reagan's close personal friend and ally, was seated next to Mikhail Gorbachev, who, in a rare tribute to his former enemy who had become a friend, had arrived earlier to pay his respects personally at the President's flag-draped coffin in the Capitol Rotunda and afterwards had gone to Blair House to embrace Mrs. Reagan.

Elsewhere in the cathedral were leaders from all over the globe: princes, kings, ambassadors (among them Prince Charles of England, King Abdullah of Jordan, Kofi Annan Secretary General of the UN and Lech Walesa, former president of Poland). Moments before the funeral began were spent for greeting each other and networking. Al Gore, whom I had known for many years, came over to hug me and ask how my son, who was waiting for a liver transplant, was doing. While I waited for the funeral to begin, I saw many familiar faces, a galaxy of the Reagan administration, among them some old friends that I hadn't seen since my Reagan days in Washington. I thought about all the meetings I had had with the President, how young and vigorous he had been in those days, how full of life, and yes, how much I would miss him. I deeply regretted that I had arrived too late to be able to call on Mrs. Reagan to pay my respects and thank her for being kind enough to invite me to share this historic event.

I was seated in the left apse, a few rows behind the honorary pallbearers, at the end of a row directly opposite the ex-president of Finland with whom I had traveled across the Atlantic, and across the aisle and a few rows behind Prime Minister Tony Blair of Great Britain and his wife, Cheri. As it happened, the former American presidents came in, not down the middle aisle, but down the aisle of the left apse, and I was lucky to be in the end seat beside the aisle. So all the presidents filed by me, close enough to touch, and I was able to observe them carefully: Gerald Ford, walking with firm step; Jimmy Carter, looking old and frail; followed by Bill Clinton, massively tall with his shock of white hair. Then it was the elder George Bush and finally George W. Bush, the sitting president, who came bouncing down the aisle—and as he passed Tony Blair, slapped him familiarly on the buttocks football-team style, a gesture that made me wince.

I had a direct view of the flag-draped coffin carried in by ramrod-straight military men—one from each service—and could diagonally observe Mrs. Reagan, very thin, pale, and porcelain-fragile, who had come in firmly supported on the arm of tall, dignified, white-gloved Army Major General Galen P. Jackman.

Despite her grief, Nancy herself had directed all the funeral planning, paying close attention to details. It was she who had personally asked Margaret Thatcher, former Prime Minister of Great Britain, Brian Mulroney, former Prime Minister of Canada, and former President George H. W. Bush to speak. A few rows behind her sat Mrs. Thatcher, dressed in black and wearing a large black hat that almost obscured her face, and immediately next to her, Mikhail Gorbachev. Too weak from her recent illness to be able to speak personally, Mrs. Thatcher had several months before recorded a video that was projected onto a large screen. Considering who she was sitting next to, I was shocked to hear her refer to the "evil empire," as did several other speakers. I think Reagan would not have been pleased. (I was gratified to hear later from my friend Teresa Heinz that Bush the elder had apologized to Gorbachev.) Other than that single discordant note, the funeral was splendid, unforgettable, dignified and yet touchingly personal.

Afterwards, Mrs. Reagan, her family and close friends were flown to California aboard Air Force One for the burial at the Reagan Library in Simi Valley, attended by many close Hollywood friends and personalities. All three of their children spoke movingly. Then his devoted Nancy, who had held herself so erect and brave through the long funeral ceremonies, finally succumbed to her grief. Laying her head on his coffin, she broke into tears…and then it was slowly lowered into the earth as the last rays of a brilliant sunset illuminated the western sky and the faraway glittering Pacific Ocean.

I was to see Nancy Reagan again in California at the Reagan Library. Situated at the top of a winding road, it is a beautiful place that crowns a mountaintop in Simi Valley, overlooking a wild expanse of California countryside. Built in Spanish hacienda style with a dark red tiled roof, the library is surrounded by orange trees and flowering bushes. There is a spacious entrance courtyard with comfortable benches and, in the center, a bubbling fountain. It is elegant yet welcoming. I have been there several times and always looked forward to working in the quiet research section and having lunch on the sunny back patio with its magnificent view to the distant Pacific.

The first time I visited there was when Mrs. Reagan invited me to give a lecture in the Library's auditorium. The last time I was to glimpse her was in October, 2005 when she included me in what was called a "family celebration" (a cast of many hundreds) for the inauguration of the new exhibit in an enormous additional wing that had been added to the library. As I thought it might be the last time she would appear in public, I flew from Maine to California to attend.

This impressive new building was built over a mountaintop, and one entered in what was the third floor. I looked up to see an extraordinary sight. Suspended high above my head was a shining Boeing 707 with the presidential shield—Air Force One—looking as if it were in flight. Reagan had been the last of six presidents who had traveled the world in that plane. It was scheduled to be demolished, but fulfilling his desire to have it be part of an exhibit that would show children what it was like to be a president, and thanks to a wealthy Texan, Boone Pickens, who financed the project, the plane was cut apart and its parts hauled up the mountain and reassembled in the new hangar-sized building where it was hung. President Reagan, who didn't like to fly, had flown 630,000 miles on that plane.

The gleaming plane was the star, but downstairs the exhibit also included a Marine One helicopter and a presidential limousine. On the upper floor, there was an exhibit showing the many countries Reagan had visited. Also, strikingly heralded by huge flags of both the United States and the Soviet Union hanging on the walls, visitors passed through "Checkpoint Charlie" (the name given by the Western Allies to the best known Berlin Wall crossing to the East) into a room where films were shown of the two leaders meeting. From there, curving metal stairs suspended from the ceiling led into the plane. A photographer stood ready to photograph delighted visitors waving in presidential style at its entrance. In the cockpit, I discovered that the plane was so high and artfully suspended that one could not see the earth below, only clouds in the sky ahead, so it seemed to be flying.

Replaced today by a humongous Boeing 747, this 707 seemed modest and small, intimate. All the worldwide communications were tucked into a closet-sized compartment. The cabins were narrow; in one, Reagan's flight jacket hung from a chair in front of a table where his favorite yellow legal pads lay, and, to my surprise, there were only a few seats in the back for the press. (Today, there is usually a special plane provided for the huge press corps that accompanies a president.) The whole exhibit was marvelous, well worth a visit to the Reagan Library. Everybody loved it and, as Reagan had hoped, the children most of all.

It was a wonderful, nostalgic celebration, pure Reagan. His favorite foods (macaroni and cheese, barbecued meat) were served. An Irish pub in Tipperary that was named after him had been carefully recreated, and draft Guinness (a dry Irish beer) was served to all comers. The Irish owners, treated as honored guests, occupied a table in the center of the room, laughing and toasting. Children from a California dancing school performed Irish jigs. Hugh Sidey, the veteran journalist who had covered the White House and the American presidency more than four decades for TIME magazine and had traveled often with presidents as a member of the press, spoke and ventured the opinion that, if Reagan had been there, he would surely have told a joke. He then proceeded to quote Reagan as once saying to him, "Hugh, did you know the Irish built most of our prisons?" ("No," said Sidey.) The President continued jovially, "And then they proceeded to fill them!"

It was an unusually cold day for California, and Nancy was dressed warmly in a tweed suit. That day, she was not the radiant princess of the presidential days, beaming at the side of her handsome prince. She had recently been ill and looked very fragile. She gave a short speech, expressing her thanks, and, at the end, touchingly recited her husband's favorite Irish blessing :

> *May you always have walls for the winds*
> *A roof for the rain, tea beside the fire*
> *Laughter to cheer you, those you love near you*
> *And all your heart might desire.*

And then, overcome with emotion, she broke into tears. She was engulfed by the crowd as she left and was whisked away before I could reach her to wish her well.

I have thought of her often over the years that have passed, always with the hope that her children and close friends have provided her with a measure of comfort during the painful years that followed her halcyon days in the White House. In the words that Ronald Reagan often used, heartfelt thanks to you, Nancy, for all that you did for him, for our country—and, so graciously, for me.

EPILOGUE

"Perhaps we are all witnesses in a great trial whose outcome is unknown but whose outlines we can glimpse, as behind the clouds we can sometimes glimpse the silhouettes of angels."
Oleg Okhapkin, Russian poet

There can be and still is much controversy over President Reagan's actions and aspects of his domestic policies. Yet ironically, members of both political parties these days keep trying to hang onto his coattails. Perhaps this is because politics for him was, above all, a moral cause, not a mere pursuit of power, his belief rooted in a deep idealism about the role of America—something sadly missing today in our national life, more than ever ruled by special interests and money.

In foreign policy, he was a revolutionary who bucked his advisors and went his own way toward his deeply held hope of abolishing all atomic weapons.

His great achievement was that, often against ferocious opposition from his advisors, he was able for the first time since the Communist takeover of Russia to forge a relationship—not of agreement, but of trust—with a Soviet leader. He did this when others wanted only to keep a more "realistic" status quo, and went directly against the establishment position that the best we could do was contain and accommodate the Soviet Union because it would never change. He believed that it would, as did I. On his watch, the perilous years of the Cold War ended without the firing of a single shot. Of course, he was not singly responsible for this; Gorbachev and the Russians also deserve great credit, but I am certain it would not have happened as it did without Ronald Reagan. He managed the difficult transition that led to a new and less demonic relationship between our two nations. Long after Reaganomics and Iran Gate are forgotten, this will remain his most important and lasting legacy, the one that supersedes all others.

At his funeral, many moving words were spoken by his friends. Former Prime Minister of Great Britain, Margaret Thatcher, said of him, "Nothing was more typical of Ronald Reagan than his large-hearted magnanimity, and nothing was more American. While resolute in purpose and guided by an unwavering moral compass, he saw many sides of truth." The former Prime Minister of Canada, Brian Mulroney, observed that, "Ronald Reagan does not enter history tentatively," and added that it was pure Reagan to disdain "the moral equivalency occasionally in fashion when talking about the West and the old Soviet Union and paint his vision of the future in bold, bright colors." A moving homily was delivered by the former Missouri senator, Reverend John Danforth. But one phrase has stuck in my memory above all others, the words of his Vice President, George Bush, who said of him that "He never turned an adversary into an enemy."

Eloquent testimony to this fact is that, long after his death, at a conference in England in 2011, a British academic remarked that he had always considered Reagan "rather an intellectual lightweight." Gorbachev, who was present, rebuked him, saying, "You are wrong. President Reagan was a man of real insight, sound political judgment, and courage."[1]

At the Reagan Library there is a re-creation of Reagan's Oval Office, where a tape plays his familiar voice delivering a moving description of his last day in that office, the last message he wrote before he drifted into the shadows of the cruel Alzheimer's disease that robbed him of his memory. He speaks of his feeling about the Oval Office, how he felt the presence of former presidents—and ends with a description of his final briefing by his last National Security Advisor, Colin Powell, who concluded by saying, "Mr. President, the world is quiet today." What president has heard those precious words since President Reagan left?

Yes, he was always an optimist. At times, lesser men mocked him and called him "unrealistic," but I say to this, "Amen." We have too few of such men in political life today, in our cyber age of machines, cynicism, greed, and vulgarity. Reagan was a man who could and did play many roles, but he was a man who, in his heart of hearts, clung to his deepest dreams and beliefs even when all others did not, and who made many of them happen. We can find some clues to his complex and sometimes enigmatic personality, but that he kept many secrets unspoken is perhaps the mark of all great dreamers.

On the horseshoe-shaped monument of his tomb on a mountain in California, overlooking the beauty of the state he loved to the far-off horizon and the vast reaches of the sparkling Pacific Ocean are engraved words taken from a speech he gave at the dedication of the Reagan Library on November 4, 1991 that leave us with his deepest belief:

> *"I know in my heart that man is good, that what is right will always eventually triumph and [that] there is purpose and worth to each and every life."* [2]

So ends the story of those extraordinary four years in my life. These days I live and work on the Maine coast by the ever-changing Atlantic Ocean in a log house in the forest. I continue to write and to go to Russia whenever I can. Official Washington is once again a faraway and impenetrable place. When I reflect on those unforgettable four years, they remain a proof that even the most far-fetched things are possible and that life holds extraordinary surprises for us all. We are, indeed, all witnesses. As my father always told me, each one of us can make a difference in the world. Believe in your convictions and your dreams. If you care strongly enough, persevere. When it comes to human relations, nothing is impossible.

And always remember that anyone in the world is only two introductions away.

SELECTED BIBLIOGRAPHY OF BOOKS AND ARTICLES

BY RONALD REAGAN:
Reagan, Ronald, An American Life. Edited by Kiron Skinner, Annelise Anderson & Martin Anderson. New York: Simon & Schuster, 1990.
Reagan: In His Own Hand. Edited by Douglas Brinkley. New York: The Free Press, 2001.
The Reagan Diaries. New York: Harper Collins, 2007.
Reagan: A Life in Letters. Edited by Kiron Skinner, Annelise Anderson and Martin Anderson. New York: The Free Press, 2003.

SOURCES CONSULTED:
Anderson, Martin, *Revolution: The Reagan Legacy*. Stanford CA: Hoover Institution Press, 1990.
Beschloss, Michael, *Presidential Courage: Brave Leaders & How They Changed America, 1789-1989*. New York: Simon & Schuster, 2007.
Bourdeaux, Michael. *Faith on Trial in Russia*. London: Hodder & Stoughton, 1971.
Risen Indeed:Lessons in Faith from the USSR. Crestwood, NY: St.Vladimir's Seminary Press, 1983.
Cannon, Lou. *President Reagan: The Role of a Lifetime*. New York: Touchstone, 1991.
Chernyaev, Anatoly. *My Six Years with Gorbachev*. Translated by Robert English & Elizabeth Tucker. University Park, PA: Pennsylvania State University Press, 2000.
Deaver, Michael K. *A Different Drummer: My Thirty Years with Ronald Reagan*. New York: Harper Collins, 2001.
Behind the Scenes. New York: William Morrow & Co., 1987.
Dobrynin, Anatoly. *In Confidence: Moscow's Ambassador to America's Six Cold War Presidents (1962-1986)*. New York: Times Books, 1995.
Gorbachev, Mikhail S. *Gorbachev: Mandate for Peace*. Toronto: PaperJacks Ltd., 1987.
Gorbachev, Mikhail S. *Memoirs*. New York: Doubleday, 1996.
Hersh, Seymour M. *The Target is Destroyed*. New York: Vintage Books, 1987.
Hoffman, David E. *The Dead Hand*. New York: Doubleday, 2009.
Kengor, Paul. *God and Ronald Reagan: A Spiritual Life*. New York: Regan Books, 2004.
Korchilov, Igor. *Translating History*. New York: A Lisa Drew Book/Scribners, 1997.
Mann, James. *The Rebellion of Ronald Reagan: A History of the End of the Cold War*. New York: Viking, 2009.
Matlock, Jack F., Jr. *Reagan & Gorbachev: How the Cold War Ended*. New York: Random House, 2004.
Rogers, Will. *There's Not a Bathing Suit in Russia and Other Bare Facts*. New York: Albert & Charles Boni, 1927.
Shultz, George. *Turmoil & Triumph: My Years as Secretary of State*. New York: Scribners, 1993.
Solzhenitsyn, Aleksandr. Translated by Alexis Klimoff. *Rebuilding Russia: Reflections and Tentative Proposals*. New York: Farrar, Straus & Giroux, 1991. Translated by Michael Nicholson & Alexis Klimoff. *The Moral Danger: How Misconceptions About Russia Imperils*

America. New York: Harpers, 1980.
Strober, Deborah Hart and Gerald S. Strober. *Reagan: The Man & His Presidency: The Oral History of an Era*. New York: Houghton Mifflin Co., 1998.

ARTICLES:
"Arthur Hartman Planning to Quit as Envoy to Moscow in Early '87." *The New York Times* (December 19, 1986).
"A Russian Expert Who Has the President's Ear." *The New York Times* (September 26, 1985).
Bailey, Norman A. "The Strategic Plan that Won the Cold War." *National Security Decision Directive No. 75*. McLean, VA: Potomac Foundation, 1999.
Barnes, Fred. "Chums." *The New Republic* (July 14, 1988): 10-12.
Belyakov, Vladimir V., ed. "Summit Washington D.C." *Soviet Life: Special Supplement for Subscribers* (December 7-10, 1987).
Editorial. "Our 'Man' in Moscow Should be Mrs. Massie." *New York City Tribune* (December 30, 1986).
Friedman, Saul. "Leaders Come Out on Top." *Newsday* (December 13, 1987).
Gailey, Phil. "President's 'Tutor' on U.S.S.R. Chats about Ordinary Russians." *St. Petersburg Times* (December 18, 1987).
Kandel, Bethany. "Ron's Secret Advisor." *New York Daily News* (October 8, 1984).
Kaplan, Fred & Alex Beam. "Reagan Prods USSR on Rights." *The Boston Globe* (May 28,1988).
Lydon, Christopher. "Agent of Influence." *The Atlantic* 271:2 (February 1993): 28-30, 39-40.
Santini, Maureen. "Nancy, Raisa—They'll Mien [sic] Well." *New York Daily News* (May 29, 1988).
Seaman, Barrett. "Has Reagan Gone Soft?" *TIME* (October 13, 1986): 38.
Watson, Russell, Robert B. Cullen and Thomas M. DeFrank. "Reagan in Moscow." *Newsweek* (June 6, 1988):16-19.
Whittemore, Thomas. "Rebirth of Religion in Russia." *National Geographic Magazine* (November, 1928).
Wilson, Page Huidekoper. "The Summit's Godmother." *The Washington Post* (May 22, 1988).

ELECTRONIC SOURCES:
"Alexander Yakovlev and the Roots of the Soviet Reforms." *National Security Archive Electronic Briefing Book No. 168*.
http://www2.gwu.edu/~nsarchiv/NSAEBB/NSAEBB168/index.htm
Blanton, Thomas and Svetlana Savranskaya, eds. "The Moscow Summit 20 Years Later." *National Security Archive Electronic Briefing Book No. 251*.
http://www2.gwu.edu/~nsarchiv/NSAEBB/NSAEBB251/index.htm
Beckhusen, Robert. "New Documents Reveal How a 1980 Nuclear War Scare Became a Full-blown Crisis." *Wired.com*. May 16, 2013, http://www.wired.com/dangerroom/2013/05/able-archer-scare/.
Birch, Douglas. "The USSR and US Came Closer to Nuclear War Than We Thought." *The Atlantic*. May 2013, http://www.theatlantic.com/international/archive/2013/05/the-ussr-and-us-came-closer-to-nuclear-war-than-we-thought/276290/.

Cobb, Tyrus W. "Reagan & the Strategic Defense Initiative: Key to the End of the Cold War?" *National Security Forum*. March 21, 2013, http://nationalsecurityforum.org/wp-content/uploads/2013/03/Reagan-and-SDI-Final-version.pdf.

"To the Geneva Summit: Perestroika and the Transformation of U.S.-Soviet Relations." *National Security Archive Electronic Briefing Book No. 172*. http://www.gwu.edu/~nsarchiv/NSAEBB/NSAEBB172/index.htm.

ADDITIONAL READING:

Aldous, Richard. *Reagan and Thatcher: The Difficult Relationship*. New York: W.W. Norton, 2012.

Andrew, Christopher & Oleg Gordievsky. *KGB:The Inside Story of its Foreign Operations from Lenin to Gorbachev*. London: Hodder & Stoughton, 1990.

Arbatov, Georgi. *The System: An Insider's Life in Soviet Politics*. New York: Random House, 1992.

Berezhkov, Valentin. *History in the Making: Memoirs of World War II Diplomacy*. Moscow: Progress Publishers, 1982.

Cohen, Stephen F. *Failed Crusade: America & the Tragedy of Post-Communist Russia*. New York: Norton, 2000.

Deaver, Michael K. *Nancy: A Portrait of My Years with Nancy Reagan*. New York: Harper Collins, 2004.

Fitzgerald, Frances. *Way Out There in the Blue: Reagan, Star Wars and the End of the Cold War*. Simon & Schuster, 2000.

Hayward, Steven F. *The Age of Reagan: The Conservative Counterrevolution 1980-1989*. New York: Crown Forum, 2009.

Kaligin, Oleg with Fen Montaigue. *The First Directorate*.New York: St. Martin's Press,1994.

Matlock, Jack F. Jr. *Autopsy of an Empire: The American Ambassador's Account of the Collapse of the Soviet Union*. New York: Random House, 1995.

Medvedev, Zhores A. *Andropov*. New York: W.W. Norton, 1983.

Oberdorfer, Don. *The Turn: From the Cold War to a New Era: The United States and the Soviet Union 1983-1990*. New York: Poseidon Press, 1991.

Roosevelt, Selwa. *Keeper of the Gate*. New York: Simon & Schuster, 1990.

Swan, Jack. *A Biography of Patriarch Tikhon*. Jordanville, NY: Holy Trinity Russian Orthodox Monastery, 1964.

Ulam, Adam B. *The Bolsheviks*. New York: Macmillan, 1968.

FOOTNOTES

All the descriptions of and conversations with the President and Mrs. Reagan are taken from my copious notes and tapes dictated after our meetings.

PROLOGUE
1. Hemophilia is a potentially fatal defect in the process of blood coagulation that causes prolonged and acutely painful bleeding and destruction of the joints as well as bleeding in internal organs, kidney, liver and brain. It is a recessive defect of the X chromosome that determines sex. Incorrectly called "the royal disease" because of Queen Victoria of England whose third son, Leopold, was born with the condition. Her daughters passed the condition to many royal families of Europe, most famously, Russia. Occurring in all races worldwide, 30% to 40% are caused by a mutation, cause still unknown. As I had twenty-one male first cousins and my sisters have healthy boys, I was judged to be a mutation. Once hemophilia occurs it is passed by the mother, suffered with only rare exceptions only by boys. Girls do not exhibit the condition but can be carriers. In families who have mainly girls it can skip generations.
2. *Glasnost*: Introduced by Gorbachev in the mid-1980s an official policy of the Soviet government emphasizing candor in discussions of social problems and shortcomings along with *perestroika*: economic, political and social restructuring.

CHAPTER 1: THE LONG ROAD
1. There are two mass siege graves in St. Petersburg. One, the Piskaryov cemetery where 850,000 bodies are buried and the other, the Semyenov, for 350,000 others.
2. The town of Pushkin, fifteen miles from St. Petersburg, originally named Tsarskoe Selo (the Tsar's Village), was founded in 1710 as an imperial summer residence. The name was changed to Pushkin in 1937 to commemorate the 100th anniversary of the death of the poet Alexander Pushkin.
3. Prononciation of "*St. Petersburkh*" by Constantine is as it was written and pronounced in Peter the Great's time. When I told my friend the late Evgenia Lehovich (born Princess Ourussova of the distinguished aristocratic Russian family), administrative head of George Balanchine's School of Ballet in New York, that I was going to Leningrad, she made the statement, "I know the poets are there. I wonder who they are?" Her question remained indelibly in my mind when I got to Leningrad.
4. *BUFETT* is the Russian prononciation of the French word "buffet." In the Soviet Union every theater had one where, at intermisson, is served coffee, tea, sometimes cheap Soviet champagne, and more or less elaborate snacks. This one had nothing but coffee.
5. He meant Grand Duke Vladimir Alexandrovich, brother of Tsar Alexander III and uncle of Nicholas II. "Great Prince" was his literal English translation of the Russian term for Grand Duke: *Veliki Kniaz*.
6. In Soviet years called the Kirov Theater (and the Kirov Ballet) after the assassinated Communist boss of Leningrad. Since 1991, returned to its former name, Mariinsky (Marie's Theater), after the daughter of Nicholas I.
7. *Manège*: a building where horses train and exercise. Here a ballet term referring to a male dancer's circle of high leaps around the stage.

CHAPTER 2: THE WORM TURNS

1. When our publisher wanted to have *Nicholas and Alexandra* read for accuracy by a professor whose field it was, none could be found in the United States and the only one they could locate at all was one who had done work on the trains of the time.
2. Former Soviet dissident Natan Sharansky wrote in his 2004 book, *The Case for Democracy*, (p.3): "Kissinger saw Jackson's amendment as an attempt to undermine plans to smoothly carve up the geopolitical pie between the superpowers." Jackson believed that the Soviets had to be confronted, not apeased. Andrei Sakharov was another vociferous opponent of détente. For him, it was also a matter of international security. As he succinctly put it: "A country that does not respect the rights of its own people will not respect the rights of its neighbors." Solzhenitsyn called it a "charade."
3. Senior staff member, NSC 1969-74, then Counselor U.S. State Department, known for his philosophical affiliation with and influence on Henry Kissinger, architect of foreign policy in Nixon and Ford administrations.
4. *Knout*: A scourge-like multiple whip used in Russia, usually made of a bunch of rawhide thongs attached to a long handle, sometimes with metal wire or hooks. A few blows of this lethal whip could maim or kill its unfortunate victims.
5. The former George Pullman mansion at 1125 16th Street in Washington. Built in 1910, became the Embassy of Russia in 1913 then Embassy of the Soviet Union until 1994 when the Soviets built a large new modern Embassy on Wisconsin Avenue. It remains the residence of the Russian ambassador.
6. Quote reported by historian Douglas Brinkley, *American Spectator*, August, 2010.
7. I was to meet her in Moscow in 1986.
8. This was a premature judgement. Since 1975 more than 500,000 refugees, many of whom were Jews, evangelical Christians, and Catholics from the former Soviet Union, have been resettled in the United States. An estimated one million Soviet Jews have immigrated to Israel in that time. Jackson-Vanik also led to great changes within the Soviet Union. Other ethnic groups subsequently demanded the right to emigrate and the Soviets had to face the fact that there was widespread dissatisfaction with their governance.
9. My former husband Robert Massie's book, *Peter the Great*, published at the same time was also negatively attacked the following day after mine by the same *Times* reviewer who called Bob's book, "boring." It was later selected for a Pulitzer Prize.
10. Solzhenitsyn expressed his thanks, writing that he imagined "that I had met opposition in my work and that the passage of this book may not be light" but that he hoped this would not shake "my noble impetus to enlighten my fellow countrymen on the truth of an earlier Russia." When *Firebird* was published, he sent a telegram to the publisher's party—his first public endorsement of any book in the United States. This was not worth mentioning in our press, and when, a year later, a quote was put on the front cover of the paperback edition, the editors at Simon and Schuster turned down Nobel Prize-winner Solzhenitsyn's endorsement in favor of one from journalist Hedrick Smith.
11. *Land of the Firebird* was not published in Russia until 2000.
12. When William Odom was named Military Advisor to President Carter, and he and his wife moved to Washington, I introduced Anne Odom to Hillwood Museum where she became a docent and then in later years chief curator of the museum.
13. *Pavel Livinov:* Physicist, writer, human rights activist and Soviet-era dissident. Grandson of Maxim Litvinov, Stalin's Foreign Minister. Born and raised among the Soviet

elite he became a critic of the system and in 1968 demonstrated in Red Square against the Soviet invasion of Czechoslovakia and was sentenced to five years exile in Siberia. Able to leave Soviet Union after his exile, he lives in the United States today.

Major General Petro Grigorenko: 1907-87, one of the main voices of conscience in the Soviet Union, heroic member of the Soviet dissident movement, friend and defender of the Crimean Tatars, founding member of the Ukrainian Helsinki Group in Moscow. Placed in a psychiatric "punitive" hospital from 1969-74, he was finally released due to pressure from the international community and plunged back into human rights work. He died in forced exile in the United States, stripped of all his military honors.

14. SCUSA: Student Conference on Military Affairs. The largest conference of its kind in the world, held at the US Military Academy each year. Delegates from colleges all over the USA spend four days discussing current topics affecting foreign policy with military officers, professors, and State Department specialists.

15. Lieutenant Colonel Tyrus Cobb served in the European and Soviet Directorate, NSC, from 1983-1988.

16. Edwin Meese: Attorney General in the Reagan administration, 1985-88.

17. War Colleges are for advanced study and training for top military leadership of senior U.S. officers. There are five War Colleges: Army War College, Carlisle PA; Naval War College, Newport, RI; Air Force War College, Montgomery, AL; and two National War Colleges in Washington DC. I spoke at the Army, Navy, and Air War Colleges.

18. General Andrew Jackson Goodpaster, 1915-2005. Distinguished American hero, quintessential soldier-scholar. Recipient of thirteen medals for valor and service including the Presidential Medal of Freedom and the Medal of Freedom. Retired in 1974, he returned to active duty in 1977, giving up one star to serve as Superintendent of the U.S. Military Academy in order to clear up a notorious cheating scandal that had happened there. His fourth star was returned after he retired for the second time.

19. The great mathematician and computer scientist Seymour Papert of MIT tells me that the military also took the most important steps in the early computer years.

20. IREX: International Research and Exchanges. A LJS-based nonprofit organization committee for international education in academic research, professional training and technical assistance.

21. IMEMO: Institute of World Economy and International Relations, Moscow. One of the world's leading research institutes. A highly reputed center for fundamental and applied socio-economic, political and strategic research.

22. ISKRAN: Institute for U.S. and Canadian Studies. A Russian think tank, part of the Russian Academy of Sciences, specializing in comprehensive studies of the United States and Canada. The main Soviet, and later Russian center of research of American and Canadian foreign and internal policy. Founded by Dr. Georgy Arbatov in 1967 who led the Institute until 1995.

CHAPTER 3: BACK TO THE USSR

1. George Shultz. *Turmoil and Triumph: My Years as Secretary of State.* New York: Scribners, 1993, p. 5.
2. G. Arbatov, A Yakovlev, Y. Primakov.
3. *Rus:* Name of early Russia.
4. Orthodox Easter is celebrated on a different date from Western Easter.
5. *Pood*: An Imperial Russia weight measurement equal to 36.11 pounds.

CHAPTER 4: BACK IN THE USA: A STEP CLOSER

1. The U.S. now has eighteen Trident ballistic missile submarines. Each submarine carries over 1,000 times the destructive power of the Hiroshima atomic bomb. The 18 submarines carry fifty percent of the total US strategic warheads. At least five, each with hundreds of warheads, are on constant patrol in the Atlantic and Pacific.
2. Timothy Wirth: U.S. House of Representatives (Colorado) 1975-1987, U.S. Senator (Colorado) 1987-1993, President of the United Nations Foundation 1998-2013.
3. Senator John Heinz died in a tragic plane accident in 1991. Teresa Heinz is now married to John Kerry, former Senator from Massachusetts, now Secretary of State.
4. Early Spanish princesses, often accompanied by a dwarf as contrast to their beauty.
5. Rick was thinking of Bud's father, William, a congressman from Texas (1933-39).

CHAPTER 5: FIRST MEETING

1. National Security Council, Senior Director of Soviet and European Affairs, 1983-87.
2. Back channel: an unofficial and private channel of communication between political entities.
3. The so-called "Doomsday Clock" is an invention of the editors of *The Bulletin of the Atomic Scientists* who, at the end of WWII began to dramatize the professional journal's annual assessment of global nuclear danger. Since 1947, *The Bulletin* periodically moves the Atomic Clock either forward towards midnight or backward, depending on how close civilization may be to nuclear Doomsday.
4. No women were directly involved in Soviet policy until 1985 when a 29-year veteran of the State Department, Rozanne Ridgway, was named Assistant Secretary of State of European and Canadian Affairs, becoming the highest ranked woman in the department. A specialist in Soviet arms control policy, she was chief negotiator for all Reagan and Gorbachev summit meetings.
5. The Imperial Russian Duma, initially an advisory organ to the tsars, was given broader powers in 1905 and became the precursor of the Russian constitution.
6. Michael Deaver described that first meeting with Reagan: "I'll never forget how the CIA, the State Department, the National Security Administration would set up these meetings on the Soviet Union for him. After about fifteen minutes he would glaze over and sometimes doze a little. Bud McFarlane brought Suzanne Massie to see him...I sat in that first meeting with Suzanne Massie. She wasn't talking about throw-weight and the military of the Soviet Union. She was talking about the people and the spirit and boy, the old radar homed right in on it—and he had a lot of meetings with her. She was the one who was responsible for getting Reagan ready for summits, not the experts over in the State Department or the CIA. That was exactly what he wanted. He wanted to learn how these people were made up." (Miller Center Oral History Interview, March 21, 2013.)

CHAPTER 6: MISSION TO MOSCOW

1. Today blessedly destroyed, replaced by the super expensive and luxurious Ritz Carlton hotel. The street has been returned to its original name, Tverskaya.
2. Arthur Hartman, U.S. Ambassador from 1982-1987.
3. Our embassy in Moscow today numbers some 1200 people, many housed in a walled compound in the middle of Moscow, complete with American supermarkets and stores, sports facilities and movie theaters. The embassy personnel once had a contest to see who could stay in their compound longest without going out.

4. A measure of Glazunov's popularity among the Russian public was demonstrated in 1985 at one of his large exhibitions in the Moscow Manege—in Imperial times a huge ring for excercising the mounts of the Horse Guards. This enormous building in the shade of the Kremlin in central Moscow was mobbed by three million people—many who had to wait for hours to get in. The U.S. Embassy reaction was that it was "not important."
5. She was to tragically commit suicide only a year later.
6. Russian translation: "*daryonomu konyu v zuby ne smotryat.*"
7. MID: The Ministry of Foreign Affairs, Soviet counterpart to the US State Department.
8. I later met Bessmertnykh when he came to Washington with General Chervov and a Soviet delegation for congressional meetings in 1984. In following years we became friends.
9. Proven after the Soviet Union itself collapsed.
10. Richard Burt: State Department in 1983. Assistant Secretary of State for European and Canadian Affairs and, from 1985, Ambassador to Germany. Richard Perle: Reagan Assistant Secretary of State, known in Washington as "The Black Prince." Both hawks.
11. A stunning example was when, at the United Nations in the '60s, a highly-placed Soviet diplomat I met argued passionately that it was Rockefeller who controlled Kennedy, that everyone knew this, and couldn't be shaken from his position.
12. One that caused a furor was the showing of the Garbo film *Ninotchka* which made fun of the Soviet system and was taken as a deliberate insult.
13. At that time (1982-84) Lawrence Eagleburger was Deputy Secretary of State.

CHAPTER 7: LUNCH IN THE OVAL OFFICE
1. The rodeo idea was greeted with great enthusiasm by several western senators. When I brought it up in the Soviet Union the reaction was the same. They had horse clubs all over their country and had immediately gotten in touch with their Olympic champion horsewoman who eagerly offered her help. The idea percolated and was about to come to pass until I discussed the ongoing plans with Jack Matlock who had become our new ambassador in 1987. Alas, he scotched the whole idea saying, "Somebody might fall off a horse." Despite this inevitable risk, I still think it would have been a good idea.
2. A Metropolitan is equivalent to a Cardinal in the Catholic Church. Philaret is a monastic name.

CHAPTER 8: THE ACHILLES' HEEL
1. Will Rogers. *There's Not a Bathing Suit in in Russia and Other Bare Facts.* New York: Albert & Charles Boni, 1927, p.155.
2. At the Harvard Russian Research Center, where I was a Research Fellow for twelve years, discussion of religion was discouraged. Admiral Inman confirmed that I was the first, and indeed the only, analyst or Russian expert who brought up the subject when he was Deputy Chief of the CIA.
3. Ronald Reagan's 9/9/81 letter to John O. Koehler: "I have had a feeling, particularly in view of the Pope's visit to Poland, that religion might very well turn out to be the Soviets' Achilles' heel."
4. A much revered, courageous, and outspoken man, Tikhon had served nine years in the United States (1898-1907) as Bishop of the North American Diocese and Alaska and kept warm memories of his stay in our country which had made a strong impression on him. He spoke out forcefully against the Bolsheviks and openly condemned the killing of the tsar's family. In 1923, he was accused of counter revotutionary activities and imprisoned

in the Donskoi Monastery. In 1924 he fell ill (rumored poisoned by the Bolsheviks), was hospitalized and died in 1925. From the time of his death he has been considered a martyr and was canonized in 1981 by the Synod of Bishops in the Church Outside Russia and in 1989 by the Moscow Patriachate during the glasnost period.
5. Ringing of church bells was prohibited and I remember my shock in the early '80s when I heard a church bell ring in Moscow for the first time.
6. There is a poignant film showing this destruction. The cathedral was to be replaced by the tallest skyscraper in the world with a gigantic statue of Lenin on top. This building could never be built and the cathedral was finally replaced by a swimming pool.
7. See *National Geographic Magazine,* November, 1918.
8. A Russian once told me, "No soldier dying on the field ever called out, *For atheism!"*
9. Evgenia Ginzberg, Aksynov's mother, was arrested in 1937, condemned to the gulag for ten years and exiled for five more. She finished her searing book, *Journey into the Whirlwind,* about her years in the camps in 1967. It could not be published in the Soviet Union but was smuggled out and published in the West.
10. This was possible because of a loophole. The Orthodox Bishop of Antioch had a church in Moscow by special agreement because the Orthodox church in Antioch had been destroyed in an earthquake in the 10th century and the seat moved to Damascus. His church in Moscow was under fewer regulations than Russian churches so there was a bustling business in baptisms and marriages.
11. This remark seemed to have a particular resonance for President Reagan, perhaps thinking of his own mother, a deeply religious woman.
12. The Russian definition of art: "The purpose of art is to uplift mankind and serve God." The Soviets changed only one crucial word in their official definition: "The purpose of art is to uplift mankind and serve *the State."*(italics mine)
13. *Kulich* is a tall cake with a rounded top, baked in a cylindrical mold. *Paskha* (means Easter in Russian), made of butter, farmer cheese, heavy cream and egg yolks, a bit similar than our cheesecake, molded in a triangular mold, is its obligatory rich companion.
14. Reagan never stated publicly or in any account exactly what he meant by "mission."
15. Edwin Meese in *Reagan: The Man & His Presidency: The Oral History of an Era,* by Deborah Hart Strober and Gerald S. Strober (New York: Houghton Mifflin, 1998.) p. 55
16. Author interview with Robert McFarlane, 1998.
17. Nancy Reagan had two meetings alone with Pope John Paul II.
18. Gorbachev *Memoirs*, p. 328.
19. Mikhail Gorbachev *On My Country and the World.* New York: Columbia University Press, Pgs. 20-21.

CHAPTER 9: MOSCOW INVITES, WASHINGTON CALLS

1. The date brought to my mind two prophetic books: George Orwell's *1984* (published 1949) and Andre Amalrik's *Will the Soviet Union Survive until 1981?* (published 1969).
2. One of the four skyscraper-tall buildings that dot Moscow called "Stalin Wedding Cakes."
3. Arkady Shevchenko, *Breaking With Moscow*, New York: Alfred A. Knopf, 1985. The memoirs of the Soviet diplomat and highest-ranking Soviet official to defect (1978) to the West.
4. As a follow-up to our meeting, I wrote a long memo to the President about my ideas about Russian attitudes and the realities of life in the Soviet Union, as well as my own

sense of Gorbachev. Although I had been strictly warned that any "position papers" for the President could only be one and a half pages, mine was eleven pages. I hesitated and asked the advice of my Episcopalian minister about whether I could dare to send it. He advised me jovially, "Go ahead. He can always read it where the king goes alone."

CHAPTER 10: GENEVA
1. Shultz, p. 586.
2. Matlock, Jack F. Jr., *Reagan & Gorbachev:How the Cold War Ended*. New York: Random House, 2004, p. 143.
3. Matlock, p. 144.
4. Shultz, p. 586
5. Matlock, p. 152.
6. I had urged, "Talk for two years!" They nearly did..
7. Author phone interview with McFarlane, 2010
8. Matlock, p. 134
9. Mann, James, *The Rebellion of Ronald Reagan,* New York: Viking, 2009, p. 66.
10. Ronald Reagan, *An American Life*, New York: Simon and Schuster, 1990, p. 640.
11. Today, The Academy of Russian Ballet.
12. Author interview with McFarlane, 1999.
13. Matlock, pp. 152-3.
14. Matlock, p. 164.
15. Anderson, Martin, *Revolution, The Reagan Legacy* Hoover Institution Press, 1988, p. 83.
16. Shultz, p. 376
17. Shultz, p. 376
18. Shultz, p. 466
19. Author interview with McFarlane, 1998.
20. Matlock, p. 166.
21. Ronald Reagan, *An American Life*, p. 567.

CHAPTER 11: LUNCH ON THE PATIO
1. On President Reagan's desk in the Oval Office was a card that read "There is no end to the power you can have if you don't care who gets the credit."
2. Pentecostalists were released on April 12, 1983.

CHAPTER 13 REYKJAVIK
This account is a personal observation gleaned from my study of that historic near-miss meeting, and not a detailed account of the complicated negotiations. For any of my readers who wish to consult the voluminous official accounts and the word-for-word exchanges between Reagan and Gorbachev, I have listed the main sources I have consulted in addition to newspaper and correspondent coverage.
1. Shultz, p. 750
2. Shultz, p. 758
3. Shultz's joking translation to the press of the Russian proverb was the American saying "In God we trust, but all others pay cash."
4. Mikhail Gorbachev. *Memoirs,* New York: Doubleday, 1996, p. 416
5. Shultz, p. 755

6. Shultz, p. 757
7. Shultz, p. 763
8. Paul Nitze (1907-2004). Distinguished and often controversial government official who served in high ranking posts in several administrations. Always convinced of the Soviet Union's military and nuclear threat. At the time of Reykjavik he was Special Advisor for Arms Control to President Reagan and Secretary Shultz.
9. Shultz, p. 763
10. Matlock, p. 214
11. Gorbachev, pp. 415-16
12. Matlock, p. 222
13. Shultz, p. 774
14. Gorbachev, pp. 415-16
15. Matlock, p. 232
16. Shultz, p. 780
17. Shultz, p. 780
18. Yet, his idea did not die. In 1996, General Goodpaster, along with General Lee Butler and Rear Admiral Eugene Carroll, co-authored a statement for the Global Security Institute advocating a complete elimination of nuclear weapons because they "constituted a nuisance and a danger" and were of "no military utility."
19. Shultz, p. 778
20. Shultz, p. 777
21. *Ronald Reagan an American Life,* New York: Simon and Schuster, 1990, p. 674
22. Shultz, pp. 776, 780.
23. Gorbachev, p. 419
24. Gorbachev, p. 419
25. Gorbachev, p. 419
26. Gorbachev, p. 419

CHAPTER 14: NANCY

1. The public was far less critical. In every annual Gallup Poll from 1981 on, the American public voted her as one of the ten most admired women in the world. In 1985 and 1987, she topped the list.
2. Her trademark in clothes was "Nancy red," the President's favorite color.
3. She confessed to Merv Griffin, "I'm scared every time he leaves the house and I don't think I breathe until he gets home. I cringe every time we step out of a car or leave a building." Patti Davis, *Angels Don't Die*, Harper Collins, 1995, pp. 26-27.
4. Among the major naysayers: Clark, Casey, Weinberger, Brezinski and Kissinger.
5. Calculating that it would antagonize viewers and increase anti-American feelings, the authorities had the film shown on Soviet television.
6. Their horoscopes might have provided a warning clue: Nancy was Cancer (July 6), "touchy, unforgiving." Raisa, Capricorn (January 5), "over-exacting, rigid."
7. Tellingly, this question and Gorbachev's answer was deleted when the interview was shown on Soviet television.

CHAPTER 15-GORBACHEV COMES TO WASHINGTON

1. Anatoly Dobrynin was Soviet Ambassador from 1962-86, serving during the terms of six U.S. presidents.
2. Korchilov, Igor. *Translating History*. New York: A Lisa Drew Book/Scribners, 1997, p. 12
3. Among the obligatory: Vice-President George Bush, Secretary of Defense Frank Carlucci, Secretary of State George Shultz, Protocol Chief Selwa Roosevelt, White House Chief of Staff Howard Baker, Assistant Secretary of State for European and Canadian Affairs Rozanne Ridgway, National Security Advisor Colin Powell and Deputy Chief of Staff Kenneth Duberstein.
4. Baron de Bodisco arrived from Russia in 1838 as Envoy Extraordinary and Plenipotentiary and rented the house at 3322 O Street. That year he gave a Christmas party for his two nephews, students at Georgetown College, and met a beautiful 16-year-old girl, Harriet Beall Williams, with whom the 54-year-old diplomat fell madly in love. They were married in 1849 and he bought the O Street house for her as a wedding present where they lived happily until his death in 1854. He urged his wife to remarry when he died in order to make some other man "as happy as she had made him" which she did, marrying a British diplomat in 1860.
5. I was told by Ambassador Beyrle that sometimes imitating Reagan's pronunciation, Gorbachev would repeat the proverb with an American accent.
6. Mrs. Reagan also extended this courtesy to the other ladies who came alone: Claudette Colbert, Mrs. Ralph Bunche, Chris Evert and Mary Lou Retton.
7. Alexander Yavoklev: How wrong these earlier estimates were of Yakovlev. He is known now as the "godfather of *glasnost*" and to have been the intellectual force behind Gorbachev's program of *glasnost* and *perestroika* and a beacon of moderation and democratic political process in Russia.
8. *President's table:* President Reagan, Mrs. Gorbachev, Ambassador Vernon Walters, Mrs. William Crowe, Jr., Mr. Donald Peterson (Chairman & CEO,Ford Motor Co.), Mrs. Ralph Bunche, Dr. Edmund Edward Teller, Mrs. Jeane Kirkpatrick. *Mrs. Reagan's table:* Mrs. Reagan, Mr. Gorbachev, Rep. Dick Cheney, Mrs. Zubin Mehta, Dr. James Billington, Mr. Robert Strauss, Mrs. Richard Helms, Mr. Richard Perle.
9. Different than the French who give two kisses, one on each cheek. Russians give three kisses each on alternating cheeks because they say, "God loves three."

CHAPTER 16: KGB "PRINCES"

1. KGB Komitet Gosudarstvennoy Bezopasnosti (The Committee for State Security).
2. *TIME*, February 14, 1983.
3. "A person could become a KGB officer only through a very careful selection process. You couldn't make a career without being really smart, professional, disciplined and organized. It was probably the only meaningful part of society which was not touched by corruption." Former KGB officer, now Moscow businessman.
4. In December, 1825 after Emperor Alexander I died leaving no heir and Nicholas I accepted the throne, there was an uprising of high ranking officers and liberal aristocrats known as the "Decembrists" who refused to swear allegiance to the new emperor and wanted to establish a republic and abolish serfdom.
5. Six weeks after he became general secretary, Gorbachev reached a working majority in the Politburo and notably numbered KGB chief Viktor Chebrikov as a full member, along with Yegor Likachev, Nikolai Ryzhkov as his closest advisors. On February 26,

1986, only months after he took power, the Party congress brought major changes in the Party Central committee and 40% of the members resigned. In his massive book Matlock writes, "Gorbachev's consolidation of power in his first year was a stunning political maneuver."*Autopsy of an Empire*, p. 54.

6. In 1984, when he accepted an invitation to a July 4th party at the US consular residence, my friend Dmitry Shagin, an artist, was called into the KGB and warned against attending because "Americans were all spies." Shagin cheekily replied, "Well if they are all spies and you know it, why don't you arrest them?" and went to the party.

7. Chief in charge of Intelligence and Espionage.

8. There are instances of icons known as "weeping" because sometimes some moisture seeps out that smells like incense and these drops are considered miraculous.

9. *Nicholas and Alexandra, Land of the Firebird, The Living Mirror.*

10. DCM: Deputy Chief of Mission.

11. *The New York Times*, August 21, 1987.

12. Luke 10:25.

13. Known today as the avant garde of the new Russia.

CHAPTER 17: THE AMBASSADOR FLAP

1. Today re-named the Davis Center for Russian and Eurasian Studies.

2. Letter from Senators William Cohen and John Heinz to the Honorable Ronald W. Reagan, June 3, 1986, Presidential library WORM files PEOO2 case file.

3. Alexandra Kollontai, the world's first female ambassador in modern times, was appointed Soviet Ambassador to Norway in 1923. She later served as Ambassador to Mexico (1926-27) and Sweden (1930-1945).

4. Peter Klebnikov, a courageous Russian-American investigative journalist working for *Forbes* magazine, was assassinated outside his office in Moscow in 2004. The case has never been solved.

CHAPTER 18: CROCODILES IN WASHINGTON

1. Once, in a single week, 150 reporters called me.

2. There was only one exception to my press rule. In 1987 before Gorbachev's arrival in Washington, one particularly tough reporter from *Newsday* kept asking me incessantly, "How did you meet the President?" So I called McFarlane and asked, "Can I say you sent me?" He answered, "It's about time!" But I told the reporter only that I had been sent on a back-channel mission and that "both sides had picked up the phone again."

3. The size and budget of the EOP is a bit of a mystery since many of the employees are detailed from the other agencies. Staff estimates range from 2,000 to 6,000 employees with an annual budget of $300 million to $750 million.

4. The traveling entourage of President George W. Bush included 250 Secret Service agents, 150 National Security advisors, 50 White House political aides, 200 representatives from other US departments, a personal chef with a team of four cooks, and 15 sniffer dogs. Two identical Boeing 747-200's and a third chartered jumbo jet, a Sikorsky Sea King helicopter, a Black Hawk helicopter, two identical motorcades of 20 armored vehicles, including limousines.

5. Frank Carlucci served as NSC advisor for only one year, 1986-87, and as Secretary of Defense from 1987-89.

6. James Mann, *The Rebellion of Ronald Reagan: A History of the End of the Cold War*. New York: Viking, 2009, p. 105.
7. Mann, p. 107.
8. Reagan, Ronald, *An American Life*. Edited by Kiron Skinner, Annelise Anderson & Martin Anderson. New York: Simon & Schuster, 1990.
9. Mann, p. 108.
10. Interview with Frank Carlucci, Miller Center, University of Virginia , August 28, 2001.
11. *Klukva* (cranberries): stems from the writings of Alexander Dumas, père, the French writer who, while visiting Russia, wrote that Russians often took their ease under the shade of a klukva tree(!?), so klukva came to mean all the nonsense and untruths that foreigners write about Russia.

CHAPTER 19: SHULTZ
1. Shultz resigned as Treasury Secretary in 1974 to join Bechtel, one of the world's largest construction and engineering conglomerates. He became president of the firm the following year and remained until 1982 when he was appointed Secretary of State.
2. George Shultz, p. 720.
3. Evidently Shultz learned after we met that the relation of Chernobyl's explosive power was equivalent to that of a single nuclear warhead. Shultz, p.724.
4. Shevernadze and Shultz met three times in Washington and four times in New York in intense personal meetings attended by only one person on each side. The final resolution, the result of Shultz's heroic efforts to find an acceptable solution for both sides, included freedom for Daniloff and also for a leading dissident and his wife and two Jewish "refusniks" who arrived in the United States in early October, a conviction of Zaharov who was given five years probation and allowed to return to the USSR.
5. Wikipedia, William J. Casey, https://en.wikipedia.org/wiki/William_J._Casey.
6. Shultz, p. 570.
7. Reagan diary (February 25, 1987).
8. In the years after the Khrushchev "Thaw" in the '70s and '80s, a group of writers became known as the "Village Writers"—a literary genre of poignant and nostalgic stories about the life and decline of villages in the Soviet Union. These included Valery Rasputin whose moving story, "Farewell to Matyora," was made into a hugely popular film. A harrowing Soviet film was also made at the time about a village terrified by ex-gangsters released from the gulag.
9. *Repentance* won a special prize in Cannes in 1987 and amazingly the entire trilogy won a Lenin Prize in 1988.
10. Shultz, p. 879
11. Plenum in the Soviet Union was a plenary session of all members of the Communist Party Central Committee required to be held every six months, attended by full and candidate members. All decisions adopted at a plenum became formal Communist Party policy.
12. Helena Marie O'Brien, known throughout her lifetime as O'bie, served as a first lieutenant in the Army Nurses Corps during World War II and was a member of the invasion force in the capture of the Philippines in 1944. She married Shultz in 1946 and actively supported her husband throughout his career.
13. Obie died at age of 80 in 1995. In 1997, Shultz remarried San Francisco powerhouse socialite Charlotte Mailliard Swig.

CHAPTER 20: REAGAN WOWS MOSCOW

1. In 1990, after the death of Patriarch Pimen, Alexey II the first Patriarch in Soviet history to be chosen without government pressure. Candidates were nominated from the floor and the election conducted by secret ballot.
2. The bells remained at Harvard for 77 years until 2007 when wealthy industrialist Victor Vekselberg bought them and paid for both their transportation back to Russia and the cost of new bells to replace them.
3. Igor Korchilov, a top Soviet translator for 29 years, whose book *Translating History* about his long career devotes a colorful chapter to the Moscow Summit as seen through the eyes and ears of a Russian. Korchilov, who had been translator for Gorbachev's visit to Washington in 1987, was deeply impressed by Reagan. Korchilov, p. 151.
4. Korchilov, p. 154.
5. Korchilov, p. 155.
6. This had been a suggestion of George Shultz who calls it "my personal triumph." Shultz, p. 1104.
7. Over the years I have often had the pleasure of staying at Spaso House. Ambassador Hartman once graciously put me up in that grand suite.
8. Reagan diary, Sunday, May 29, 1988.
9. Members of the American delegation: George Shultz, Frank Carlucci, Howard Baker, Colin Powell, Paul Nitze, Edward Rowny, Rozanne Ridgeway, Jack Matlock.
10. National Security Directive, #305.
11. An example of American stubborn disbelief in Gorbachev: In February 1988, in a conversation with George Shultz, Gorbachev announced that Soviet troops would leave Afghanistan starting in May and would be completely gone by spring 1989, an outcome that CIA chief Robert Gates and the NSC Soviet Advisor had bet $25 and $50 respectively would never occur. (It did.)
12. Memorandum of conversation, Second Plenary Meeting, June 1, 1988, Reagan Library.
13. Korchilov, p. 179.
14. Matlock, p. 299.
15. I have not gone into the weary minutiae of these stubbornly inconclusive weapons discussions. For any of my readers who would like to consult these documents closely see National Security Archives Electronic Books Numbers 251 and 305 and also Shultz's and Matlock's lengthy accounts.
16. National Security Archives, #305.
17. Korchilov, p. 141.
18. Korchilov, p. 142.
19. Korchilov, p. 165
20. All Reagan quotes from full text of his Danilovsky Monastery speech, Reagan Library.
21. Matlock, p. 302.
22. Matlock, p. 300.
23. Doder and Branson, *Gorbachev*, p. 320.
24. Matlock, p. 302.
25. Matlock, p. 302.
26. Gorbachev, *Memoirs*, p. 457.

CHAPTER 21: MILLENIUM AND LAST LUNCH
1. Kievan Rus: The historic name of early Russia until Kiev was destroyed by Mongol invasions in the 13th century.
2. Mann, p. 93.
3. Shultz, p. 720.
4. Six months after he left office, on July 4, 1989 at a private ranch in Mexico, Reagan was thrown from a wildly bucking horse and hit his head on a rock, suffering a massive brain contusion. Two months later Reagan underwent surgery at the Mayo Clinic to relieve fluid on his brain. This accident is now believed to have accelerated the onset of Alzheimer's. Ronald Reagan, *Reagan: A Life in Letters*. New York: The Free Press, 2003, p. 79.

CHAPTER 22: A FEW LAST WORDS
1. Reagan dictated this letter and when the tape ran out added this written fragment (circa 1980). Ronald Reagan, *Reagan: A Life in Letters*. New York: The Free Press, 2003, p. 79.
2. Reagan exercised every day, even on the road. While recovering from the assassination attempt, a special exercise room was set up outside his bedroom.
3. Out of respect for the presidency, Reagan always wore a jacket in the Oval Office.
4. Author interview with Gorbachev in Moscow, 1999.
5. As my favorite Leningrad hairdresser, Zenaida, used to say, "God gave me a tongue and means me to use it!"
6. George Shultz, Strober, p. 119.
7. Reagan notes exhibited in Reagan Library museum: Reagan Presidential Foundation.
8. Introduction, *Reagan: A Life in Letters*, p. xiii
9. Judge Abraham Sofaer: Legal Advisor to State Department until 1990, Senior Fellow at The Hoover Institution, Strober, p. 99.

EPILOGUE
1. Matlock, p. 326
2. The text in brackets is also engraved on the tomb.